Healing Parents

*Helping Wounded Children
Learn to Trust & Love*

Michael Orlans, M.A.

and

Terry M. Levy, Ph.D.

CWLA PRESS

www.cwla.org

CWLA Press is an imprint of the Child Welfare League of America. The Child Welfare League of America is the nation's oldest and largest membership-based child welfare organization. We are committed to engaging people everywhere in promoting the well-being of children, youth, and their families, and protecting every child from harm. All proceeds from the sale of this book support CWLA's programs in behalf of children and families.

CHILD WELFARE LEAGUE OF AMERICA, INC.
HEADQUARTERS
1726 M Street NW, Suite 500
Washington, DC 20036
www.cwla.org/pubs

CURRENT PRINTING (last digit)
10 9 8 7 6 5

Cover and text design by Marlene Saulsbury
Edited by Jennifer M. Price
Printed in the United States of America

Library of Congress Cataloging-in-Publication Data

Orlans, Michael.
  Healing parents: helping wounded children learn to trust & love / Michael Orlans and Terry M. Levy.
      p. cm.
  Includes bibliographical references.
  ISBN-13: 978-1-58760-096-8 (pbk.)
1. Problem children—Family relationships. 2. Attachment disorder in children.
3. Parenting. 4. Child rearing 5. Special needs adoption.
I. Levy, Terry M. II. Title.

  HQ773.O67 2006
  649'.154—dc22

2006030214

Dedications

To my wife Jeri, for being my partner on our journey to creating a healing relationship. I thank her for all her love and support. To my parents and siblings who taught me the meaning of attachment. To my children Jesse, Raina, Ushi and Jon, Julie and Adam, and my grandchildren Rhyan and Taylor for showing me who I really am.

M.O.

I dedicate this book to my family. To my loving and supportive wife, Suzanne. To my wonderful children, Mia, Eliah, and Matthew. To my grandchildren, Anika, Mariah, and Jordana. To my sister, Laurie, and to my parents, Donald and Renée. You have all helped me learn about attachment and love.

T.M.L.

Contents

Dedications iii

Acknowledgements vii

Author's Note and Confidentiality Statement vii

List of Figures vi

List of Tables vi

I.   Introduction 1

II.   Attachment: The Core 17

III.   Know Your Child 37

IV.   Know Yourself 89

V.   Corrective Attachment Parenting: Basic Principles 119

VI.   Corrective Attachment Parenting: Skills & Solutions 145

VII.   Attachment and the Adoptive Family 229

VIII. Attachment and Foster Care 259

IX.   Epilogue 277

About the Authors 279

References 281

Index 293

List of Figures

Figure 1. First Year of Life Attachment Cycle 22

Figure 2. Triune Brain 23

Figure 3. Attachment: The Core 72

Figure 4. The Autonomy Circle 148

List of Tables

Table 1. Child Assessment 48

Table 2. Connection vs. Control 131

Table 3. Punishment vs. Consequences 161

Table 4. One-Liners 175

Table 5. Minimizing the Trauma of Moves: Developmental Considerations 268

Acknowledgements

I would like to express my gratitude to my colleague, Dr. Anthea Coster, for her friendship and contributions to making this book a reality. I would also like to give special heartfelt recognition to all the healing parents in the world. There is no more important job and no more important gift one can give to society than to help a wounded child heal. For all the families on the front lines, this book is for you.

M.O.

I express my appreciation to the many adults, parents, adolescents, and children I have worked with over the past 35 years. Your courage, commitment, motivation, and hard work have inspired me. Thank you to the Child Welfare League of America for your patience and support during the long process of preparing this book. I want to acknowledge the contributions of the many therapists, researchers, and teachers that I have learned from, and who have laid the foundation of theory and practice in the fields of psychology and child welfare. This book is built on your solid foundation. Thank you to Dr. Anthea Coster for your support and many contributions as a part of Evergreen Psychotherapy Center. A special thank you to Suzanne and Matthew for your endless love, support, and patience. You make it all possible.

T.M.L.

Author's Note and Confidentiality Statement

The parenting examples, drawings, and case vignettes throughout this book come from children and families we have seen in our treatment and parenting programs. The names and other identifying characteristics have been changed to protect privacy and confidentiality. For the ease of explanation and to avoid sexist language, we alternate between the personal pronouns, he and she, throughout the book.

1

Introduction

*B*efore you were born you were floating warmly, comfortably, and securely in your mother's womb. You were snug, safe, and content. You basked in the biochemical messages that you are loved, wanted, and all is well. Then suddenly one day you were thrust into a frightening world of bright lights, loud noises, and unfamiliar smells. To add insult to injury, you were torn away from your source of security and abruptly poked and prodded. Finally, with great relief, you are reunited with the familiar heartbeat and soothing voice that you have known for nine months. You are held in loving arms and relax into adoring gazes and smiles. You snuggle into the splendor of a soft warm breast and its life-giving nurturance. Soon your sensitive and responsive caregivers learn which cry means "I'm hungry," "I'm uncomfortable," or "Pick me up." You and your caregivers are in-sync. You soon realize you have the power to have an impact on your surroundings.

You experience that your needs will be met, and you learn patience and the ability to manage your impulses and feelings. You learn to trust caregivers to be reliable, the world to be safe and good, and to feel good about yourself. The connections in your brain are developing and expanding. You begin to develop confidence, and over time, become independent, resilient, optimistic, and compassionate toward others. You are on your way to becoming a responsible person, a good friend, a loving spouse, and an affectionate parent.

Now imagine that before you were born you received messages of ambivalence about your value or were flatly unwanted. You are overcome with your mother's stress hormones, anxiety, depression, and fear. A poor maternal diet, drinking, smoking, and drugs also assault you. Every time your mother takes a drag on a cigarette your tiny heart races, as you struggle with a flood of carbon dioxide which cuts off life-giving oxygenated blood. You bathe in a noxious soup of more than 2,000 toxic chemicals, including nicotine by-products such as arsenic, cyanide,

1

and formaldehyde. You are thrust into a state of chronic anxiety, waiting for the next onslaught.

After experiencing the trauma of birth you are not held and reassured, but left alone to wallow in fear and helplessness. Your cries of protest are ignored or met with anger. Soon you become discouraged and withdraw into despair and hopelessness. You quickly learn that your caregivers are unresponsive, unsafe, and cannot be trusted. Since you were not properly regulated by soothing and calming attention, you don't learn how to self-regulate impulses and feelings. You lack confidence in your ability to impact others and become closed-off and disconnected. With no experience of emotional connection, you become selfish and incapable of intimacy and closeness. You feel separate from yourself and others. You develop a cynical view of humankind, seeing others as untrustworthy. You believe since your needs are not met, you must be "bad." You later become unwilling to play by society's rules or see the value in helping others. You feel like a victim of life; you blame others and take no personal responsibility.

You haven't received the experiences necessary to correctly "wire" your brain. You lag behind developmentally, can't handle stress and adversity, and become depressed or violent. Fear of abandonment is a force that runs your life. You are distant and controlling to hide your vulnerability. Anger and argumentativeness cover your fear. You become pseudoindependent and lack resilience, empathy, and compassion. You become a neglectful or abusive spouse and parent, perpetuating the cycle of maltreatment and emotional disconnection with the next generation.

The above anecdotes illustrate the difference between starting life with secure versus compromised attachment. When we refer to *wounded* children, we are describing those who lacked safe, secure, and loving attachments in the early part of life. Instead, these children experienced neglect, abuse, abandonment, and other attachment disruptions. Disrupted and compromised attachment is more common than many people realize. Numerous studies in the United States and in other countries have found that about 33% of children in middle-class families are insecurely attached (Levy & Orlans 1998). As many as 82% of children develop severe attachment disorders in high-risk families (i.e., parental depression, substance abuse, and unresolved psychological problems; abuse and neglect; multiple moves and caregivers) (Hesse et al. 2003; Lyons-Ruth & Jacobvitz 1999).

When you have a cut your body forms scar tissue, which toughens and thickens the flesh. The purpose of the scar is to provide a protective shell around the injury. This is nature's way of preventing further injury in the same location. Similarly, if we have tight fitting shoes, nature responds to the discomfort by forming a callous. Emotional wounds occur in much the same way. If we have an emotional injury, we harden our hearts, become callous toward others, and withdraw into a protective armor. This strategy is designed to protect us from the original perpetrator and from all others who can potentially hurt us (Maltz 1960).

The title of this book—*Healing Parents*—has a double meaning. First, the title refers to the role of a therapeutic parent. Your job as a therapeutic and healing parent is to provide the correct blend of ingredients to promote emotional, mental, social, and moral growth in your child. You are creating the opportunity for your child to heal wounds from the past and develop positively in the future.

Sensitivity and responsiveness to children's needs leads to the development of trust and the ability to internalize the wishes and values of caregivers. Securely attached children are motivated by the desire to please, to put a smile on Mom and Dad's face, to be just like them. They learn quickly from consequences. Without adequate nurturing and protection early in life children do not develop trust or the motivation to please caregivers. They take pleasure in defying rules and don't care about receiving parental disapproval. Punishment doesn't work because they believe they deserve harsh treatment ("I'm not worthwhile or loveable"). They make the same mistakes time and time again. Parents often respond by being punitive, giving in, or giving up.

This book is designed to provide parents of wounded children with the information and skills necessary to create a healing environment. Parenting concepts and methods that typically work well with the general population of children are usually unsuccessful with children who have compromised attachment. The approach described in this book—*Corrective Attachment Parenting*—is designed for children with disrupted and compromised attachment: children who have had damaging and painful experiences early in life and, consequently, do not trust caregivers, do not like or believe in themselves, view the world as unsafe and threatening, and are emotionally and biochemically unbalanced due to the absence of security and support when they were young and vulnerable.

Compromised attachment is basically a condition of emotional detachment. The child perceives others as unsafe and, therefore, keeps away. He is controlling and pushes you away as a defense—to survive. The "cure" is connection; helping your child learn to trust, be emotionally vulnerable, and really connect with another human being in a safe and satisfying way. *Your goal is connection, not control.*

The second meaning of the title—*Healing Parents*—refers to you, the parent or caregiver, and the importance of self-understanding and personal growth. As you understand more about yourself and evolve as a person, you are in a much better position to help your child recover and succeed. Generally speaking, all parents need to be stable and mature to successfully raise children. However, parenting children with special needs, such as histories of abuse, neglect, and lack of secure attachment, is particularly challenging. They will "push your buttons," test your coping abilities, and make you question your competency. To be a healing parent you must be able to "look in the mirror," take stock of your own life, know your emotional triggers, seek healthy relationships and plenty of support, and pursue personal growth and well-being.

Our Background and Experience

This book is based on more than 60 years of combined experience doing therapy, teaching, consulting, and research related to children, families, and society. We have had the privilege of being friends and colleagues for almost 45 years. Our clinical work with challenging children—victims of abuse, neglect, and disrupted attachments—and their biological, foster, and adoptive families, has given us many insights and lessons. We understand these children, parents, and families, and, most importantly, know how to promote positive change and healing.

In our seminars in the United States and around the world, we have taught thousands of mental health and child welfare professionals, educators, and parents. This book is based on our experiences working with parents of challenging children and the professionals who try to help these families. Parents have voiced their needs, questions, and frustrations. This book addresses those needs and answers those questions.

We began working with children and families in the late 1960s and early 1970s, during the heyday of the family therapy movement. The mental health community came to the realization children couldn't be understood or helped alone, apart from the family and social systems that influence their lives. Family therapy focused on how people related and communicated, and the way these patterns and dynamics influenced child growth and development.

This family systems approach worked well for many families, especially biologically-intact children and parents who had some foundation of attachment and connection. However, by the 1980s, we began to realize something was missing. Many children did not start life with a safe, loving, and dependable connection with a parent or caregiver. When placed in adoptive families, many of these children failed to attach, the parents had no idea how to handle their angry and mistrustful children, and even mental health professionals were often at a loss to help. Child and family therapy did not seem to work for these challenging children and families.

It was out of this need for a more effective approach that we developed *Corrective Attachment Therapy* and *Corrective Attachment Parenting*. These combine ideas and methods from the fields of trauma, family dynamics, child development, biology and the brain, and attachment theory (Levy & Orlans 1998; Levy 2000). In 1989, we cofounded the Association for the Treatment and Training in the Attachment of Children, or *ATTACH*. This was the first national organization to include both parents and child welfare professions, focusing on children and families dealing with attachment-related problems.

Children and Society

There has been an explosion of research in recent decades in the behavioral and social sciences and in neurobiology that has enabled us to gain a deeper understanding of childhood health and development. We now know the factors that contribute to healthy emotional, mental, social, and moral development. We also know what causes children to become delayed and damaged in these crucial areas. Despite all this knowledge, the children and youth of our society are showing increasing signs of distress and poor

health. Growing numbers of our children are suffering from mental, emotional, and behavioral problems and related conditions—depression, anxiety, attention deficit disorder, conduct disorders, suicidal thoughts and attempts, substance abuse, and violence.

Consider the following statistics (Quartz & Sejnowski 2002; Institute for American Values 2003; Annie E. Casey Foundation 2004).

- One in 10 children and adolescents in the United States today has emotional problems so severe they cannot function normally.

- In the United States, 21% of children ages 9 to 17 have diagnosable mental or addictive disorders.

- The current generation of children is more likely to be depressed and anxious than its parents' generation; the number of children and teens taking medication for depression (Prozac) and ADHD (Ritalin) more than doubled between 1987 and 1996.

- Since the 1980s, the number of murders committed by youths has soared 168% and suicides increased 140%; suicide is the third leading cause of death among young people.

- In the United States, 2,000 children die each year from abuse and neglect.

- One in four adolescents is at risk of not achieving a productive and fulfilling adulthood; 50% report smoking marijuana, 30% use other illicit drugs, and 33% engage in binge drinking; 20% consider suicide; 40% witness serious violence; and 11% drop out of high school.

- Almost 4 million young adults are not in school or working, a disturbing trend; 15% of 18 to 24 year olds are "disconnected."

Why are we seeing so many problems? The answer to this question is both simple and complex. The simple answer is: *children do poorly when they lack close connections—loving and safe attachments—during the first few years of life.* We know, without a doubt, that early attachment affects every part of a child's life and development—mind, brain, emotions, relationships, and morality.

The answer is also complex because children form close connections in families, and families are part of larger communities. In recent generations, the social institutions (e.g., nuclear and extended family, community networks and support systems) that foster and sustain those close connections have deteriorated. Changes in the American family, for example, have had a negative impact on the health and well-being of infants and young children. Increases in poverty, inferior childcare, severely stressed single-parent families, and other influences, have contributed to a lack of stable and loving attachments.

Poverty during early development is very harmful due to family stress and limited access to enriching experiences; preschoolers today are more likely to be from poor families than 25 years ago. Record numbers of women with young children work outside the home, resulting in increased reliance on daycare for infants and toddlers; 66% of women with children under six years old are in the workforce, compared to 38% in 1975. Many daycare centers fail to meet Federal guidelines. And, in the last 25 years the proportion of children in single-parent families has almost doubled, from 18 to 31%; 70% of African American children live with one parent, typically mother, leading to increased financial hardship, stress, and lack of male role models (U.S. Department of Health and Human Services 2002). Under these conditions it is difficult to create the necessary stable and loving attachments children need.

Core Concepts of Childhood Development

In order to develop effective solutions to the problems of children and families we must first understand the nature of child development. Many of the brightest and well-respected individuals from the fields of psychology, medicine, education, and sociology have described the basic ingredients of early childhood development (see Institute for American Values 2003; National Research Council 2000). This is what we know about how children develop, described as six core concepts that form the foundation necessary to prevent and solve significant problems.

1. **Nurturing and dependable relationships are the building blocks of healthy childhood development.**

   Secure attachments develop when parents and caregivers are dependable, available, and sensitive to the child's needs, enabling that child to count on the parent for continued protection, need-fulfillment, and guidance. Even infants and children fostered or adopted from harsh and neglectful conditions, such as abusive families or crowded orphanages, can become securely attached when parents provide sensitive, responsive, and consistent care. Secure attachment leads to healthy development in all-important areas—emotions, relationships, self-esteem, core beliefs, self-control, brain growth, and morality.

2. Human beings are hardwired to connect.

All babies are born with the ability to attach, but this "prewired" instinct can only develop in close harmony with a loving and responsive caregiver. Attachment forms within a close, cooperative, reciprocal relationship—the give-and-take of minds, emotions, and biochemistry. For example, as a loving mother holds and nurses her baby, the hormone oxytocin floods both bloodstreams, relaxing the baby and mother, and strengthening the bonds between them. Babies with unresponsive or depressed mothers miss-out on the emotional and social cues of attachment. As they grow older, they have more behavioral, social, and cognitive problems, compared to babies whose caregivers are attuned and responsive to their needs. When secure attachment is not triggered by sensitive and nurturing care, such as in cases of neglect, abuse, or repeated disruptions, children often become angry, depressed, defiant, impulsive, and hopeless.

3. Attachment changes the brain.

The presence or absence of sensitive, nurturing, and loving care during life's early stages not only determines emotional and social development, but also affects the way the brain develops, profoundly influencing long-term health. The early attachment relationship alters the brain's structure, chemistry, and genetic expression. The brain's limbic system, which governs how children feel, relate, and self-regulate, requires exposure to nurturing and attuned care for healthy growth. A baby and parent achieve limbic resonance—attuned to each other's inner states via eye contact, loving touch, and a connection of their brain's limbic systems. The nature of the child's attachment to his caregiver determines if brain connections will grow to full potential or waste away. Children without secure attachments often have altered levels of brain chemicals (e.g., noradrenaline, cortisol, and serotonin), resulting in aggression, lack of impulse control, depression, and a high risk for substance abuse.

4. Child development is shaped by the interplay of nature and nurture— biology and experience.

Scientists used to argue about which was more powerful, nature (biology and genes) or nurture (experience and the environment). This debate is obsolete. It is not nature versus nurture but nature through nurture. Biology, including genetic tendencies and vulnerabilities, may provide the starting point, but it is the child's relationships with caregivers that shape the course of her growth and development. A safe, positive, and loving environment can overcome depression, anxiety, or other tendencies, and even transform these vulnerabilities into strengths. Research with rhesus monkeys, for example, has shown some baby monkeys have a genetic trait of anxiety and others a tendency to be aggressive. When nurturing and protective "foster mom" monkeys raised these babies, the nervous babies relaxed and the aggressive ones became less violent (Suomi 1991). Fortunately, this is also true of human children; sensitive and nurturing foster and adoptive parents can counter the effects of an unhealthy genetic background and maltreatment.

5. Learning self-regulation is essential for child development and lifelong health.

Babies are born helpless and totally dependent upon caregivers for survival. Development involves the increasing capacity for self-regulation and self-control; the transition from helplessness to competence, from dependence on others to the ability to manage one's own emotions and behaviors. The ability to learn self-regulation is deeply rooted in early attachment, beginning with dependency and evolving toward autonomy. The mother's body first accomplishes this with the fetus in the womb, then through the infant's signaling needs to the responsive parent, and later by developing the capacity for self-regulation. Children must have supportive and attuned caregivers to develop the ability to regulate their emotions, impulses, and attention. The inability to self-regulate contributes to the development of conduct disorders, attention deficit disorders, anxiety, depression, and other serious problems in childhood and later life.

6. The balance between risk factors and protective factors has a powerful effect on development.

Risk factors, such as difficult-to-soothe infant temperament, neglectful or abusive parenting, poverty, and family violence, increase the likelihood of serious problems in childhood and throughout life. Protective factors, including easy temperament, mature and supportive caregivers, and social support, buffer children from undue stress and results in resilience—the ability to "bounce-back" from adversity. Children who start their lives with compromised attachments have the double burden of both biological and environmental risk factors; a family history of severe psychological and biochemical problems, and the absence of loving, dependable, and responsive care. Children do better when protective factors are increased. For example, preschoolers could become securely attached when their high-risk mothers (i.e., high stress, irritable, unresponsive) participated in a program where they learned to be sensitive and responsive (Zigler 1994). The basic objective of therapeutic parenting is to reduce risk and increase protective factors by providing nurturing, consistent, and sensitive care. Children learn to expect support, guidance, and understanding, rather than betrayal, neglect, and disinterest.

Secure and Disrupted Attachment

*The capacity to make intimate emotional bonds is a principal
feature of effective personality functioning and mental health.*

— John Bowlby

Attachment is the deep and enduring heartfelt connection that children and caregivers establish in the early stages of life. This connection is basic to every aspect of a child's development—mind, brain, emotions, relationships, and morality.

Children who start out securely attached are healthier and more well-adjusted over time in the following areas:

- positive self-esteem;
- loving and respectful relationships with parents and others;
- the ability to trust, be emotionally close, and feel empathy and compassion;
- effective coping skills, such as anger-management, impulse control, and frustration tolerance;
- positive and hopeful view of self, others, and life;
- the ability to develop independence and resilience;
- success in school, both behaviorally and academically; and
- maturity, loyalty, and the ability to be caring partners and parents.

The opposite is often true for children lacking sensitive, protective, and loving caregivers. Children who experience compromised and disrupted attachment are high-risk for serious problems, including:

- negative sense of self;
- distant and defiant relationships with parents and others;
- lack of trust, empathy, conscience, and remorse;
- poor coping skills, including inadequate control over impulses and emotions, and inability to handle frustration and stress;
- pessimistic and hopeless view of self, family, and life in general;
- inability to function independently and bounce-back from adversity;
- school failure, both behaviorally and academically; and
- severe relationship and parenting problems as adults; perpetuate the cycle of maltreatment and disrupted attachment in their own children.

Our Philosophy

Our treatment and parenting programs, as well as the concepts and methods described in this book, are grounded in a foundation of basic principles and theories of behavior, relationships, and the process of change. The following describes the six key elements of our philosophy and what we believe to be true.

1. Focus on family and community systems.

A system is a set of connected parts that work together to form a whole. In families, all members affect one another, in ongoing patterns and dynamics—*an interpersonal dance*. Children can only be understood and helped in the context of the social systems that affect their lives—family, community, school, and child welfare systems. Thus, the focus should not be on your child alone, but rather on the bigger picture, the family and social systems that shape everyone's lives. Change the system and your child will change.

2. Attachment is the core.

The type and quality of attachment formed in the early stages of development set the foundation for the rest of your life. Attachment is at the core of our beliefs, attitudes, emotions, behaviors, relationships, and values. The mind and brain of the baby and young child is formed, to a large extent, by emotional experiences with attachment figures. When attachment goes wrong with vulnerable infants and young children, numerous symptoms and conditions are likely to occur: depression, behavior disorders, anxiety, posttraumatic stress disorder (PTSD), attention deficit and hyperactivity disorder (ADHD), and antisocial personality. Disrupted and compromised attachment is often at the core of these problems. Thus, the "cure" resides in the experience of a healthy and healing relationship. You, the healing parent, hold the key.

3. Embrace the process of change.

When you understand the basic principles of change, you are able to promote growth in yourself, child, and family. You can only change yourself. However, you can create opportunities for others to change via your attitude and actions. Information and skills are essential for change. Using *Corrective Attachment Parenting* (CAP) ideas and skills, as described in this book, can build your confidence and lead to success. You must believe in the possibility of change: maintain a positive attitude, be a role model of change, reinforce little steps, focus on the future not only the past. Experience is the basis of change. Provide your child with new and positive learning experiences, resulting in new expectations ("I can trust you") and positive feelings ("I feel secure and loveable"). Have a plan with specific goals and ways to achieve your goals. Change is a team effort, something you, your spouse/partner, and child work on together. Your relationship with your child is the primary vehicle for change. Change is not easy; it is a step-by-step, back-and-forth process, and it is normal to be anxious and ambivalent. Hope is essential. A positive expectation of success allows you to convey optimism and encouragement to yourself and your child.

4. Attachment begins with the parents.

Your own family background and attachment history play a major role in the way you live your life, engage in relationships, and parent your children. Your mindset about attachment—the way you think about your own attachment history and deal with your emotional and relational issues—is the number one factor in determining your child's type of attachment. This is true in biological, adoptive, and foster families. Wounded children are experts at triggering unresolved issues and sensitivities left over from your childhood. By becoming self-aware—looking in the mirror—you will be proactive, not reactive; able to respond constructively and therapeutically to your child's angry, controlling, and distancing behavior, rather than reacting in a destructive "knee-jerk" manner.

5. Create a healing environment.

Parents cannot "fix" a child, but they can create and maintain the emotional, social, and moral climate in which children learn and heal. Healing parents understand they are in a therapeutic role. You are aware of the way you label and interpret your child's behavior, because those labels and perceptions guide your actions. You provide a balance of love and limits. Nurturance and compassion meet deep emotional needs and teach your child that heart-felt human connections are safe and rewarding. Structure, including limits, rules, and consequences, helps your child feel secure and learn from her mistakes. As a healing parent you maintain a mindset of opportunity rather than crisis. Stressful and challenging situations are viewed as opportunities for teaching and learning, rather than as crises to be dreaded and avoided. You are proactive, not reactive; set the emotional tone of your family, maintain the rules, and provide a positive role model by remaining calm and not taking your child's behavior personally. You are parenting with intention; you have a plan and a purpose, and work deliberately toward achieving your goals. You respond to your child in ways that do not reinforce his script—*change the dance, change the child.* You look beyond your child's negative behaviors and understand the beliefs and mindset at the root of his actions. You help your child develop more hopeful and healthy core beliefs. Your primary goal is connection, not control. The relationship you establish with your child is the vehicle for teaching about the value of secure, safe, and loving connections. You show by example how to effectively communicate, cope with stress, manage emotions and conflict, solve problems, and care about yourself and others. You have confidence that you can promote positive changes in your child's mind, brain, and behavior by maintaining a healing environment.

6. Connection is your goal.

A person's philosophy and beliefs determine what he does and how he does it. In the past, some therapists believed wounded children must release their rage and submit to the therapists' authority in order to become vulnerable and then learn to trust. They believed anger was the primary cause of defiance. This led to a parenting approach that emphasized control over the child and a focus on "Who's the boss?" Our belief, as well as many others in the field, is that therapists and parents become trusted figures for wounded children by being sensitive and responsive to their needs, providing appropriate limits and consistent structure, and being empathic, supportive, nurturing, and a positive role model. We believe fear is the primary cause of defiance—fear of additional loss, pain, and maltreatment. Our parenting approach emphasizes respect, reciprocity, and the creation of deep emotional connections. This helps children develop positive core beliefs, internalize parental values, establish trust, and become motivated to be compliant rather than defiant. In other words, children need connection, not control (see Table 2, page 131).

Parent Frustration and Struggles

A Mother's Story

Morning in our home is chaotic. Brice wakes up first and usually makes noise so his sister wakes up. Next he gets out food and milk, which he often spills. The counter is a mess. Then he hits the family room and watches T.V. Until he has his Ritalin, he bumps into tables, walls, and counters and goes from one area to the next leaving mess after mess.

Our typical response is frustration and dread of even getting up. As soon as I get up, Brice and Abby seem to start fighting or telling on each other. I give Brice his medicine and have a cup of coffee. I ignore all of his behavior until I've had some coffee. Once he has had his medicine, he doesn't bump into things and he doesn't argue constantly.

My husband's typical response is anger and then he and Brice start fighting. Brice and Abby argue a lot. They both want to be the first to do anything—sit in the front, play outside, watch their program, play a game. Brice gets mad, screams, or throws something down.

The behaviors that bother my husband the most are sneaking around at night, sucking his thumb, constantly and always blaming others for not getting what he wants. The behaviors that disturb me the most are the way he destroys a room in seconds, wets or messes in his clothes and then stuffs them into clean clothes, and the escalation of inappropriate behaviors like stealing, drinking, and setting fires. He also can't stand to be alone.

Brice acts much younger than the children in his class. The other kids tease him and tire of his silly behaviors. His first year he was with us, he was in four different schools before we could find one that could handle him. Now he is in a small class with strict discipline.

Brice's positive behaviors are his sense of humor and helpfulness. He is very charming and intelligent. He can figure out any puzzle or take any object apart. My sisters have only seen us once since getting the children. They thought we were too strict and yet they thought the kids were exhausting to be around. Don's parents don't visit us as much as they used to and are pretty tired of Brice's behavior.

As for our marriage, it has been difficult to describe what an impact Brice has had. It must be strong to have survived for so long under so much adversity. We are both deeply saddened that things have not worked out better. We had such hopes of having a happy family life. Instead we seem to argue a lot and disagree on parenting techniques. Don goes into a rage when Brice misbehaves, and I get upset.

I don't know of any parenting techniques that work the way I want or for any length of time. I feel like I'm the head of a military school. I feel depressed. I wish I could send both kids off to camp for the summer. It would give some respite but detrimental in the long run. The children are even worse when we have been apart for two-week summer camp. After having it calm, it's horrible when the chaos returns.

Helping your child is not just about learning techniques. To be a healing parent you need the right attitude. However, being positive and confident is very difficult when feeling alone, confused, helpless, and exhausted. Foster parents tell us they do not receive the training and support to deal with very angry and defiant children. Adoptive parents express frustration and anger because they were not given much information about their child before adoption, and were not provided with parenting education or therapy services following adoption.

Parents and caregivers are often angry at "the system" and don't know where to turn and who to trust. They are confused due to conflicting advice about parenting and treatment, and baffled by their children's behavior. Numerous books offering different parenting philosophies and strategies perplex them. They are worn-out due to the constant demands and challenges and often feel guilty and inadequate in their parenting roles. Over time, high levels of stress associated with relationship conflicts create a climate of tension, despair, and hopelessness in the family (Levy & Orlans 2000a). The mother of 10-year old Brett reports:

"How am I feeling? I feel totally helpless and hopeless. I feel tired of all this craziness and manipulation. I feel depressed a lot. I have not had much energy lately and sleep more than I used to. I feel like I have no control over how a normal day is going to go at home with Brett. I feel like I have lost control of my own life. I feel very inadequate as a mother."

I try to hurt my parents, mostly my Mom.

There is a paradox here: you need patience, confidence, and love to be a healing parent, but you may be too frustrated and fed up to respond therapeutically. It is normal to not want to open your heart to your child, fearing more rejection, grief, and abuse. We have found, however, with the right information, skills, and support, parents do become more emotionally available, confident, and successful. Our hope is this book will help you to become a healing parent.

Most parenting books focus on the children's problems and how to get them to change their behavior: less defiant, depressed, angry; better self-esteem, compliance, mood, and motivation. This book focuses on you—the parent or caregiver—and how you can change yourself and the dynamics in your relationship with your child. Only by having the right viewpoint, behavior, and attitude can you be a healing parent, which results in your child learning to connect in trusting, secure, and loving ways.

Goals of This Book

The primary aim of this book is to create positive change by giving you—the parent or caregiver—the *information, tools, support, self-awareness,* and *hope* you need to help your wounded child. The more you understand yourself and your child, the more effective you will be in creating a healthy environment. You must have tools—skills, methods, and strategies—to respond in a constructive and helpful way. Consider this book as a tool box, a practical manual to be a healing parent and all the tools you will need. You will learn how to help your child heal emotional wounds and improve behaviorally, socially, and morally, through the development of secure attachments.

Support is crucial. As the saying goes, "It takes a village." You cannot do this alone. You need support systems: spouse, partner, extended family, school, community and religious groups, professionals. Unfortunately, parents often feel alone, isolated, and misunderstood. When reading this book we hope you feel understood; we know what you are going through and dealing with. We hope you feel a measure of comfort, become more confident, and feel less alone. We also encourage you to reach-out for support from others who are caring and helpful.

Many parents and caregivers feel hopeless, demoralized, and powerless. They do not know how to help their child or create family harmony. When you are demoralized you lack energy, motivation, and determination—"Why bother, I'll only fail again." Having hope is an important part of change. Burned-out parents convey their pessimistic feelings to their children, making it more difficult for them to change. Children rely on adults for encouragement, guidance, and hope. Hope is communicated verbally and nonverbally. Your words, deeds, and confident demeanor send messages of optimism and hope; "I believe in me and you—this *will* work out."

The information, ideas, and tools offered in this book will help you combat demoralization. As you understand yourself and your child, and learn constructive ways to help your child, you will feel more confident, successful, and hopeful. You will realize you *can* do this, and know *how* to do it. You will develop a positive expectation of success, and convey this positive attitude and indomitable spirit to your child.

The second goal of this book is to help you understand attachment in children and families. Chapter Two explains the functions of attachment—the ways in which a young child's attachment relationship affects his or her developing brain, self-regulation, trust, reciprocity, core beliefs, morality, and resiliency. Chapter Three shows you how to assess and understand your child. You will gain a deep appreciation for the effects of abuse, neglect, and compromised attachment on your child's behavior, brain, mindset, and patterns of relating. You will learn to understand your child using the *Three Pillars of Assessment:* history, symptoms/diagnoses, and the attachment histories of the biological parents (or other primary caregivers).

The third goal of the book is to tell you why it's so important to *look in the mirror*— to have self-awareness and self-understanding in order to be a healing parent. You can complete the *Life Script,* found in Chapter Four, a self-evaluation tool that will enable you to understand your own attachment history, beliefs, styles of relating, and emotional triggers. Self-awareness will empower you to be a healing parent. You can develop the ability to be proactive rather than reactive, confident and composed, maintain an optimistic attitude, and be a positive role model.

The fourth goal is to bring together information from various disciplinary fields, including psychology, neurobiology, child welfare, trauma therapy, education, criminal justice, family systems and attachment theory, and parent training. Integrating and blending together knowledge from these many fields will help parents and professionals appreciate the importance of secure attachment as basic to the future of children, families, and society. This will also hopefully lead to better communication between parents and professionals (mental health, social work, education, and legal), working as a team for the benefit of children and families. Improved cooperation and teamwork will reduce the feelings of alienation and isolation that many parents feel.

Parents who participate in our treatment programs and parenting seminars often tell us that the concepts and skills learned are constructive and helpful with their children, themselves, their marriages, and entire family. Over the years parents and professionals in the mental health and child welfare fields have requested we write a book to share this information with a wider audience. Thus, the final goal of this book is to reach out to more people about how to help wounded children and families. You will find practical parenting skills and strategies in the remaining chapters. By writing this book our hope is to let parents know how to help their children by having the right attitude, information, skills, and support. Believe in miracles. Any child and family can heal from applying this information, so why not yours?

Summary

- To be a *healing parent* means to be therapeutic with your child and to pursue personal healing and growth.
- Your goal with wounded children is connection, not control.
- Children develop emotional, social, and behavioral problems when they lack close connections—loving and safe attachments—during the first few years of life.
- Human beings are prewired for attachment. Nurturing and dependable relationships are the building blocks of healthy childhood development.

- Attachment affects the brain's structure, function, and genetic expression.
- Children who begin their lives with secure attachment are healthier in all areas—mentally, emotionally, socially, morally, and biochemically.
- Your *mindset about attachment* is the primary factor in determining your child's attachment pattern.
- You can't "fix" your child, but you can create a healing environment.
- The primary goals of this book are to give you the *information, skills, support, self-awareness,* and *hope* to be a healing parent.

2

Attachment: The Core

It is better to build children than repair adults.
—**Anonymous**

Attachment is the deep and enduring biological, emotional, and social connection caregivers and children establish early in life. The attachment relationship is the core of a child's world and the foundation on which life is built. Attachment security is the most powerful predictor of life success.

The creation of attachment occurs as a combination of both nature (biology) and nurture (experience). We are hardwired to connect. Babies are instinctively motivated to seek closeness and communication with their parents. Parents instinctively love, nurture, and protect their young, and promote secure attachment via smiles, eye contact, positive feelings, loving touch, gentle soothing, and other forms of need-fulfillment. Attachment is mutual, a deep sense of security that children and parents create together in their ongoing reciprocal interactions. Children learn to trust dependable caregivers who provide the right balance of love, limits, protection, and guidance.

The development of attachment is not only a result of the parent-child relationship, but is also influenced by the larger emotional network of family and community. Family system influences include the role of father, siblings, the quality of the marital relationship, and extended kin (e.g., grandparents). Social systems, such as school, religious and community organizations, and child welfare agencies, also affect the family and subsequent attachments (Levy & Orlans 1998).

Attachment affects us throughout our lifespan. Studies have shown the importance of secure attachment for adults. Men and women who feel loved and supported are more often happier and healthier, less likely to develop a serious illness, and recover more quickly from medical problems, than those without loving connections. Adults who do not have close emotional attachments have five times the risk of premature death than those with close family ties and supportive friends (Hafen et al. 1996).

Vital Functions of Secure Attachment in Child Development

Children learn the basics of how to think, feel, relate, and communicate from the quality of their early attachments. Secure attachment serves the following vital functions in child development. Each will be discussed in detail later in the chapter.

- *Basic human need* creates a strong desire (instinct) in the parent and baby to stay close to one another for safety, protection, and survival.
- *Safe haven* enables the child to explore his environment with feelings of safety and security (secure base). Children become confident, competent, and learn best, when they explore and interact without undue anxiety.
- *Trust and reciprocity* teaches basic trust, intimacy, and reciprocity, the give-and-take of all healthy relationships. This serves as a foundation for sharing and cooperating, and is a template for meaningful relationships throughout life.
- *Brain development* affects the structure, function, and growth of the brain. Attachment is the most important social factor shaping the growth of the child's brain and mind.
- *Self-regulation* leads to the ability to control impulses and emotions, a cornerstone of early childhood development. Parents' soothing and stimulation eventually becomes internalized and the child learns self-control.
- *Core beliefs* form the basis for a child's mindset about self, caregivers, and her world in general (internal working model). This results in self-identity, including feelings of self-worth, competency, and the balance between dependence and independence.
- *Morality* fosters prosocial morality, including empathy, compassion, and the development of a conscience. Antisocial morality (selfishness, vindictiveness, lack of remorse) often results from compromised attachment.
- *Resilience* promotes resiliency, the ability to bounce back from life's challenges. Reduces the negative effects of stress and trauma throughout life.

A Basic Human Need

In the 1940s, psychiatrist René Spitz studied orphaned children raised in foundling homes and institutions (Spitz 1945). They were bathed, fed, and clothed, but were not touched, hugged, or played with. The rationale was to prevent the children from getting sick by exposing them to human contact and germs. These children became withdrawn, depressed, thin, and sickly. The death rates in these sterile institutions around the turn of the century were between 75 and 100%! Spitz had discovered what is now called "failure to thrive syndrome;" lack of human contact and interaction is gravely damaging and, in fact, lethal to babies and young children.

Attachment between infant and caregiver is a basic human need; it is instinctual. Babies are born with their brains *prewired* to connect. Their very survival is dependent upon the care they receive. Human infants require a longer period of protection and nurturance than any other mammal, making the parental responsibility also the greatest. Babies possess an inborn drive to be close to and communicate with their mothers or other primary caregivers, and feel distress when that connection is absent. The helpless and vulnerable infant feels safety and security over time as the caregiver meets his emotional and physical needs in a sensitive and timely fashion. John Bowlby, a pioneer of attachment theory in the 1950s, called this a *secure base,* the foundation necessary for children to explore, learn, and develop in healthy ways (Bowlby 1988).

What is obvious to most people—that secure attachment is healthy and neglect is damaging—has been demonstrated by decades of animal studies. Baby monkeys were given a choice of two substitute "mothers," one made of wire mesh holding a bottle filled with milk, and another made from terrycloth that offered no milk. The babies spent most of their time with the soft and furry "mom." They communicated with her, held her tight, and used her as a safe haven when frightened (Harlow 1958). Monkeys, just like humans, have an inner need to connect with a cuddly attachment figure.

Monkeys reared without their mothers and in social isolation show signs of severe disturbances when older: unpredictable aggression and violence, inability to form normal relationships, self-mutilation and self-stimulation (e.g., bang their heads, prolonged rocking), eating disorders, learning disabilities, and the inability to raise their own offspring (they reject and attack their babies). These traits are also found in human children and adults who experience a lack of secure and loving attachment in the first few years of life (Suomi 1991).

A Safe Haven

Secure attachment provides a safe haven for the vulnerable child; a shelter, sanctuary, and place of safety. Infants and toddlers are dependent on their parents or other caregivers to provide protection, security, and meet basic needs. Babies instinctively stay close to their attachment figures.

Toddlers with a secure base can wander off and explore their environments without undo stress and anxiety knowing they have reliable caregivers to protect them. They will look back and go back seeking reassurance from their attachment figures. This safe haven reduces the child's fear in novel and challenging situations, allowing him to explore and learn with confidence ("Stay here so I can do it myself"). The result is healthy cognitive, emotional, and social development.

Toddlers without a secure base and safe haven do not learn to count on a dependable caregiver for safety and protection. They will wander off without checking back and often do not develop *stranger anxiety.* This is very dangerous because they will go to anyone. Their high levels of stress and anxiety also interfere with their ability to learn.

The ability to explore and learn with security and confidence leads to feelings of self-efficacy, a building block of good self-esteem. The child learns he can produce a desired result, influence others, and affect his world. He begins to feel competent, a sense of mastery that brings about optimism and a solid sense of self. Compare this to the feelings of helplessness and pessimism of the child lacking secure attachment. Children with compromised attachment act pseudoindependent; their self-assured and independent behavior is a façade covering insecurity, neediness, and fear.

Emotionally sensitive parents give children a haven of safety when they are frightened or upset, helping them cope with sadness, fear, and other stressful emotions. An emotional relationship is established in which the parent's responses increase positive emotions, such as joy, love, and serenity, while reducing negative emotions, including anxiety, fear, and shame.

Children develop different attachment patterns as a result of how caregivers treat them, especially regarding caregivers' sensitivity and availability. The child who can rely on his parents to be available in loving and reassuring ways, especially in times of need or distress, forms a *secure attachment*. His experience tells him he can expect his parents to be dependable and protective in the future.

I pretend I don't need anybody.

Some parents cannot be counted on to be sensitive, responsive, and meet their children's needs, usually because of mental and emotional problems (e.g., depression, violence, drug and alcohol abuse, immaturity, unresolved psychological wounds, unwanted pregnancy). These children learn caregivers are not reliable and safe, and therefore, expect the same harsh, insensitive, and painful treatment in the future. They learn to adapt to these unfortunate circumstances in order to survive, and develop insecure attachment strategies to cope with their caregivers, especially when frightened or distressed.

When young children have parents who are emotionally unavailable and rejecting, they learn to turn away, as if to say, "I don't need you." *Avoidant attachment* patterns develop; they dismiss their caregivers just as they were dismissed. Children turn-off or deactivate attachment behavior, because they have learned to tune-out and avoid.

When young children have caregivers who are inconsistent, sometimes meeting their needs and other times unavailable, they never know what to expect. *Resistant or ambivalent attachments* develop. They are anxious, not easily soothed, and seek-out but then pull away from caregivers, as if to say, "I need you but can't trust you; I'll give you the same mixed signals that you give me." These children can't seem to turn off their attachment behavior (overactivated). They work hard at getting their caregivers to respond and are constantly filled with anxiety.

The most dangerous and destructive scenario is when caregivers are physically, emotionally, or sexually abusive, or neglect their children's basic needs for love, security, or protection. These children are traumatized and have a total breakdown in their reaction to caregivers. They have no idea how to adapt or respond, and develop *disorganized-disoriented*

attachments. They appear confused, scared, and often dissociate and act in bizarre and "crazy" ways. As many as 80% of abused, neglected, and traumatized children have these very disturbed attachment patterns (Lyons-Ruth 1996).

Disturbed and compromised attachment patterns also develop in biologically-intact families. Factors such as unwanted pregnancy, premature birth, postpartum depression, domestic violence, and abuse and neglect, can contribute to insecure or disorganized-disoriented attachment patterns. Damage to these children can be prevented by effective interventions. For example, there is considerable research on the health benefits of premature babies being touched, massaged, and stimulated by caregivers. They gain weight quicker, have fewer medical complications, and leave the hospital sooner than the babies who are left alone more (Field et al. 1996).

Trust and Reciprocity

The development of trust is a basic task that must be accomplished in the early stages of life. Trust provides a foundation for future emotional and social growth, and serves as a template for all future relationships. Trust is learned within the context of child-parent attachment—an ongoing *reciprocal partnership*.

One of the primary long-term effects of secure attachment is the development of socialization skills. An important way this is accomplished is by learning reciprocity—the give-and-take of relationships. The reciprocal relationship begins in the womb. Physical and emotional communication between the unborn baby and her parents (particularly Mom) has a major impact on future health and development. Every sensory system of the fetus is capable of functioning. For example, a 5-month-old fetus can recognize the voice of his mother and father (DeCasper & Fifer 1980). Mother and unborn baby are in-sync, already forming a reciprocal attachment. They even coordinate sleep and activity schedules. Pregnant women instinctively rub their abdomen gently in response to their baby's kicks and talk in soft and soothing ways. Many believe this is the beginning of the child feeling loved and wanted.

A newborn baby's nervous system is not well-organized. It is through the mutual give-and-take between infant and caregiver/parent that organization and development occurs. For example, the baby's smile brings joy and pleasure to the enchanted mother, motivating her to cuddle and stay close. Conversely, mother's familiar smile soothes and relaxes her baby. Her love and sensitivity actually regulates her baby's body and brain—maternal touch stimulates growth hormones; her milk changes the baby's heart rate. By three months of age, more than 50% of the moods and behaviors of mothers are influenced by her baby, while 40% of the infants' behaviors are a reaction to Mom. Mothers and babies continuously affect each other—the *dance of reciprocity* (Tronick & Weinberg 1997).

This reciprocal relationship relies on the baby's ability to communicate needs, as well as the parents' ability to accurately read their baby's signals and respond in a timely and sensitive way. This occurs in the First Year of Life Attachment Cycle (see Figure 1). The infant communicates his needs through arousal (e.g., crying, facial expressions, motion), and the parent meets the baby's needs. Through the ongoing alleviation of arousal and discomfort, and gratification of basic needs, the baby develops trust and security. This also directly affects a child's developing sense of self, impulse control, and ability to form loving and compassionate relationships in the future.

Figure 1. First Year of Life Attachment Cycle

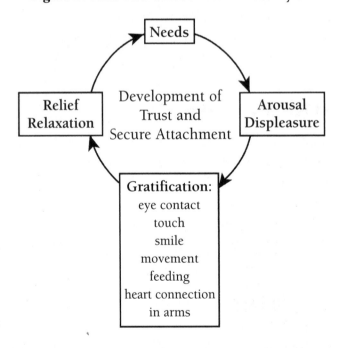

The Developing Brain

Scientists have learned more about the brain in the last 10 years than in all of history. Advanced technology has given us amazing insights into the workings of the brain. The human brain is the most complex structure, natural or artificial, known: 20 billion neurons, 2 million miles of neuronal fibers, 100 billion brain cells, trillions of connections (Kutulak 1996).

The old concept of the brain was of a self-contained, hardwired machine that was unchangeable after childhood. We now realize our brains continually develop new connections, and experiences actually change our brain's chemistry, structure, and genetic expression throughout life (you can teach an old dog new tricks). It is relationship experiences in the first few years of life, however, that are most important in shaping the development of the brain and behavior. This is because a child's brain grows at the quickest rate during the first three years of life. The brain reaches 75% of its adult size by the third or fourth year.

There has been an ongoing debate about the influence of genetics or environment on the child's development—known as nature versus nurture. We now know development is a result of the combination of both nature (biology and genetics) and nurture (experience and environment). Nature supplies the blueprint or potential, and nurture is the architect that determines the final result. This partnership between your genes and your environment is at the heart of who you become. A child's environment consists primarily of close emotional relationships, and *these attachments are the most important social factor that affects the developing brain.* The social world of the child during the first 45 months (9 months in the womb, 3 years after birth) actually determines how the brain and mind are formed, and how well they work.

The human brain is composed of three distinct but intersecting areas—*brain stem, limbic system,* and *neocortex*—a triune brain (see Figure 2). The *brain stem* is the most primitive part, and controls basic states of arousal, alertness, and physiology (e.g., heart rate, breathing, body temperature). The *limbic system* is the center of emotion, social behavior, and attachment. It regulates emotion, memory, motivation, and stress. The *neocortex* is in charge of complex information-processing functions, such as abstract thinking, reasoning, and awareness, the ability to observe our own thoughts, feelings, and actions (MacLean 1990).

Figure 2. Triune Brain

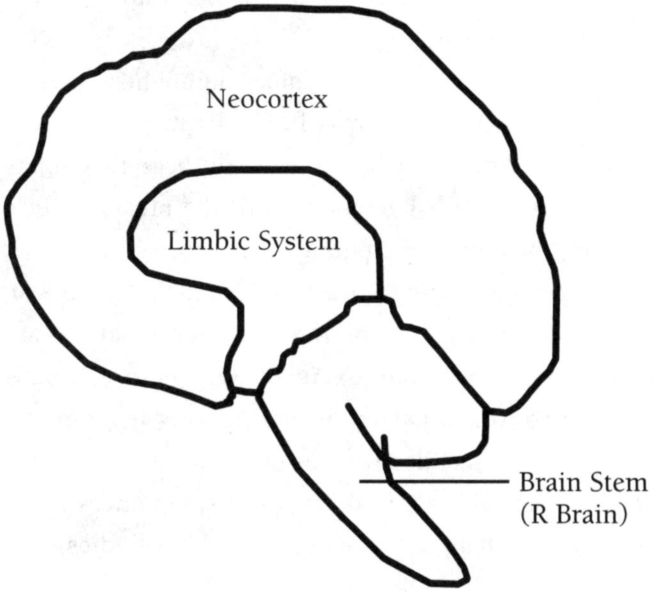

Neocortex

Limbic System

Brain Stem
(R Brain)

The three parts of the brain continually exchange information. Under conditions of threat and heightened emotion the limbic system takes control with automatic reactions of self-preservation, commonly known as the "fight-flight-freeze" response. When feeling secure, safe, and calm, logic and reasoning are switched on by the neocortex. Thus, children who feel frightened and insecure because of the absence of nurturing and protective caregivers are less apt to use logic and more likely to remain in their limbic brains—emotionally aroused, highly anxious, and reacting on the basis of self-preservation. Children learn best when they feel calm, safe, and nurtured. When attachment is disrupted, a child's brain is focused more on self-preservation and survival and less on being inquisitive and learning.

The limbic system plays a pivotal role in the emergence of attachment and is most altered by the stress of compromised and insecure attachment. To better understand this, it is necessary to know the difference between a closed-loop and open-loop system. A *closed-loop system* regulates itself, with no help from the outside world. For example, our circulatory system is closed-loop; our blood keeps flowing inside our body regardless of how others behave. The human brain, especially the emotional limbic system, is an *open-loop system*; it relies on attuned and caring input from attachment figures for healthy growth and functioning (Lewis et al. 2000).

A baby's experiences with caregivers actually shape the way her brain forms and operates. Most affected are the parts of the brain that regulate self-control, the release of stress hormones, and the way genes are expressed. Thus, it is common for children with histories of abuse, neglect, and compromised attachment, to have elevated stress hormone levels and problems with self-control. They are often impulsive, inflexible, and have temper tantrums. Inherited tendencies, such as mental illness, alcoholism, and hyperactivity, are also more likely to emerge without the buffer of secure attachment.

A study with premature babies highlights the open-loop nature of an infant's physiology (Ingersoll & Thomas 1994). Premature infants slept with either a regular teddy bear or a "breathing bear"—a teddy bear that inflates or deflates in-sync with the breathing of the baby. Infants with the breathing bears were able to sleep better and develop healthier respiration than those with static teddy bears. Of course, it would have been even better if they slept in their mother's arms!

Another example of the open-loop nature of the infant-mother connection involves the hormone oxytocin. Oxytocin is a substance released during birth to induce contractions and during nursing to promote caregiving and attachment. As the newborn suckles the mother's breast more oxytocin is released in the mother's body, which helps shrink the uterus, enhances the follow of milk, and relaxes both mother and baby, affecting one another's bodies, emotions, and attachment (Quartz & Sejnowski 2002).

Self Regulation

Stress is a natural part of living, but too much stress is damaging, especially to the young and vulnerable brain. Humans have a built-in mechanism to deal with threatening situations—the *stress response*. When faced with danger, a flood of chemical messengers is released into our brain and body. These stress hormones (e.g., adrenaline, norepinephrine, and cortisol), originating in the limbic system, shift energy away from non-critical tasks, such as digestion, and towards survival-oriented tasks. This alarm reaction rivets our attention on the threat, quickens our heart rate and breathing, and increases energy to our muscles (fight-flight-freeze). This automatic reaction is very useful when coping with short-term challenges. For example, we all know the purpose of an "adrenaline rush" is to avoid danger or have more available energy in a crisis. However, when the stress response is activated continually, as in abuse, neglect, and compromised attachment, it leads to damage to the brains, bodies, and behavior of children.

Infants under acute and chronic stress often respond with apathy, withdrawal, loss of appetite, and failure to thrive. They are overaroused, cry excessively, have trouble sleeping, and eventually become detached and emotionally unreachable. Over time, these children become hypervigilant, fearful, aggressive, have impaired memory and cognitive skills, and are at risk for health problems. Serious psychological and social problems often result later in life, including depression, anxiety, post-traumatic stress disorder (PTSD), eating and dissociative disorders, and alcohol and drug abuse. One of the most alarming results of chronic stress in children is their inability to control emotions and behavior, leading to aggressive, impulsive, and antisocial reactions.

I am very energetic.

How does secure attachment facilitate self-regulation? Initially, the sensitive and loving parent helps regulate her baby's mind and body by attunement to signals and needs. Eventually the child internalizes her parents' ongoing comfort and support, and learns to soothe and regulate herself (self-control). The sensitive parent provides a balance of *up-regulation,* such as playful stimulation, and *down-regulation,* including gentle touch and a calm voice. For example, the well-attuned mom holds, rocks, and soothes her crying baby, who then goes to sleep feeling safe and relaxed. Infants and young children without loving and supportive caregivers fail to learn the crucial life skill of self-regulation. They commonly lack frustration tolerance and impulse control, are chronically inflexible, exhibit intense anger and aggression, and cannot handle stress and anxiety.

As previously stated, the human infant is the most helpless mammal on earth, depending on the caregiver for his very survival. The responsive and sensitive parent serves as a protective barrier or cushion, shielding the child from danger, threat, and damaging levels of stress. For instance, the stress hormone cortisol naturally lowers at night in securely attached babies, allowing for calm and restful sleep. Cortisol levels remain high, however, in children with histories of insecure attachment and maltreatment. They remain over-aroused and stressed. Securely attached babies have lower levels of stress hormones in their systems even after stress, compared to babies with disrupted attachment (Dozier et al. 2002b).

An important job of parents is to buffer their children from stress. The absence of a protective and dependable caregiver leaves children without the necessary help in regulating distress. These babies and young children experience stress as overwhelming, unmanageable, and disorganizing. As they grow older they are not able to effectively manage emotions and impulses, and lack the skill to handle external challenges, such as peer relationships, authority, or school.

Core Beliefs

Early experiences with caregivers shape a child's core beliefs about self, others, and life in general. It is necessary to understand how memory works in order to appreciate the way core beliefs form and affect a child's life. Memory links our past, present, and future. Images stored in the brain become expectations about future events. There are two types of memory that develop in the early years. The first, *implicit memory* is present at birth. An infant's brain is capable of creating "mental models" which involve images and emotions based on experiences with caregivers. Implicit memory does not involve conscious processing but nevertheless affects the baby's behavior and reactions. For example, babies with secure attachments have positive images encoded in their minds—"Parents are safe, nurturing, and dependable"—and anticipate more loving care in the future. Insecurely attached babies encode negative images—"Parents are threatening, unloving, and unavailable"—and learn to expect continued harsh or neglectful treatment.

Explicit memory, the second type, develops by two years of age. A child is now learning language, has conscious awareness, and can remember himself in a specific past event. By now the toddler can bring up a sensory image of his parent or caregiver, including pictures, body sensations, and emotions. The secure child feels calm and relaxed. The insecure child feels anxious and tense.

Experiences of the baby and young child are encoded in the brain. Emotional experiences of nurturance and protection are encoded in the brain's limbic area, the emotional center. Over time, repeated encoded experiences become internal working models—core beliefs about self, self in relation to others, and the world in general. These core beliefs become the lens through which children (and later adults) view themselves and others, especially authority and attachment figures. Core beliefs serve to interpret the present and anticipate the future. You get what you expect, and your expectations are based on past experiences. The brain is an anticipation machine (Siegel 1999).

A child's core beliefs become deeply engrained and operate outside of conscious awareness, affecting how he perceives himself and interprets events and social situations. Children who lack secure and loving attachments commonly blame themselves, and develop a self-image as helpless, bad, and unlovable. These children see danger even when it is not there. They misinterpret social cues, assume the worst, and over-react emotionally and behaviorally. The result is ongoing conflict with parents and peers, aggressive and controlling behavior, and further damage to self-esteem.

The core beliefs of children who have experienced secure and compromised attachments in the early years are as follows:

SECURE ATTACHMENT.
- *Self.* "I am good, wanted, worthwhile, competent, and lovable."
- *Caregivers.* "They are appropriately responsive to my needs, sensitive, dependable, caring, trustworthy."
- *Life.* "My world feels safe; life is worth living."

COMPROMISED ATTACHMENT.
- *Self.* "I am bad, unwanted, worthless, helpless, and unlovable."
- *Caregivers.* "They are unresponsive to my needs, insensitive, hurtful, and untrustworthy."
- *Life.* "My world feels unsafe; life is painful and burdensome."

The goal of *Corrective Attachment Parenting* (CAP) is not merely to change children's behavior, but rather to change their negative core beliefs. This is quite challenging, because core beliefs are rigid, automatic, and associated with self-protection and survival. Your relationship with your child becomes the pathway to change and healing. Without change, negative core beliefs formed early in life remain fixed into adulthood, with severe social and emotional consequences.

Morality

Culturally, the development of prosocial morality had survival value. Our ancestors shifted over time from isolated gatherers to cooperative hunter-gatherers. As the only animals that lacked built-in weapons, such as claws and fangs, humans relied on intelligence and cooperation to survive. Small tribes could only survive if the members helped one another; the needs of the community overrode the needs of the individual. Values that included empathy, sensitivity, sharing, and altruism became keys to our survival.

We are still social animals, and the family is the primary social environment in which children learn values and a moral code of conduct. Prosocial morality, including empathy, cooperation, and conscience, are learned in early secure and loving attachment relationships. Traits are formed, such as identifying with the needs and feelings of others, knowing and acting in right and decent ways, and being respectful, tolerant, charitable, and fair. A child learns the content of her parents' moral code and has the desire to follow that standard. Children who experience maltreatment and compromised attachment commonly develop conduct disorders and antisocial morality. As early as elementary school and into preadolescence, they show a lack of remorse and empathy, are deceitful, manipulative, and selfish, and have a total disregard for the rules of society. They lack an inner voice, or "conscience," to help make correct decisions and restrain destructive impulses (Levy & Orlans 2000a).

Empathy is at the root of morality. The ability to feel for someone else leads children and adults to follow moral principles. Assuming there is safety and security, empathy begins in infancy. Infants are upset when they hear another baby's distress, and cry when they see another baby's tears. At one year old, children feel upset when a playmate gets hurt and try to help soothe the child. By age two, children realize they are separate and distinct from others, and are even more sensitive to another's feelings (Zahn-Waxler et al. 1992). Empathy becomes more complex by late childhood. Children not only feel for another's pain, but can also have compassion for groups, such as the poor or oppressed. This is the foundation for following moral principles.

I can be good sometimes.   *But then I do something that screws me up. I go back to my devilish ways.*

Prosocial morality evolves within the secure parent-child relationship by four psychological processes: *modeling, internalizing, attunement,* and *self-identity.* Children learn more from modeling than by any other means—they do what we do, not what we say. When parents model empathy, honesty, integrity, and caring about others, they rear children who have these same values. Securely attached children are more caring toward peers and more likely to be chosen as playmates by age three, compared to those with insecure attachments. By age five, children with secure attachments are more compassionate and better friends, while those with compromised attachment are often insensitive and cruel, taking pleasure in another child's distress (Sroufe 1983).

To be an effective positive role model you must set a strong moral example—*walk your talk*. Do you control your anger and manage stress well? Show patience and follow rules? Indulge in unhealthy habits, such as excessive drinking, smoking, eating, or gambling? Treat your spouse and children with love and respect? Treating children with respect gives them the experience of being respected. They are then more likely to show others respect.

In order to be an effective role model you must be available. Parents who do best at fostering empathy are emotionally available and actively involved in their children's lives. Today's parents spend 40% less time with their children than parents 30 years ago. Mothers working outside the home spend an average of 11 minutes a day in quality interactions with their children. Mothers who do not work outside the home spend 13 minutes a day. Fathers spend only 8 minutes a day on weekdays and 14 minutes a day on weekends. Children need quality time with their mentors and role models (Greenspan 1999).

I try to be good but then my anger takes over.

Children also develop empathy and morality through internalization; they absorb the values and actions of parents and other attachment figures. A child raised with loving care wants to please her parents, to see a parent smile, and feels upset when Mom or Dad is unhappy with her behavior. Over time, children are not only motivated by rewards and punishments, but internalize a moral inner voice. Securely attached children internalize a prosocial inner voice that guides them toward empathy, honesty, and self-control. They become self-directed, can think for themselves, and judge their own choices and actions. They develop the following characteristics: high self-esteem, self-confidence, and a sense of competence; high moral character, integrity, and self-discipline; and the desire to contribute to the family and other social groups.

Children with compromised attachment typically internalize antisocial standards, such as selfishness, aggression, and dishonesty. Their inner voice tells them not to trust. Instead, they are guided by self-preservation and often by a lack of conscience and feelings of remorse. They are externally directed; scanning their environment for danger, fearing disapproval and abuse, lacking an inner compass to guide and motivate them toward success and fulfillment (Medhus 2001).

Emotional attunement and reciprocity is the third process that leads to empathy and morality. The capacity for empathy stems from emotional attunement, being aware of your own feelings and mental states, and attuned to the inner states of others. For instance, a loving mother is in-sync with the needs and feelings of her baby—emotionally and mentally attuned. By looking into his eyes and understanding his gestures, Mom knows when to cuddle or let him be, when to stimulate or soothe. Mother and child are becoming attuned to one another—*limbic resonance*—the key to emotional connection and secure attachment. He is learning how to be aware of the feelings and needs of another person by being in-sync with his caregiver. Secure attachment involves heightened awareness of another's mental and emotional states, a primary ingredient of empathy and prosocial morality (Siegel & Hartzell 2003).

The capacity for attunement is based on one's talent for reading nonverbal cues, such as facial expressions, gestures, and tone of voice. This is important because 90% or more of emotional communication is nonverbal—not just what you say, but *how* you say it. Studies show children who are skilled at reading nonverbal messages are the most popular and emotionally stable. They also do better academically than the children less skilled at nonverbal communication, even though their average IQ's are not higher. Their emotional intelligence, including competencies such as empathy, cooperation, and the art of listening, help them achieve intellectual and social success (Goleman 1995).

The fourth factor contributing to prosocial morality is a positive self-identity. Caring for others starts with a solid and positive sense of self. As previously described, a child's self-identity develops as a function of the way in which attachments are formed. A solid foundation of safe and secure attachment, with positive messages, healthy boundaries, and sufficient support, leads to a positive self-image. Children lacking this healthy foundation develop a weak, fragmented, and negative self-image. Feeling insecure and frightened, they fight to survive in a world perceived as threatening and unsafe, preventing the development of empathy, kindness, or other prosocial values. Instead, they assume a controlling, defensive, and hostile stance toward others in order to survive (Trevarthen 1993).

Sometimes I can handle things.

Resilience

Resilience is the ability to recover or bounce back following adverse and stressful life events. The study of resilience explains why some children who experience maltreatment and compromised attachment develop serious emotional and social problems over time, while others overcome these obstacles, rise above their traumatic beginnings, and lead healthy and fulfilling lives.

Resilience is established as a result of the balance between a child's *protective factors* and *risk factors*. Protective factors reduce the effects of adversity and promote resiliency. Risk factors increase the likelihood of severe and harmful difficulties in the future, especially under detrimental and stressful conditions. There are three types of protective factors in childhood: 1) *qualities of mind and character,* such as sociability, cognitive skills, high self-esteem, communication skills, and accountability for one's actions (rather than a victim mindset and blaming); 2) *family ties,* including emotional support (especially during stressful times), stability at home, and parents who set appropriate rules, respect individuality, and foster security in the parent-child relationship; and 3) *external support systems,* consisting of community, extended kin, school, and religious affiliations that render support, as well as positive principles and guidelines to live by (Brooks & Goldstein 2001).

Secure attachment, although not a guarantee of mental health, has been found to be the most important protective factor. Secure attachment serves as a buffer against later problems caused by adversity and stress. The quality of parent-child attachment actually determines how well children cope following early loss. In a 40-year study, one-third of the children who experienced early adversity, such as poverty, parental substance abuse and serious psychological problems, and family breakup, became well-adjusted and caring adults. The quality of their primary attachment relationships was found to be the most significant ingredient regarding future functioning (Werner 1989). Infants and young children who have supportive, sensitive, and reliable caregivers are healthier and happier over time in many ways: better coping skills, resistance to stress, self-esteem, family ties, and friendships; greater trust, intimacy, empathy, and success in school and work.

Although not all infants and toddlers who have compromised attachment develop severe psychosocial problems, it is clear that insecure attachments are pathways toward such problems. Children with anxious attachment are at risk for becoming aggressive and depressed, developing anxiety and personality disorders, and having ongoing difficulties in relationships. Limited social support leaves them without a buffer or cushion in dealing with stress and uncertainty, which only makes matters worse. Children with *disorganized-disoriented* attachment, a result of chronic and severe abuse and neglect, are vulnerable to dissociation, antisocial personality, and other severe forms of psychological dysfunction.

Compromised attachment is also a risk factor due to the damaging biochemical effects in the brain of young children. The increased levels of adrenaline and reduced levels of serotonin, associated with maltreatment and lack of loving and sensitive care, leads to aggression, impulsivity, anger, and fear. They become children, and later adults, who see danger around every corner, trust no one, fail repeatedly, take-out their pain and anger on others, lack social skills, and end up alone and alienated.

Healing parents, those who value self-growth and know how to create a healing environment for their children, foster resiliency. As a healing parent, you know your child can overcome challenges with the proper guidance, support, structure, and love. You know the difference between victims and survivors: victims focus on what they can't change, while survivors focus on what they can and will change.

The Healing Power of Family

Humans are genetically programmed to form kinship bonds through which we learn the lessons of love, caring, and attachment. The family is the classroom in which this learning occurs. The powerful benefits of loving attachments in families come from several sources: the feeling of being loved and cared for; the experience of being valued and

esteemed; the sense of belonging to a clan with responsibilities and obligations to one another. Nurturing and supportive relationships in families act as a buffer against stress and help prevent physical and emotional illness. Members of strong families enjoy many health benefits, including the following (Ornish 1998; Rowe & Kahn 1998):

- recover more quickly from surgery and follow medical instructions better,
- manage chronic illness better (e.g., children in healthy families manage diabetes better),
- are less likely to develop heart disease and more likely to survive a heart attack,
- are better able to handle unemployment,
- do better in stressful situations, including the death of a loved one,

- live longer than people in unhealthy or weaker families, and
- experience less stress from hospital procedures when parents are present with the children.

Abuse, neglect, unresolved loss, and other damaging experiences in early relationships result in children who are emotionally, socially, and physically injured and/or delayed. A healing family environment, however, can repair prior damage as well as encourage growth and development. How do you make right experiences that were so wrong? How can you foster trust in a child after so much hurt and betrayal? How do you help children feel deserving of and accept love when they see themselves as defective and unlovable? How do parents remain "centered" and committed to a child who constantly challenges, rejects, threatens, and manipulates? The chapters to follow will describe the factors that make the family a healing environment, and provide specific solutions and skills to achieve that goal.

Love, Support, and Health

It is a well-known fact loving and supportive relationships play a powerful role in determining illness and health from infancy to old age. Children who have secure and stable attachments do better in every important realm of life. Adults with loving and supportive relationships are healthier and happier—they live longer, are better at managing stress and adversity, and recover more quickly from disease. Healthy attachments are also protective; they enhance our immune system, strengthen resistance to disease, and act as a buffer to reduce the harmful effects of risk factors. Love, support, and intimacy are healing. Conversely, experiences that lead to isolation, loneliness, loss, hostility, and depression create illness and suffering.

One of the first studies to show the power of human connections was done by French sociologist Emile Durkheim more than a century ago. He found people who were a meaningful part of social groups and families were much less likely to commit suicide than those who were alienated and isolated. They felt a sense of belonging, of loving and being loved, of being important to others (Durkheim 1951).

The Harvard Mastery of Stress Study demonstrates how loving relationships affect susceptibility to disease. In the early 1950s, male students were given questionnaires to determine how they felt about their parents. Thirty-five years later their medical records were reviewed. The results were profound: 91% of the men who did not have a warm relationship with their mothers had serious diseases by midlife (e.g., heart problems, high blood pressure, ulcers, alcoholism), compared to only 45% who had more loving relationships. Similar differences were found for father-son relationships (82% versus 50%). These findings were not caused by other risk factors, such as family history of illness, stress, smoking, or divorce. The researchers concluded the perception of being loved could act as a buffer, reducing the negative impact of factors that cause disease, while promoting immune function and health (Russek & Schwartz 1997).

A similar study asked the question: is the quality of human relationships a factor in the development of cancer? More than 1,000 medical students, in the 1940s, were asked about their emotional closeness with their parents. Those who developed cancer 50 years later were much more likely to have lacked close and loving family relationships. They also suffered more from loneliness and relationship difficulties, and more often were hospitalized for mental illness and committed suicide (Thomas & Duszynski 1974).

Adults missing supportive and loving relationships have up to a five times greater risk of premature disease and death from all causes (Cohen 1988). One study found men and women who felt the most support and caring in their network of relationships had much less blockage in the arteries of their hearts. The quality of their emotional relationships was a more important predictor of coronary artery blockages than other factors, such as diet, smoking, cholesterol, genetics, or exercise (Seeman & Syme 1987).

Feeling isolated and lonely is a major health risk factor. Even research with animals shows the health risks of loneliness and benefits of connection. Affectionate petting by humans reduces stress in cats, dogs, and horses. People benefit from the companionship of pets as well. One study of the elderly found pet owners enjoyed better health and had fewer visits to the doctor (Lynch 1977).

The effects of loneliness and support are far-reaching. In a study of labor and delivery the results were striking: 75% of mothers who underwent labor alone developed complications, while only 12% of mothers with supportive partners had complications. Unsupported mothers had an average length of labor of 19.3 hours; the mothers with support had an average labor time less than half as long (Ornstein & Sobel 1987). College students who are lonely and feel less supported were found to have a poorer response to the flu vaccine, visit the health services clinic more frequently, and have longer recovery times when ill, than students with better relationships. Social factors are important, the researchers concluded, because they encourage healthy behaviors, such as eating well, sleeping, and exercise, and also strengthen the immune response (Adelson 2005).

Feeling connected in a loving relationship can overcome risk factors. More than 10,000 married men with no history of angina (chest pain) were studied. Those with the most risk factors (high cholesterol and blood pressure, smoking, diabetes) were more than 20 times more likely to have chest pains in 5 years. However, men who felt most loved by their wives had significantly less angina—even with other risk factors. The wife's love and support diminished the harmful effects of risk factors. In other words, while diet, smoking, blood pressure, and other factors play an important role in developing disease, a loving relationship can actually reduce the negative impact of these forces, helping a person stay healthier (Medalie & Goldbourt 1976).

Many large-scale community studies examined the relationship between human connections and health. One of the most remarkable studies took place over a 50-year period in Roseto, a small town in Pennsylvania. The people of Roseto had a significantly lower death rate from heart attacks compared to those of nearby towns. The risk factors for heart disease in all the towns were the same (diet, smoking, diabetes, water supply). So what accounted for this difference? The residents of Roseto were descendants of settlers from the same village in Italy in the 1880s, and maintained close family ties and a very cohesive community. Beginning in the 1960s, however, there were profound social changes, and a breakdown occurred in traditional values, multigenerational households, and community cohesiveness. There was a significant increase in death due to heart attacks as the community became fragmented and families less close-knit. The researchers concluded the strong sense of community and close family relationships had previously protected the people of Roseto from death (Egolf et al. 1992).

In another study, 7,000 men and women in Alameda County, California, were studied for more than 17 years. Those with the strongest social and community ties had much lower rates of disease and premature death than people who were isolated and alone. Women who lacked closeness and emotional support had a much higher death rate from breast cancer (Berkman 1995; Reynolds & Kaplan 1990). Men and women in foreign countries who are lonely and isolated were found to have four times the risk of death, compared to those who had close and fulfilling relationships (Kaplan et al. 1988).

Marriage provides another arena to understand the benefits of love, support, and attachment. Four decades of research shows how marriage leads to healthier, happier, and longer lives for both men and women. This is due to several factors: emotional support, having a partner who is committed and cares, depending on one another, and giving special meaning and purpose to our lives.

Adults who are not married (including single, widowed, and divorced) are far more likely to die from all causes: 50% higher for women and 250% higher for men. Being unmarried is a greater risk to one's life than cancer or heart disease. Having heart disease shortens the average man's lifespan by about 6 years, while being unmarried reduces the lifespan by almost 10 years. Married men and women are healthier and are less likely to suffer from long-term illnesses (Ornish 1998).

The emotional and social support marriage offers can boost the immune system and improve both physical and mental health. Emotional and social support has important physical as well as psychological effects. Men who have high levels of support were found to have less stress hormones (epinephrine, norepinephrine, cortisol) in their bodies. Reduced stress results in better health (Rowe & Kahn 1998).

Some of the health benefits of marriage also come from having a partner to talk to about feelings and stressful events. Married people have less depression, anxiety, and other psychological problems, than the unmarried. Divorced and widowed persons are three times more likely to commit suicide than those who are married. The health benefits of marriage continue into old age. A study of married Medicare recipients found men are less likely to die, women are less likely to become disabled, and both men and women do not enter nursing homes as often, compared to unmarried seniors (Schoenbach et al. 1986).

The physical and emotional benefits of marriage cannot be explained by the idea of simply living with someone else. There is something very special about marriage itself. Marriage increases the sense of meaning in people's lives. Cohabitation (living together) just does not result in the same kinds of health benefits for either men or women. Spouses know they are deeply connected, their lives are intertwined, and there is a feeling of responsibility for one another. People who live together without being married are typically more interested in autonomy—remaining separate and independent. On the whole, the deep and enduring attachment that is found in a loving marriage makes people healthier and happier.

Summary

- Attachment is the deep and enduring biological, emotional, and social connection caregivers and children establish early in life. It is a basic human need.

- Attachment security is the most powerful predictor of life success, and directly affects learning, brain development, self-control, trust and reciprocity, core beliefs, morality, and resilience.

- Children with disrupted attachment are more focused on self-preservation and survival, and less on being inquisitive and learning.

- Maltreatment and compromised attachment result in elevated stress hormones and lack of self-control.

- Positive images are encoded in the minds of securely attached children— "Parents are safe, nurturing, and dependable"—and they anticipate more loving care in the future.

- Insecurely attached children encode negative images—" Parents are threatening, rejecting, and unavailable"—and they expect harsh treatment in the future.

- Your relationship with your child is the pathway to change and healing.

- Limbic resonance—caregiver and child attuned to one another—is the key to emotional connection and secure attachment.

- Love, support, and intimacy protect us from illness. Isolation and loneliness are major risk factors for illness.

3
Know Your Child

The lotus is a flower that grows in the mud. The thicker
and deeper the mud, the more beautiful the lotus blooms.

—Zen saying

Y ou must understand your child before you can help her. Before getting into
the details of assessment, however, there are a number of important factors to
consider. First, it is essential to focus not only on problems, but on strengths
as well; not just on "what's wrong," but also on "what's right" with your child.
Acknowledging your child's positive attributes, special talents and abilities, and

underlying desire for a better life, leads to positivism and hope. Second, remember your child is not her label or diagnosis. Diagnostic categories and labels are meant to guide our understanding and planning, not to define everything about your child. Look beyond the labels so you can understand and appreciate your child completely.

Third, children are products of their environments and behave differently under various conditions. Thinking, feeling, and behavior often change based on the type of structure, level of support, expectations, dynamics of relationships and roles played, and the child's perceptions of events and people. Therefore, it is necessary to observe your child in diverse settings—home, school, friends and family member's homes, and other places. Notice what type of settings bring out the best and worst in your child. Build on the positive.

Fourth, don't overlook the bigger picture. Children live in families, but families are part of larger social, community, and cultural systems. How do school, neighborhood, social services, extended kin, and religious affiliations influence the lives of your children, yourself, and your family?

Fifth, knowing about developmental issues is crucial. Understanding normal child development helps you see where your child is in comparison to other children. Each stage of development has its own characteristics and challenges. Knowing your child's developmental stage at the time of loss, stress, or trauma will enable you to appreciate how he was affected and where to put your healing focus. For example, trust and self-control are learned in the early stages of development when there is secure attachment. The capacity to trust and ability to exercise self-control can be learned later, but requires a consistent and determined effort on the part of caregivers and role models.

Lastly, being sensitive to cultural factors is very important, especially when your child has a different background than your own. Each child is born into a *cultural niche*—beliefs, values, customs, rituals, and behaviors shared by members of a community. These cultural models help people to organize knowledge, interpret events, and know how to act in situations (Finn 2003). For example, each culture has its own beliefs and practices about pregnancy, birth, and childrearing. It is critical to respect the diversity of beliefs and practices of different ethnic, racial, and cultural groups, and to understand how your child is affected. Does your child fit into the culture of your family and community? How can you respect your child's background while also helping her achieve a sense of belonging in your family and community?

Understanding your child completely—mindset, feelings, patterns of behavior, biology, values, and history—is necessary to be a healing parent. This chapter will explain the causes of compromised attachment, the three pillars of assessment, and describe the most common symptoms, traits, and issues.

Causes of Compromised Attachment

Three major factors place children at risk for developing serious attachment problems: *parent/caregiver, child,* and *environmental.* The first factor involves the way in which babies and young children are treated by their parents or caregivers. Abusive, inconsistent, and insensitive care is associated with disrupted attachment. The second factor involves the contributions of the child—what the child brings to the family. For instance, children with fetal alcohol syndrome/effects (FAS/E), failure to thrive, or difficult-to-soothe temperaments are particularly challenging for parents and caregivers. The third factor includes high-stress, chaotic, and unsupportive environments. Violence, poverty, multiple moves in the foster care system, and crowded orphanages are examples of environmental contributions. The following lists cover the situations and experiences that typically result in childhood attachment difficulties.

Parent and Caregiver Factors include:

- abuse or neglect;
- severe psychological problems: depression, bipolar disorder, borderline personality, and other mental illnesses;
- alcohol and drug addiction;
- adolescent parenting;
- prolonged absence: prison, hospitalization, abandonment; and
- family history of maltreatment and compromised attachment.

Child Factors include:

- failure to thrive;
- FAS/E and in-utero drug exposure;
- difficult temperament: inconsolable, moody, colicky;
- poor "fit" between child and parent (for example, outgoing, energetic child and introverted, quiet parents);
- medical conditions: premature birth, chronic pain (e.g., untreated inner ear infections), hospitalizations; and
- genetics: family history of mental illness, criminality, substance abuse.

Environmental Factors include:

- high stress: violent home or neighborhood, chaotic and disorganized family, severe marital conflict;
- out-of-home placements: multiple moves and caregivers (e.g., foster care system, foreign orphanages);
- lack of support: absent parent or extended kin, isolation, lack of medical, mental health, or other services; and
- poverty.

Old Dad/Mom.

Maltreatment

Official statistics indicate between 1 and 3 million children are abused and neglected each year. Anywhere between 16% of men and 20% of women have experienced some type of abuse during childhood (U.S. Department of Health and Human Services 2003). Children younger than age three have the highest rates of victimization.

Abuse and neglect are commonly associated with serious attachment problems. Maltreated children have a high incidence of anxious and disorganized-disoriented attachment. More than 80% of children in high-risk, maltreating families were found to develop disorganized-disoriented attachment—the most severe type of compromised attachment (Lyons-Ruth et al. 1991). Another study found more than 85% of maltreated children in foster care were avoidantly attached; they developed belief systems and expectations that their needs will not be met by others (McWey 2004). Maltreated children develop many emotional, social, and cognitive problems, such as anxiety, depression, conduct disorders, aggression, and delinquency. Child maltreatment interferes with the learning of important developmental tasks, including self-control, self-identity, cooperation with peers, and adapting to the school environment. Abuse and neglect leave their mark on the child's brain, leading to depression, anxiety, posttraumatic stress symptoms, and impulse control problems.

One of the most concerning aftereffects of child maltreatment is the increased risk for violence. Children who are physically and sexually abused are much more likely to perpetrate physical or sexual violence when older and are more likely to be abused again. Witnessing violence in the home or neighborhood has similar effects as maltreatment: PTSD, depression, fear, somatic complaints, social withdrawal, and aggression (Cicchetti 2004; Johnson et al. 2002).

Maltreatment in childhood often leads to antisocial behavior in adolescence and adulthood—crime, aggression, cruel and heartless acts, and lack of remorse and conscience. Two reasons have been found for this link. First, the lack of behavioral and emotional self-control is a common consequence of child maltreatment. These children do not have the ability to regulate their impulses, anger, and stress. Alienation is the second factor that underlies the relation between child maltreatment and later antisocial behavior. Maltreated children lack trust in caregiver's availability, support, and guidance. Thus, they learn to avoid their caregivers, and therefore, have no secure base to provide comfort when distressed. Over time, alienation from others becomes a primary characteristic, leading to antisocial thinking and behavior (Egeland et al. 2002).

The costs of child maltreatment are enormous. The effects on children can last a lifetime. Child maltreatment impacts law enforcement, judicial, social services, school, medical, and mental health systems, as they deal with the incidents and long-term aftermath. Beyond the pain and suffering of children and families, Prevent Child Abuse America has calculated that child abuse and neglect costs the United States more than $94 billion per year (Cicchetti 2004).

Neglect

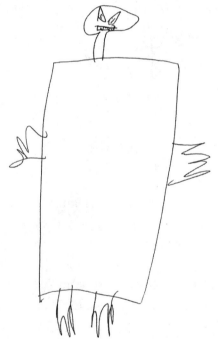

Child neglect is the most frequent form of maltreatment, accounting for about 65% of child abuse reports. Birth parents are responsible for neglect in more than 90% of the cases (NCCAN 1995). Several types of neglect have been identified: physical, emotional, medical, mental health, and educational (Erickson & Egeland 1996).

Emotional neglect, due to inattention to a child's needs for nurturing, support, and comfort, is more harmful than physical neglect or other forms of maltreatment. Babies with emotionally neglectful mothers were found to be anxiously attached at one year of age; angry, noncompliant, and developmentally delayed by three years old; impulsive, excessively anxious, and negativistic in preschool; and by the school years, they were depressed, unpopular, and socially withdrawn (Erickson et al. 1989).

The most extreme form of neglect results in *failure to thrive*, in which infants' emotional, physical, and social needs are unmet. This produces stunted growth, physical illnesses, severe attachment disorders, and is often fatal. Babies must have emotionally responsive caregivers when hungry, tired, or frightened. When such support is lacking, babies develop compromised attachment; they expect to be rejected in the future and live their lives pushing away love and support from others.

Abuse and neglect often lead to different consequences for children. Abused children tend to be more angry and aggressive, while neglected children are more withdrawn, passive, helpless under stress, and show more significant developmental delays (Crittendon & Ainsworth 1989).

Sexual Abuse

Surveys report about 16% of men and almost 30% of women have been sexually molested at some time during childhood (Finkelhor et al. 1990). Sexual abuse is relatively common among children who have severely compromised attachment. Children who have been sexually abused suffer from serious emotional and social problems, not only in the present, but also enduring as adults. Symptoms of sexual abuse include: depression, anxiety, guilt, shame, somatic complaints, disruption of normal development, negative core beliefs, PTSD, and sexual behavior problems. PTSD occurs in almost 50% of sexually abused children (McLeer et al. 1988).

Sexually abused children are likely to be depressed and suicidal, and as adults are four times more likely to suffer from major depression (Stein et al. 1988). Due to the traumatic nature of the sexual experience, these children are often inappropriately sexual (e.g., masturbate openly, molest other children, seductive with adults). They typically blame themselves—"It must be my fault, and I am bad"—resulting in guilt, shame, and self-contempt. They feel powerless, helpless, and profoundly betrayed. Sexual assaults by adults in positions of trust, such as parents (incest) or other authority figures, are even more traumatic because of the intensity of the confusion and betrayal.

Many factors affect a child's reactions to sexual abuse. The characteristics of the abuse are important to understand: "hands off" offenses include witnessing another person expose sexual organs; "hands on" offenses range from fondling to intercourse. More invasive abuse is more damaging. Long-term repetitive abuse is commonly more damaging than a single episode. Abused children are more psychologically wounded when a close family member perpetrates the abuse. Guilt caused by succumbing to the molestation without fighting back is a factor that results in more trauma.

The child's age and stage of development play a role in the outcome. Children have different perceptions and understandings at different stages. A child's "cognitive appraisal" (i.e., what the say to themselves about the experience) is one of the most important mediating factors. The child's history is important: Have there been other traumatic events? What was the child's life and functioning like before the abuse? A child with a history of trauma and loss will have more severe reactions than a stable and secure child.

Support from a parent or caregiver is the most powerful factor determining a child's recovery. Children who can disclose the abuse to a supportive and protective parent are likely to suffer fewer long-term consequences (Kendall-Tackett et al. 1993). Family dysfunction will increase the effects of abuse. The effects are worse in families with more conflict, violence, psychological and substance abuse problems, and less support and cohesion.

In Utero Alcohol and Drug Exposure

Fetal alcohol syndrome (FAS) is the result of heavy drinking by a pregnant woman and has devastating effects on the unborn baby's brain, body, and later development. Symptoms of FAS include: prenatal and postnatal growth deficits; central nervous system dysfunction; mental retardation; impaired learning, memory, impulse control, and judgment; hyperactivity; and attention deficit disorder (ADD). FAS is the most common cause of mental retardation in the United States; the average IQ is 70. Children with FAS have a distinctive look: short, thin, small heads, drooping eyelids, upturned nose, thin upper lips, bulging foreheads, receding chins. They often become teenagers who are depressed and isolated, and adults who get involved in crime, alcoholism, and drug addiction. Children who have a milder form of the syndrome are diagnosed with fetal alcohol effects (FAE). Nearly 12,000 children are born each year in the United States with FAS, and at least 4 times as many with FAE. The rate is 5 times higher among African Americans, and up to 15 times higher among Native Americans (Harvard Mental Health Letter 2004; McCreight 1997).

The increase in out-of-home placements is a direct result of the growing drug abuse problem. Some county social services agencies, for example, cannot keep up with the number of children placed in foster care due to the explosion of methamphetamine use among parents. A psychoactive substance (e.g., cocaine, heroin, methamphetamines) used during pregnancy affects the developing brain and lead to behavioral, developmental, and biochemical problems later in childhood. Cocaine, methamphetamine, and other drug exposure cause premature birth and low birth weight, and leads to painful and damaging withdrawal in the newborn. Cigarette smoking during pregnancy diminishes the flow of oxygen and blood to the placenta and can lead to prematurity (Jaudes & Ekwo 1997).

Drug and alcohol exposure before birth can disrupt later attachment. Infants who are biochemically irritable, agitated, and anxious are often unable to take in the care and nurturance provided by caregivers. They are inconsolable; not able to be soothed, calmed, and comforted. Attachment is disrupted when babies are not able to experience safety, need fulfillment, and a reduction in arousal and discomfort with their parents or caregivers.

Violence

Violence in our society is commonplace, and children are typically the victims. Homicide is the third leading cause of death for children between 5 and 14 years old (Children's Defense Fund 1997). Children are exposed to violence in their homes, schools, and 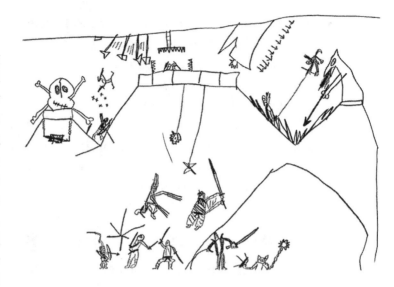 neighborhoods, with severe and damaging emotional, social, developmental, cognitive, physical, and academic consequences. A common reaction in children is posttraumatic stress symptoms: reexperiencing the trauma (nightmares, night terrors); numbing and avoidance (disassociation, emotional detachment); and hyperarousal (anxiety, hyperactivity). Other symptoms include sleep disturbance, separation anxiety, aggressiveness, difficulty concentrating, and depression. When these natural and biological reactions to stress and trauma are not properly addressed and the children are not given the nurturing they need or the means to properly process and cope with what occurred, posttraumatic stress disorder (PTSD) can develop. Violence creates fear and insecurity in children and often results in compromised attachment. The following are the primary factors that lead to violence (see Levy & Orlans 2000a).

FAMILY INFLUENCES. Aggressive and violent children often have parents who have antisocial personalities, use harsh physical punishment, do not provide adequate supervision, and lack involvement in their children's lives. Children who witness violence in their homes are high-risk for developing distress symptoms (depression, anxiety, impulsivity, sleep problems) and violent behaviors themselves. It is estimated 10 million children are exposed to marital violence each year. Children are often drawn into the conflicts of parents and are frightened and traumatized when they see their parents hurting one another. Children living in homes where domestic violence occurs are neglected and physically abused at a rate 15 times higher than the national average. Further, they are high-risk for becoming perpetrators and victims of violence in later years (Osofsky 1995).

ENVIRONMENTAL FACTORS. Human aggression is largely learned. Children learn violence is an acceptable way to solve problems by experiencing and witnessing violence. Boys who learn to be aggressive are more likely to be violent towards their wives and children when they become adults.

HABITS OF THOUGHT. From preschool years through adulthood, violent individuals have thought patterns and beliefs that endorse the use of violence: "aggression is a legitimate way to express feelings, solve problems, enhance self-image, and attain power."

BIOLOGICAL FACTORS. There is no single "violence gene," but violence is related to traits that may be partially heritable: a difficult, fearless, and uninhibited temperament; hyperactivity; and attention problems. Biochemical dysregulation, resulting from prenatal drug and alcohol exposure, can lead to later problems with impulse control, aggression, and rage.

MEDIA. The average American child spends 900 hours a year in school and 1,500 hours a year watching TV! Forty years of research has documented that violence can

be learned from TV and movies. Preschoolers who watch violent cartoons are more likely to hit playmates, disobey class rules, and argue than children who watch nonviolent shows. Children who watch extensive violence on TV can become less sensitive to the suffering of others, more fearful, and more harmful. By the time a child leaves elementary school, he has seen 8,000 murders and more than 100,000 other violent acts on TV (Huston et al. 1992).

ALCOHOL AND DRUGS. Drugs and alcohol have the power to disinhibit, often resulting in violent behavior. Drugs and alcohol are involved in more than 60% of all homicides (NCIPC 1989).

GUNS. The widespread availability and use of guns has broadened the scope and severity of youth violence. Guns have become a staple of childhood and teenage life in many American cities. In one study, every child living in public housing in Chicago had witnessed a shooting by age five. A child is killed every 90 minutes by someone with a gun (Bell & Jenkins 1993).

The creation of secure attachment is a protective factor against later violence and antisocial behavior. Children with secure attachments have emotional experiences and learn specific skills that prevent violence, including:

- to control impulses and emotions;
- to develop empathy and other prosocial values;
- to establish a positive sense of self;
- to cope with stress and adversity; and
- to have emotionally close, reciprocal, and fulfilling relationships.

Three Pillars of Assessment

Understanding your child rests on three pillars: 1) *developmental history,* 2) *symptoms and diagnoses* (current and previous), and 3) the *attachment history of parents/caregivers,* as shown in Table 1. The following goes into more detail about the type of information and data that builds each assessment pillar.

Developmental History

- Background information collected about the child's biological parents and family includes psychological and social functioning before and during pregnancy (feelings about pregnancy, family background, prenatal care, stress level) and after birth (quality of the birth experience, prematurity, bonding immediately after birth).

- Assessment of the child's temperament, responsiveness to caregivers, growth patterns, and completion of developmental tasks (e.g., exploration, trust, self-control) that influence development is made.

- Attachment and relationship history during the first three years is studied to include:
  - nature of relationships, length of time, and disruptions with birth parents and family;
  - circumstances of out-of-home placements;
  - availability and competency of primary caregivers;
  - attachment patterns (secure, avoidant, resistant, disorganized); and
  - maltreatment: abuse, neglect, abandonment; age, duration, severity, effects, and prior efforts to help child.

- Information is gathered regarding school history, including behavioral and academic performance, ability to learn, and special school programs.

- Sexual attitudes and behaviors associated with sexual abuse or exposure are determined and assessed.

- Strengths and resources, including positive traits and talents, resilience, desire to change, and supportive people in the child's life (e.g., extended kin, social workers, friends, mentors, teachers, therapists) are combined with other data and assessments collected to create a complete picture of the development history of the child.

Symptoms and Diagnoses

- There are six symptom categories: behavior, thoughts, emotions, social, physical, and moral/spiritual. Each of the symptoms and traits are described in this chapter.

- It is necessary to know your child's current, as well as prior, symptoms and characteristics. The frequency (how often), duration (how long the symptom lasts), and severity (degree of damage and disruption for the child and family) of each symptom are important.

- Symptoms exist along a continuum, from mild to severe. Children vary in the types of symptoms they have and in the severity of their symptoms.

- Children commonly have a number of concurrent conditions and diagnoses, including ADHD, PTSD, depression and bipolar depression, and oppositional defiant disorder (ODD). It is beneficial to know current and prior diagnoses.

- Your child's behavior, symptoms, and patterns of relating can only be understood within the context of family and social systems, both currently and historically. For example, how do you and other family members perceive, feel about, and react to your child; what solutions have you tried, and how did they work out; what are your resources and support systems; are family dynamics constructive or destructive?

- A special emphasis is placed on understanding how your child views self, parents, and life in general—referred to as the *internal working model*. These core beliefs and attitudes, formed early in life based on how your child was treated by caregivers, have a major impact on how he feels and behaves. (A comparison of the internal working models of children with secure and compromised attachment is presented in Chapter Two on pages 22–27.)

- Symptoms in children with compromised attachment vary from mild to severe as a result of the following factors:
  - developmental stage at time of trauma and loss as children react differently at various stages;
  - prior attachments and the quality of those attachments before trauma;
  - subsequent attachments and the quality of attachment experiences after trauma and loss;
  - duration and number of disruptions—more moves result in more damage;
  - constitutional factors such as temperament and genetic background; and
  - protective factors such as support and help from extended family, foster parents, and others.

Children with moderate to severe attachment problems typically display the following symptoms: being angry, aggressive, controlling, manipulative; lying and stealing; lacking empathy, remorse, and genuinely loving relationships; and having self-contempt, shame, and depression.

Children with severe attachment difficulties will often exhibit three very troubling additional symptoms—*cruelty to animals, preoccupation with fire,* and *bedwetting.* They find satisfaction in venting anger and frustration on helpless pets and other animals, to compensate for their own feelings of inadequacy and powerlessness. They do not have empathy for the animal's suffering. Many of these children are fascinated by fire and its attributes of power and destruction. Starting fires allows children to express their rage, achieve revenge, and attain a sense of power. Enuresis (bedwetting) may be a result of physical or stress-related causes, such as sexual abuse.

Attachment History of Parents/Caregivers

- Your *state of mind* regarding attachment is the strongest predictor of your child's attachment pattern.
- Your unresolved issues and patterns of relating can be "triggered" by your children. It is important to *look in the mirror*—know yourself—to respond in a therapeutic manner (i.e., calm, patient, firm, and loving).
- The *Life Script* is a self-report tool to increase your self-awareness (see Chapter 4).

Table 1. Child Assessment

Developmental History

- Birth parents and family
- Infancy and early childhood: experiences and developmental milestones
- Attachment and relationship history
- School history
- Sexual history
- Strengths and resources

Symptoms and Diagnoses

- Six symptom categories: behavior, thought patterns, emotions, social, physical, and moral/spiritual
- Current and previous symptoms
- Frequency, duration, and severity of symptoms
- Diagnoses: current and previous
- Family context: family and social system influences
- Internal working model: mindset, core beliefs, and expectations
- Severity of symptoms

Attachment History of Parents/Caregivers:

- Current parents/caregivers: psychological, social, and attachment history; parent's/caregiver's "state of mind" regarding their own attachment history influences parenting style and competency

---

Common Traits, Patterns, and Problems

In addition to the symptoms described in this chapter, the traits, patterns, and issues explained below will help you gain a deeper understanding of your child. Children with disrupted and compromised attachment will typically display the following patterns of behavior and relating.

Fear of Closeness

Children who feel secure with their parents and caregivers become anxious when that parent is absent. Anxiety is reduced when they reunite. The opposite happens when children have compromised attachment. These children learn they cannot depend on caregivers for protection and comfort. Thus, their anxiety rises as they make contact, and they feel less anxious with distance. Keep in mind your child has anxiety and fear about getting emotionally close to you because he expects a negative reaction.

My heart.

Defenses

Defenses are mental operations and protective strategies designed to reduce fear and minimize emotional pain. Defenses can be conscious and unconscious; people use them on purpose or without being aware. Your child developed defenses early in life to cope with the fear and pain of maltreatment and lack of protection, security, and love.

Fear activates attachment needs in young children. A child with a secure attachment can rely on caregivers to calm, soothe, and protect him when frightened. Without this secure base, the child must cope with fear and insecurity alone. He builds defenses to cope and survive. These

I have to protect myself from getting hurt.

defenses are for self-protection but prevent connection later on—pushing you away, shutting down emotionally, and being very bossy and controlling. See pages 170–171 for a list of defenses.

Core Beliefs

I mostly feel all alone.　　　　*I feel weird, like I'm from outer space.*

Core beliefs, also called internal working models and mindsets, are how we see others and ourselves. It is the mental lens through which we perceive and interpret reality. Core beliefs are developed in early childhood based on our attachment experiences. A child who experiences maltreatment and attachment disruptions is likely to have negative core beliefs. She views herself in a negative light, "I'm inferior, unlovable, helpless, bad;" and does not trust caregivers, "You are unreliable, frightening, selfish." The brain is an anticipation machine. Your child expects you to hurt and betray her just as she was hurt in the past.

Brain and Biochemistry

The infant's brain is designed to develop in concert with a nurturing and protective caregiver. The *limbic dance* of the securely attached mother and baby soothes the nervous system, regulates stress hormones, and allows for normal exploration and learning over time. Children without an attuned and protective caregiver are deprived of this buffer from undo stress. Chemical messengers of stress (cortisol, epinephrine, norepinephrine) flood their brains and bodies, while other brain chemicals (for example, serotonin) do not flow enough. The result is impulsivity, aggression, depression, attention deficits, and anxiety.

You must counter these biochemical reactions by being a healing parent and providing a secure base. A consistent, predictable, and calm environment is crucial. Your style of communication—calm, soothing, reassuring—will help to "down-regulate" your child, and reduce the effects of stress.

Defiance

I can be really mean.   *I start fights with everyone.*

It is common for children with attachment problems to be diagnosed with oppositional defiant disorder (ODD) and conduct disorder. They don't listen and follow rules at home or in school. There are many reasons for this defiance. First, it gives the child a feeling of control, and control equals survival—"If I can control you, I feel safer." The second reason for defiance is it maintains emotional distance. If your child can provoke anger and frustration in you, then emotional closeness is avoided. The next reason is about anger. Your child will express anger by opposing you. The fourth reason for oppositional behavior involves negative core beliefs. Your child feels inadequate, lacks trust, and does not feel she belongs—"I'm not on your team, so I'll do things differently."

Attachment Patterns

There are four attachment patterns, which usually remain with us throughout our lifetime, that are learned early in life: *secure, avoidant, resistant/ambivalent,* and *disorganized/disoriented.* Babies and young children develop attachment patterns based their caregiver's reactions, sensitivity, and availability. Children who can depend on their caregivers to be available in loving and reassuring ways, especially during times of stress, form *secure attachments.* They expect their caregivers will be dependable and protective in the future. Some caregivers, however, cannot be counted on to meet their children's needs. Due to drug abuse or alcoholism, violence and chaos in their lives, depression and psychological problems, not wanting the baby, or other reasons, these caregivers are not available in loving ways. Their children learn caregivers are not reliable and safe, and therefore, do not expect love or protection in the future. Therefore, these children develop anxious attachment strategies to relate to those caregivers, especially when distressed or frightened. They adapt in order to survive.

When babies and young children have emotionally unavailable and rejecting caregivers, they learn to turn away, as if to say, "I don't need you." These children have *avoidant attachments;* they dismiss their caregivers just as they were dismissed. Because they have learned to tune-out and avoid, the result is the ability to turn-off (deactivate) their attachment behavior as well.

When children have caregivers who are inconsistent, sometimes meeting their needs and other times unavailable, they never know what to expect. These children develop *resistant* or *ambivalent attachments.* They are anxious, not easily soothed, and seek-out but then pull away from their caregivers, as if to say, "I need you but can't trust you; I'll give you the same mixed signals that you give me." These children can't seem to turn-off their attachment behavior (overactivated). They work too hard at getting their caregiver to respond, and they are constantly filled with anxiety.

The most dangerous and destructive situation is when caregivers are physically, emotionally, or sexually abusive, or neglect their children's basic needs for love, security, protection, or food. These babies and children are frightened and have a total breakdown in their reaction to caregivers—they have no idea how to adapt or respond. They develop *disorganized* or *disoriented attachments.* They appear confused, scared, out-of-it (dissociated), and often acting in bizarre and "crazy" ways. Data shows as many as 80% of abused, neglected, and traumatized children have this type of very disturbed attachments (Lyons-Ruth 1996).

Projection and Reenactment

Children with compromised attachment typically experienced abuse, neglect, rejection, chaos, and emotional isolation in the past. They anticipate more harsh and insensitive treatment in the future. Your child will project his fears and anger on to you; he will take it out on you. If you become triggered and respond in nontherapeutic ways—impatient, abusive, and rejecting—then you and your child reenact negative patterns of relating.

When I'm mad, I like to hurt people. It seems like there's a monster that bursts in me when I get mad all the way.

Lie Man

Lying

Most all children lie at times as a part of growing up. Securely attached children will lie on occasion in order to avoid getting in trouble. However, they are more likely to feel bad about it, tell the truth when confronted, and accept a consequence. Children with disrupted attachment will maintain their lies even in the face of overwhelming evidence or "crazy lying," not feel guilty or remorseful, and not take responsibility for their behavior. There are a number of reasons why these wounded children lie chronically and severely. Again, it furnishes a feeling of power and control; "I know the truth and you don't." Second, these children often had examples of antisocial behavior and morality that demonstrated how to be deceptive and dishonest. It is easy to lie and manipulate when lacking empathy and remorse. Lastly, lying maintains emotional distance in the parent-child relationship. You cannot trust a liar. Parents feel extremely hurt, frustrated, and betrayed when their children chronically lie, resulting in a tense and mutually hostile relationship.

Shame

Shame is an emotional state of disgrace, discredit, and humiliation. Children who feel shame view themselves negatively and assume others view them with disdain. Shame involves four elements: *emotional misattunement, blaming self for abuse, toxic parenting,* and *family background.*

EMOTIONAL MISATTUNEMENT. Emotional misattunement entails a disconnect between caregiver and child. The caregiver does not understand or tune into the child's thoughts, feelings, or needs. Missed opportunities for connection occur in all families, but healthy parents notice the situation and do something

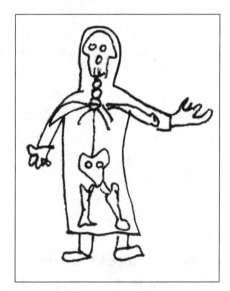

If people saw the real me, they wouldn't like me.

actively to remedy or repair it. The emotional connection is reestablished and the child feels secure and loveable. When emotional attunement is in short supply, or not available at all—as is often the case with depressed, angry, or rejecting caregivers—the child's needs are unmet, and the sense of self is damaged: "I am worthless, inferior, and unlovable." Shame is based on a profound feeling of inadequacy.

BLAMING SELF FOR ABUSE. Young children are by nature egocentric; they accept responsibility for other's actions toward them. Thus, children typically take on the blame when abused by parents or others in positions of authority, resulting in guilt, humiliation, and shame. A child will feel guilt and self-hate for having done something to deserve abuse, rather than face the reality that someone in a position of trust has betrayed her. Shame is the product of a failure in trust.

TOXIC PARENTING. Some parents and caregivers use shame intentionally as a form of control and punishment. They criticize, reject, and convey disgust, causing their child to feel "wrong" and ashamed. The child develops a deeply scarred, fragmented, and lost sense of self. Parents who use shame as a tool of cruelty raise children who become cruel to themselves, and brutal to other children, parents, and pets.

FAMILY BACKGROUND. Children can either feel pride or shame about their family background. Shame by association occurs when the legacy involves alcoholism, drug addiction, crime, maltreatment, lack of education, poverty, abandonment of family, and dysfunctional lives. These children feel ashamed of their heritage and, therefore, ashamed of themselves: "the apple doesn't fall far from the tree."

Traits and Symptoms

There are six categories of traits and symptoms of attachment disorder: behavioral, cognitive, emotional, social, physical, and moral-spiritual. Children vary in regards to the number of symptoms they have and in the severity of their symptoms. Each trait and symptom is described followed by specific examples given by parents.

The symptoms and symptom checklist described in the following pages are *not* meant for parents to use to diagnose their children. Qualified mental health experts should only provide diagnoses. Use the following descriptions and the *Symptom Checklist* on page 71 to further understand your child and to measure your child's progress over time.

Behavioral

1. Lack of impulse control

Not able to control impulses, arousal, emotions, and behaviors. Acts rashly without thinking of the consequences, on the spur of the moment. Cannot delay desires.

> *"She does not seem to be able to control her temper, her rage, or her words when angry. Her words and comments are quick, meant to be hurtful, and she says she can't stop herself. She speaks when the thought strikes her and moves when she feels like it, rarely with thought to the consequences. For instance, while waiting outside a restaurant before a concert she took off her shoes and rolled up her pants and ran through a fountain dodging the water. She gave no thought to being soaked and didn't care."*

"When given a job, he does not stay on task if there is any possible distraction, and sometimes even if there are no distractions. He regularly is sent from the table for gross table manners. He does not stop himself from baiting the other children. He lies before he thinks."

2A. Physically self-destructive

Hurts or mutilates self, including head banging, pinching, cutting, picking, or scratching; running into things.

"She is always picking at her skin until it bleeds. She spent some time with my Mom and had some mosquito bites. By the end of the summer she had turned them all into sores with the constant picking at the scabs. I don't know how many teeth she has pulled out looking for money from the tooth fairy. She just shakes them until they become loose, no matter how long it takes, until they fall out."

2B. Psychologically self-destructive

Acts in emotionally or socially self-defeating ways, such as sabotaging closeness and trust, and setting oneself up to lose rewards or privileges.

"He pulls out his hair and breaks all his toys. He even destroys things he really loves. When we are going to go somewhere fun he makes sure he blows it so he can't go."

3. Destruction of property

Breaks things—their own or often someone else's property—particularly when angry or frustrated; includes trashing bedroom, putting holes in doors and walls, peeling wallpaper, carving on furniture, breaking toys, cutting up things, and throwing objects.

"She will break things in her room out of anger. Throw objects in her room, slam doors, kick the wall. She recently sprayed blue silly string throughout her room, staining her bedspread and carpet. She has little regard for her property or the property of others. She has broken a sewing machine and a dishwasher, dented a pickup repeatedly with a stick or broom handle, poked holes through the dog water dish, scratched woodwork in several areas of the house, added water to shampoo bottles, broken erasers and pencils, etc."

"He destroyed the guest bathroom because he was mad at me. Countless toys and presents are broken when he gets mad or to get even. He kicked his shoes at an antique picture I had on the wall causing it to fall from the wall and break. He destroyed a brand new pair of leather shoes because I did not go back to Chuck E. Cheese's to look for his birthday sunglasses, and the list goes on."

4A. Aggression towards others—physical

Punches, kicks, bites, and pushes parents when frustrated or angry, usually when they don't get their way. Physically aggressive with other children during play. Often targets mother or younger and more helpless children.

"When she is really angry and feels her control is being threatened she feels no fear in moving to stand toe-to-toe in our faces to challenge us. She will physically push us—grab our arms to make us stay in her room so she can argue with us. She hits and has kicked her siblings. Her 12-year-old brother has told me that on occasion he has been afraid to go to sleep because he went to bed with her angry at him and he was unsure of what she would do to him when he fell asleep. When she was 6 she pulled a knife on a babysitter and threatened to hurt her. She threatened me (Mom) that if I told her counselor about her behavior that she 'would get me'. That same day she wrote me a note saying if I told on her she would kill me."

4B. Aggression toward others—verbal

Verbally threatens bodily harm. May curse, scream, and threaten to shoot you or kill you with a knife. Often picks names they believe will hurt you ("Fatty," "Baldy").

"He spat in the faces of children, hit them in the head as they are sitting on the school bus. He regularly abuses me verbally and physically. He screams at the top of his lungs at his aunt. He is very aggressive towards the other children at his school and after school center. He baits them and dares them to come after him. He will trip them, and throw a soccer ball at them."

5. Consistently irresponsible

Complains and resists when asked to pitch in and help. Rarely completes chores and other tasks correctly. Often says the task is completed when it isn't. Forgets or loses homework and other things they should be responsible for. Lacks emotional maturity expected for their age.

"She can't find anything and loses everything. She always lies about her home-work saying she doesn't have any or she finished it. It takes 15 to 20 minutes every-day to get the homework agenda from her from all her excuses and explanation. She never completes her jobs right the first time. It's never her fault."

"He cannot keep track of anything. When given a deadline for family chores, he usually misses it. He pretends he has done things when he clearly hasn't. The same applies for school assignments. We have rarely ever seen him appropriately handle responsibility."

6. Inappropriately demanding and clingy

Makes relentless and inappropriate demands for your attention much of the time, particularly when you are busy with something. Acts out in anger and vindictiveness when jealous of attention given to others. Uses whiny or clingy behavior to annoy, manipulate, and get your attention.

"She hangs all over her dad. She grabs onto him sometimes making it difficult for him to walk. We have noticed other teenage children do not act like this around their parents. Ever since we can remember, she has always done this with her dad."

"If anyone comes to the house he always has to talk with me that moment. On the phone, he is saying every 30 seconds, 'Excuse me, Mom. Excuse me, Mom.' I usually have to make him leave the room to finish a phone call. He has to be the center of attention all the time. He hugs everyone. He hangs on your leg and sits on your lap. Sometimes I feel smothered."

7. Stealing

Money or small objects turn up missing. Comes home from school with things and says they either found them or they were a gift. Takes things off the teacher's desk, from other children, or while visiting others' homes. Mother's valued possessions are particular targets.

"She steals constantly—at least 2 or 3 times a week. She has stolen money, every manner of lipstick, nail polish, toys, whatever. She has stolen from Target, Wal-Mart, a grocery store. She has stolen money from my Mom; she has stolen from her teachers. If we visit anyone's home, heaven forbid do not let her go use their bathroom because she will search rooms near it and steal something. At her school or daycare, if anything is missing, she is automatically the first suspect and she has usually stolen the thing."

"He has stolen things that he can hide in his pocket from kids at school. He has robbed his 3-year-old brother's piggy bank. We have to check his pockets whenever we go into a store. It seems to be getting worse as he gets older."

8. Deceitful

Lies to avoid getting in trouble, but also lies habitually when the truth will serve just as well. Does not admit a lie even in the face of convincing evidence to the contrary. Shows no remorse when caught—only annoyance for being caught. Boasts or exaggerates stories in order to manipulate and appear better. Tells you what ever it is they think you want to hear. You never know if they are telling you the truth.

"You cannot believe 90% of what she says. Even if she just says the sky is blue. You'd better check because I can guarantee you it's not true. None of her teachers or any students trust her or anything she says. Don't try to tell her you don't believe what she is saying, even if she is caught red-handed. She always denies it, always. Then you get the actress and drama queen with the tears and hysterics until she realizes it's not getting her out of trouble; then she abruptly stops. She frequently tells new teachers that I don't give her anything to eat and that I beat her a lot. The teachers have gotten pretty good at wising up to what she says and to double check everything."

"He has become so good at lying that we have a really hard time discerning between truth and lies. He can look us straight in the eye and lie, even when he doesn't have to. He does not consider revealing only the partial truth as lying. He admitted to his Dad that lying makes him feel powerful because he knows something that we don't know."

9. Hoarding

Has a cache of food, particularly sweets, and other items stashed under pillows, mattresses, beds, and in closets or drawers.

"Whenever I return from a trip I routinely look under her bed, in the drawers, her desk, and closet for food she has hidden or half eaten in her bedroom. I have since put an alarm on her bedroom door because she would sneak downstairs to the refrigerator when we go to sleep. She says she steals the food because she thinks I will say no if she asks for it. Candy she routinely steals from the teacher or whoever has it."

"We find food in his room, some partially eaten, some still in wrappers, and candy wrappers, stuffed under his bed. He snacks constantly and sneaks out of his bedroom at night and treats himself to something out of the pantry."

10. Inappropriate sexual attitudes and conduct

Has interest in and knowledge about sex that is beyond their years. A history of sexual abuse places them at risk for sexually acting-out with other children. You may feel a sense of discomfort when they hug you. It just doesn't feel quite right. "Accidentally" touches private areas of siblings, parents, and others. Exposes self, masturbates excessively, or masturbates in public.

"Last summer I found her locked in the playhouse with her girl cousin. When I banged on the door for her to open it she jumped down and pretended they were playing. Her cousin looked traumatized. She used to masturbate regularly. She asked my best friend if she wanted to have sex with her at 3 and a half years old. She sneaks into the bathroom when her girl cousins are taking a bath by pretending she forgot something and stares at their private parts. If I play with her, tickling her, or sometimes I hold her as I am talking to her, her play becomes suggestive."

"When left alone he frequently reverts to masturbation as a form of entertainment. His attitude toward sexual violence on TV worries me. He seems to revel in it. He uses a lot of disrespectful sexual talk."

11. Cruelty to animals

Very rough with pets—squeezes too hard, kicks, or pulls their tails. Pets often growl or avoid their presence. Neglects pets' needs. In severe cases tortures or kills animals.

"She is very nice to the animals as long as someone is watching. She will kick them or pinch them if no one is around. We have had gerbils and birds mysteriously die."

"He picks on animals, swings sticks at them and throws things at them. He pulls the dog's ears and bangs its head. The dog and cats run away from him."

12. Sleep disturbance

Has difficulty transitioning to sleep, remaining asleep, or awakening. Gets up and wanders during the night. Nightmares or night terrors are common.

"She talks in her sleep and grinds her teeth. She is plagued by nightmares and several times a week wanders into our room wanting to sleep with us because she is scared. Usually we guide her back to bed and occasionally we make her a bed on the floor next to our bed depending on the severity of her fear. She has night terrors several times a month. It is difficult for her to fall asleep until between 10 PM and 12 AM. Nobody likes to wake her up in the morning; she's a real crab."

"He doesn't go to sleep until I go to sleep because he thinks I am going to leave. He takes hours to fall asleep. I have him remove the comforter and pillow every night, otherwise they are all wrapped around his head by morning. He also uses the pillow to hide stuff he steals to take to his room."

13. Enuresis and encopresis

Soils self (urination or defecation) as a strategy to express anger, defiance, or control. Urinates in pants, bed, closet, floor, or heater grates. Often refuses to flush toilet or wipe after a bowel movement. In severe cases, smears feces on clothes, floor, or walls.

"She has wet her pants and occasionally pooped in her pants during the day. She does wet the bed most nights."

"We bought an enuresis monitor for him about three months ago. After using it for approximately three weeks he has not had to use it but once since then. He doesn't like to wear it. He would urinate on the pillow, in the bed, in the trash can, and on the floor in the bathroom."

14. Frequently defies rules (oppositional)

Does not follow rules at home or school. Shows little regard for adult authority figures. Gets angry or defiant when asked to do anything. Also shows defiance by passively ignoring rules.

"If I am not in the house and someone else is babysitting her, all bets are off. She is in charge. She says she has to yell and scream and be disrespectful because she doesn't like anyone to tell her what to do."

"Frequently defies rules? How about constantly? It is what he lives for. He doesn't understand why he can't make his own rules. He hates being 'bossed around'. He will do whatever he can get away with. He will argue every single point, all day long."

15. Hyperactivity

Always in motion. Activity often seems chaotic and purposeless. High energy, fidgety, and restless. Bumps into tables, walls, and people. Constant "motor mouth". Has difficulty focusing for any length of time, even on pleasurable activities.

"She is constantly fidgeting, chewing her nails, chewing on her sleeve. She wiggles and can't sit still. In the car, she can be irritating by singing and making noises. Her laugh is giddy at times when she is hyper."

"He has a hard time sitting still. He is always wriggling, even while reading books. He is nicknamed the 'Tornado'. He is constantly going."

16. Abnormal eating habits

Uses food as a means of control. Refuses to eat certain foods, eats slowly or picking at food. Eats larger amounts of food for their size. Craves sweets, particularly sugar. Has poor table manners, such as eating with mouth open or making noises at the table.

"Her manner of eating, if she likes something, is as if she has never been fed before in her life. If she doesn't like it, she takes forever to eat it. If you leave the room, she dumps everything in the trash. She asks for food whether she wants it or not. The rule is, if you ask for it you have to eat it. That has helped to slow down the constant asking."

"He sneaks food from the pantry. When he is supposed to be in bed, he will sneak downstairs and get food to eat. He craves sweets and carbohydrates and he will eat sugar right out of the sugar packet. At mealtime he will eat more than two adults could. We wonder where he puts it all."

17. Preoccupation with fire, gore, or evil

Has a fascination with the power and destructiveness of fire. Sneaks unattended matches. Parents often find bits of burned tissue or paper. Clothing found singed. In severe cases, burns down homes and barns. Relishes violent or gory movies, and intrigued with accidents or dead animals on the road. These themes can be seen in their drawings or stories.

"I have caught her lighting candles in her room a few times. She loves to light candles. She can't pass a candle without playing with the fire or wax. When she was younger she told us she was going to burn the house down. We found matchsticks lying on the floor upstairs."

"When given free reign on library checkout he chooses the scary and violent books or the books about disasters. He chooses those kinds of movies when he visits his grandparents and recounts the details of them with great relish. He is fascinated with gore, war, and fire."

18. Persistent nonsense questions and incessant chatter

Asks questions that are unimportant or that they already know the answer to. Continues to ask a question again, even if you already have given an answer. Talks on and on about anything and everything, often making little sense. Interrupts and dominates conversations, particularly when they have a captive audience (in car) or when you are busy with something (on phone).

"When people first meet her they think she is so cute, polite, and well-mannered until she starts talking and never stops. Then you see the look of delight on their faces change to one of 'Oh my God, when is she ever going to shut up?' She will ask you 20 questions in five minutes all making no sense. She constantly asks questions that she clearly knows the answer to."

"Sometimes you have to wonder, 'Is he going to come up for air?' He can dom-
inate a conversation and then leave you asking, 'What did we just talk about?' He
can switch topics mid conversation and go off on a completely different subject. I
have often wondered if he talks so much because he is afraid that once he stops talk-
ing he will lose our attention. It's exhausting."

19. Hypervigilant

Acts continually on-guard, scanning the environment. Very aware of everything around them. Notices minute details. Overhears and remembers every conversation.

"She knows what's going on around her at all times. She amazes us with her awareness of details. She remembers every word we say."

"He's constantly staring at people. He stands back, never really participating. Sometimes I think he's like a jackrabbit ready to take off. He hears every conversa-tion, even if we are in another room."

20. Difficulty with novelty and change

Becomes agitated in new situations or with any changes in routine. Always wants to know where they're going and why. Does not like to try new things. Anxiety regard-ing change leads to behavior problems.

"She does not do well with change. She can cry, refuse to go along, protest con-tinually and loudly. No telling what could set her off. If she doesn't know the plan—or you change plans on her—she erupts."

"He only has difficulty with novelty and change if he is changing to something he doesn't want to do. He can transition beautifully all day long such as while traveling if we are doing things he thinks is fun. But the minute he has to transition to something he doesn't want to do—like bed or homework or going to the grocery store instead of the toy store—he blows up and screams mean names to the person in charge like 'I hate you. You're an idiot,' etc. And he becomes unreachable until it passes."

Cognitive Functioning

21. Lack of cause and effect thinking

Appears to not learn from experiences. Repeats the same mistake over and over again. Does not seem to care about consequences or punishment. Does not connect the dots, "If I do this, then this will happen."

"She doesn't connect her behavior to any consequence. Things just spontaneously happen to her or she just says it's because people are being mean to her. It is pointless trying to connect the dots for her between her behavior and consequence. She doesn't learn from experience."

"He does not seem to learn by his mistakes. He could be disciplined for behaving a certain way and 15 minutes later turn around and do the same thing again. He seems to know what will happen but just doesn't care."

22. Learning disorders

Lags behind for their age level or developmental level, particularly prevalent in children who did not receive adequate stimulation as infants and toddlers. Often misdiagnosed; knows more than they let on in order to manipulate and control teachers and parents.

"She is mildly dyslexic, but also has trouble with reading comprehension and math concepts. She's about two grades behind her class."

"He has severe learning disorders. Although he is very smart and savvy, he has had a very difficult time learning to read. He can do a little math but not at grade level. He loses interest quickly and doesn't pay attention to explanations."

23. Language disorders

Acts like they don't understand what you're saying; can be genuine or used as a ploy, particularly if English is a second language. Also includes speech impediments such as stuttering or saying words incorrectly.

"She doesn't speak in complete sentences. Sometimes she will say one word, and the listener has no clue what she means. She frequently baby talks or talks so softly you can't hear her."

"He also has a lot of difficulty with language. His testing shows his receptive speech is better than his expressive, which we agree with. He hears everything, sometimes seems to remember whatever is useful to him."

24. Perceives self as a victim

Complains others pick on them and treat them unfairly. Does not recognize they are responsible and accountable for the consequences of their behaviors. "Poor me" attitude. Sets themselves up to be treated poorly by others. Feels no one is on their side or understands them. Acts helpless in order to shun responsibility.

"She believes she is always being picked on. Her parents are against her, her brother hurts her feelings, her classmates think she is bossy, and her teacher does not like her. She is always complaining and crying about her life. She seems to enjoy self-pity. Sets herself up to be a victim. We frequently hear, 'It's not my fault. You're all against me', and 'Everyone is picking on me!'"

"People are always being mean to him as far as he is concerned. He spends a great deal of time trying to get even. When pushed about his behaviors he complains that he can't help what he does because he was abused and is still angry about that."

25. Grandiose sense of self-importance

Believes the world revolves around them. Does not take into account the feelings and needs of others. Always wants to come first or be first in line. Acts as though they know everything and thinks they can handle things they can't. Believes every conversation is about them. Acts like the world owes them.

"She believes it's her way or the highway at home. She has to have control or know what is going on in every situation. She interrupts my phone conversations, demanding to know to whom I am speaking. She believes the world owes her."

"When asked to do a chore and he refuses, his reason is because he doesn't want to do it and someone else should have to do it instead of him. When given a consequence he acts surprised and enraged. He is extremely selfish. He always thinks of himself first."

Emotional

26. Not affectionate on parents' terms

Avoids parent-initiated closeness and hugs. Often says, "No", pulls away, or stiffens if parent asks for a hug. Allows hugs when others are around for show. Has no problem asking for hugs on their terms or at inappropriate times; usually feels disingenuous.

"She is not generally an affectionate person. She has the 'heart' of affection, but she is resistant when you approach and try to hug or kiss her. She comes to me for a hug when she wants something from me."

"He will not accept any affection from us. This has gotten a lot worse over the past 6 months. He screams every time I hug him or put my hand on his head. He is telling me now not to snuggle with him at night."

27. Intense displays of anger (rage)

Quickly escalates into temper tantrums when frustrated or does not get way. Making a request or saying no can set off "hair trigger". Includes screaming, hitting, throwing things, threatening, and destroying property. Outbursts can end quickly or last hours.

"There is no telling what may set her off. If we assert our parental authority she can absolutely go into a rage: yelling, screaming, 'I hate you!' At times I (Mom) avoid disciplining her to avoid being at the other end of her rage. When she gets out of control and verbally abusive it takes all my self-control to keep my hands off her. I usually try to walk away even with her at my heels screaming at me. It's exhausting."

"Up until about a month or two ago, roaring was his primary method of communication and he could do it for an hour or more at a time. He will also throw things (like chairs) or push people. He still roars occasionally, but now relies on the looks that could kill as his main method of registering his disapproval. In the morning I don't say anything to him for fear of setting him off into a rage."

28. Frequently sad, depressed, or hopeless

Appears flat, listless, and lethargic. Tends to pout or sulk. Prefers to avoid social interaction, and will isolate themselves in their rooms or with TV, music, computers, or video games. Easily irritated or frustrated. Little interest in interactive activities. Discouraged and unmotivated about life and the future.

"She cries quite often when she is in her room listening to music. Perhaps it makes her melancholy. She cries easily at nighttime or when she is tired. She has made comments in anger that she will kill herself, but I believe she intends it as manipulation. She can also be carefree and happy. It just depends on the circumstances and the day."

"He attended one school where the kids were actually more aggressive than him. He spent a lot of time sad and depressed because he couldn't control anyone or bother them to the point of where they got upset. There are days when he is quiet, unresponsive and off on his own. He is afraid he won't ever be normal and happy like other children."

29. Inappropriate emotional responses

Tendency to overreact to situations, particularly when angry or upset. Often escalates emotionally in public (supermarkets, restaurants, etc.) when they feel parents are more reluctant to intervene. Might laugh at things that are not funny or fail to show sadness when sadness is appropriate. Overreacts to incidental injuries and ignores more serious ones.

"A minor infraction from her brother can set her off. When I correct her behavior she will stomp her feet and glare at me, 'MOM...stop it now!' Like SHE is parenting ME. She laughs when she hurts someone's feelings in our family. A minor injury is cause for hysteria and when she had to have blood taken the entire main floor of the hospital could hear her screaming. I often remind her that she is 'way' overreacting to the circumstances. She doesn't show appropriate empathy for the feelings of others."

"If someone falls down or gets hurt he cracks up laughing. He overreacts to comments by getting defensive. He shows either overwhelming sadness, anger, happiness, or excitability that doesn't fit the situation at hand."

30. Marked mood changes

Emotionally unpredictable. Moods can change very quickly. Can be in a good mood, go into a rage, and then be laughing again within a few moments. Moods can vary over hours, days, or weeks.

"She can be sweet and compliant one minute, and angry and defiant ('You can't make me,') the next. It just depends what sets her off. She can slide between tender and nurturing to irritable and bossy in the blink of an eye. She doesn't want to talk and then you can't get her to stop talking and making plans."

"His mood swings are dramatic and unpredictable. Can go from happy-go-lucky to a rage within seconds. Can also go from hyper to calm very quickly."

Social

31. Superficially charming and engaging

Doubts their own value and compensates by putting on a front of likeableness. Learns through trial and error that pleasing others gets them noticed, and is charming, witty, or coy. Often unable to maintain this façade with those they are closest to (immediate family).

"This is probably the hardest part of dealing with her. She can be whatever the situation requires (sweet, helpless, hurt, helpful, giving). Most people just think she's a doll. Our dentist wanted to take her home. When she was younger, she would go to anyone. Once when her dad and brother had surgery, she spent the whole time drawing pictures for the receptionist. She was about 9 and we were surprised she showed no concern for her father or brother."

"He is very charming while he is sizing up the situation. Once he figures out what's up, he loses the charm and becomes more controlling. That can take as little as one hour or a couple of months. It depends on the stakes in his estimate. I get more compliments on his behavior from strangers who are around him for an hour or less. He asks about their families, he compliments them, he says, 'Excuse me,' in the right moments, everything."

32. Lack of eye contact for closeness

Avoids feeling the vulnerability involved in eye contact. Only uses direct eye contact when lying, manipulating, or threatening. Eye contact is an important component in the development of secure attachment and is associated with closeness and intimacy.

"She won't look at me when I'm talking to her. She looks away, down, at the TV, or clock. When you force her to maintain eye contact, the look she gives you sends chills up your spine. I feel like I'm looking at Damian in The Omen and then she adds that awful half grin that says, 'I'm going to get you for this'."

"Almost all eye contact is initiated by us. He is uncomfortable with it and sometimes it feels more like staring. He only looks straight at me when he is lying."

33. Indiscriminately affectionate with strangers

Is inappropriately friendly with unknown people and acquaintances. Does not show a natural caution of strangers. Will go to and with anyone. Hugs, kisses, and says, "I love you" to unknown adults.

"If someone takes the time to show an interest in her she comes alive with the attention. She sits too close, she is casual about her physical affection, and she can be just too friendly. She will get into a car with a complete stranger. She will hug and sit in the laps of men she has just met."

"He treats his family like the strangers and strangers like his best friends. People who don't know him will think he is so cute and sweet, they don't know what we go through every day. They can't understand why I am so angry."

34. Lack of or unstable peer relationships

Has difficulty maintaining long-term friendships. Makes friends easily but can't keep them. Reports they have good friends but rarely are invited over to play, to parties, or to spend the night. Friends they do keep are usually other children with problems. Gravitates towards either much younger children who they can control or much older children who manipulate them.

"The friends who last with her usually have more problems than her or are extremely bossy. The others last a little while until they get tired of her stealing their things, lying, trying to get them in trouble, bossing them around, or just generally being obnoxious. Her best friend in third grade was a first grader. She generally plays with kids about 3 to 4 years younger than her."

"He is never invited to other boys' birthday parties or invited over to play. The phone seldom rings for him. He can be overbearing and bossy, and his honesty can be biting and mean. He usually goes too far when playing."

35. Cannot tolerate limits and external control

Has difficulty following instructions and obeying rules. Does not accept guidance from parents, teachers, and other adults. Misinterprets limits and guidance as threats and control. Engages adults in power struggles.

"She resists anyone telling her what to do. She has enormous control issues with everyone. This is the one area where we battle a lot. She is passive aggressive with me. I give her a chore and it takes her three hours to do it."

"'You can't make me.' 'I don't have to obey you.' 'No!' 'Who said you're the boss of me?' He hates control and authority. He will obey when it pleases him, but he still must maintain some sort of control. He argues constantly and is uncooperative and defiant both at home and at school."

36. Blames others for own mistakes or problems

Does not take responsibility for own actions. Comes up with excuses (even the absurd) in order to shun ownership of problems and blame others. This includes anything from losing a coat to missing an assignment deadline. It is never their fault.

"She only does stuff or gets in trouble because of what other people make her do, not because of her actions. She had to hit her brother because he wouldn't play with her. She has to lie because she tries her best to tell the truth and nobody believes her. She did not do her homework because the teacher didn't explain it, etc. She blames me for losing her shoes or losing her homework."

"I don't think he has ever taken the full responsibility for his actions. Someone else teased him or hit him first; they made him do it; Mom is the one who made him lose his temper. We made him mad, therefore it is our fault he yelled and screamed. It's always someone else's fault. I don't think he has ever voluntarily admitted that he was in the wrong."

37. Victimizes others (perpetrator, bully)

Does not respect the boundaries, needs, or wants of others. Physically, verbally, and often sexually aggressive. Tries to bully other children regardless of their size. Tends to seek revenge for any perceived slight.

"She can be really mean to her younger sister. Last week, her younger sister ran into the house wailing she did not want to go to the doctor's office to get her shots for school again. She had told her this just to be cruel, knowing how her sister hates shots (what kid doesn't) and when I asked her about why she had said something that was a complete lie she got this satisfied sick smile on her face. Like 'Mission accomplished. I intended to scare my sister and I succeeded.'"

"Tripping people is a favorite thing to do. Bumping into them as well. Annoying them by singing right next to them and generally being annoying until they get mad. Then he has reason to get even. He talks loud and gets in other people's faces. He is very bossy and tattle-tales. He likes to be a bully."

38. Victimized by others

Sets self up to be a "victim." Purposefully loses privileges. Perceives self as deserving of punishment. Confesses to things they haven't done. Relishes in the role of helpless martyr. "Poor me" mentality.

"Interestingly enough, she is easy to victimize. Kids who are more aggressive or manipulative can easily control her. Funny thing is she tries very hard to be accepted by these types of kids. She is easily taken advantage of. She does not know how to protect herself."

"He has been punched in the stomach twice in the past couple weeks by two different kids. Kids love to pick on him because of his behavior and because he overreacts."

39. Lacks trust in others

Does not believe caregivers and others are safe, reliable, and will truly meet needs. Has difficulty allowing vulnerability, sharing deep feelings, and asking for help. Does not make progress in developing the trust one would expect over time.

"She lacks trust in people. She feels more freedom with strangers—I think—because it is easier to trust when there are low expectations of love. She distrusts people who desire vulnerability most. She protects herself by desiring control of trust. She is very good at recognizing motives."

"He is quick to think that others don't care. He will barely let me put on a bandage or take out a splinter. He takes awhile to warm up to adults. He says he doesn't want to trust anybody."

40. Exploitative, manipulative, controlling, and bossy

Takes advantage of others for their own gain. Only thinks "What's in it for me?" Has desperate need to be in control. Determined to use power over others. Gets satisfaction from refusing to comply with authority. Attempts to control only intensify the opposition.

"With her there is always an angle to everything. She uses charm to get what she wants. If that doesn't work, she becomes controlling and bossy. I've never seen her have a normal interaction with anyone where one of the above didn't apply.

She knows how to say or do just the right thing to get people to give her what she wants."

"When he has any free time he uses it to boss the other children and keep track of their behaviors. He likes to control who plays with who and how, if he can. He gets close to people and then uses what he knows to hurt them. He tries to pit us (Mom and Dad) against each other when he is angry, or trying to get his way, or for the fun of it. He is bossy and tries to parent all of us. He stomps his foot and meets your eyes with a look that says, 'Don't cross me.'"

Physical

41. Poor hygiene

Is reluctant to keep up proper conditions and practices for maintaining cleanliness, such as brushing teeth, combing hair, and showering. Often takes showers or baths without using soap or shampoo. Would wear the same clothes for days at a time.

"Bath! What is that! She routinely doesn't bathe. She may bathe 1 or 2 nights a week unless someone else bathes her or stands in the bathroom and watches her do it. She has run the water and not stepped foot in the shower or she will get in but not use any soap. The same for brushing her teeth. If you don't stand there and watch her it doesn't happen. She never flushes the toilet or uses toilet paper."

"He has very poor hygiene. He hates brushing his teeth, and would never wash his hands if I didn't ask him to. He never thinks about washing before a meal. He likes showers and baths, but more for the calming effect or the warming effect than for cleanliness. He blows his nose on his t-shirts constantly and uses his shirt for a napkin. His clothes are worn dirty. He doesn't use toilet paper. His underwear is always dirty."

42. Chronic body tension

Appears stiff and robotic with shoulders pulled back, rigidity, and shallow breathing. Tightens up more when others get too close. Muscles are in a condition of chronic tension and contraction.

"She is never physically relaxed except when she is asleep. When she is angry she is tense and doesn't want to be held. She tenses during snuggling."

"He just tenses up when touched. He startles easily if touched. Never snuggles in."

43. Accident prone

Trips and falls often, bangs into furniture and other people. Always says, "It was an accident" when spilling, breaking things, or hurting other children.

"She has cuts and scratches, from all her 'accidents'. A lot of times she wants medicine so there is always something wrong. She comes up with weird accidents,

bruises and bites. No one else sees the incident happen. She has sprained her ankle three times in the past two years."

"He lacks judgment about what could severely injure him. He will swing too high in a swing or jump seven feet off the stairwell. An 'owie' is an enormous deal. He is fearless and careless."

44. High pain tolerance/overreaction to minor injury

Endures serious injuries without complaint. However, overreacts to slight injuries to gain attention. Goal is to not feel but be numb to physical pain.

"If she has a little cough, she swears she has pneumonia again. Any little cut she watches it and guards it moaning, but she will have a big gash and does nothing. She will tolerate pain, if it is a result of something she did. She can really howl in the doctor's office."

"I often see him just keep going after hurting himself, saying, 'That didn't hurt'. He has to be injured badly before he cries or needs assistance. He rarely cries in pain."

45. Tactilely defensive

Avoids any parent initiated physical contact for closeness. Dislikes stroking cheek or caressing hair. Pulls away and stiffens with attempts to hug or kiss. Often says, "No," or "You're hurting me." Hugging them is like hugging a board. Hugs or kisses on their terms, usually inappropriately.

"She went through a period where she would recoil from Dad's hugs and kisses. It took him about six months of constantly seeking her out to let him hold her for brief moments until she was comfortable with hugging and snuggling with him."

"He hates being touched. He also hates his head being touched. He also reacts strongly to being touched on his back."

46. Genetic predispositions

Inherited genetic traits that can be passed on in families include: aggressiveness, unipolar and bipolar depression, excitability, alcoholism, psychosis, shyness, vulnerability to stress, obesity, diabetes, and risk-taking behavior.

"Maternal grandfather—alcoholic, aggressive, rage issues, verbally abusive.

Maternal grandmother—never dealt with her childhood abuse, periods of depression.

Mom—depression, attachment issues from own childhood.

Paternal grandfather—alcoholic, depression.

Paternal grandmother—deceased at age 31 of brain tumor. Addiction runs in her family.

Dad—depression."

"Birth mother is schizophrenic and was institutionalized. Father—smoking, drinking, marijuana, cocaine abuse."

Spiritual/Moral

47. Lack of meaning and purpose

Believes life has no meaning, significance, or purpose. "What's the use?" attitude. Lacks exuberance, vitality, and zeal. Not a participant but watches from the sidelines. Has no internal motivation to purposefully enjoy life.

"She has been raised in a Christian home, but I doubt if her desire to honor God is what motivates her to choose good things. She may be her own God or at least she seems headed in that direction."

"He seems to have little direction or purpose. Sometimes it is like he floats through life and comes up for air occasionally."

48. Lack of faith, compassion, and other spiritual values

Lacks ethical convictions, and doesn't act in right and honorable ways. Is unable to recognize and respond to the needs of others. Does not treat others with respect, tolerance, and fairness. "If there was a loving God, I wouldn't feel the way I do."

49. Identification with evil and the dark side of life

Believes they are bad; therefore, they identify with bad (evil) pictures and stories that reflect evil themes. If parents have strong faith, they go in the other direction, often without the parents' awareness.

"She wears black a lot. She has stolen black nail polish. She's attracted to magic."

"His stepfather claimed to be psychic and to be training him to be psychic as well. Although he now says that he does not believe this he still has trouble believing that God loves him or that he would go to heaven if he died. He is certainly attracted to any media that has evil magical themes."

50. Lack of remorse and conscience

Has no inner voice to do the right thing and stay on the moral path. Doesn't care about hurting others. Delights in seeing or causing pain. Lacks guilt. Not genuinely sorry, only of getting caught.

"She seems to delight in the hurt feelings and abuse she gives to her brother and sister. She will tease and pester while she giggles in a high-pitched, hyper sort of laugh. It is not genuine, but she is delighting in someone else's frustration. Her only true remorse is in being exposed. There is a coldness about her. I have never once seen her truly sorry for anything she has done."

"At three years old I asked the first therapist he had if he was a sociopath because he didn't appear to have a conscience. He told me he would eventually develop one. Well, he is nine and a half, and it hasn't happened. He will scream at you, steal your things, try to hurt you, and then take revenge if you don't play with him. He steals and doesn't feel sorry. He actually gets mad when he has to return the stuff. He has never ever expressed any remorse about what he has done or what he has broken or destroyed."

Symptom Checklist

Child's Name: _____   Date: _____

Completed By: _____

Please place a mark in the appropriate column for each symptom as it pertains to your child. On a separate sheet of paper, please give a brief description of your child's behavior regarding each of the symptoms checked as moderate or severe.

	None	Mild	Moderate	Severe
1. Lack of impulse control	____	____	____	____
2. Self destructive, physical/psychological	____	____	____	____
3. Destruction of property	____	____	____	____
4. Aggression toward others, physical/verbal	____	____	____	____
5. Consistently irresponsible	____	____	____	____
6. Inappropriately demanding and clingy	____	____	____	____
7. Stealing	____	____	____	____
8. Deceitful (lying, conning)	____	____	____	____
9. Hoarding	____	____	____	____
10. Inappropriate sexual conduct and attitudes	____	____	____	____
11. Cruelty to animals	____	____	____	____
12. Sleep disturbance	____	____	____	____
13. Enuresis and encopresis	____	____	____	____
14. Frequently defies rules (oppositional)	____	____	____	____
15. Hyperactivity	____	____	____	____
16. Abnormal eating habits	____	____	____	____
17. Preoccupation with fire, gore, or evil	____	____	____	____
18. Persistent nonsense questions and incessant chatter	____	____	____	____
19. Hypervigilant	____	____	____	____
20. Difficulty with novelty and change	____	____	____	____
21. Lack of cause and effect thinking	____	____	____	____
22. Learning disorders	____	____	____	____
23. Speech disorders	____	____	____	____
24. Perceives self as victim (helpless)	____	____	____	____
25. Grandiose sense of self-importance/entitlement	____	____	____	____
26. Not affectionate on parents' terms	____	____	____	____
27. Intense displays of anger (rage)	____	____	____	____
28. Frequently sad, depressed, or hopeless	____	____	____	____
29. Inappropriate emotional responses	____	____	____	____
30. Marked mood changes	____	____	____	____
31. Superficially engaging and charming	____	____	____	____
32. Lack of eye contact for closeness	____	____	____	____
33. Indiscriminately affectionate with strangers	____	____	____	____
34. Lack of or unstable peer relationships	____	____	____	____
35. Cannot tolerate limits and external control	____	____	____	____
36. Doesn't like criticism and blames others for own mistakes or problems	____	____	____	____
37. Victimizes others (perpetrator, bully), revenge	____	____	____	____
38. Victimized by others	____	____	____	____
39. Lacks trust in others	____	____	____	____
40. Exploitative, manipulative, controlling, bossy	____	____	____	____
41. Poor hygiene	____	____	____	____
42. Chronic body tension	____	____	____	____
43. Accident prone	____	____	____	____
44. High pain tolerance/overreaction to minor injury	____	____	____	____
45. Tactilely defensive	____	____	____	____
46. Genetic predispositions	____	____	____	____
47. Lack of meaning and purpose	____	____	____	____
48. Lack of faith, compassion, and other spiritual values	____	____	____	____
49. Identification with evil and the dark side of life	____	____	____	____
50. Lack of remorse and conscience	____	____	____	____

Concurrent Conditions and Diagnoses

We conceptualize attachment disorder as the core or "hub," with other disorders as spokes on a wheel (Figure 3). A lack of secure attachment in the early stages of development, combined with abuse, neglect, and multiple moves, commonly results in a number of problems, symptoms, and conditions: ODD, conduct disorder, ADHD, major depression and dysthymic disorder depression, bipolar disorder, and PTSD.

Figure 3. Attachment: The Core

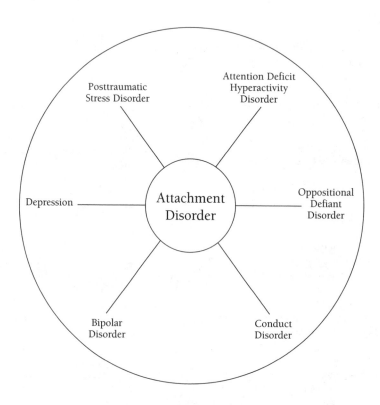

The following section will describe the symptoms of the disorders most commonly found to coexist with compromised attachment (adapted from American Psychiatric Association 2000). Medications typically given to children and adolescents with these diagnoses and symptoms will also be noted (Wilens 2004).

Oppositional Defiant Disorder (ODD)

All parents know about the "Terrible Twos"—the time when young children assert their independence and autonomy by oppositional behavior (e.g., saying "No" to parental requests and having temper tantrums when not getting their way). Children with compromised attachment never grow out of this stage of development. They are defiant and hostile toward parents and other authority figures, due to their lack of trust and need to control.

Symptoms.

- Defiant, negative, and hostile behavior lasting at least six months, including four or more of the following:

    - often loses temper and argues;
    - refuses to comply with adults' requests and rules;
    - deliberately annoys people;
    - blames others for own behavior and mistakes;
    - is touchy, easily annoyed, and inflexible; and
    - is angry, resentful, spiteful, and vindictive.

Medication.

Medication is used for specific symptoms, as there is no medication available for the disorder itself. Medication can be used for ADHD (Ritalin) and mood disorders (Imipramine, Wellbutrin) that co-occur with ODD.

Conduct Disorder

Conduct disorder is the next step up in severity of harmful behavior from ODD, and includes behaviors that violate the basic rights of others and oppose the rules of society. These children and adolescents are showing true signs of antisocial personality, often a result of severe maltreatment and compromised attachment (see Levy & Orlans 2000a).

Symptoms

- Aggression toward people and animals where the child:

    - bullies, threatens, and intimidates others;
    - initiates physical fights; uses weapons (e.g., bat, knife, gun);
    - is physically cruel to people or animals;
    - steals while confronting a victim (e.g., mugging, armed robbery); and
    - forces someone into sexual activity.

- Deliberate destruction of other's property including fire setting.
- Deceitfulness including lying and "conning" or theft of items through shoplifting, forgery, or by breaking into a house, building, or car.

- Serious violation of rules:
    - stays out at night despite parents' rules, beginning before age 13;
    - runs away from home overnight; and
    - is truant from school.

Medication.

As with ODD, medications are used to target specific symptoms, such as depression, bipolar disorder, and aggression. Antipsychotics (Seroquel, Risperdal, Zyprexa) are often used for severe agitation and aggression.

Attention Deficit/Hyperactivity Disorder (ADHD)

ADHD is a neurologically-based disorder that is present in about 5% to 9% of school-age children. About half grow out of it by adolescence, while for the remainder it continues into adulthood. ADHD is characterized by hyperactivity, inattention, and impulsivity. Children with compromised attachment are often misdiagnosed with ADHD, due to the similarity of symptoms.

Symptoms.

- Inattention characterized by six or more of the following, and persisting for at least six months:
    - fails to give close attention to details and makes careless mistakes,
    - has difficulty sustaining attention in tasks,
    - does not listen when spoken to directly,
    - does not follow through on instructions and fails to finish schoolwork or chores,
    - disorganized and often loses things,
    - dislikes and avoids tasks that require sustained mental effort (e.g., homework), and
    - is easily distracted and forgetful.
- Hyperactivity:
    - fidgets and squirms;
    - leaves seat in classroom;
    - runs around, talks, and climbs excessively; and
    - has difficulty playing quietly.
- Impulsivity:
    - blurts out answers,
    - has difficulty awaiting turn, and
    - interrupts and intrudes on others.

Medication.

Stimulants are most often prescribed, including Ritalin, Concerta, Dexedrine, Cylert, and Adderall. They increase the levels of the neurotransmitters dopamine and norepenephrine, by stimulating release or blocking reabsorption. Side effects include insomnia, loss of appetite, and irritability. A "rebound effect" may occur, whereby behavior worsens when the stimulant wears off.

Second-line medications include antidepressants, such as Imipramine and Wellbutrin, when there is co-occurring depression and anxiety. Antihypertensives (Tenex, Clonidine) are often given to young children who are especially overactive, aggressive, and have sleep problems.

Major Depression

Mood disorders in children are classified as major depression, dysthymia (less severe depression), and bipolar disorder—which includes both the "lows" of depression and the "highs" of mania. Major depression affects about 1% to 2% of elementary-age children and 5% of adolescents. Depression in children is often overlooked and not diagnosed, because the symptoms shown include irritability, fatigue, and lack of concentration. Depression can be genetic; between 30% to 50% of children with depression have a family member who also has depression. Depression is associated with grief and loss, and therefore is almost always present in children with compromised attachment.

Symptoms.

- At least five of the following symptoms occurring simultaneously for at least two weeks and impairing the child's social, family, and academic functioning:
  - depressed or irritable mood most of the time;
  - diminished interest, lack of enjoyment and pleasure in activities;
  - too little or too much sleep;
  - lack of or increased appetite; significant weight loss or gain;
  - slow movements/speech or agitation;
  - poor concentration and indecisiveness;
  - fatigue and lack of energy;
  - feelings of worthlessness and excessive guilt; and
  - suicidal thoughts and behaviors.

Medication.

The most commonly used antidepressants are selective serotonin reuptake inhibitors, or SSRIs, including Prozac, Zoloft, Paxil, Luvox, Celexa, and Lexapro. Other antidepressants used include Wellbutrin, Serzone, and Remeron. Ativan is given for depression with anxiety. Seroquel is prescribed for depression with psychotic symptoms (e.g., hallucinations, out-of-touch with reality).

Dysthymic Disorder (Depression)

Dysthymic disorder is a low-grade, long-term form of depression that is the most common mood disorder in children and teenagers. Dysthymic disorder—commonly called depression—is characterized by a negative and irritable mood, tiredness, low self-esteem, poor concentration, and hopelessness. This ongoing depression is very common among children who have a history of maltreatment, unresolved loss and grief, and compromised attachment.

Symptoms.

- Depressed mood for most of the day, for at least two years. Mood is often irritable in children and teens. Two or more of the following symptoms, causing significant distress and impairment in family, social, and school functioning:
    - low self-esteem,
    - hopelessness,
    - poor concentration and difficulty making decisions,
    - poor appetite or overeating,
    - low energy and fatigue, and
    - trouble sleeping or sleeping too much.

Medication.

The most commonly used medications are the SSRIs—Zoloft, Prozac, Paxil, Luvox, Lexapro, and Celexa. High levels of serotonin are associated with aggression, moderate levels are associated with relaxation and sleep, and low levels are linked to depression. The Federal Drug Administration (FDA) recently issued a warning that antidepressant medications (especially Prozac) can increase emotional agitation and suicidal thoughts and attempts in children and teens.

Bipolar Disorder

Bipolar disorder, formerly known as manic-depressive illness, is characterized by mood cycles or swings between depression and mania. During depression the child is sad, tired, irritable, argumentative, and spends much of his time alone and isolated. During time of the manic or high mood, he becomes impulsive, very talkative, goes without sleep, feels invincible, and engages in high-risk behaviors. The risk of bipolar disorder is higher when there is a family history. About 1% of the teenagers in the United States, or about 400,000 teens, have bipolar disorder (Birmaher 2004). There is a significant overlap between the symptoms of ADHD and bipolar disorder, which makes diagnosis more challenging. Children who have both ADHD symptoms and bipolar symptoms have more severe behaviors, are more impaired psychosocially, and have a poorer long-term prognosis than those with ADHD alone.

Symptoms.

- Mania—a persistent elevated, expansive, euphoric, or irritable mood for at least one week, and has at least three of the following:

    - inflated self-esteem or grandiosity,
    - decreased need for sleep,
    - increased talkativeness,
    - racing thoughts,
    - increased distractibility,
    - increased activity or agitation, and
    - daring and dangerous behaviors.

- Depression—see section under Major Depression.

Medication.

Mood stabilizers are most often used, including Lithium, Tegretol, and Depakote. Lithium toxicity can be dangerous, resulting in confusion, fatigue, muscle weakness, slurred speech, and nausea. Depakote and Tegretol may cause sedation, nausea, heartburn, tremors, weight gain, and diarrhea. Antipsychotics (Risperdal, Zyprexa, Serquel, Geodon, and Abilify) are used for acute mania, hallucinations, and when mood stabilizers are not effective. It is important to note antidepressant medications can make bipolar children worse, potentially increasing mania, more frequent cycling, increased agitation, aggression, temper outbursts, paranoia, and psychosis.

Posttraumatic Stress Disorder (PTSD)

PTSD is one of the most serious anxiety disorders, and is common in children and teens with histories of severely compromised attachment, abuse, and neglect. PTSD develops after a child experiences very stressful and frightening events, such as physical or sexual abuse, or being a victim of or witnessing violence or a disaster involving threatened or actual serious injury or death to self or others (for example, hurricane, 9/11 type event). During the trauma, the child feels intense fear, helplessness, and horror.

These reactions are normal and part of the fight-flight-freeze response of the brain's limbic system. When these symptoms are not processed and the child—or an adult—lives in a constant state of arousal for 1 to 3 months or longer, than the more severe and long-term disorder and its symptoms develops (Brohl 1996).

There are four primary symptom categories of PTSD: 1) *reexperiencing the trauma,* such as flashbacks, nightmares, and painful memories; 2) *numbing of responsiveness and avoidance* of reminders of the trauma, including dissociation; 3) *experiencing hyperarousal,* which involves impulsiveness, agitation, hyperactivity, and hypervigilance; and 4) *experiencing physical complaints,* which include frequent illness, eating disorders, elimination disorders, and psychosomatic pain. Additional traits and symptoms of PTSD include sleep disturbance, separation anxiety, fearfulness, aggression, difficulty concentrating and staying on task, emotional detachment, depression, and substance abuse.

Symptoms.

- Reexperiencing the trauma
    - has recurring and distressing images, thoughts, and repetitive play (in young children themes of trauma are expressed in play);
    - has frightening dreams and nightmares (sleep disturbances);
    - acts or feels as if the traumatic event were recurring; flashbacks, hallucinations, a sense of reliving the experience; and
    - has intense anxiety and distress, physically and psychologically, to cues that symbolize or resemble the traumatic event.

- Numbing of responsiveness and avoidance
    - avoids thoughts, feelings, and conversations associated with the trauma;
    - avoids activities, people, or places to the point of developing phobias;
    - is unable to recall aspects of the trauma;
    - has diminished interest in activities and is extremely cautious about trying new things;
    - detaches from others;
    - has restricted range of emotions;
    - senses a foreshortened future—does not expect to live a normal lifespan— with depression and suicide ideation;
    - practices self-mutilation;
    - experiences *fugue*—sudden, unexpected travel from home, for example, with the inability to recall the event;
    - feels separate form one's body;
    - engages in fantasizing and magical thinking (wishes he were a superhero or that he had different parents);
    - engages in high-risk behavior and endangers others while playing;
    - engages in drug and alcohol use;
    - has short- or long-term memory loss;
    - practices compulsive behaviors, such as repetitious hand-washing or hoarding;
    - develops separate and multiple personalities;
    - expresses developmental regressions (for example, separation anxiety);
    - experiences time-learning confusion;
    - experiences panic attacks;
    - is preoccupied with criticism or social rejection; and
    - engages in inappropriate and unusual sexual behavior, particularly if the trauma was sexual abuse (adapted from Brohl 1996).

- Experiencing hyperarousal
  - has difficulty sleeping,
  - is irritable and has anger outbursts,
  - has difficulty concentrating (walks into obstacles) and attention-deficit;
  - is hypervigilant (watches for threat or danger), and
  - has an exaggerated startle response (loud noise may cause panic reaction).
- Experiencing physical complaints
  - has sleep deprivation and disturbances such as insomnia, sleep walking, nightmares, excessive sleeping;
  - is more susceptible to infections, unexplained rashes, double vision, even paralysis or localized weaknesses;
  - has headaches, loss of balance, unexplained choking, dizziness, and breathing disorders;
  - has psychosomatic pain;
  - develops eating disorders (anorexia nervosa or bulimia); and
  - develops elimination disorders (encopresis, enuresis, or constipation) (adapted from Brohl 1996).

As can be seen from this shopping list of symptoms, PTSD is complicated. The traumatized child's mind may pick one or more symptom from each of the four categories. In this way, PTSD is highly individualized. When a child develops such disorders as obsessive-compulsive disorder (OCD), anorexia, or depression in addition to flashbacks and an abnormal fear of playing outside, it as a result and response to the trauma and an attempt to survive and control. It is important to note, for example, just because a child is anorexic does not mean she has PTSD. Rather it is the traumatic event(s) *combined* with multiple symptoms (including other disorders) that characterizes PTSD. It is these multiple symptoms and disorders that make PTSD such a serious anxiety disorder and difficult to treat.

In children and teens with histories of severely compromised attachment, abuse, and neglect, this disorder often severely impairs normal functioning. Parents are at a loss and overwhelmed. Understanding the mental defenses can often manifest in physical symptoms can greatly help parents and caregivers to respond appropriately to their child's needs. For example, a parent needs to be aware of the possibility of psychosomatic pain in an abused child, even if that child is a habitual liar. Understanding these mental and physical symptoms can alleviate some of the frustrations felt by the parents or caregivers of these children and help to facilitate healing and attachment.

Medication.

No specific medication has been found for PTSD, but medications are used to target certain symptoms: antidepressants (SSRIs), anxiety-reducing medications, and antipsychotics (for dissociation and "breaks with reality").

Your Child and Medication

One in five children and teens in the United States suffers from mental health problems, and the number is growing. Experts believe this is a result of increased stress in children and families as well as better diagnosis of existing problems. Studies have shown a combination of counseling and medication is most effective for some children and teens with severe problems, but the issue of medication has become controversial (DeAngelis 2004).

Twenty million Americans take antidepressants. In adults, about 60% of depressed patients improve with these drugs (improvement is defined as a 50% reduction of symptoms). Roughly 40% have similar improvements with a placebo (sugar pill). One of the best classes of medications for fighting depression in adults is the SSRIs, which includes Prozac, Paxil, Zoloft, Lexapro, and Wellbutrin.

More than 6% of American children and teens are on psychiatric medications. The use of antidepressants among children and teens increased threefold between 1987 and 1996 (DeAngelis 2004). It is certainly understandable why medication is prescribed. It is very painful to watch your child suffer from emotional problems such as depression. Untreated depression has a lifetime suicide rate of 15%—with even more deaths caused by related behaviors, such as self-medicating with alcohol and illegal drugs.

There are many unanswered questions, however, about medicating children and teens. The majority of these medications, with the exception of those for ADHD, have been tested and approved by the FDA for *adults only,* and are being used "off label" for children. This practice is legal but risky for a number of reasons. The brain chemistry of children is different from adults. The brain's frontal lobes, vital to "executive functions" like managing feelings and mature decision-making, do not fully mature until about age 25. Children metabolize medications differently than adults. Many experts believe the use of these medications is experimenting on children and they are concerned about what these drugs are doing to still-developing brains. Further, how does medication affect a child's ability to learn emotional and social skills? For example, do antianxiety drugs prevent a child from learning to manage stress and anxiety without medication? Side effects can also be alarming and dangerous, including weight gain, high blood pressure, jitteriness, and flat emotions. Another concern is many children get their medications not from a specialist in child psychiatry and psychopharmacology but rather from a pediatrician or family doctor who does not typically have the time or training for extensive evaluations and follow-up.

On October 15, 2004, the FDA issued a "black box" warning, its strongest safety alert, linking antidepressants to increased suicidal thoughts and behavior in children and teens. Prescriptions for antidepressants for children have since dropped by 20%. Dr. Ronald Brown, the Chair of the FDA's research group and Dean of Temple University's College of Health Professionals, said, "… the bottom line is there's more use of psychotropic medication with children than there is research data on it"

(DeAngelis 2004). One theory regarding the suicidal tendencies is antidepressants lift fatigue and passivity, resulting in a more energized but still very depressed person.

The response in England has been even stronger. British regulators have banned the use of antidepressants for children. The National Institute for Clinical Excellence recommends doctors encourage children to improve diet, get more exercise, and provide therapy focusing on the family, school, and social network. In cases of severe depression when antidepressants are absolutely necessary, they recommend using Prozac, which has shown the weakest link to suicidal tendencies, monitoring children weekly for adverse reactions, and using the medication only in conjunction with ongoing therapy. The Institute says Paxil and Effexor should never be used for children and teens, as they have shown the strongest link with suicidal thoughts and attempts (Cooper 2005).

On February 9, 2006, the FDA suggested issuing a "black box" warning for ADHD drugs, including Adderall, Ritalin, and Concerta. It was found between 1999 and 2003, 25 people died suddenly and 54 others developed serious cardiovascular problems after taking these medications. Children accounted for 19 of the deaths and 26 of the cases of cardiovascular problems. The FDA reported "uncertainty" about the safety of these medications (Bridges 2006).

There are four factors—managed care, symptom-focused treatment, increased severity of problems, and lack of understanding attachment—that contributed to the widespread use of psychotropic medications for children and adolescents in the United States.

Managed Care

Pressure from insurers and health maintenance organizations (HMOs) has dramatically shifted the way health care services are delivered to children and families. In an attempt to reduce costs, HMOs dictate to psychotherapists how many sessions they can provide and how much they can charge for services. Managed care views short-term therapy and medication as a more economical approach. Consequently, psychotherapists are finding it difficult to remain in practice, pharmaceutical companies are increasing profits, and children are not receiving adequate care. Pediatric medications are big business to drug companies. The American Medical Association (AMA) reported the use of behavior-altering medications for 2 to 4 year olds has tripled in the last decade. Pharmacies fill 11 million prescriptions for Ritalin every year ($100 million in sales). The United States accounts for 90% of the total consumption of Ritalin—five times more than the rest of the world combined (Breggin 1999).

Symptom-focused Treatment

Critics fear we are overreliant on chemical solutions for emotional problems in children. Some prescribers and parents focus on the suppression of symptoms rather than addressing the underlying issues that contribute to problem behaviors. We want a quick fix, a magic pill to make the disturbing behavior go away, and are chemically restraining children to control their behaviors rather than teaching them self-control. A growing number of mental health professionals realize children are being medicated for impulse control problems and thought patterns caused by a combination of unfavorable social influences and ineffective parenting, not for true neurological disorders. No medication has ever taught a child how to think; only positive role models can do that. Medication alone is not enough. Children need a comprehensive treatment approach that examines all the factors in their lives.

Increased Severity of Problems

The most recent survey of mental illness in the United States found almost half of the population has or has had a serious psychological illness at some point in their lives, and that treatment is usually delayed and inadequate (Kessler 2005). Daniel Goleman, in his classic book *Emotional Intelligence,* summarized the results of a nationwide survey in which 7 to 14 year olds were randomly selected and rated by parents and teachers. The study, which was conducted in the 1970s and repeated in the 1980s, concluded children deteriorated on all of the 42 indicators of emotional health and improved in none (Goleman 1995).

Today, things are not any better. In the two decades since the alarming results of this survey were disclosed, the number of diagnoses for ADHD has risen 700%, and the number of children identified as suffering from depression has risen 1,000%. Children's emotional health is rapidly declining. They are more reckless, disobedient, disrespectful, anxious, and violent than ever before. Violent crime among juveniles has quadrupled in the past 25 years. The number of youths held in juvenile facilities has increased 41% in the past 10 years. The incidence of juvenile homicide has doubled (Levy & Orlans 2000a). The World Health Organization (WHO) estimates by 2020 psychosocial disorders in children will increase by 50%, making them one of the five leading causes of childhood illness, disability, and death (DeAngelis 2004). As the number of children with serious problems rises so does the use of powerful medications.

Lack of Understanding Attachment

Although the identification of disturbances of attachment are becoming more common, many mental health professionals still lack adequate training and experience in diagnoses and treatment. The symptoms and traits of compromised attachment are also commonly found in the major childhood disorders (ODD, conduct disorder, ADHD, major depression and dysthymic disorder depression, bipolar disorder, and PTSD). Treating the symptoms of these disorders, while ignoring the underlying relationship and attachment problems, is often ineffective.

Misdiagnosis can lead to ineffective treatment. Conventional therapeutic methods typically do not work with this population. Insight oriented "talk therapy" addresses the wrong part of the brain (neocortex). Attachment occurs in the emotional brain (limbic system). This part of the brain learns best by being provided with corrective emotional experiences. You cannot blame desperate parents for seeking relief any way they can. If psychotherapy is continually tried with inadequate results chemical restraint becomes more attractive. Medication may temporarily reduce symptoms but does not produce long-term emotional and relationship changes.

Child-centered approaches that do not address family interactions and influences miss the boat. Attachment disorders are created in relationships and can only be healed in relationships. Effective therapy needs to address the child's prior attachment-related traumas while also promoting secure attachment in the current parent-child relationship. A parental structure is required that includes appropriate limits, rules, and boundaries delivered with sensitivity and love. These children need a safe, loving, and secure environment. Without this security and consistency they will remain anxious, angry, and acting-out. We have found when the right type of help is provided for children, parents, and the family system, there is a reduced need for medication.

The decision whether or not to medicate your child is difficult, and many parents are now more confused than ever. Many mental health experts believe even if antidepressants do increase suicidal tendencies in a small number of children and teens, these drugs save many more children overall. Statistics seem to support that idea; between 1992 and 2001, as the use of antidepressants rose, suicides among 10 to 19 year-old children dropped by 25% in the United States (Raeburn 2004). Under the right circumstances children can benefit from medication. Advocates argue there can be negative consequences for not using medication in the early years for children who lack impulse control, cannot concentrate, or are depressed. An out-of-control child does not feel good about herself or function successfully at home or at school. If brain chemistry is out of balance due to inherited genetic factors or maltreatment, medication can help in gaining control of behavior and emotions. Medication can also lower a child's frustration level to facilitate learning.

When considering medication for your child, you would be well-advised to choose mental health professionals who do the following:

- conduct thorough evaluations, including a review of past and present symptoms, a detailed developmental history, and discuss with caregivers the dynamics of current family relationships and social networks (school, extended kin, and social services);

- take the time to listen to and address your questions and concerns;

- have a good knowledge of the latest research, including the side effects and interactions of medications;

- consult with a skilled psychotherapist and have knowledge of the benefits of nonmedical interventions;

- start conservatively with the lowest possible dose, and use medications with the fewest side effects;

- monitor your child's progress consistently and carefully over time; and

- are interested in your observations and those of others who are regularly involved in your child's life (e.g., teachers).

Diet, Allergies, and Behavior

Diet is often overlooked as a serious factor contributing to problem behaviors in children. In fact, decades of research have found what children eat has a direct effect on brain performance, mood, and behavior. There are some foods that nourish the body and mind and promote health and well-being, and there are others that interfere with health. Some foods trigger a stress response, releasing adrenaline and cortisol into the body, which increases anxiety and attention difficulties. Other foods can actually prevent a stress response, enhancing calmness and mental focus. Nutritional deficiencies early in life (e.g., protein, iron, zinc, B vitamins) are associated with hyperactivity, aggression, and defiance in older children.

Unhealthy foods and lack of exercise have resulted in an epidemic of childhood obesity, linked to heart disease, diabetes, and behavior problems. More than 9 million children and teens in the United States are overweight or obese, four times as many as only 40 years ago. The current generation of children may be the first in American history to have a shorter lifespan than their parents (Atkinson 2005, Clinton 2005).

Many studies have shown the connection between food and mood. Anxiety and depression are correlated with low levels of serotonin in the brain. Serotonin is found in certain foods, including milk, eggs, chicken, and bananas. Omega-3 fatty acids, found in tuna and salmon, have a positive effect on mood and performance. Children with ADHD who received Omega-3 supplements had a reduction in symptoms of inattention, anxiety, and learning problems. Up to 60% of children with ADHD became more overactive and aggressive after eating foods with synthetic colorings and preservatives (Atkinson 2005).

Foods such as sweetened cereals, soft drinks, candy, potato chips, and fast foods containing high levels of fat, sodium, and sugar fuel disruptive behavior in children. Sugar in particular contributes to hyperactivity, irritability, lack of concentration, and aggression. Refined sugars are quickly absorbed into the bloodstream causing a burst of energy. This triggers the release of endorphins, natural opiates, which create euphoric feelings. During this temporary high, blood sugar levels escalate. The body recognizes the situation as an emergency and stimulates the pancreas to produce insulin, which shuts down the production of glucose (the fuel of the brain). This sudden release of insulin causes blood sugar to plunge to below normal levels. Once your child crashes, her body compensates by releasing stress hormones that can lead to moodiness, distractibility, impatience, and aggression. She may also experience hunger and weakness, causing a craving for yet another "hit" of sugar, creating a hormonal roller-coaster of hyperactivity, anxiety, and irritability (Null 2000).

Two hundred years ago the average American ate less than 10 pounds of sugar per year. We now consume a world-leading 137.5 pounds per year. Most of our processed foods and soft drinks are loaded with sugar. An average of 25% of our total calories are empty, devoid of vitamins, minerals, enzymes, and other important nutrients necessary for healthy growth and development. Refined sugar actually depletes the body of B vitamins, zinc, and chromium. Children whose brains have experienced the stress of maltreatment and compromised attachment may be more susceptible to the ill effects of sugar. They already have high arousal levels and problems with self-control. Sugar literally fuels the fire.

Studies done at juvenile detention centers have shown a substantial drop in angry, defiant, and violent behavior when sugared foods were cut from the menu (Howard 1994). One of the most dramatic examples of the effects of food on mood was at Wisconsin's Appleton Central Alternative High School, a school for high-risk children with many discipline problems. A full-time police officer was required to maintain order with the unruly students. All candy and soda machines were replaced with bagels and water coolers, and the cafeteria replaced processed high fat and sugar foods with healthy, balanced, freshly prepared meals. The students' behavior immediately began to improve. Teachers noticed improved attentiveness and the disappearance of outbursts and other classroom disruptions. Since this change, the school has had no dropouts, expulsions, or suicides. The program was so successful it was expanded to all the elementary, middle, and high schools in the district (Atkinson 2005). The Prevention of Childhood Obesity Act in 2005 aims toward "junk-food-free" schools throughout the United States by banning soda and candy from schools and increasing funding for programs that encourage exercise for children (Chamberlin 2006).

Some children have allergic reactions that affect their behavior and moods. An allergy is an overreaction by the immune system to a foreign substance, which is inhaled, eaten, or touched. Food allergies have been linked to depression, anxiety, poor concentration, and behavior problems in children. The number of children with food allergies and the frequency of occurrence have increased dramatically in recent years. A primary reason for this increase appears to be due to high levels of artificial ingredients and preservatives. The Center for Science in the Public Interest reviewed many studies and concluded certain foods and additives can trigger adverse behavioral and emotional reactions in children (Hansen 2003).

A child's allergic reactions do not only affect her, but can have a dramatic impact upon the entire family. Chronic discomfort, incessant crying and whining, and the inability to be comforted can easily lead to parental anger and frustration. Allergic reactions are triggered and magnified by emotion and excitement, and a vicious cycle may develop. The child's response to an allergic reaction triggers the parent into a stress-driven response, which makes the child's reaction worse and further frustrates the parent. This is a recipe for disaster.

Nutrition tips for parents:

Avoid processed convenience foods and snacks that are loaded with fat, salt, and sugar, and low on nutrition and fiber.

Ideal foods and snacks are minimally processed, rich in vitamins and minerals, and have few or no additives, including fruits, vegetables, natural juices, yogurt, high-fiber cereals, nuts and whole grain bread, crackers, and pasta.

Breakfast is very important. A child's brain has 2-3 times the energy needs of an adult's. When a child misses breakfast his body draws fuel from existing energy sources triggering irritability, fatigue, and the inability to learn. Breakfast should contain a balance of protein and complex carbohydrates to calm the body and stimulate the mind.

Healthy mid-morning and afternoon snacks can help minimize behavior problems that occur when children go without nourishment. Nibbling on healthy foods every 2-3 hours prevents your child's blood sugar from falling too low.

Don't use sweets with refined sugar to reward good behavior. We tend to equate love with sugar; we call our loved one's sweetie, honey, and give candy on Valentines Day to express our endearment. Provide natural forms of sugar, such as fructose and honey, found in fruit and healthy treats.

Your Child and Therapy

Parents routinely tell us they have endured years of therapy for their children with limited results. They also share their confusion and frustration in being given different types of, and often contradictory, parenting advice.

The first step in helping your child and family is to get a proper assessment. Assessments should only be done by knowledgeable and skilled mental health professionals who can determine the proper diagnosis and who understand child development and family systems issues. It is particularly important they have a thorough understanding of attachment. The following are recommendations regarding assessment of children with histories of maltreatment and compromised attachment.

- *Ecological.* Always involves an understanding of the family and social systems that influence children (for example, nuclear and extended family, school and social service systems).

- *Comprehensive.* Focuses on diverse aspects of the child's and family's functioning. Includes emotional, mental, social, physical, and moral behavior and symptoms, as well as strengths, coping abilities, and the desire for growth inherent in most people.

- *Eclectic.* Involves a variety of methods and settings. Children's behavior often varies in different contexts, and it is necessary to observe and understand their behavior and relationships under different conditions (i.e., home, school, day care, and friends).

- *Culturally sensitive.* Must be careful not to apply their own beliefs and traditions to families from different cultural backgrounds. Behavior considered normal in one culture may be labeled as abnormal in a different culture or society.

- *Developmentally sensitive.* Understands and evaluates behavior in the context of normal childhood development. The developmental stage of the child during trauma will influence psychosocial aftereffects.

- *Ongoing.* Provides continuous feedback about your child's and family's progress using a four-step model: *assess* ▸ *goals* ▸ *intervene* ▸ *reassess.*

Once a qualified professional has completed a thorough assessment of your child and family, you are ready to identify an appropriate therapist or treatment team. It is important the therapist is a qualified mental health professional and someone you and your family feel comfortable with. You should see measurable progress within a few months. The following are treatment recommendations.

- *Systems model.* Therapy should involve the child, parent/caregivers, and other family members. The focus should never be on the child alone and always include family and external influences (e.g., social services, school, and community resources).

- *Didactic and experiential.* Therapy should be both educational- and experience-based. Positive change occurs as a result of information, skills, and participation in growth-enhancing activities.

- *Reputable and respected.* Treatment techniques and parenting approaches should be safe, ethical, and based on solid theory and research. Treatment and parenting methods should never involve physical or psychological coercion, domination, or control. Intrusive approaches that threaten and retraumatize children are not appropriate. If it doesn't feel good, don't do it.

- *Secure base.* Treatment that focuses on facilitating secure attachments should include secure-base behavior by therapists and parents: emotionally available, sensitive and responsive to needs, supportive, appropriate limits and boundaries, and genuinely helpful. Treatment should focus on improving your child's *internal working model* (core beliefs), not merely modifying behavior.

- *Skill building.* Treatment should include constructive skill building for children and parents. Children need to learn impulse-control, anger-management, problem-solving, and communication skills. Parents must learn the skills associated with being a healing parent: self-awareness; understanding their child's core beliefs; being proactive, not reactive; engaging positively; staying calm; down-regulating their child; communicating for attachment; and constructive coparenting.

Look for the following characteristics in a therapist. Therapists should be:

- tolerant, empathetic, patient, and compassionate;

- emotionally nonreactive, and have a professional demeanor;

- accepting, nonjudgmental, and supportive;

- comfortable with anger and other strong emotions;

- confident and able to instill confidence;

- devoid of sarcasm and ridicule, and have a genuine sense of humor;

- resolved with regard to grief, loss, and other personal issues;

- growing and evolving as therapist and person;

- sensitive to cultural backgrounds and differences;

- adept at dealing with resistance in a creative and flexible manner;

- able to work effectively with a treatment team and colleagues;

- able to maintain hope and optimism;

- knowledgeable and skillful regarding attachment and both child and family systems therapy; and

- fully trained, qualified, and licensed as a mental health professional.

Summary

- Causes of compromised attachment: parent or caregiver, child, and environmental factors.

- Three Pillars of Assessment: developmental history, symptoms and diagnoses, and attachment history of parents/caregivers.

- Common traits, patterns, and problems: fear of closeness, defenses, negative core beliefs, biochemical dysregulation, defiance, anxious attachment patterns, projection, lying, and shame.

- Six symptom categories: behavioral, cognitive, emotional, social, physical, and moral/spiritual.

- Concurrent conditions include ODD, conduct disorder, ADHD, major depression and dysthymic disorder depression, bipolar disorder, and PTSD.

- Factors contributing to increased use of psychotropic medications: managed care, symptom-focused treatment, increased severity of problems, and lack of understanding attachment.

4

Know Yourself

*There is only one corner of the universe you can be
certain of improving, and that is your own self.*
—**Aldous Huxley**

In this chapter we ask you to focus on yourself, as individuals, as parents. We will explain why it is so important to look in the mirror—to understand your attachment history and current mindset—so you can truly be a healing parent. We have provided the *Life Script*—an effective tool to increase your self-awareness and prompt reflection.

Attachment styles affect people "from the cradle to the grave" (Bowlby 1969). You bring your past experiences, feelings, expectations, and relationship patterns into your parent-child and adult intimate relationships. Your experiences in earlier relationships create core beliefs and attachment styles, which then determine how you perceive and relate to your children and adult partners.

Once formed, our belief systems and attachment patterns operate automatically and unconsciously, making them difficult to change. Change, however, is possible. As you increase self-awareness you are no longer on automatic pilot. You now have choices and are open to creating new experiences with your children and partners.

As previously stated, enhancing attachment is crucial for a child's health, development, and success. "Intimate attachments to other human beings are the hub around which life revolves" (Bowlby 1980). It is not possible, however, to promote security of attachment using parenting techniques alone. Techniques and strategies will not work when a parent has unfinished business, unresolved emotional issues.

To be a healing parent you need the ability to look in the mirror regarding your mindset, feelings, and attachment history. This is called *mindful parenting* because your state of mind is focused on your thoughts and feelings, as well as those of your children (Siegel & Hartzell 2003). Knowing yourself—making sense of your life and coming to terms with your past—is the first step in helping your child heal and grow. When looking in the mirror and learning to know yourself, it is important to be aware of the following:

- *Mindset:* your core beliefs, created in early attachment relationships, which affect how you interpret your child's behavior, your emotional reactions, and your parenting attitudes and style.

- *Emotional reactions:* strong negative feelings, triggered by your child's actions and demeanor, usually associated with your own early attachment experiences.

- *Attachment history:* past relationship experiences and patterns that still influence your perceptions, attitude, and behavior.

- *Coping strategies:* style of responding to emotionally-laden events; how you deal with issues such as threat, anger, confrontation, rejection, frustration, disappointment, and loss.

- *Body signals:* physical reactions, especially to stress and threat, such as racing heart, clenched jaw, and shallow breathing.

Why Look in the Mirror

Be the change that you wish to see in others.
—**Gandhi**

Healing parenting is a combination of head and heart. Intellectual understanding of how to help your child is only half of the picture. You must also be emotionally available in sensitive, composed, and mature ways. The benefits of looking in the mirror are as follows.

Avoid Being Triggered

You cannot avoid bringing your emotional baggage into your relationship with your children. However, these unresolved issues can get in the way of being an effective parent, especially with challenging children. For example, if you were often rejected as a child, you might overreact (as known as being *triggered*) when your child pushes away your love and support.

You know you are getting triggered when your reactions are excessive or out-of-proportion to the situation, you react in a "knee-jerk" fashion, and you repeat old patterns, even though you realize this is not helpful. The ability to look in the mirror enables you to avoid these negative reactions by identifying your particular triggers and your responses to them, and instead, to provide the most constructive and healing responses possible.

Your State of Mind and Your Child's Security

There are four attachment patterns learned in childhood based on the type of caregiving received: *secure, avoidant, resistant-ambivalent,* and *disorganized-disoriented.* These attachment patterns (previously discussed in Chapter Two) typically remain into adulthood and affect feelings of security, safety, and closeness in relationships. Parents who honestly and openly deal with their thoughts and feelings about early relationships are more likely to have children who are securely attached. Parents who lack self-awareness—do not look in the mirror—more often have children with anxious and insecure attachments.

You can *earn* attachment security as an adult, even if you lacked it as a child, by looking in the mirror, learning positive communication, and creating secure and loving adult relationships. Self-understanding promotes new and healthy choices, leading to secure relationships for you and your children. This concept is discussed in more detail later under Adult Attachment Patterns.

Being a Positive Role Model

The best way to facilitate a change in your child's actions and attitudes is by example. As a healing parent, you model empathy, boundaries, coping skills, problem solving, and communication. Parenting your challenging child is difficult and demanding, and it is common to feel anxious, frustrated, angry, helpless, and even hopeless. Children are vigilant, watching your reactions, including the way you cope with stress and emotions, and the solutions you offer. Looking in the mirror enables you to be a positive role model for your child by becoming aware of the behaviors your child sees from you and making changes in yourself accordingly.

Your Relationships Affect Your Children

The quality of your relationships with spouse, partner, extended family, friends, teachers, and professional helpers influences your parenting and your children. The healthier your relationships, the more your children benefit. For example, parents communicating well and working as a team will avoid triangulation—situations where the child plays one parent against the other. Another example is of a single parent with a supportive network of friends, family, and others who help to reduce stress, increases hope, and results in better parenting. By looking in the mirror—assessing and improving the quality of your current relationships—you benefit yourself and your children.

Taking Good Care of Yourself

The Number One Rule of good parenting is *take good care of yourself.* If you are tired and stressed-out you will not be of much use to your child. You will not have patience, the ability to think creatively, or the desire to be a healing parent. Thus, it is essential to be aware of your stress level and make certain your needs (emotional, physical, social, and spiritual) are being met. You can only ask for what you need if you are aware of what you need.

State of Mind

Attachment patterns are passed down from one generation to the next. Children learn attachment from parents, and they in turn pass it on/teach the next generations. Your attachment history plays the most important role in determining how you perceive and relate to your children, as well as how you behave in intimate adult relationships. However, it is not what happened to you as a child that matters most, it is how you deal with it.

A common misconception is early life experiences determine how you will be as a parent. Following this idea, if you were abused, neglected, and experienced severe losses as a child, you will naturally end up being a flawed and inferior parent. This is not true. It is not what actually happened to you during your childhood that decides your parenting attitude and behavior. What *matters* most is your mental sate or mind-set with regard to those early attachment experiences. This is called your *state of mind*—your way of processing and dealing with the emotions and memories of your own attachment history. If a parent's state of mind is positive and resolved, they can overcome the attachment patterns learned through negative childhood experiences.

A parent's state of mind with regard to attachment is the strongest predictor of infant and child attachment. In biological families, a parent's state of mind regarding attachment determines their child's attachment pattern 75% of the time (Main et al. 1985; Van Ijzendoorn 1995). This has also been found in foster families; a foster mother's state of mind is associated with their foster baby's attachment pattern 72% of the time (Dozier et al. 2001). Even *before* a baby is born, the parent's state of mind will predict their child's attachment pattern at one year old (Fonagy et al. 1991)!

Adult Attachment Patterns

Those who cannot remember the past are condemned to repeat it.
—George Santayana

There are four adult attachment patterns: *secure, dismissing, preoccupied,* and *unresolved.* Each adult pattern corresponds to a child attachment classification (see Chapter Two, pages 20–21).

Adults are *secure* when they make sense of their attachment experiences in an honest and realistic way, understand the connection between the past and the present, and deeply value attachment. They have a "coherent" state of mind and most likely have securely attached children. Their emotional baggage does not get in the way of being a sensitive and responsive parent. They are proactive rather than reactive.

Adults who are *dismissive* are unable or unwilling to deal with their prior attachment experiences in a clear and logical way ("incoherent" state of mind). They dismiss and devalue the importance of attachment, avoid their own feelings, and reject their children. They typically have children with avoidant attachment patterns.

Adults are referred to as *preoccupied* when they are confused about and over-focused on early family problems. They are still emotionally entangled with past-unresolved issues. They commonly have children with resistant or ambivalent attachments because their own issues cause them to be inconsistent and unpredictable.

Unresolved adults had painful losses and serious traumas as children, including severe abuse and neglect, and have not resolved these early emotional wounds. They threaten, abandon, and frighten their own children, who often develop the most insecure and dysfunctional attachment pattern called disorganized-disoriented attachment.

Each of the four adult attachment patterns is described in detail below, including behavior in romantic relationships as well as parenting attitudes and behavior (Rholes & Simpson 2004; Siegel 1999).

Secure-Autonomous Adults

These adults have a coherent view of attachment. They are able to process and talk about their early family and attachment experiences logically and clearly. There is no self-deception; the details support their memories. They value close and trusting relationships, understand the importance of secure attachment, and are able to trust and depend on others. They do not idealize their past or portray their childhoods as trouble-free and are objective about their parents' positive and negative qualities. They are able to reflect on their own thoughts and feelings and those of others. They have confronted and worked through painful childhood issues and can discuss those events without undo anxiety. Their past, present, and anticipated future are integrated, and they have achieved a meaningful level of acceptance and "forgiveness" with their parents. They communicate in a clear, direct, and honest way.

In romantic relationships, secure adults find it relatively easy to get close to, trust, and depend on their partners. They open-up emotionally, make a solid commitment for the long-term, and are comfortable having their partners depend on them. They are tolerant of differences, compassionate, and responsive to their partner's needs.

These adults were securely attached to at least one parent or caregiver as children (continuous security) or developed secure attachment later in life (earned security of attachment). The adults with *earned* security experienced problems in their families growing up, but were able to deal with and make sense of those early experiences, understand how those experiences influenced their lives, and form healthy relationships as they got older. They formed a close, trusting, and healing relationship with a friend, romantic partner, therapist, or other significant person.

Studies have shown there is no difference between children of parents with continuous or earned security. Children are just as likely to be securely attached to their parents in both groups. Even under stressful conditions, parents with earned security did just as well, providing warm, sensitive, and responsive parenting (Phelps et al. 1998; Roisman et al. 2002).

Parenting Style and Behavior.

As parents they are emotionally available, sensitive, warm, and caring. They are attuned to their children's needs, cues, and signals, and meet those needs in a sensitive and timely fashion. They are able to balance closeness and separateness, engagement and disengagement, and respect their children's age-appropriate autonomy. They set appropriate boundaries and limits and can reflect on the "state of mind" of their children as well as themselves. They play with their children and have fun together. Most children of these parents are *securely attached*. Their children are not afraid to express anger or other emotions to them. Communication is open, honest, and reciprocal. They are good listeners, and share their thoughts and feelings in assertive and non-threatening ways.

Dismissing Adults

For these parents, their state of mind regarding attachment is not coherent. Memories and stories of the past are not consistent with the facts. They tend to idealize their parents, deny unpleasant events, do not recall much about early experiences, and are unaware of the impact their past has had on their current lives. They minimize and dismiss the importance of relationships and emotional attachments. Their parents were emotionally unavailable, rejecting, and insensitive to their signals and needs. They developed defenses to survive in their emotionally empty families—avoid closeness, be "independent," don't need.

In romantic relationships dismissing adults are most comfortable being self-reliant, not seeking or accepting support from their partners. They are anxious with closeness, maintain emotional distance, and find it difficult to trust. Their partners want more intimacy and connection from them than they are able or willing to give.

They are often cool, in control, ambitious, and successful. They are good in a crisis because of their ability to react with intellect while setting emotions aside. They avoid conflict and tend to be sarcastic and passive-aggressive.

Parenting Style and Behavior.

These parents are insensitive and rejecting with their children, and their parent-child relationships are characterized by physical and emotional distance. Their children learn to deactivate and deny their attachment needs, feelings, and behavior to avoid the constant rejection. Seventy-five percent of their children develop *avoidant attachments*.

Preoccupied Adults

These individuals are confused and incoherent regarding memories and preoccupied with unresolved issues from the past. Their childhoods were filled with disappointment, frustrating efforts to please their parents, and role reversals, where they became caregivers to their parents (parental child). Their parents were inconsistent, alternating between warmth and availability, and coldness and rejection.

Their romantic relationships are characterized by anxiety and uncertainty. They are so sure they won't be loved and supported that they are excessively vigilant, demand reassurance, jealous, and end-up scaring others away. They are often controlling, critical, and argumentative. They have a profound need for closeness but little trust in the emotional availability of others.

Parenting Style and Behavior.

These parents are so entangled in their own unfinished business they are unable to connect with their children. Their emotional and mental states interfere with their ability to accurately tune into their children's needs and feelings. They are inconsistent, sometimes intrusive and overinvolved, and other times unavailable and disengaged. Unlike the children of dismissing adults, who keep away to avoid rejection, these insecure children are clingy. They are desperately trying to get the attention of their unpredictable attachment figures. Roughly 75% of their children have *resistant* or *ambivalent attachment* patterns.

Unresolved Adults

These individuals experienced severe trauma and loss as children, including emotional, physical, and sexual abuse. They have not mourned their losses and are frightened and confused by memories and emotions stemming from prior trauma. They are incoherent when talking about the past and will even disassociate to avoid fear and pain. They are emotionally and biochemically dysregulated and often feel overwhelmed and out-of-control.

These adults are afraid of closeness. They view themselves as defective and unworthy of love and are not capable of intimate, trusting, and mature romantic relationships. They are selfish, controlling, and refuse to take personal responsibility for their actions. They often are antisocial, disregard rules, have little empathy and remorse, and are high-risk for drug and alcohol abuse.

Parenting Style and Behavior.

It is common for these parents to abuse and neglect their own children, continuing the cycle of maltreatment and severe attachment disorders. They script their children into past emotional dramas. Their children are frightened, have no organized strategy to connect, and are afraid to come close to the very person they need. Their intense and sudden emotional outbursts frighten their children as well. *Disorganized-disoriented attachment* patterns are common in their children.

The *Life Script*

Three women started boasting about their sons. "What a birthday I had last year!" exclaimed the first. "My son, that wonderful boy, threw me a big party in a fancy restaurant. He even paid for plane tickets for my friends."

"That's very nice, but listen to this," said the second. "Last winter, my son gave me an all-expenses-paid cruise to the Greek islands. First class."

"That's nothing!" interrupted the third. "For five years now, my son has been paying a psychiatrist $150 an hour, three times a week. And the whole time he talks about nothing but me."

—Readers Digest

Our childhood experiences with attachment figures are where our scripts are written. These experiences develop into core beliefs; the mindsets, attitudes, and expectations that define who we are, how to relate to others, and what roles we play. A child's beliefs about herself are based on how her parents or caregivers act toward her. For example, messages such as "You can't do anything right," or "Why are you so stupid?" communicate to a child that she is inadequate and incompetent. Unspoken messages can be even more powerful. For example, a parent who abandons a child conveys the message, "You are not worthy of love and connection."

From before birth and well into childhood, our subconscious receives a tremendous amount of input from which we formulate our beliefs about self, others, and the world. This is how we are taught to view ourselves as capable or inept, good or bad, deserving of love or unacceptable. This is how we learn to expect and anticipate certain behaviors from caregivers and others—safe or dangerous, kind or mean, available or rejecting. Children also learn how relationships operate by observing how their parents treat one another; how they deal with conflict, power, intimacy, and communication. For example, witnessing father abuse mother teaches a child that domination and violence are acceptable ways to solve problems and females should fear males.

Many adults have some degree of emotional baggage from their pasts—unhealed pain, losses, resentments, and fears stemming from early life experiences. As explained, these childhood experiences develop into "working models"—the core beliefs, mindsets, and expectations about whom we are and how to relate to others. Without self-awareness, we will be controlled by these outdated beliefs. Awareness of why we make certain choices frees us to make healthier choices. The *Life Script* is an excellent tool for becoming aware of your early programming, and the associated perceptions, emotions, and behaviors.

While completing your *Life Script,* it is important to realize we often view our childhood experiences through rose-colored glasses. This is done unconsciously to minimize the impact of painful childhood memories. Thus, the more honest you are in completing your *Life Script,* the more value it will have for you. Also, our parents often mellow with age; who they are now may not be who they were when you were a vulnerable child. Therefore, do your *Life Script* from the viewpoint of your "inner child," between birth and around 11 years old. Finally, if you have a spouse or partner, it is helpful for you both to complete a *Life Script.* It is best to do so separately, and then discuss your responses and insights together. This can serve as a powerful vehicle for improving both your coparenting and adult-adult relationships. If you do not have a significant other, choose someone you trust to talk to about your *Life Script* (close friend, mentor, sponsor, or counselor).

Life Script Questions

1. List 4 to 6 descriptive words or phrases to describe your mother or other maternal caregivers. Include stepmothers and grandmothers if they played a key role during your childhood. Examples: caring, loving, mean, scary, angry.

2. List 4 to 6 descriptive words to describe your father or other paternal caregivers. Include stepfathers and grandfathers if they were significant influences during your childhood. Examples: strict, involved, funny, hard worker, abusive.

3. List 4 to 6 descriptive words that describe yourself as a child—the way in which *you* perceived yourself during childhood. Examples: shy, sad, happy, needy, pleaser, lonely, angry.

4. Give 4 to 6 descriptive words to describe your siblings, including significant stepsibling relationships. Examples: stubborn, bossy, sneaky, leader, hero.

5. What were the major messages your mother(s) gave you about who you are and how to deal with life? Did you agree or disagree with these messages? Remember, an absent parent still conveys a powerful message, such as "You're not important to me."

6. What were the major messages your father(s) gave you about yourself and how to deal with life? What was your response to these messages? For example, if the major message was "You are a burden," your response may have been, "I'll keep trying to please you and win your love."

7. What did your mother(s) model regarding women (mothers and wives)? Examples: women are good housekeepers, obedient to their husbands, victims, independent.

8. What did your father(s) model about men (husbands and fathers)? Examples: men are providers, overbearing, uninvolved, protective.

9. How did your parents handle conflict, communication, emotion, and discipline of the children? Who had the power in their relationship? Who was the disciplinarian? Examples: "Mom would yell and Dad would give in." "We didn't talk about feelings." "We were spanked with a switch." "My Mom ruled the roost." How did these things affect you as a child? How does it affect your parenting now?

10. Did alcohol or drug abuse play a role in your family? Example: "Dad would come home from work and drink until he passed out."

11. When you were upset as a child (emotionally distressed or frightened, physically ill or hurt), to whom did you turn to for comfort and support? What happened?

12. Name the people in your life with whom you have had significant romantic relationships. List 4 to 6 descriptive words to characterize each one. Include your current partner. Examples: caring, abusive, selfish, intelligent, driven, domineering.

13. Who was your favorite childhood hero or heroine? Why? This can be a sports figure, historical figure, family member, etc. Example: Superman, because he was invincible and helped people.

14. What would you write on the tombstone or epitaph for father, mother, self, and spouse/partner? For example, "Here lies a caring but troubled person."

15. How do you think your childhood relationships and experiences affected you as an adult, including how you think about yourself and how you relate to your partner and children? What behaviors and patterns of relating do you want to change, and how difficult is it to change?

Making Sense of Your Life Script

Questions 1 and 2: How you describe maternal and paternal figures will give you a deeper understanding of your core beliefs about yourself and your expectations of relationships. Father's example shows us how to be a husband and father, or who to pick as a husband. Mother's example teaches us how to be wives and mothers, or who to pick as a wife. In relationships, we either replicate these familiar patterns or reject them by choosing someone with opposite qualities. Either way, our parents' modeling influences our choices. A characteristic of a parent that you do not like may be a trigger for you if you perceive this same trait in your partner or child. How many of your mother's or father's traits match your own? How many match your partner's or child's? Which ones push your buttons?

Question 3: How were the adjectives you used to describe yourself as a child influenced by the messages you received from your parents? What do the adjectives tell you about how you felt as a child? How are you the same now? How are you different? How have those old messages helped or impeded your success in reaching your goals? Do you ever put your inner child's face on your children, thereby addressing your unmet needs rather than theirs?

Question 4: Relationships with siblings serve an important function in our emotional and social development. Many important lessons about sharing, competition, conflict, intimacy, and love are learned in sibling relationships. What lessons did you learn from your siblings? How did these messages and experiences impact your life?

Questions 5 and 6: When children are young and helpless, parents appear all powerful and all knowing. Children internalize the messages their parents give them about themselves. They then pass down these learned attitudes and rules of interacting to the next generation. How have the messages you received from your mother and father influenced your feelings of self worth? Did these messages help you to feel confident or powerless? What were the messages you received about your appearance, intelligence, and value in your family?

Questions 7 and 8: These two questions further explore how your mother and father are the models by which you measure what it is to be a woman or man. You learned many basic assumptions about relationships by the way your mother and father treated you and each other. How does your father's description compare to yourself if you are a man, or your partner if you are a woman? How does your mother's description compare to yourself if you are a woman, or your partner if you are a man? How are they different?

Question 9: In well-functioning families, parents cope with the pressures of life by working out problems. Open and honest communication is encouraged, options are explored, and outside help is sought when necessary. The expression of feelings, individuality, and personal responsibility is supported. In other families, open and honest communication is discouraged, boundaries are poorly defined, and others are wrongly blamed. How did your parents deal with conflict? Were they "rage-oholics" or did they avoid conflict at all costs? How do your parents' styles compare with your own? Who had the power in your parents' relationship? Was power shared? Who has the power in your relationship? How did your parents' model affect your view of power? How did your parents handle discipline? Were they consistent? Did they use threats, humiliation, guilt, or violence? How do you discipline in comparison to your parents?

Question 10: Parental alcohol or drug abuse might be more damaging than you realize. Abusers act in ways that hurt and always result in disruptive consequences to their families. Children who grow up in these homes suffer from damaged self-esteem and a confused sense of self-identity, and often become enablers or irresponsible. High levels of stress are created by the abuser's unpredictability, negativity, and volatility. Abusers tend to use criticism and blame to control their children. Substance abuse in the home destroys a child's trust and the ability to be open and vulnerable. Adult children of alcoholics frequently marry alcoholics, and one in four becomes an alcoholic. How has parental substance abuse affected your life and your relationships?

Question 11: Secure attachment develops when a child's needs are met, especially during times of stress or discomfort. When you needed comfort, protection, or reassurance, what happened, and how did that affect you?

Question 12: By looking at the adjectives you used to describe your romantic relationships you might begin to see a pattern of similar traits. Be aware of themes in these relationships and how they ended. How many adjectives match your parents? How many are opposite?

Question 13: Your favorite hero can reveal a lot about what you thought was important as a child. Why did you pick this individual? What were the qualities of your hero that were appealing to you? If you had no hero, what does that say about your role models?

Question 14: How do you sum up your own and others' lives? What would you want your epitaph to be? You can work toward that goal.

Question 15: Your core beliefs, formed early in life, affect how you think, feel, and relate. What have you realized by doing your Life Script? What do you want to change, and how will you achieve those goals?

Adult Attachment and Communication

Attachment theory gives us a way of understanding the intricacies of intimate adult relationships, including issues such as trust, support, loss, emotional reactions, patterns of interacting, and core beliefs. Just as children need their parents and caregivers to be a secure base and safe haven, adults need their partners to provide safety and security. It is important you view your partner as emotionally available, responsive to your needs, and dependable, especially during stressful times.

When you turn to your partner for support and comfort, and he or she is not there for you, an *attachment wound* often occurs. Trust is damaged and there is a predictable response to the loss of connection: angry protest, despair, and detachment. Depression often occurs as a response to the loss.

There are two basic strategies people use in these situations. The first is characterized by increased attachment behaviors (hyperactivated), including anxious clinging, pursuit, and other frantic attempts to connect with their partner. The second strategy is detached avoidance; attachment needs and behaviors are reduced (deactivated) to avoid the pain of loss. Couples can get stuck in ongoing, repetitive patterns using one or both of these strategies, which is extremely damaging to the relationship. For example, there is a high incidence of divorce among couples with a pattern of angry accusations followed by avoidance and emotional distance by the partner (Gottman 1999).

Many of the interaction behaviors and patterns in couple relationships can be traced back to the internal working models formed early in life. These mindsets become biases and expectations—the lens through which we view our partners and ourselves. Secure adults see themselves as worthy of love and trust that their partners will be dependable and supportive. Those with insecure and anxious attachments view themselves as not deserving of love and expect their partners to reject, abandon, or abuse them. These mental models and beliefs influence behavior and emotional reactions, and eventually develop into ongoing patterns—the dance of relationships.

An effective and powerful way to change negative patterns is to learn how to communicate effectively: how to share and listen in honest, deep, positive, and constructive ways. This can be accomplished by learning the concepts and skills of *Attachment Communication Training (ACT)*. After you have completed your *Life Script*, you are now ready to create positive connections, using the communication skills outlined in the next section.

Attachment Communication Training (ACT)

Effective communication is the basis of meaningful relationships and secure attachment. It promotes understanding, empathy, support, and need fulfillment, and is a vehicle for positive problem solving. The communication method that we have developed and teach—*Attachment Communication Training (ACT)*—has the following desired results:

- Provides a framework conducive to safe and constructive confiding and connecting; fosters a healthy and healing emotional environment.

- Enables you to practice and learn effective communication skills, including listening and sharing skills.

- Requires the use of ground rules that increase positive ways of interacting and prevents destructive behaviors, such as criticism, contempt, defensiveness, or stonewalling, which predict divorce (Gottman 1999).

- Facilitates constructive verbal and nonverbal communication, including mental, emotional, and physical connections.

- Results in attunement to each other's needs, feelings, messages, and states of mind (feeling "felt").

- Encourages empathy, warmth, and genuineness; allows for nonthreatening confrontation and constructive conflict management.

- Offers a way to change current patterns of relating as well as prior attachment patterns; the marital relationship serves as a healing environment.

- Allows a partner to be a "secure base" for one another, an emotional support system in times of distress.

Ground Rules

Prior to practicing the communication skills and methods described later, the two people communicating must agree to follow these basic ground rules:

- No blaming, criticism, contempt, defensiveness, or stonewalling.

- Agree to disagree; each person is allowed to have and share his or her own feelings, opinions, and viewpoints.

- No interrupting.

- Discontinue until a later time if you can't talk without destructive emotions.

- No running away; work through an issue to completion.

- Practice communication skills. Set aside enough time to learn the skills prior to a "crisis."

- Agree to get help if you become "stuck," unable to resolve a problem (e.g., see a therapist who is familiar with effective communication).

ACT Steps

As previously stated, effective communication is the basis of healthy relationships, resulting in empathy, emotional closeness, and constructive problem solving. ACT is recommended for any two-person dialogue (e.g., husband-wife or parent-child). Initially, using this communication method may seem unnatural, but with practice you will find it to be helpful and rewarding (see example of ACT in use in Chapter 7, pages 253–254). It is very important to follow the guidelines and steps closely, and practice the skills as described, to insure success. There are six steps: *share* ▸ *listen* ▸ *restate* ▸ *feedback* ▸ *reverse roles* ▸ *discuss results.*

SHARING. One person speaks while the other person listens. Use the following sharing skills:

- Be honest with yourself and partner about what you are thinking, perceiving, and feeling, even if you are worried about "making waves."

- Share both thoughts and feelings; "The way I see the situation is _____, and this makes me feel _____."

- Make "I" statements. You are taking responsibility for your own perceptions and emotions. No questions, blaming, or criticizing.

- Be specific, clear, and give concrete examples. Don't talk in generalities or expect your partner to "mind read." "When you did _____, I viewed this as _____, and then I felt _____."

- Be brief. Say one or two things, and say it once. Lengthy speech is annoying and difficult to follow.

- Be aware of your nonverbal messages as well as your verbal messages. What is your body language communicating: eyes, facial expressions, tone of voice, posture? Your nonverbal messages may determine how much your partner wants to listen.

- Be assertive and positive. Do not attack, blame, or criticize.

LISTENING. While your partner is expressing his or her thoughts and feelings, your job is to be a good listener. Use the following listening skills:

- Be empathic. Understand what your partner is telling you, whether you agree or not. "Walk in your partner's shoes." Really *hear* your partner's ideas, opinions, perceptions, emotions, and needs, even if you see the situation differently.

- Be nonjudgmental. Don't judge your partner's comments as right or wrong, good or bad. Put aside your judgments for a while so you can hear and understand your partner.

- Don't censor what you hear (selective listening) or silently rehearse your rebuttal. Try your best to relax your mind and body so you can totally hear your partner's messages without being defensive.

- Be aware of your nonverbal messages. Do your eyes, facial expressions, gestures, and body positions let your partner know you are safe, supportive, and interested?

- Tune into both content and process. The content is the words, ideas, and topic. The process is the deeper meaning, the meta-message—the "message behind the message." What is your partner's emotional message?

RESTATING. When your partner is done expressing his or her thoughts and feelings, you now restate what you heard; "I heard you say _____." This is called "reflective listening," as you are reflecting back the messages you received.

FEEDBACK. Your partner will now tell you how well you did as a listener. "Yes, you heard me accurately; you got my message, thank you." If you did not think your partner heard all your messages accurately, or misinterpreted your message, you can say, "No, I did not say what you heard; let me try again." It is ok to clarify your thoughts and feelings, giving your partner another chance to listen. The goal is: message sent; message received. No "spin on it," distortions, or misinterpretations.

REVERSE ROLES. The speaker becomes the listener, and the listener now takes a turn at sharing. Follow the same rules and guidelines previously described. You and your partner have several chances to practice sharing and listening skills.

DISCUSS RESULTS. After you and your partner have had several turns sharing and listening, talk with one another about how it was to use the ACT method. Share your thoughts and feelings considering the following:

- What was it like to communicate in this way?

- How does it feel to share honestly? How do you feel when you sense your partner is really hearing you or not hearing you?

- What was more difficult for you, sharing or listening?

- How will your relationship be improved by using ACT?

- What are some of the issues you want to discuss in the future using ACT?

Constructive and Destructive Communication

The following are traits and characteristics of constructive and destructive communication (McKay et al. 1995). Your goal is to practice and learn constructive communication skills.

Destructive Communication

A person with destructive communication skills

- mind reads, labels, predicts, personalizes, generalizes, distracts, "kitchen-sinks," "cross-complains," "yes-butts", placates, and compares;

- is judgmental;

- focuses on negative rather than positive;

- uses polarizing language; pushes other's buttons;

- does not listen or validate; focuses only on self;

- complains, nags, criticizes, insults, attacks, blames, or threatens;

- pseudo-listens—placate, rehearse comeback, avoid conflict to seek approval;

- interrupts;

- gets into a standoff—must maintain own position, plays "win-lose," stonewalls, defensiveness;

- is vague and general;

- is rude and impolite;

- airs old resentments; and

- does not take a "time-out" when necessary.

Constructive Communication

On the other hand, a person with positive and constructive communication skills

- is empathic and validates other's thoughts and feelings;

- listens to and paraphrases other's thoughts and feelings;

- gives clear, honest, and immediate feedback without being judgmental and blaming;

- asks for feedback;

- has congruent content and style;

- shares thoughts and feelings;

- stays focused on issue or theme;

- asks clarifying questions;

- is open-minded and reserves judgment;

- sends assertive, not aggressive, messages;

- makes sure message sent is message received;

- is aware of nonverbal messages (eye contact, facial expressions, tone of voice);

- edits comments to avoid conflict and provocation;

- calls "time-out" when helpful;

- stays committed to positive communication even if upset, angry, or frustrated; and

- gives whole messages (perceptions, thoughts, feelings, and needs).

Successful Adult Relationships

In the United States, 2.5 million couples get married each year, but more than 60% will end in divorce. Even more will fail if it is a second marriage. There are many apparent reasons for unsuccessful marriages: incompatibility, substance abuse, domestic violence, lack of communication, and affairs. Unhappy couples are far more likely to resort to four behaviors—criticism, defensiveness, withdrawal, and contempt—that destroy trust and love and often lead to divorce (Gottman 1999).

Most of us are poorly trained for marriage; we are pitifully unprepared for life after infatuation. Movies, television, and magazines are saturated with images of lust-driven romance, but do not present a model of long-term love. Many people have grown up in families where they lacked role models of healthy, long-term love and commitment. Couples do not realize problems can be solved, and they can work their way back to trust and romance. In a feel good, disposable society, it is easier to throw away a relationship and find a new one, rather than be uncomfortable and work at the relationship.

There is a heartening trend in the last few years, though, showing couples working harder to strengthen and preserve their marriages. Almost 5 million couples per year seek help from more than 50,000 licensed marital and family therapists (Levy 2001).

More people are realizing that in a marital relationship one can acquire knowledge about hidden parts of the self. Marriage recreates the environment of childhood, with many of the same issues: acceptance/rejection, connection/loneliness, love/hate, safe/threatened, empowered/victim. When partners are open to creating a healthy marriage, old wounds can be healed and new paths toward growth pursued.

Healthy and happy couples will have the following characteristics.

- Both partners have "come to terms" with their pasts. They have separated emotionally from their families-of-origin and have truly become mature individuals, able to fully invest in the relationship.

- They are able to balance togetherness and autonomy, intimacy and individuality. They can be independent without being distant.

- They trust, depend on, and support one another; serve as each other's emotional support system and safe haven in times of distress or crisis.

- They practice good communication and problem-solving skills. They share their views and feelings in constructive ways and are both good listeners. They share thoughts, feelings, needs, hurts, desires, and hopes with one another.

- There is a feeling of true partnership between equals. Power and control are shared with important decisions made jointly. The division of labor is fair regarding roles and responsibilities, both inside and outside of the family.

- They meet the basic emotional needs of one another. Both parties are satisfied with the degree and frequency of love, affection, and sexual intimacy.

- Both are willing to take responsibility for their part in problems and solutions— "take your own inventory"—rather than blame, judge, or criticize the other person. Both work on making the relationship better.

- They both make their relationship a priority. They spend enjoyable time together and show their love and caring regularly in special ways (for example, flowers, notes of appreciation, massage, or breakfast in bed). They use humor and laughter to connect and keep things in perspective.

- They do not take out hurt, anger, or frustration about other things on their partner. They exercise self-control and use good stress-management techniques.

- They deal with and make peace with past hurts, disappointments, and breaches of trust in the relationship. They are able to talk about, work through, and resolve such wounds, and therefore, have confidence that problems can be solved.

- They find ways to successfully adapt to the changes and challenges of having children. They are a united team in raising their children.

- They find ways to keep their relationship alive and vital over time. They realize needs, perspectives, and emotions change as time goes by, and they must learn to adapt.

- They share basic values and moral codes of behavior. They can also agree-to-disagree respectfully when there is a difference of opinion or outlook.

Secondary Traumatic Stress: The Cost of Caring

Secondary traumatic stress (STS) is a natural consequence of helping a traumatized or suffering person. For example, social workers are exposed to significant stress through the trauma of their clients. Child welfare workers, as well as foster and adoptive parents, deal with the painful details of the awful things some adults have done to their children. Empathy and caring, so important to building a relationship with a child, is also a channel through which a caring adult is exposed to traumatic stress (Figley 1999).

STS, also called compassion fatigue, vicarious traumatization, and covictimization, can result in numerous symptoms: fatigue, physical illnesses, emotional numbing, social withdrawal, loss of motivation, and feelings of hopelessness and despair. Numerous studies have documented the negative effects of caring for traumatized people (see Nelson-Gardell & Harris 2003). Nurses providing emergency medical care were found to suppress their emotions, display rigid thinking, and have trouble making decisions. Trauma therapists working with holocaust survivors and their children were found to rely on defenses such as numbing, avoidance, denial, distancing, and often had feelings of guilt, rage, shame, and grief. Counselors working with perpetrators and survivors of domestic violence reported experiencing visual images of what they heard (flashbacks) and feeling horror, having loss of confidence, and become less secure in general. Symptoms of secondary traumatization were found among mental health and law enforcement professionals who help sexually abused children. Symptoms of stress and trauma were reported in 70% of these workers, including anxiety, depression, sexual problems, and eating disturbances.

What if the person providing caring and helping services has a history of trauma in his or her own background? How does a personal trauma history affect STS? Trauma therapists who reported a personal trauma history showed more negative effects from their work than those without such a personal history. A recent study of child protection workers in two southeastern states confirmed these findings. Child welfare workers who reported abuse and neglect in their own childhoods had a higher risk of STS symptoms. Emotional abuse and neglect in a person's history placed them most as risk (Nelson-Gardell & Harris 2003).

Stress-related problems are an occupational hazard for those who help others in need. This is especially true when the person helping has a personal history of trauma. We have found many adoptive and foster parents trying to make a difference in the lives of wounded children are sustaining blows to their own emotional and physical well-being. The parents who have a personal history of maltreatment and compromised attachment often have a good deal of empathy for their children, but are also more susceptible to psychological harm and symptoms of STS. They are more likely to get triggered by the anger, defiance, manipulation, and ongoing stress of dealing with their children. This can cause flashbacks to the loss and abuse of their own childhoods, making it very difficult to remain calm and not take it personally. There are destructive effects on their emotional stability, marriages, and family relationships.

If you are aware of issues in your past that make it difficult to be a healing parent, it is very important to take the proper steps: talk to someone you trust, use stress-management methods, maintain support, get the right help, and equip yourself with the correct parenting skills, such as Corrective Attachment Parenting.

The helping individual who develops STS, whether or not compounded by their own personal histories, is subject to burnout. The following are some tips to prevent and recover from burnout (Simmons 2005).

Keep clear of denial.

It is common to deny there is a problem until things get out of hand. Admit you are under stress, identify the sources of your stress, and then you can learn better ways to cope.

Avoid isolation.

You may not feel like relating with others, but closeness and communication help when under stress. Closeness decreases the negative effects of anxiety and depression and also increases self-awareness via communication and feedback.

Reduce the pressure.

Recognize the areas of your daily life that produce the most stress and work toward lightening your load. See if you can eliminate some tasks, take a new mental approach to them, and get some more help—share the load.

Pace yourself.

Strive for moderation and balance; there is a time to work hard and a time to rest. Make sure you build relaxing breaks into your daily schedule.

Minimize worrying.

Although normal, worrying doesn't solve problems; it leads to more anxiety and distress. Rather than brooding over your concerns, write in a journal, talk with someone you trust, use a constructive problem-solving method to find solutions, and then take action.

Take care of yourself.

Take care of your body. Get plenty of exercise, have a nutritious diet, avoid drugs and alcohol, and get enough sleep. Nurture yourself, not just others. If you are more focused on caring for others than caring for your own needs, you will become burned out. Remember, the number one rule of parenting—take good care of yourself.

You and Stress

Stress is defined as an automatic physical response to any situation that requires you to adjust to change. The stress response includes physical changes, such as faster heartbeat and breathing, triggered by stress hormones released in response to real or perceived danger. This is also called the fight-flight-freeze response.

The stress response helped our primitive ancestors deal with a dangerous world. When they encountered a wild animal they had to either attack or try to escape. When the danger passed the response would turn off. There is a positive aspect to stress; as stress or anxiety increases so does performance—to a point. When the stress response is repeatedly triggered damage occurs to the mind and body. Chronic stress is caused by constant emotional pressure one can neither fight nor flee, such as the ongoing stress of a stormy relationship with a challenging child and a traumatized family environment.

Chronic stress has been linked to many health problems, including heart disease, stroke, cancer, asthma, arthritis, ulcers, depression, and anxiety. Here is how stress takes its toll:

- *Starts in the brain.* When the brain detects a threat several structures (amygdala, hypothalamus, and pituitary gland) send signaling hormones and nerve impulses to the body to prepare for fight-flight-freeze.

- *Hormones released.* The body unleashes a flood of hormones. The adrenal glands release adrenaline (epinephrine), which makes the heart pump faster and the lungs increase oxygen to the body, and releases extra cortisol, which converts sugar into energy. Nerve cells release norepinephrine, which tenses the muscles, sharpens the senses, and shuts down digestion.

- *Damage occurs.* Stress hormones released continually can damage arteries, weaken the immune system, and cause loss of bone mass, suppression of the reproductive system, and impaired memory.

An estimated 60% to 90% of doctor visits are the result of stress-related conditions. It is now a known fact mental states and physical well-being are intimately connected. An unhealthy mind can lead to an unhealthy body, and visa versa. A vicious cycle occurs of mental and physical reactions. Depression is a perfect example of the mind-body connection. Once you have a heart attack your risk of dying from cardiovascular disease is up to six times greater if you also suffer from depression.

How do you know if you are stressed out? You need to know the warning signs so you can take the appropriate actions to reduce your stress (Dadoly 2002).

- *Physical symptoms:* body tension, headaches, stomachaches, sleep problems, rapid heartbeat, fatigue, weight gain or loss, dizziness, nausea, loss of sexual desire.

- *Behavioral symptoms:* increased smoking, drinking, or drug use; procrastination, grinding teeth, overly critical, fidgeting, isolating from others.

- *Emotional symptoms:* severe anxiety, crying, irritability, quick temper, sense of loneliness, lack of meaning, depression.
- *Cognitive symptoms:* fearful and anxious thoughts, poor concentration, forgetfulness, loss of sense of humor and creativity, indecisiveness.

No one can totally avoid stressful situations, but we can influence how these situations affect us. By using self-care measures and stress-reducing techniques, as described in the following sections, you can reduce the damaging effects of stress, increase your body's self-healing ability, and even reduce or eliminate the need for some medications (Benson 2000, Dadoly 2002).

The term "relaxation response" was coined by Dr. Herbert Benson of Harvard Medical School to describe a state of deep rest and stress release. Numerous studies have confirmed the benefits of the relaxation response: it decreases blood pressure, heart rate, and breathing, and relaxes the mind and body by reducing the flow of stress hormones (Benson 2000). You can achieve the relaxation response by various methods, including meditation, progressive muscle relaxation, visualization, yoga, and prayer. It is important that the method you choose interrupts everyday thoughts, allowing you to calm your mind and body.

Meditation

An ancient method of relaxation, meditation allows you to empty your mind and achieve a state of calm. Ten million Americans meditate regularly. Studies show meditation boosts the immune system, rewires the brain in order to lower stress, and reduces pain, depression, and anxiety. Here is how to meditate:

- *Find a quiet place.* Turn down the lights and make sure there are no distractions.
- *Close your eyes.* Shut out the outside world so your brain can stop processing information. Sit quietly in a comfortable position. Relax your muscles, from your feet up to your head.
- *Choose a word or phrase.* Repeat a word or phrase that is soothing to you ("calm", "peace"). Say your "mantra" over and over as you exhale and relax.
- *Clear your mind.* When thoughts come into your mind acknowledge them, gently let them go, and return calmly to your mantra. With each breath you become more and more relaxed.
- *Practice.* Ideally, spend 10 to 20 minutes, but even 5 minutes of meditation is beneficial. When finished, sit quietly for one minute before getting up.

Progressive Muscle Relaxation

It is common to have tension in your muscles. You might feel tightness in your neck, shoulders, back, or other areas. Progressive muscle relaxation (PMR) enables you to isolate specific muscles, tense them briefly, and then relax them. You will feel the tension melting from your muscles and also experience mental relaxation. Follow these steps:

- *Breathe.* Lie down and breathe deeply for two minutes. With each breath you become more and more relaxed.

- *Tighten and release.* Concentrate on one muscle group at a time. Tighten the muscle for a count of five, and then release the muscle while inhaling and exhaling deeply. Tighten and relax all your muscles from head to toes: forehead, eyes, neck, jaws, back, shoulders, arms, stomach, hips, legs, and feet.

- *Relax.* Breathe slowly and relax your body and mind for as long as you want. Let go. Relax.

Visualization

Also called *guided imagery,* this technique involves picturing yourself in a safe, peaceful, and relaxed environment. Start by relaxing your body and mind with PMR and deep breathing. Next, imagine yourself in a relaxing scene, one that has good memories for you: "I am on a beautiful beach, warmed by the sun, hearing the ocean and the sound of seagulls;" "I am sitting by a stream in a forest, taking in the wonderful fragrance of the pine trees, feeling at one with nature." You can also visualize yourself accomplishing a particular goal.

Yoga

This ancient form of exercise increases flexibility and coordination while also enhancing tranquility and relaxation. There are many forms of yoga, but the most popular is Hatha yoga, which has become well known in the last 20 years. Yoga is a very powerful mind and body stress-reduction tool.

Exercise

Ongoing stress keeps your body in a constant state of arousal. Regular physical exercise is essential to turning off the stress response, as well as being crucial for general good health. There are many documented benefits of exercise. Physical benefits include: strengthened heart, arteries, and blood flow; lowered blood pressure, cholesterol, and risk of heart attack; improved immunity and digestion; strengthened muscles, bones, joints, ligaments, and tendons; and increased flow of oxygen and nutrients into the cells and the transport of carbon dioxide and toxins out of the body. The mental and emotional benefits include: the release of mood-elevating endorphins which improve mental outlook and lessen depression; the stimulation of creativity; improved self-esteem and sense of well-being; reduced tension and anxiety; released pent-up emotions; and improved sleep.

For every hour of exercise you can increase your lifespan by two hours. An unfit person is eight times more likely to have a heart attack or stroke. With all the well-known benefits, why do fewer than 20% of Americans exercise? (Murray & Pizzorno 1998) The answer is the lack of motivation. Here are a few tips for increasing your motivation to exercise.

Make it fun.

As long as you raise your pulse rate, the only thing that matters is you enjoy what you are doing. If it's enjoyable you are more likely to continue. The most beneficial exercises are the ones that increase your heart rate, such as brisk walking, jogging, bicycling, swimming, tennis, cross country skiing, and aerobic dance. It also helps to have a partner to keep you honest and interested.

Set goals.

It's best to start with small successes that can lead to bigger ones. Create a chart to gauge your progress.

Vary your routine.

Take short breaks if you start to lose enthusiasm. Vary what you do to keep it interesting. A minimum of 15–20 minutes of exercise at least three times per week is necessary to gain significant cardiovascular benefits.

Diet and Nutrition

Diet affects your long-term health and vulnerability to illness. What you eat and when you eat influences your physical and psychological well-being. Nutrition is particularly important in reducing stress. If you are trying to lower your stress and anxiety level, pay attention to the following:

- *Eat the optimal diet.* The optimal diet for combating stress consists of fresh foods that are high in complex carbohydrates and fiber, low in sugar, fat, and salt, and moderate in protein. Many consider fish to be the best choice for animal protein. Researchers found people who had diets high in Omega-3 (the healthy fats in fatty fish) were less likely to suffer from depression (Atkinson 2005). Complex carbohydrates are our best source of fuel. Our diet should be 50% to 60% fresh fruits and vegetables, legumes, and whole grains. Also drink lots of water; your body needs water to regulate digestion, circulation, and detoxification. Our bodies require 4–6 pints of fluid per day. Coffee, tea, soft drinks, and alcohol do not count; they are dehydrators.

- *Limit caffeine.* Caffeine is a stimulant that heightens arousal by releasing cortisol, the same chemical released during a stress reaction. Coffee, tea, cola, and chocolate are all stimulants, which activate the sympathetic nervous system and prepare us for fight-flight-freeze. Caffeine can wear on the adrenal glands and is stressful to the body. If you are already stressed, this is a "double whammy." Caffeine can trigger anxiety, panic attacks, and problems with concentration. One cup of coffee contains 75–125 mg of caffeine. The arousal effects of one cup of coffee last approximately six hours. The average American consumes 15–225 mg of caffeine in a day (two cups of coffee). Most people can handle this, but those who suffer from depression, insomnia, stress, and anxiety should avoid caffeine.

- *Limit alcohol.* Contrary to what is commonly believed, alcohol is not a stimulant, it is a depressant. The lift we get from alcohol comes from hyperactivity of the brain, which reduces inhibitions and suppresses unpleasant feelings and anxiety. This euphoria is short lived, and soon you are feeling worse than you did before. The last thing someone who is depressed needs is a liquid depressant. Alcohol produces many chemical stresses on the body; it increases the production of stress hormones, disrupts normal sleep cycles, destroys brain cells, and can lead to premature aging. People who use alcohol as the primary method of stress management are at risk for developing alcohol dependency. If you do drink, limit yourself to one ounce per day (two beers or two small glasses of wine). It is best for people with chronic stress or anxiety to avoid alcohol entirely.

- *Limit refined carbohydrates.* Refined carbohydrates, such as sugar and white flour, are directly related to problems with blood sugar control, especially hypoglycemia. Hypoglycemia is common in individuals who suffer from depression, and depression is one of the most common causes of anxiety. Refined sugar has no nutritional value; it actually robs your body of vitamins, since it takes calcium, B vitamins, and magnesium to metabolize sugar. Sugar also has a detrimental effect on mood, particularly when combined with caffeine. Your adrenal glands are the key organ in the battle with stress; excess sugar stimulates the adrenal glands to trigger a stress response. Most packaged foods contain sugar additives. An estimated 25% to 50% of our total calories come from sugar. In 1900, people consumed about 5 pounds of sugar per year. Today we consume our body weight in sugar; approximately 300,000 empty calories per year, providing no vitamins, minerals, enzymes, or other needed nutrients (Chamberlin 2006).

- *Create a relaxed mealtime atmosphere. How* you eat is just as important as *what* you eat. A relaxed mealtime environment not only prevents stress, but also reduces the stress you already have. Stress affects the parasympathetic nervous system, which also controls our digestion. Eating in a stressful, rushed, or chaotic environment negatively impacts digestion and overall health. Do not rush eating; sit down and enjoy your meal. Engage in pleasant conversation or listen to soft music. Meals are not the time to discuss problems.

Change Your Thoughts

Your perceptions and thoughts often determine your emotional reactions. Negative thoughts, including cognitive distortions and exaggerations, can trigger the stress response. This *self-talk* (see Chapter 6, page 182), such as "I'm stupid; I can't solve my problem," leads to anger, hopelessness, and severe stress. Here is a way to identify and challenge negative thoughts:

- *Take time-out.* Do not react. Consciously decide to take a break.

- *Relax.* Breathe deeply. Relax your mind and body.

- *Reflect.* Be mindful and check out your perceptions and self-talk: "Is my belief and conclusion true?" "Can I view this situation differently?" "Am I being triggered from something in my past?" "Is there a more constructive perception I can have?"

- *Cope effectively.* Choose the best course of action based on the source of your stress. If you determine your negative self-talk is causing stress, let go and create a more constructive viewpoint. If the root of the stress is external, use practical problem-solving steps to cope and find a solution (see problem-solving strategy, Chapter 6, pages 184–187). Affirmations, which are positive thoughts and ideas, can combat negative self-talk. Make sure your affirmations are in the present tense ("I am now creating solutions;" "I am now relaxing my mind and body;" "I am a healing parent").

Sleep

Sleep is an essential part of our well-being. Studies show it is not the length of sleep that refreshes us, but the number of complete sleep cycles we experience. Each sleep cycle contains five phases, alternating between periods of REM (rapid eye movement) sleep in which we dream, and non-REM sleep. Each phase contains different brain wave patterns. One complete sleep cycle last 90 minutes. If we sleep naturally, with no alarm clocks or other disruptions, we would wake up after a multiple of 90 minutes. Sleep deprivation is very taxing to our emotional and physical health. Interrogators know depriving people of sleep is a sure fire way of "breaking" them. An infant requires about 14 hours of sleep; adults average 7.5 hours; and the elderly, about 6 hours. If you have trouble sleeping, try the following:

- If you have racing thoughts, keep a pad and pen next to your bed, and write down your thoughts. Then release them until the morning.

- Get out of bed and leave the room. Sometimes a change of scenery helps. Be sure not to put on bright lights.

- Drink a cup of warm milk with honey (melatonin).

- Read something that is not too stimulating.

- Make sure the bedroom is pitch black; if not, use a sleep mask.

- If there is extraneous noise, use earplugs.

- Meditate and relax.

- Do not put on the TV, as this will stimulate you further.

- Do not exercise before bed.

- Avoid alcohol within four hours of bedtime.

- Do not eat a heavy meal before bed.

Prayer

Prayer is another excellent way to deal with stress. People report when they pray regularly they are calmer, healthier, and more appreciative for what they have. When we feel overwhelmed, releasing our problems to a higher power can dramatically reduce stress. Connecting with a divine source brings peace and knowingness that we are loved and not alone.

Breathe

When we are under stress our muscles tense and breathing becomes shallow and rapid, in preparation for fight-flight-freeze. A simple way to short-circuit the stress response is to breathe deeply and slowly. Put your hand on your belly and take a deep breath through your nose. Feel the air filling your body. Starting in your belly, move the air up through your diaphragm into your chest. Mentally count to 5 as you inhale, and again count to 5 as you exhale. Work up to a 10 count.

Laugh

Laughter brings oxygen into the body, releases muscle tension, and stimulates the production of endorphins, which make us feel good. Find ways to laugh every day—smiling and laughing are contagious. A belly laugh lasting just 10 minutes can provide 2 hours of pain-free sleep. Laughter also appears to be an important factor in recovering from life-threatening illness. Laughter enhances respiration, increases immune cells, and decreases the stress hormone cortisol. Performance on problem-solving tests yields better results when preceded by laughter (Howard 1994).

Cry

Humans are the only mammals that cry when feeling emotion. It is part of our nature to cry as a means of releasing stress. If you place a tear under a microscope, you find stress hormones and other substances the body needs to expel. Crying is a way to release toxins and cleanse emotional stress.

Sing

Singing feels good and facilitates good breathing. You do not have to have perfect pitch to receive the benefits of singing. Anything that allows you to take in oxygen and to expel emotion is beneficial.

Dance

Dancing is joyful and allows us to move our bodies. It also occupies our minds and gives our intellect a rest. Primitive cultures used dance to grieve, celebrate, and connect to spirit. You can dance in a club, take lessons, or "let go" in the privacy of your home.

Talk

Talking to someone who is really listening makes us feel understood. Being truly heard is a major source of comfort and relief. Speaking your truth feels good. It helps us to vent and to process our feelings. Two important factors in coping with stress are warm, supportive relations, and the need to communicate.

Listen to Music

Listening to relaxing music is an excellent way to melt away stress. Any rhythm that approximates the beat of a relaxed heart (60 beats per minute) is calming. Baroque music is one example. Making music is another way to relax. If you are not musically gifted, you can beat a drum, shake maracas, or find another way to join in.

Nap

When Thomas Edison was stuck by a problem he would lie down and take a nap. Power naps are a great way to rejuvenate. Studies show people who nap regularly live longer and show a 30% lower incidence of heart disease (Howard 1994). The ideal amount of time for a nap seems to be 30 minutes. Napping any longer is sleeping, which means you have to wake up, which can cause grogginess instead of a feeling of restfulness and alertness.

Take a Bath

Showers are invigorating, and baths are relaxing. Turn off the phone, turn down the lights, and get into hot water. You can light candles, use scented oils, and listen to relaxing music. Soak away your stress.

Journal

Talking to yourself through writing is soothing to the soul. It allows you to express what you feel without judgments from others. It's for your eyes only; you can say whatever you want and spell any way you want.

Go Into Nature

Spending quiet time alone in a natural setting away from noise and stimulation allows you to fall into rhythm with nature. It rejuvenates us and helps us to adjust to a more relaxed state of being. Even a brief respite is extremely beneficial.

Time Management

An organized environment enhances harmony and security. Poor time management is a major stressor. Organize family tasks such as meal preparation and chores. Delegate as much responsibility as you can. If everyone is doing his or her share, there will be fewer burdens on you. Set priorities. Instead of trying to do everything, decide what is most important. Make lists of the things you need to remember. Keep the family schedule as regular as possible. Build in time to take care of yourself. The more organized you are, the less stressed you will be in accomplishing your goals.

Pamper Yourself

Go to a spa. Get a massage, haircut, and manicure. Sit in a Jacuzzi, steam bath, or sauna. Browse a bookstore, window shop, see a movie. Buy something you want, not need. Your car can be a sanctuary; keep it stocked with snacks, relaxing music, and good reading material. It's ok to indulge yourself sometimes.

Take a Break

Sometimes we need a vacation to rejuvenate ourselves. Getting away separates you from the daily grind. A change of scenery can recharge us. If an extended vacation is not practical, then do an overnight or weekend escape.

Summary

- Your experiences in earlier relationships create core beliefs and attachment styles, which then determine how you view and relate to your children and adult partners.

- To be a healing parent you need the ability to *look in the mirror*—knowing your mindset, feelings, coping strategies, and attachment history.

- You are emotionally triggered when your reactions are excessive, you have "knee-jerk" reactions, and you repeat old patterns.

- A parent's *state of mind* regarding attachment is the strongest predictor of their child's attachment pattern.

- There are four adult attachment patterns—*secure, dismissing, preoccupied, and unresolved*—each corresponding to a child attachment pattern.

- The *Life Script* is a tool to become aware of your early programming, mindset, and patterns of behavior.

- Effective communication is the basis of attachment with children and adult partners. *Attachment Communication Training (ACT)* is a constructive method to achieve deep and rewarding communication.

- Secondary traumatic stress (STS) is a natural consequence of caring for a traumatized person and a wounded child. It is important to use stress management techniques to avoid burnout and maintain a healthy mind and body.

5

Corrective Attachment Parenting: Basic Principles

Nothing destroys authority so much as the unequal and untimely interchange of power pressed too far and relaxed too much.
—Frances Bacon

*C*orrective Attachment Parenting (CAP) was developed to meet the needs of children who have experienced maltreatment, significant losses, and disrupted attachment. Parenting such children—being a *healing parent*—is quite a challenging task, as they are typically mistrustful, angry, defensive, defiant, and reluctant to accept or give love and affection.

Effective parenting requires the maturity to look in the mirror (self-awareness); the patience to remain calm and committed; the firmness to set appropriate limits; the heart-felt desire to give plenty of caring, compassion, and love; and the flexibility to meet the unique needs of your child. To be a helpful and healing parent, you need the right information, skills, support, and attitude.

Maintaining a positive attitude is a key to success, but not easy to do. Parents often feel hopeless, demoralized, and powerless to help their children and create family harmony. When you are demoralized you lack the motivation and determination necessary to create positive change—"Why bother, I'll only fail again." Burned-out parents project their hopeless feelings on to their children.

How can you increase your sense of hope and then instill it in your children? Hope is increased when you believe you are able to produce a workable pathway toward your goals ("I know I can do this"), and have the ability to move consistently toward those goals ("I have the skills"). This leads to success, and hope is a by-product of success. Positive feelings, reduced stress, and increased confidence result when you can envision achieving your goals and you have the requisite skills. Confident parents are more likely to succeed with their children, and children feel more hopeful when their parents are confident and optimistic.

The importance of a positive expectation of success is found in the placebo effect. A placebo is a harmless substance (sugar pill) given as if it were medicine. Research has shown many people have positive reactions because they believe they will get better—

they have a positive expectation of success. In other words, if we believe in something enough, we can make it happen—mind over matter. The following story demonstrates the power of belief and expectation.

In 1901, Manhattan State Hospital had too many patients with tuberculosis and too few beds. They transferred about 40 patients with this disease to two large tents set up on hospital grounds. The novelty of this arrangement caused excitement among staff, and patients began to improve. Outdoor tent wards were constructed by other hospitals to help more patients. However, the novelty of this approach eventually wore off, and the outdoor settings lost their "curative power."

The initial success of tent wards is a good example of the importance of novelty, hope, enthusiasm, and positive expectancy in recovery and healing. This is the nature of the placebo effect.

All experiences—especially between you and your child—have the potential of being helpful and healing. New relationship experiences lead to new expectations and behaviors from children. Through your thoughtful and corrective actions, reactions, and the maintenance of a safe, predictable, and constructive emotional environment, you will help your child achieve many positive changes. For success in life your children must learn the following skills and abilities:

- experience secure attachments with parents/caregivers; give and receive affection and love; feel empathy and compassion; and have a desire to belong;

- view oneself, others, and the world in a realistic and positive way; have positive core beliefs, mindset, and self-esteem;

- identify, manage, and communicate emotions in a constructive manner; exercise anger management, stress management, and self-control;

- make healthy choices; solve problems and deal with adversity effectively;

- utilize an inner moral compass, prosocial values, morality, conscience, and a sense of purpose;

- be self-motivated; set and persevere toward goals, and achieve a sense of mastery, competence, and self-confidence;

- maintain healthy relationships; able to share, cooperate, resolve conflicts, communicate effectively, and be tolerant of others; and

- experience joy, playfulness, creativity, and a sense of hope and optimism.

As you are learning the concepts, skills, and strategies of CAP, remember to make it your own. Don't just try to copy someone else's style. Take these ideas and tools and merge them with the values, styles, and culture of your own family. You must be genuine and authentic.

Remember two other basics. First, "it takes a village"—get the support and cooperation necessary to help you, your children, and family. The more the adults are on the same page whenever possible the better for your children (e.g., parental team, parents, and school all equally informed and clear about goals and the agreed-upon plans to achieve those goals, and presenting a unified front). Second, children test! Don't use these ideas and skills short-term and give up. Persevere; moving steadily toward your goals will result in success. Children need time to change.

Chapter 6 will explain and describe the specific skills, strategies, and solutions of CAP. The remainder of this chapter, however, will give you an understanding of the basic principles of maintaining a healing attitude and being a healing parent, including the *principles of change, creating a healing environment,* and the *10 Cs of Loving Leadership.*

Principles of Change

Change your thoughts and you change your world.
—Norman Vincent Peale

You Can Only Change Yourself

The only person over whom you have direct and immediate control is yourself. You cannot change others—not your spouse, children, parents, other family members, friends, coworkers, or employer. You can influence others and create opportunities for others to change, via your attitudes, actions, and reactions. By creating a healing environment you can have a positive impact on your child, resulting in learning, growth, and motivation to succeed. By looking in the mirror—knowing yourself and striving for personal growth—you are on the road to developing the patience, maturity, and confidence to influence your child in positive ways.

Information and Skills

Knowledge is power. By understanding your child deeply, including his history, emotions, mindset, biology, and relationship patterns, you will be in a position to help. Having the specific and practical skills of CAP, as described in this book, can build your confidence and lead to success. Teaching your child *life skills,* such as communication, problem solving, and anger management, is essential for healthy development, good self-esteem, and future success in all realms of life.

Focus on Change

Believe in the possibility of change. Your child can and will improve under the right conditions. You can change too! "Nothing is permanent but change" (Heraclitis 500 B.C.). Have a positive attitude. Create a home environment where new perspectives, experiences, and behaviors are welcomed and encouraged.

Be a role model of change. Show your children positive change is possible by improving your health, marriage, parenting, and general attitude toward life. Use a *resource model—a* philosophy or methodology that focuses on one's positive strengths and resources. In other words, focus on what's right, not just on what's wrong. "Catch your child doing something right." Look for and validate any change for the better, even tiny little steps. Always ask, "What is different, what is better?" Focus on the present and future, not just the past. Your goal is to create positive changes today, not get stuck in old negative patterns from the past.

Learning Through Experience

Intellect (insight and understanding) and "book learning" are not enough to create change if not applied and acted upon. Experience is the basis of change. People learn and change via real life experiences. Negative experiences with caregivers create attachment problems, and positive experiences with caregivers are helpful and healing. Don't just lecture to your child; provide your child with new relationship experiences— *change the dance.* New experiences with a healing parent result in new expectations ("I can trust you"), and positive feelings ("I feel love, security, and self-worth").

Motivation Is Essential

Burned-out parents convey hopelessness to their children. Combat demoralization by having information, skills, support, and the confidence that comes from success. Your child's motivation to change will increase as your parent-child relationship improves. Motivation is not a trait *inside* your child, but rather occurs *between* you and your child. Children are motivated when actively involved—"buy into"—the goals and process of change.

Have a Plan with Specific Goals

You must have a vision, a picture of what changes you want to see for yourself, child, and family. Define your goals. Goals should be specific, realistic, and defined in behavioral terms (e.g., do chores without being reminded).

Goals should be small at first. "Hit singles; don't go for the homerun." Notice and celebrate these small achievements, even though you and your child have much further to go. *Rituals* or procedures, that require your child's active participation, are part of creating change. These rituals and methods are the pathways to achieve your goals. For example, you and your child read together at bedtime, enhancing both reading skills and emotional closeness.

Partnership for Change

Change is something you and your child work on together, not something done to your child. It is a *collaborative team* effort. Your relationship with your child is the primary vehicle for change. A healing alliance—with empathy, nurturance, support, limits, and hope—will guide your child toward growth and health.

Risk and Protective Factors

Risk factors (abuse, neglect, and multiple moves/caregivers) make children frightened, frozen, and incapable of change. Protective factors (safety, support, and consistency from a sensitive caregiver) increase motivation, exploration, and positive change. Your job is to reduce the effects of risk factors and enhance the growth-producing protective factors. All children are prewired to learn, grow, and evolve. Under the right conditions, change occurs naturally. Your child will flourish in the healing environment you create.

Change Is Not Easy

Change usually is a step-by-step, back-and-forth process. Rarely is a problem solved in one try. Resistance is a natural part of change. The unknown is scary, and it is normal to be ambivalent ("I want to change, but I want to stay with the familiar"). Regression—one step forward, one step back—is a part of change. Mistakes happen, by parents and children. Your child must learn that an unhealthy choice or action is not the end of the world. Reparation—making amends, correcting the situation—is possible and healthy and models taking personal responsibility.

Have Hope

Hope is associated with positive feelings, increased confidence, reduced stress, and the ability to convey an optimistic and encouraging attitude to your child. You will be more hopeful when you understand your child, have constructive goals, skills, and methods, have confidence in what you are doing, believe in the possibility of change, and feel a sense of personal mastery and control ("I am capable of doing this").

You get what you expect. Expecting yourself and your child to change is crucial. Your positive expectation is communicated verbally and nonverbally to your child: "I believe in me and you; this will work out; we will succeed."

Creating a Healing Environment

How wonderful it is that nobody need wait a single
moment before starting to improve the world.
—Anne Frank

As a parent, you are responsible for establishing and maintaining the emotional, social, and moral climate that is healthy and healing for your children. This context—your relationship with your children and the larger family system—is the fertile soil in which children can recover from trauma and develop in positive ways. The ingredients of creating a healing environment are supplied in this section.

Cannot "Fix" a Child

Parents cannot "fix" a child, but can create a healthy environment in which the child learns and improves. You can create a context with opportunities for positive change, healthy growth and development, and secure attachment. Parents who assume the responsibility of "fixing" their child end up working too hard, getting frustrated and angry, rescuing and enabling, and blaming themselves—as well as feeling guilty—when it doesn't work out. Remember, you can only control your own choices and actions; you cannot control your child. Trying to control or change your child usually leads to increased defiance, power struggles, and "digging in his heels." You can encourage, guide, and be a role model for your child, but you cannot control him. Your job is to create and maintain a healing environment, which includes the knowledge, attitude, and actions described in the following pages. You will reduce your feelings of pressure and frustration when you let go of the idea it is your job to fix your child.

Look in the Mirror

Maintaining a healing environment is very challenging when your child is angry, defiant, and constantly looking for a fight. This requires a good deal of patience, confidence, maturity, and support as a parent. Your own background—how you were raised and the type of attachments you formed—play a major role in how you parent your children. This is especially true with challenging children. Your child will trigger unresolved issues and sensitivities left over from childhood. For example, if you felt unloved as a child, you may overreact when your child rejects and distances you. This is because we stack emotions—one on top of the other—and you are reacting to prior feelings from similar situations. By knowing yourself well—looking in the mirror—you are more likely to be proactive rather than reactive. You will be able to respond constructively to your child's attempts at blaming, distancing, and controlling you, rather than reacting in a destructive knee-jerk manner.

Research shows a parent's *mindset about attachment*—how you think about your childhood and family background, and deal with those emotional and relationship issues—is the number one factor that determines your child's attachment. There is a 70% to 75% correlation between the parent's mindset regarding attachment and their children's attachment patterns. In other words, securely attached parents—foster, adoptive, and biological—typically have children who are also securely attached.

What happened to you in the past is less important than how you deal with it. Parents who are *unresolved* about their past often have emotional and relationship problems, such as depression and marital conflicts, and are easily triggered by their children. Parents who openly and honestly face their past usually have more fulfilling lives and can create and maintain a healing environment for their children. Chapter Four goes into greater detail on the importance of looking in the mirror.

Labels Affect Solutions

The way you interpret, explain, and label a child's behavior will determine how you intervene to help that child. In other words, "what you *see* is what you get." This is true for parents, therapists, teachers, and others who work with children. For instance, children labeled as biochemically imbalanced (e.g., bipolar disorder) are given medicine to change their behavior; children described as impulsive, aggressive, and out-of-control, are placed in highly structured milieus (e.g., hospitals or residential treatment centers); parents who see their child as emotionally and socially delayed often become "helicopter parents" —hovering over the child, rescuing, and overprotecting—thereby reinforcing the very incompetency they worry about.

We invite you to understand your child's behavior as symptoms of compromised and disrupted attachment. This interpretation and label will enable you to use the concepts and skills of CAP. Your goal is to find a way to connect with, not control, your child. To accomplish this goal, you must be a confident, nurturing, and limit-setting role model, and avoid becoming triggered into destructive reactions and interactions.

Family and Community Systems

A system is a set of connected parts that work together to form a whole. For example, your cardiovascular system is composed of separate parts, including heart and blood vessels, which must work together to function correctly. In families, all members affect one another, in ongoing, circular patterns—the *dance of family dynamics*. Everyone works together to keep the dance going, either in a healthy or dysfunctional way. For instance, a nurturing mother helps her baby feel secure and relaxed; the cuddles and smiles of her baby encourages mom to keep the loving care flowing. Another example shows how the quality of the marriage affects mother-infant attachment. Breast-feeding mothers who feel support from their spouses have babies who thrive more than babies whose moms have distant and unsupportive partners (Pedersen et al. 1978). All parts of the family system affect each other. When you change what you are doing, your child will change in response. *When the system changes, your child changes.*

Children can only be understood and helped within the context of the family and social systems that shape their lives—the bigger picture. Attachment develops within the larger emotional network of the family system, including birth, foster, and adoptive family relationships, the roles of other siblings, the marital and coparenting relationships, and extended kin (e.g., grandparents). Social and community systems also affect the child, parents, and development of attachment. Schools, community programs, religious organizations, and social services (e.g., foster care, protective services, juvenile justice, and mental health systems) all have a major influence on children and families. Foster and adoptive families take in children with histories of maltreatment and compromised attachment, and therefore, face complex challenges from both inside and outside their family in order to create a healing environment.

Creating a healing environment involves looking at the bigger picture—how the family operates, including the rules, roles, boundaries, and the nature of the family's connection to outside social systems. This is illustrated by the family-school connection. It is crucial for parents and school personnel, such as teachers and counselors, to be a cooperative team for the benefit of the child.

Love and Limits

Balancing love and limits is important for all children, but especially crucial when creating a healing environment for wounded children. Nurturing and loving care fosters the learning of trust, empathy, and a positive mindset. It teaches your child that closeness and heart-felt human connections are safe and rewarding, leading to future closeness in adulthood with partners and children, and giving a special meaning to life. Loving and nurturing care results in positive core beliefs: "I am wanted and important; caregivers are dependable and trustworthy; life is good."

Providing limits and structure, including rules, clear expectations, and appropriate consequences, helps children feel safe, secure, and learn from their mistakes. A sense of order and predictability is particularly important for children who come from chaotic and frightening backgrounds. It is essential that limits and consequences be given with patience and understanding, and without anger or threat, for your child to benefit.

Limits must also fit the developmental stage of your child. Creating secure attachment during infancy requires consistent and sensitive fulfillment of your baby's physical and emotional needs. Toddlers, on the other hand, need limits along with love. You must communicate "no" and offer gentle consequences, so your child begins to learn impulse control and cooperation. Over time, you maintain a healing environment by teaching the four R's: respect, responsibility, resourcefulness, and reciprocity. As development continues, the *autonomy circle* is very useful, especially for teenagers. Your child can earn privileges and independence by demonstrating competency in four areas: knowledge, skills, judgment, and self-control (see Chapter 6). Children who have these abilities and skills need fewer limits, while those who lack these skills do best with more structure and parental involvement.

Opportunity versus Crisis

The word opportunity means a favorable chance or opening offered by circumstances. When your child acts out, it is a red flag; she is telling you something about her needs, feelings, or conflicts. For example, defying authority or being disrespectful may be your child's way of remaining in control to avoid closeness, fearing abandonment and loss if she becomes connected to you. Parents who react with hostility or withdrawal miss the opportunity for problem solving, teaching coping skills, and strengthening the parent-child relationship.

In order to create a healing environment you must be aware of your mindset. Healing parents don't just do things differently—they *see* things differently. Do you view stressful and challenging situations as crises to be dreaded or as opportunities for teaching, learning, and growth? Your frame of reference will determine how you respond.

The opportunity for learning and growth is not only available for your child, but for you as well. When your child triggers you into a strong emotional reaction, take a look in the mirror and ask yourself the following questions: "What can I learn about myself; what is my lesson; what do I need to change?" Let's take the same example of the defiant child, from the parent's perspective. The parent who overreacts to his child's defiance or disrespect may have unresolved feelings from childhood; maybe he had an abusive or disrespectful parent, and is therefore being triggered. The goal is family learning and growth, not merely a focus on your child's needs for improvement. Parents often tell us their most challenging children are their "gurus"—providing the richest opportunities for personal and marital growth.

Proactive versus Reactive

To create and maintain a healing environment you must be proactive: you create the emotional climate, take the initiative, and maintain the rules. When you are reactive, you are allowing your child to set the emotional tone, placing her in a position of control. To be proactive, you have to know your goals and *stay the course*—persevere toward those goals. Children feel more safe and secure when they can count on their caregivers to be in charge in a sensitive and caring way.

Being proactive involves remaining calm and not taking your child's behavior personally. When you escalate emotionally with your child—for example, yelling when your child yells—you only intensify the conflict and place your child in control. In order to remain calm during the storm, you must learn to not take it personally. Your child's negative attitudes and actions are often a result of prior wounds. Your current actions and attitudes, however, will either diminish or magnify those old injuries and patterns.

Being proactive also means you deal with issues and problems as soon as they occur—on the front-end—not waiting until the situation escalates out of control. Ignoring negative behavior is not a good idea. This only leads to an escalation of negative behaviors, culminating in negativity that can't be ignored. Stepping in quickly, firmly, and with a caring and calm attitude, will nip it in the bud, reduce emotional and behavioral escalation, and let your child know you can handle her provocations and problems.

Children are very predictable; you know how your child will typically react to situations. Being proactive means you are prepared—not caught off-guard—to deal constructively with your child's behaviors. Children reenact or project their problems and patterns on parents. Being proactive prevents the negative dance, offering your child the opportunity for change and healing.

Positive Role Model

All parents—biological, adoptive, and foster—are role models for their children. It matters less what you say (you could lecture all day long) and more what you do. Your job is to show by example how to effectively communicate, solve problems, cope with stress, manage emotions and conflict, and care about others. This is very challenging when your child is pushing you away, disrespectful, or defiant. But this is exactly the time in which being a positive role model is most crucial. You must maintain your equilibrium, be proactive not reactive, and show your child the healthy way to be. It will be easier to be a positive role model when you know yourself and your triggers, possess effective parenting skills, and have adequate support.

By presenting your child with a positive role model *you will make a difference*. Remember, the mind of the developing child is mostly formed by experiences with significant others—parents and caregivers. You can actually promote positive change in your child's brain, mind, and behavior. The concepts and skills of CAP will enable you to create a healing environment and foster these positive changes.

Faith Helps

Studies have shown regardless of the particular religion, people with strongly held spiritual beliefs are more satisfied with life (Gerwood et al. 1998). Faith enhances your conviction that having the right attitude and tools leads to positive results with your child. Faith helps you stay focused and committed to your goals.

10 Cs of Loving Leadership

We cannot change the wind, but we can adjust our sails.
—Unknown

The 10 Cs of Loving Leadership are the foundation for creating a healthy and healing relationship with your child, based on compassionate care, appropriate structure, and mutual respect. CAP incorporates the 10 Cs, and is a blend of love and limits, considering the unique needs of each child.

Discipline comes from the root word disciple, which means "follower of a leader or teacher." Effective discipline depends on building the right relationship with your child, not merely about using a particular technique. Discipline is not just about responding to "bad" behavior, but what you can do to encourage your child's total development—mind, body, emotions, relationships, and values.

If you want to have a positive impact on your child, you must abandon the notion you can demand obedience through the use of physical or psychological coercion or force. Withdrawing from your child by holding back love, attention, and connection is also nonconstructive. Your child has already experienced enough rejection, criticism, and abandonment.

The truth is, you cannot control children's behavior. Only they can control their behavior. You might temporarily impose your will on a younger child through constant surveillance and domination. However, your child is merely learning to comply to external pressure, rather than developing a healthy inner voice and moral compass. Using excessive force and control with older children encourages them to fight back.

What are the key ingredients of therapeutic parenting? You can have a positive influence on your children if you use the following guidelines—the *10 Cs of Loving Leadership.*

1. Connection
2. Calm
3. Commitment
4. Consistency
5. Communication
6. Choices and Consequences
7. Confidence
8. Cooperation
9. Creativity
10. Coaching

Connection

When the heart speaks others must respond.
—Anonymous

Connecting with your child involves empathy, support, nurturance, and love. Your child needs to sense you are genuinely interested in her as a person. Limit setting is also a part of connecting. Children need structure, including consistent, predictable, and reasonable rules, for a feeling of safety and security. This leads to respect, trust, and secure attachment.

The ability to form and maintain positive connections is essential for healthy childhood development. This involves taking into account the needs, feelings, and opinions of others, and is accomplished by understanding and respecting another's point of view. The resulting rapport makes it possible for your child to develop trust, be open to influence, and seek out your guidance. Parents who successfully connect with their children are emotionally available, actively involved in their lives, and model respect and compassion.

Many parents are unclear about the difference between the use of power and force. True power is based on love, compassion, and understanding. Compassion gives you the capacity to be patient, persistent, and positive in the face of ongoing adversity. Laws of Physics teach us the use of force automatically creates a counterforce. The more we use a strategy utilizing violence, domination, and control, the greater likelihood of escalating the conflict. Gandhi was able to use the power of gentleness, persistence, and implicit will to defeat the entire British Empire without raising a hand in anger. The use of force is never a permanent solution (Hawkins 2002).

Children are most influenced by those with whom they feel the deepest respect and strongest connections. You cannot make lasting changes in your child's attitudes and behavior by lecturing, coercing, punishing, or humiliating. Children learn best when encouraged, not criticized. This is particularly true of children with low self-esteem and negative self-images. Your child will only follow your lead if he wants to, and he will only want to if he feels good about you—feeling positively connected.

Parenting approaches are based on either connection or control. The goal of connection-oriented parenting is to establish a respectful, trusting, and reciprocal relationship. This results in your child being motivated to accept your advice, follow your lead, and internalize your values. The goal of control-oriented parenting is to change the child by modifying behavior. This results in your child being motivated to struggle for power, reject your suggestions, and keep away from you.

Table 2 shows the difference between connection- and control-oriented parenting philosophies and methods. Parenting for connection is reciprocal and interactive, a sharing of ideas and influence. Parenting for control is dominant-submissive, with the emphasis on compliance to overbearing authority. Parenting for connection focuses on the positive (e.g., compliments); "catch your child doing something right." Parenting for control involves criticism, focusing on the negative. Connection-oriented parenting is characterized by two-way respect, with parent and child respecting one another. Respect is one-way in control-oriented parenting. The child is expected to show respect for his parent; respect is demanded not earned. Cooperation is encouraged in connection-oriented parenting, such as working together to solve a problem. Control-oriented parenting uses confrontation, which leads to hostility and defiance. Parents using a connection approach teach through providing reasonable consequences. Parents using a control approach tend to be punitive, angry, and vindictive. Connection-oriented parenting highlights the primacy of the parent-child relationship, whereas a control-orientation places the focus on changing the child's behavior.

Parenting for connection is based on a health and resource model, building skills and encouraging resources leading to positive outcomes. Parenting for control is based on an illness model, focusing on the child's pathology and deficits. Connection-oriented parents use an assertive communication style; clear, direct, and nonthreatening. Control-oriented parents are aggressive in their communication—hostile, offensive, and threatening.

Learning is internalized and endures for children with connection-oriented parents. Changes are temporary for children with control-oriented parents; lessons are superficial and short-lived. A connection approach results in a desire to comply due to genuine caring. A control approach leads to fear-based compliance; fear of punishment and disapproval. Parenting that emphasizes connection offers children choices, and helps them learn to be responsible and accountable for the consequences of their choices. Parenting that emphasizes control gives ultimatums, demanding certain behaviors and discouraging the learning of responsibility.

Table 2. Connection vs. Control

Connection	**Control**
Reciprocal	Dominant-submissive
Compliment	Criticize
Respect one another (two way)	Respect authority (one way)
Cooperation	Confrontation
Consequences	Punishment
Focus on the relationship	Focus on the behavior
Health, resource focus	Illness focus
Assertive	Aggressive
Enduring	Temporary
Comply out of desire	Comply out of fear or intimidation
Choices	Ultimatums

A Horse Story

There are many things we can learn from nature's wisdom. A great deal of knowledge we have today about human behavior was learned through the observation of animals. Mark Rashid is a gifted horse trainer who specializes in working with abused and troubled horses. His methods have transformed disobedient, skittish, and unpredictable horses into reliable and confident animals that follow willingly (Rashid 2000).

The apparent leader of the herd is the alpha horse. This horse uses intimidation and force, such as biting and kicking, to control the herd. Many horse trainers believe that by mimicking the alpha horse's behavior, using force and intimidation (spurs, whips, yelling), the other horses will see them as the dominant member of the herd and submit to their direction. Mark noticed when previously maltreated horses were trained with this "heavy handed approach" they responded out of fear and complied unwillingly. Many later became problem horses, being aggressive, defiant, avoidant, and unreliable.

What Mark discovered was when the alpha horse or alpha human went into the corral, all the other members of the herd would withdraw and avoid contact. He observed there was another horse in the herd that he called the "passive leader." This was a horse with a gentle temperament that the herd members actually sought out. The passive leader was dependable, confident, consistent, and lead by example. His quiet and unassuming nature had a calming effect on the herd. He did not force his way into leadership, but was chosen by the members of the herd as the one they wanted to follow.

Mark decided to mimic the behavior of the passive leader with astounding results. He gained the trust of the abused horses through patience, consistency, and a willingness not to use force. He took belligerent, noncompliant, and lazy horses headed for the glue factory and transformed them into horses that were easy to train, responsive, and dependable, no matter who rode them. The keys to his success were: 1) consider the horse's point-of-view (what does the horse need based on his history); and 2) it matters less what techniques and strategies you use, and matters more that they are applied with dignity and respect. Attitude is everything.

Calm

> *He who gains victory over others is strong, but he*
> *who gains victory over himself is all powerful.*
> —Lao Tzu

To be calm is synonymous with being levelheaded, peaceful, patient, and composed. Remaining calm, however, is difficult to do with challenging children. The usual reactions of frustrated parents are to impose their wills, retaliate, or withdraw to avoid a fight. The only effective way to positively influence children is to gain their trust, making them willing to follow your direction. A calm and consistent approach works best. There are several unhealthy payoffs for children when parents are emotionally agitated rather than remaining calm.

- You are not in a leadership role. You are reacting to your child, who is now taking the lead. This erodes your child's confidence in you as a reliable caregiver and safe authority figure. "How can I trust you when I have the power to make you so emotionally upset?"

- You are allowing your child to replicate the stressful and dysfunctional patterns of relating that your child experienced in a prior family or institution. "I'm used to turmoil and conflict; I can do this well, and never have to change."

- You are reinforcing your child's negative core beliefs; "Your anger and disapproval affirm my belief that I am bad and undeserving of love."

- You are likely to expect less of your child—keep the bar low—in order to avoid more stress and conflict. "I can wear you down, you'll leave me alone, and I'm off the hook."

- You are feeding into your child's discomfort with and desire to avoid emotional closeness, by perpetuating an adversarial and emotionally distant relationship. "As long as we are mad at each other, I don't have to be close."

Although it is important to be calm and centered with all children, it is critical to remain emotionally balanced with children who have compromised attachment. These children did not receive adequate emotional regulation from caregivers; they missed the necessary balance of up-regulation (stimulation) and down-regulation (soothing). Over time, securely attached children internalize parental care and learn self-regulation. These children, however, did not develop the ability to regulate their emotions and impulses. They became behaviorally and biochemically disorganized, resulting in hyperarousal, aggression, impulsivity, and distractibility. They overreact to stimulation, stress, and anxiety. Therefore, you must teach your child to be calm by providing an example of calmness. Calmness reduces your child's "alarm reaction" (fight-flight-freeze), and allows her to feel safe and secure enough to think rationally and learn.

Commitment

Perseverance and spirit have done wonders in all ages.
—George Washington

You cannot create secure attachment without a commitment. Commitment is a promise and a pledge to be available to a child through thick and thin; a moral obligation to take certain actions and respond in certain ways, which leads to safety, security, and trust. Your commitment is to:

- *Keep your child safe.* Protect your child from physical danger or injury, and be a reliable caregiver who provides emotional safety and security.
- *Truly know your child.* Have a deep understanding of your child's history, temperament, strengths, and sensitivities, in order to meet his needs and promote positive improvements.
- *Provide necessary structure.* Create and maintain the appropriate rules, boundaries, and consequences, based on your child's developmental stage and emotional needs.
- *Have compassion for your child's pain.* Feel and show empathy for the underlying anguish and distress your child experiences due to past hurts and current fears.
- *Be a positive role model.* Show your child, via actions and attitudes, examples of love, honesty, self-control, and decency.
- *Support growth and healthy development.* Maintain a healing environment that encourages your child's physical, emotional, social, and moral growth.

A commitment requires looking at the big picture. Raising a challenging child is a long-term, not a short-term, undertaking. No matter how disappointed you become, and no matter how defeated you sometimes feel, if you hang in there, you can make a dramatic difference in your child's life.

How can you assure your child you will not abandon her when her history tells her you will? You can talk until you are blue in the face and it will not work. It's actions over time, not merely words. Children must *experience* commitment and stability over and over before it sinks in. Never stop trying. Never give up. If you make a mistake, try again. Do not worry; she will give you plenty of opportunities to get it right. Remember her difficult behavior is the result of learned attitudes and beliefs. If she learned one way of being, she can learn another. This will only occur within a compassionate, ongoing, committed relationship. *It's never too late to have a happy childhood!*

As a healing parent you are making a commitment not only to your child, but also to your own emotional, social, and spiritual health. Helping your challenging child requires you to be on top of your game. Being a healing parent involves total focus on the job at hand with commitment and intention.

Two Chicago Stories

George Harnett, a professional colleague, shared with us two interesting stories by e-mail on January 9, 2003. They provide thought-provoking illustrations of commitment.

I

During World War II, Lt. Commander Butch O'Hare served as a fighter pilot on the aircraft carrier Lexington in the South Pacific. On February 20, 1942, his entire squadron was sent on a mission. Once airborne, he noticed someone had neglected to top off his fuel tank. This meant he would not have enough fuel to complete his mission and return to the ship. He was ordered to return to the carrier and reluctantly headed back to the fleet. On his way back a horrified O'Hare discovered a squadron of Japanese bombers approaching the defenseless American fleet. He couldn't reach his squadron in time to bring them back, nor could he warn the fleet of the approaching danger. Putting aside all thoughts of personal safety, he single-handedly attacked the Japanese planes. He fired at as many planes as possible, breaking up their formation and downing five enemy bombers. After his ammunition was spent, he continued to dive at the planes, hoping to clip off a wing or tail. He was desperate to keep the attackers from the fleet. Finally, the exasperated Japanese squadron broke off the engagement and headed for home. For this action he became the Navy's first Ace of World War II and the first naval aviator to win the Congressional Medal of Honor. A year later he was killed in combat at the age of 29. Chicago's O'Hare airport was named in honor of this courageous man.

II

Some years earlier, another Chicagoan was known for less heroic exploits. Al Capone was notorious for bootlegging, prostitution, and murder. Capone had a very skilled lawyer named Easy Eddie who kept Big Al out of trouble. He was so good at it Capone gave him big money and a large estate complete with live-in help. Eddie lived the high life with little concern for the atrocities that paid for it. Eddie had a son who he cherished dearly. He saw to it his son had the best of everything. Despite the way he made a living, Eddie wanted his son to have strong moral values and to be a better man than himself. Two things that Eddie could not pass on to his son were a good name and a good example. Eddie realized these two things were more important than all the wealthy he could lavish on him. One day, Eddie went to the police and decided to testify against Capone. He knew the cost would be great, but it was worth it to him, in an attempt to give his son a good name, to rectify all the wrong he had done. Within the year, Eddie was shot dead in the street. He had given his son his greatest gift at the greatest cost. Butch O'Hare was Easy Eddie's son.

Consistency

We are what we repeatedly do.
—Aristotle

All children need consistent nurturance and stability, as a supportive framework to guide, organize, and regulate their behavior. Children who have endured adverse conditions—lack of protective, loving, and secure attachments—need even more. Failing to receive the requisite nurturance and structure in the early stages of development has left these children emotionally, behaviorally, and biochemically disorganized and unbalanced. Your child desperately needs a lifeline of consistent routines, guidelines, and love.

Your child will benefit greatly from a predictable and consistent sense of order. For example, studies show stress hormones decrease to normal levels when children in foster families become securely attached. Over time, they internalize the parental structure and develop the ability to self-regulate (Dozier et al. 2002a). Consistent and appropriate structure—rules, limits, and consequences—enable the child to depend on a reliable caregiver, who he begins to respect and then trust. *Providing structure engenders feelings of safety and security in children, anchoring them for the rest of their lives.*

Inconsistent care leads to resistant or ambivalent attachment. Children become anxious, demanding, and mistrustful, not knowing what to expect. They are crying out for the stability and security that comes from clear and consistent parameters. They will constantly test limits, searching for the resistance that defines their boundaries. Your mantra needs to be "slow and steady"—consistency over time. Remember, the tortoise won the race. It is better to hit singles than strive only for the homerun.

It is important for consistency to occur among all the adults in your child's life. Teachers, counselors, daycare providers, child welfare workers, and family members, must all be on the same page. Your child will be more likely to learn and improve when everyone provides consistent messages.

Communication

When you feel understood, you feel better
about those who understand you.
—Anonymous

Communication is at the heart of attachment; it is how we convey thoughts, needs, and feelings to others. To communicate is to connect. There is no greater gift to your child than to be attuned; he sees it in your eyes, hears it in the tone of your voice, and feels it in his heart. *Parental sensitivity to the child's signals is the essence of secure attachment.*

Communication begins in the womb, via a neurohormonal dialogue between mother and unborn baby. Mother's physical and emotional states are transmitted to her baby. As early as six weeks the fetus responds to touch and at five months in utero can react to her parents' voices.

From the moment of birth, babies communicate with their caregivers verbally and nonverbally through facial expressions, gestures, crying, cooing—the language of infancy. Loving caregivers are able to read these signals accurately and respond to meet their baby's needs in a prompt and sensitive manner. The baby learns to trust, expect more love and care in the future, and to feel good about her; "I am heard, understood, important, and loveable."

Effective communication is the foundation of all relationships—parent-child, marital, friendship, and work. Communicating for attachment creates the conditions in which your child is more likely to confide and connect. Because so much of communication is nonverbal (eye contact, facial expressions, tone of voice, body language, touch), your style or delivery is often more important than your words. Your messages register in the emotional region of your child's brain (limbic system), and affect learning, trust, stress response, memory, and development. Effective communication promotes empathy, intimacy, problem solving, and secure attachment.

Choices and Consequences

> *It is the function of parents to see that their children habitually experience the true consequences of their conduct.*
> —Herbert Spencer

One of your most important jobs as a parent is to prepare your children to function in the real world. To accomplish this, children must learn to make choices and live with the consequences of those choices. This leads to the development of responsibility, accountability, and maturity.

Parents typically make two types of mistakes when it comes to offering choices. Some constantly tell their children what to do and how to be, which denies them the opportunity to learn how to think for themselves, and often results in power struggles and rebellion. Others provide insufficient guidance, allowing their children to make too many decisions without the skills and support necessary to succeed.

All children have an innate need for mastery and control. This is the desire to explore, interact with the environment, and learn new abilities; "I have an impact on my world." Because children have a need for control, why not give it to them in a constructive way. Sharing in the decision-making process helps children feel important and shows respect for their talents and abilities. By offering choices, you are using a *resource model*—focusing on positive strengths by allowing your child to make age-appropriate choices, which leads to cooperation and good self-esteem.

Although it is necessary to give children consequences for their actions and choices, many parents end up giving punishment instead. There is a big difference between consequences and punishment. Your goal in giving a consequence is to teach a lesson. This encourages your child's self-examination, acceptance of responsibility for his actions, and the ability to learn from mistakes. It also helps your child develop an inner voice, which leads to feeling confident with decision-making and problem solving.

The definition of punishment is to cause to suffer. Although many parents mean well, being punitive backfires. Punishment is harmful to your child's sense of self, emotional development, and the parent-child relationship. Corporal punishment, including hitting and slapping, hurts children physically and emotionally. Psychological punishment—threatening, yelling, criticizing, humiliating, and sarcasm—is emotionally damaging, particularly to a child with a traumatic background.

Why do parents resort to punishment? First, it is a convenient way to vent anger and frustration. Second, they are often doing to their children what was done to them when they were young. Third, they don't know what else to do. They lack alternative ideas and parenting skills. Fourth, believing they must maintain control and exert authority, they resort to punishment. Lastly, they want an immediate change in their child's behavior. Children often respond quickly out of fear, but the changes are short-lived.

Regardless of the reasons for using punishment, there are many damaging results. Punishment causes resentment, leads to revenge, and rarely results in learning. It teaches your child force, aggression, and intimidation are acceptable. You are not providing a role model of healthy conflict-management or self-control. It teaches your child to listen to an *outside* voice, which prevents thinking for himself. Punishment reinforces hurtful prior patterns of relating, recreating abuser-victim roles from your child's past, including negative core beliefs: "I am not loveable and deserve to be punished." It leads to *reactive parenting*—your child is controlling the relationship by determining the negative emotional tone. When you are angry and punitive, you are no longer in charge, your child is. For many children, being in control is more important than any punishment you impose. Finally, punishment maintains emotional distance, preventing the trust and closeness necessary for secure attachment.

Confidence

Whether you believe you can do anything or not, you are right.
—Henry Ford

Confidence is the ability to rely on yourself with assuredness and certainty. Confident parents have trust in what they are doing to help their children. If you have confidence in yourself, then your children will also. Children feel safe with confident parents, who they see as capable and dependable.

It is understandable to lack confidence when dealing with challenging children. Parenting approaches that work well with securely attached children are typically ineffective when children have histories of trauma and compromised attachment. Parents often feel inadequate, demoralized, exhausted, and guilty.

In order to develop confidence you must have *information, skills, support,* and *hope.* Knowledge is power. The more information and understanding you have about your child, yourself, and your family, the more confident you will feel. The first step in solving any problem is identifying and understanding the nature of the problem. When you understand your child's attachment issues and the effect on your family, you will be more likely to take the correct steps to solve the problem.

Learning CAP skills can lead to success, and success builds confidence. The right tools can make all the difference. You must be realistic. These skills are not developed overnight. The more you practice the better you become. When you fall back into old patterns, do not beat yourself up—this happens to everyone. Judging yourself negatively is counterproductive. Instead, recall your successes and get back in the saddle. Work toward improvement, not perfection. Act as if you know what you are doing, and eventually you will—fake it till you make it.

Parents often feel isolated and alone. Having support is crucial; it provides the encouragement, understanding, and caring that is so helpful during difficult times. You can receive support from friends, family, spiritual fellowship, support groups, and knowledgeable professionals. Having a mentor is particularly helpful. This could be a counselor, social worker, or a more seasoned parent who has expertise with challenging children.

Knowing your child can change under the right conditions creates hope and optimism. Many professionals and parents are negative and pessimistic in their outlook, believing some children are too psychologically damaged to get better. "Nothing works with wounded children" is a myth. Time and time again, we have seen traumatized children make healthy changes in their actions and choices, under the right conditions. Creating a healing environment—by having the right information, skills, support, and hope—provides the conditions in which positive change will occur.

Cooperation

*Let every man shovel out his own snow
and the whole city will be passable.*
—Ralph Waldo Emerson

Sharing and cooperation are in the best interest of families and society. Being unselfish, considering the needs of others, and being a team player, was essential for the survival of our ancestors. Cooperation and altruism are learned through early secure attachments. Children with compromised attachments become self absorbed, believing their survival depends upon "looking out for number one." Your child needs opportunities to learn about the give-and-take of relationships, including cooperation, empathy, and reciprocity.

Cooperation has to be won, not demanded. Remember, you cannot make your child do anything. The more you try to impose your will on him, the more he will resist and rebel. You need to lead in a way that encourages, not demands, cooperative behavior. The goal is to promote a cooperative attitude so your child wants to listen. He needs to realize cooperation is in his self-interest.

Parents who are *resonant* in their attitude, style, and delivery are more likely to have children who are motivated to cooperate. Resonant parents are tuned-in to the feelings, needs, and mindsets of their children. On the other hand, parents who are dissonant are out-of-sync with their children, and their children are not motivated to cooperate. These parents perpetuate the self-centered and defiant tendencies of their children.

You must model cooperation if you expect your child to be cooperative. Model cooperative attitudes and behaviors with your children, spouse, extended kin, friends, and others. Children learn by watching what we do, not what we say. Practice what you preach.

A common expression when it comes to raising children is "it takes a village." This means it is imperative that everyone is on the same page regarding the ways and means of helping your child. Cooperation among teachers, child welfare workers, therapists, parents, coaches, and others is essential for your child and for yourself.

Creativity

Problems are only opportunities in work clothes.
—Henri Kaiser

Creativity means to invest with a new form, to produce through imagination, to bring into existence something new. To create is to be proactive, as opposed to being reactive and repeating actions taken before. An important rule when dealing with wounded children is: *if something doesn't work, do different, not more of the same.*

As previously described, the human brain is a hierarchy of three brains in one, each with a different structure and function. The *brain stem* controls survival mechanisms and automatic functions of our body. The *limbic system* is the emotional brain, regulating attachment and the human stress response (fight-flight-freeze). The *cerebral cortex* allows us to be logical and creative. The Reticular Activation System (RAS) is a toggle switch between the various parts of the brain. When we feel threatened or emotionally aroused, the RAS switches the limbic system into high gear, activating the fight-flight-freeze response. This response to stress prepares us to challenge or withdraw from a perceived threat. In this situation, the RAS shuts down the cerebral cortex, and we go into "survival mode," focusing on the threat at hand. When the threat is removed, and we begin to relax, the RAS switches the cerebral cortex back into action. This allows rational thinking and creativity to return.

When I get mad, I blow my top.

When children experience ongoing threat due to abuse, neglect, and disrupted attachment, they get stuck in their limbic systems. The adrenalin is flowing, the brain is primed for a fight, and they remain in a state of high stress and arousal. The part of the brain responsible for controlling rational thinking, problem solving, and creativity is unavailable and does not function normally. Creativity is the "language of childhood." To create is to be inventive, constructive, and resourceful. The opposite is to destroy, demolish, and shut down. These children are focused on survival at the expense of flexibility and imagination.

A child's negativity can have a ripple effect on the entire family. Parents also go into survival mode, feeling threatened and overwhelmed. Remaining in the limbic brain hampers the ability to be creative for both children and parents. Learning and applying the concepts and skills of CAP can enable you to think logically and become creative.

An important aspect of creativity is humor. Laughter is the best medicine. It reduces stress, creates positive connections, and gives you a new perspective on your situation. Laughing with, not at your child, increases emotional bonding and helps you to get out of a rut.

Your child is very predictable, repeating the same strategies, defenses, and patterns of behavior. Being creative interrupts negative patterns and leads to positive change. Use your own style; don't just copy someone else. To be creative is to be genuine and authentic. Initially you might feel "mechanical" as you are learning new parenting skills. Over time, you must find a way to make them your own—a part of your own personality, values, and beliefs.

Coaching

By learning you will teach; by teaching you will learn.
—Latin Proverb

A coach is an experienced mentor who guides, teaches, supports, motivates, and inspires positive values and characteristics in children. As a healing parent you are a role model and coach, and are more influential than you might realize. You set an example of who to be and how to behave. *Children learn more from modeling than by any other way.*

A number of critical social factors, detrimental to children's development, have been eroding in our society. There is a lack of adequate adult supervision, admired models of moral behavior and spiritual development, personalized education, and community cohesiveness and resources. Children are deeply in need of mentors, role models, and coaches, as positive examples of moral, ethical, and value-based thinking and choices.

Educating children is more than merely giving them information. We teach children what to think instead of how to think. A good coach does not only impart knowledge, but also facilitates the attainment of wisdom. Wisdom is knowledge applied: figuring out a problem for yourself by using critical thinking and problem-solving skills. Coaches teach life skills not just facts, including self-awareness, self-control, conflict resolution, communication, and cooperation. Coaches also encourage the development of positive traits such as tolerance, enthusiasm, industriousness, integrity, loyalty, and perseverance.

We can learn many valuable lessons on how to positively influence young people by following the example of John Wooden. Coach Wooden was the head coach of UCLA's basketball team from 1948 to 1975, and is considered the greatest college basketball coach of all time. His accomplishments of 88 consecutive victories and 10 national titles in 12 years have never been equaled. His success was not only for his many championships, but more importantly, because of the extreme respect, adoration, and loyalty he received from his former players and assistants. His teams were known for unselfish play and hard work. He built team players in a laid back, low-key way by gaining their respect through personal example. He practiced all the qualities he wanted to instill. He believed respect is the most important thing for a leader to have, and it starts with giving respect. By respecting his players they did what he asked and more.

Great coaches do not have to tell others they are in charge; set a proper example and others will want to follow. Great coaches are effective motivators, instilling confidence in their players by making them feel good about themselves. Confidence cannot be built through criticism. As Coach Wooden said, "We cannot antagonize and positively influence at the same time." He believed discipline is meant to correct or improve, not to punish. When a player can discipline himself others don't have to.

Wooden's teams were all very disciplined, yet he never punished players; he held them firmly accountable for their actions. He was a master of using choices and consequences. One day a star player informed Coach Wooden he had no right to make him cut his hair. He responded by calmly saying, "You're right, son, I don't. I only have the right to choose who plays. Goodbye, I'll miss you." Guess what the player (Bill Walton) chose to do? (Wooden 2005)

Character-building coaching is based on a bond of affection, respect, and trust. Studies show even in the most disturbed families, one variable—a positive attachment outside the home—raises the probability a child will be successful later in life. All it takes is one person who cares. Believing in a child builds confidence and reduces fear of failure. This is encouraging for teachers, volunteers, mentors from groups such as Big Brothers and Big Sisters, and other role models who are trying to make a difference. You can have a dramatic lifelong influence on a child's life. If peripheral relationships can be so significant, imagine what a committed parent can do.

Recently a student graduated Magna Cum Laude from a local college and was honored with the alumni award for excellence. Following tradition, the student was asked to name his most important mentor. In the past, this has always been a professor or administrator. "A lot of professors made a big impact on me, but I don't think anyone made as big an impact as Bob." Bob was the school janitor, with whom he worked part-time. Bob genuinely cared and provided the student with emotional support, an open ear, and a kind heart. He learned much more about what really was important in life from Bob than from all his classroom experiences. You never know who will have a powerful impact on a life.

Summary

- *Corrective Attachment Parenting* (CAP) was developed to meet the needs of children who have experienced maltreatment, significant losses, and disrupted attachment.

- To be a healing parent you need hope, a positive attitude, and the right information, skills, support.

- Effective parenting requires the maturity to look in the mirror, the patience to remain calm, the firmness to set limits, the desire to give compassion and love, and the flexibility to meet your child's unique needs.

- New relationship experiences lead to new expectations and behaviors from children.

- Children must learn the following skills and abilities for success: secure attachments, positive core beliefs, effective communication and coping skills (e.g., anger management and problem solving), prosocial values and morality, resilience, self-motivation, healthy relationships, and a sense of hope and optimism.

- Principles of change: you can only change yourself; you need information and skills; believe in change; be a role model of change; we learn and change through experiences; motivation is essential; have a plan, goals, and a vision; teamwork helps; change is difficult—allow for resistance, regression, and mistakes; hope and positive expectations are crucial.

- Healing parents create a healing environment: you cannot "fix" a child; look in the mirror; labels affect solutions; understand the family system and *dance* of family dynamics; balance love and limits; have an opportunity rather than crisis mindset; be proactive, not reactive; you are always a role model.

- Follow the *10 Cs of Loving Leadership:* connection, calm, commitment, consistency, communication, choices and consequences, confidence, cooperation, creativity, and coaching.

6

Corrective Attachment Parenting: Skills & Solutions

When nothing seems to help, I go and look at a stonecutter hammering away
at his rock perhaps a hundred times without as much as a crack showing in it.
Yet at the hundred and first blow it will split in two, and I know it
was not that last blow that did it—but all that had gone before.

—Jacob Riis

In the prior chapter we presented the principles of *Corrective Attachment Parenting* (CAP). This chapter describes and illustrates the practical skills, strategies, and solutions you can use to be a healing parent. Having constructive parenting skills will increase your confidence, enable you to convey a healing attitude, and lead to positive changes in your child and family.

It is essential that you use these skills and solutions in a genuine way. Take these tools and blend them into your own style and values, as well as your child's temperament and abilities. You have to feel comfortable and "real," not merely copying an approach you've seen or read. Remember, however, it will take some time and practice before these methods feel natural. Have patience. Persevere. Move steadily toward your goals. Keep your vision in mind.

The skills and solutions presented in the following pages are grouped into various categories and headings. We have provided separate categories for the purpose of clarity and understanding. In reality, all these skills and tools are interrelated. They all go together. Thus, you will find a skill or strategy appear under several headings.

The skills and solutions described will show you how to:

- maintain a healing attitude;

- provide constructive limits, choices, and consequences;

- practice competency-based parenting;

- serve as a secure base;

- avoid negative emotional reactions;

- improve core beliefs and behavior;

- stay calm;

- engage positively and enhance connections;

- be proactive, not reactive;

- create a sense of belonging; and

- communicate effectively.

Limits, Choices, and Consequences

Knowing is not enough; we must apply. Willing is not enough; we must do.
—Goethe

All children need structure from parents and others in authority; a supportive framework to guide, organize, and regulate behavior. Children who have experienced a lack of nurturing, protection, and secure attachment need even more structure. Failing to receive enough love and limits in the early stages of development has left these children emotionally, behaviorally, and biochemically disorganized.

Sometimes I want control so bad.

Infants and toddlers rely on caregivers to serve as a buffer against stress. Without this support they have unmanageable levels of stress. For example, securely attached children can relax and sleep well because their levels of cortisol, a stress hormone, naturally decrease at night. Children with compromised attachment, however, fail to show decreases in cortisol in the evening. They remain distressed, aroused, and have difficulty sleeping. These children benefit greatly from a predictable and consistent sense of order. Studies show stress hormones decrease to a normal level when children in foster families become securely attached. Over time, they internalize the parental structure and develop the ability to self-regulate (Dozier et al. 2002b).

Children who did not get the necessary love and limits commonly become controlling, manipulative, and defiant. Parents and friends often call them "bossy." They became guarded and controlling because they could not rely on caregivers to keep them safe and secure. At first, your child will resist your limits and consequences because this is unfamiliar, and he feels anxious about the loss of control. With patience, consistency, and empathy, he will begin to see you as reliable and dependable, and then start to respect and trust you. *Trust always starts with respect.*

Sometimes I'm calm, and sometimes I feel good about myself.

There are three guidelines for providing structure—*the rules about the rules:*

- Always balance limits and love.

- Structure is based on your child's developmental and emotional needs.

- Structure should be clear, consistent, and realistic.

There should always be a balance of structure and nurturance, limits and love. This is a key to promoting secure attachment. Rules without love are perceived as cold and punitive. Love without ample limits does not provide a framework for healthy development. The amount of structure and support you offer should be based on your child's stage of development, emotional/social age, and competencies (i.e., abilities). Under healthy conditions, parents offer more support in the early stages and modify the structure as development unfolds. Children without this solid foundation are in need of structure and external support based on their emotional and social age, not their chronological age.

Secure attachment is developmental, requiring a change in structure and dependence over time. The helpless and vulnerable baby totally depends on caregiver(s) for protection, security, and love. As the child matures parents who are sensitive and well-attuned offer opportunities for independence and autonomy. The balance between dependence and independence, structure and freedom, changes over time based on the child's needs and capabilities.

A child with a secure foundation develops a sense of independence and self-direction as she grows older and is likely to have high self-esteem, high moral character, and a desire to be a meaningful contributor to her family. She has positive core beliefs and is confident and competent, able to exact a positive influence on her world. She can make decisions using her own mind, an inner voice of reason bringing about

I want it all for myself.

healthy choices by first considering the consequences. Such a child has a strong sense of self *and* a strong sense of belonging, including important roles with family, friends, and other social groups.

A child who lacks secure attachment does not experience dependency and vulnerability as safe. He is not likely to develop an inner voice to guide him in positive social and moral directions and is prone to think, "What's in it for me?" "How can I survive?" "I better not trust," and "I don't care about the consequences, I just want it now." This child requires more external structure and support to make up for the deficiencies in self-direction, self-control, and judgment.

This is a competency-based approach to parenting: as your child shows healthy choices, attitudes, social skills, and self-control, you reduce the external structure, and he is given more freedom to operate independently (Autonomy Circle, see Figure 4).

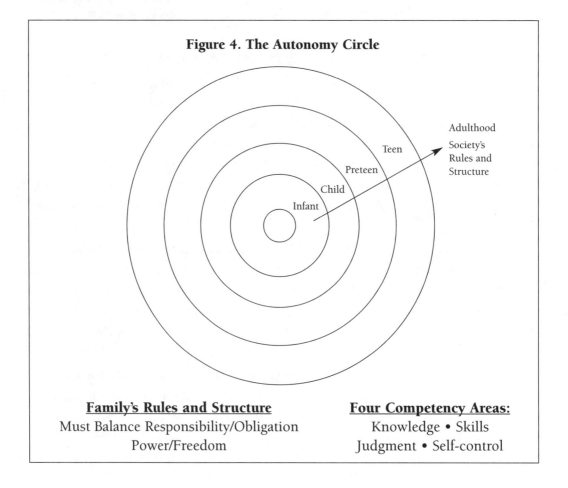

Figure 4. The Autonomy Circle

Adulthood
Society's Rules and Structure

Teen
Preteen
Child
Infant

Family's Rules and Structure
Must Balance Responsibility/Obligation
Power/Freedom

Four Competency Areas:
Knowledge • Skills
Judgment • Self-control

The rules, limits, and consequences you furnish must be clear, consistent, and realistic. Let your child know exactly what your standards, expectations, and rules are, and hold him accountable. This is the basis of a *parent-child contract*—an agreement about the rules and an understanding of the consequences for following or breaking those rules. The structure must be something the child can handle—not too loose and not too rigid. The goal is always success and a sense of mastery, with your child successfully adapting to your limits and learning to feel and be competent: "I can have a positive impact on my world." The following sections describe skills that will help you provide constructive limits, choices, and consequences.

Practice Competency-Based Parenting

How do you know how much structure or freedom to give your child? This question poses a problem for many parents. The answer is found by using the ideas of competency-based parenting: *children need to be contained within the limits of their capabilities.* In other words, the amount of structure should be based on your child's competencies in four areas: *knowledge, skills, self-control,* and *judgment.* Your child must have responsibilities and obligations, as well as power and freedom. When children have many responsibilities and little power, they become malcontent and rebellious. When they have too much power and freedom and too few responsibilities, they become "spoiled." This lack of accountability is a recipe for disaster. Parents must have as few rules as possible, but as many as necessary.

When deciding whether to allow your toddler to ride a tricycle unsupervised in the street, you ask yourself, "Does she have the knowledge, skills, self-control, and good judgment to be safe and successful?" Of course, your answer is "No; toddlers require adult supervision and guidance." Should a 5-year-old child play alone in your home? Can a 10-year old have a sleepover at a friend's house? Should a 16-year old drive a car? The answers are based on each child's capabilities in the four competency areas.

- *Knowledge:* This refers not only to inborn intelligence, but also more importantly, to a child's ability to process and apply information. Wounded children are like eight-cylinder cars with only four cylinders working. Deprived of early security and stability, their opportunity for learning has been impeded. Their cerebral cortex, responsible for higher mental functions, has been under-used, while the part of their brain that deals with survival and stress, the limbic system, has been over-used.

- *Skills:* A skill is the ability to do something well. Children with compromised attachment lack personal and social skills, such as communication, problem solving, anger management, impulse control, stress management, and delay of gratification. These are skills for living that must be learned in the context of healthy relationships; competencies modeled and taught by caring and connected role models.

- *Self-control:* The ability to regulate feelings and impulses is a fundamental skill that should be learned in the early years. Children acquire self-control in a secure parent-child relationship where a healthy balance of limits and love is furnished. When this secure framework is missing, children become impulsive, impatient, demanding, and emotionally overreactive.

- *Judgment:* This is the ability to make healthy choices using the power of reason and an understanding of the possible consequences. There is an internal dialogue (self talk) that guides the child with secure attachment to "do the right thing." It is difficult to exercise good judgment with an absence of self-control, social skills, and sufficient information-processing abilities.

The Autonomy Circle (Figure 4) is a tool used to decide how much structure or freedom to give your child. Each circle represents rules and structure beginning with the totally dependent infant and moving out toward adulthood. As your child goes through each stage of development, there must be a balance of responsibilities/obligations and power/freedom. As your child shows she is responsible and competent in knowledge, skills, self-control, and judgment, she receives more freedom and privileges. Children who demonstrate self-direction need less parental direction and guidance. On the other hand, children who lack self-direction need more external direction and guidance. Children with compromised attachment typically fall into this category. If your child does not demonstrate sufficient responsibility and, yet, has too much power and freedom, you will create an overindulged child—getting without giving.

> *"My Mary is so smart, she walked when she was eight*
> *months old," bragged one woman. "You call that intelligent?"*
> *challenged her companion. "When my Cindy was that old, she let us carry her."*
> **—A.J. Dannenberg**

Many well-meaning parents give their children too much power and freedom. There are a number of reasons for this. First, it is easy to feel sorry for a child who has suffered abuse and neglect; "I want to give her everything she missed." Second, parents may not understand their child's emotional needs and, therefore, are not aware of the proper limits to set. Third, it is common to avoid conflict and confrontation, particularly if you learned avoidance growing up in your own family. Parents also avoid conflict because they are worn out and take the path of least resistance; "I can't take it anymore, so just go ahead and do what you want." Last, parents can be embarrassed and worried about their image, not wanting to be seen as mean or unable to control their child's behavior. Thus, they back off, giving their children too much autonomy and too little supervision.

The following example shows how to use the Autonomy Circle with competency-based parenting. In this example, Zack can earn privileges as soon as, or on the condition that, he shows knowledge, skills, self-control, and good judgment in his daily life.

The Taco Bell Incident

Every time 8-year-old Zack went to a restaurant with his Mom he caused problems. At the Taco Bell, Zack ran around shouting and refused to eat. When Mom threatened to give him a consequence, he called her names and hit her. This was a set-up for failure. Mom was advised to tell Zack that, in the future, he must show he can handle a restaurant by making better decisions and having self-control. Mom told Zack, "I'll be happy to invite you to Taco Bell, as soon as you show me you have the skills, over time." It took Zack several months to learn and demonstrate these competencies at home and in other places, but he finally did it.

Keep the Bar High

It is essential to have clear and consistent expectations for your child. We recommend keeping the bar relatively high because children tend to either live up or down to our expectations. Your expectations are goals for specific behaviors, attitudes, and skills. Expect your child to be *responsible, respectful, resourceful,* and *reciprocal.*

RESPONSIBLE. The ability to act responsibly is a key to success in life. Children are expected to be responsible members of the family. There are two types of responsibility. First is personal responsibility in which you hold your child accountable for choices and actions. For example, if she lies or steals, she is expected to admit her wrongdoing and face the consequences. The second type of responsibility involves accountability for a job or role. For instance, if your child is responsible for feeding the dog or taking out the trash, he is expected to do those chores on time, correctly, and without being reminded. Having a sense of responsibility is a part of moral development, which includes sensitivity to the needs and rights of others and an inner voice that guides your child to do the right thing.

Children learn responsibility by being given responsibility, with appropriate guidance, support, and feedback from parents. Successful completion of tasks builds a sense of responsibility, enhances self-esteem, and prepares children for the challenges of the real world. Children may fail when first given responsibilities and need opportunities to learn from their mistakes. Some parents believe it is their job to prevent children from making mistakes and overprotect or rescue rather than allowing natural consequences and a subsequent learning experience. Rescuing your child is a short-term solution—you avoid dealing with the problem in the moment, but you are not helping your child learn for the future. The truth is you want your child to make mistakes when he is younger because the consequences are not as severe as later in life, and you are available as a safety net to provide support and encouragement.

RESPECTFUL. Respect is consideration shown toward others. If you want your child to be respectful toward you, you must first treat him with respect. The average parent makes many more disrespectful comments to their children than respectful ones.

Showing respect leads to self-respect, which is essential for the development of solid character and respect for others. Lacking self-respect, your child will not treat others respectfully, acting rudely and thoughtlessly, and discounting codes of proper conduct.

Respect is a stepping-stone toward trust and attachment. Children must first respect you in order to develop trust, and trust is essential for attachment. Tips for promoting respect:

Model respect.

Require respect from your children.

Call attention to disrespectful attitudes and behaviors.

Share why you consider the behavior disrespectful.

Give appropriate consequences.

There are numerous ways family members can demonstrate respect, including:

- treating others with common courtesy—say "please," "thank you," "hello," and "goodbye";

- communicating feelings verbally—without verbal abuse or physical violence;

- considering the needs of others;

- being kind; helping others who need assistance;

- showing regard for privacy and boundaries; knocking when entering, and asking before taking someone's possessions;

- using table manners; and

- using appropriate conversation skills, such as full sentences and eye contact.

RESOURCEFUL. Resourcefulness is effectively using skills and intelligence to accomplish a goal. Life presents us with a wide array of challenges. For children to be successful, you must teach them the skills to meet those challenges and instill the confidence to carry them out.

Children with histories of trauma and compromised attachment commonly act as if they are incapable and incompetent. There are several reasons for this. Negative life experiences have resulted in feelings of discouragement, helplessness, and inadequacy. They avoid trying because of a lack of self-confidence and a fear that if they fail, others will see how worthless they are. They also "act dumb" to manipulate and control others. For example, wounded children gain enormous satisfaction from "conning" a parent. The payoffs are negative attention, avoiding responsibility, and a sense of power.

Your child needs a "can do" message—communicating your belief that he is capable. Tips for encouraging resourcefulness:

Ask: "How do you think you will handle it?" "What is a better choice next time?" "Do you have a plan?"

Don't offer advice unless it is asked for and your child is receptive.

Never tell your child something he already knows or can figure out for himself.

> **Allow your child to make decisions; only become involved in the problem if it affects you directly or there is real danger.**
>
> **If your child fails, allow her to try again.**

RECIPROCAL. Reciprocity is the give-and-take of healthy relationships. It begins during infancy, as the sensitive caregiver is attuned to her baby's needs and signals. The baby responds with trust, closeness, and love; "I care about you, and you care about me;" "I do for you, and you do for me."

Many children only learn that relationships are a one-way street. They become takers, not knowing how to give back, and are only interested in what they can get from others. Tips for teaching reciprocity:

> **Everyone in the family pulls their weight by doing chores.**
>
> **Encourage your child to ask for help: ask and you will receive.**
>
> **Make sure there is a balance between giving and getting.**
>
> **Teach sharing and cooperation through games, stories, and example.**
>
> **Be aware of nonverbal communication: you smile, he smiles back; you reach out with a loving touch, she does the same.**
>
> **Practice empathy: we care about one another's needs, feelings, and opinions.**

Chores

In the past, children fulfilled a significant role in the survival of the family. Before supermarkets and Laundromats, families were burdened with a tremendous amount of work. Food had to be prepared from scratch, clothes had to be handmade, wood had to be chopped, and crops and livestock had to be tended to. Washing the family's clothes was an all day affair. The extent of the effort required was more than parents alone could accomplish. Children were a necessity for keeping the family going. The enormity of this responsibility forced children to grow up quickly.

In today's world, children are not needed to preserve the family. They have a significantly lower level of maturity and sense of responsibility compared to earlier generations. Children now spend much of their time uninvolved in the family. They are involved in sports, lessons, the Internet, video games, TV, and phone calls with peers. They have become "me" directed rather than "us" directed.

Doing chores is a way for children to increase self-confidence, internalize values, and become cooperative family members. Parents who do not have their children do chores are missing an opportunity for character building. There are three valuable benefits of doing chores.

1. Chores build responsibility.

One job of a parent is to prepare children for the real world. Thus, children need to learn to be accountable. By the time they reach their later teens, children should be well on their way to having the skills for assuming responsibility and functioning independently. They should be able to wash their own clothes, prepare meals, manage money, and be responsible for the consequences of their choices and actions.

2. Chores strengthen moral development.

Doing chores teaches family beliefs and values. Children learn to be cooperative, considerate, and contributing members of the family. They learn everyone pulls their weight and does their fair share. This promotes reciprocity, a sense of belonging, and good citizenship.

3. Chores enhance self-esteem.

Positive self-esteem is one of the most important factors for success in life. Doing chores well creates feelings of accomplishment. When children know their efforts are regarded with value, their feelings of worth and self-esteem grow. The child sees his efforts contributing directly to the well-being of the family. Praise and appreciation for a job well done helps children to feel valuable and worthwhile.

Tips for successfully using chores include:

Start early.

It is always easier to learn good habits early in life. Toddlers love to imitate their parents. Even a 3-year old can do a few simple chores, such as picking up her toys or cleaning the tabletop.

Make chores age-appropriate.

Chores must match a child's chronological, social, and emotional age. For example, a securely attached 6-year old can pick up his toys and feed the dog responsibly. However, a child of the same age with compromised attachment may be more challenged by these tasks. This child needs more guidance and external structure.

Provide guidance and structure.

First, explain what you want done. Next, demonstrate the chore step-by-step. Children learn best by being shown, rather than by only being told. Third, have your child try it for herself. The fourth step is repetition, which builds success and mastery.

Do not pay for chores.

Chores are done to be part of the family, a contributing member of the group. Paying for chores sends the wrong message; it teaches children that they do not have to contribute unless there is something in it for them. Allowance should not be tied to chores.

Be a good role model.

When you do your chores with a positive attitude, your child is more likely to do the same. One's attitude while doing chores is just as important as the chore itself.

Focus on the positive.

Rather than emphasizing what was done wrong, reinforce what was done right; "catch your child doing something right." For example, thank your child for cleaning up his crayons, rather than criticizing him for missing a few.

Accept a work in progress.

Learning and change takes time. Aim for small improvements over time. Slow and steady. One small move of a pawn can completely change the outcome of a chess game.

Show appreciation.

Positive feedback for a job well done reinforces behavior, enhances self-esteem, and strengthens attachment. Remember to praise your child's specific behavior rather than giving general praise.

Post the chores.

Place a list of the chores in a prominent location. The list should include a description, which family member is responsible, and a schedule for completion. It is important children clearly know what is expected.

Make chores a relationship building experience.

Communicating about chores is an opportunity for learning more about your child and enhancing your parent-child relationship. Chores provide an opportunity for positive change and connection.

Adapt.

Adapt the structure to the needs of your child. Younger and more resistant children need additional structure. For example, oppositional children do better with a specific schedule that is predictable and consistent. Children who are more responsible and mature can handle more flexibility.

Giving your child chores is one thing, getting her to do them is another. Your attitude and response is very important when your child refuses or "forgets" to do chores. The following example illustrates constructive and nonconstructive responses to a child who refuses to do a chore.

SITUATION: Child is asked to pick up his toys and ignores you.

Nonconstructive response: Parent becomes angry and shouts a command, "Pick up your toys now!" After 10 minutes parent again shouts, "How many times do I have to tell you, pick up your toys? I'm going to count to 10; if you don't pick up your toys, you are going to your room!" Child responds, "You can't make me."

Results: Parent feels frustrated and helpless, and the child is firmly in control. The child learns he has extra time to play with his toys if he ignores his mother.

Constructive response: Parent gives the child notice and transition time: "Honey, I need you to pick up your toys in 5 minutes." Child ignores the parent. After 5 minutes, the parent says, "Honey, you have a choice. You can pick up your toys now or I will pick them up. If I pick them up, they will be put away and you will have to earn them back. Which would you like to do?" Child continues to ignore. Parent calmly says, "I see you made your choice," and places the toys in a box. The child can earn the toys back at a later time by doing chores. (Note: If your child is likely to have a meltdown when you take the toys, remove them later when he is not present. If you do remove the toys when your child is present and he has a temper tantrum, give another choice: "Honey, you can have a tantrum and it will take longer to earn your toys back, or you can handle this better and earn them back sooner.")

Results: Parent is proactive rather than reactive, remaining calm and in charge. Child learns that there are consequences to his choices, and he cannot maintain control through noncompliance. By having the opportunity to earn his toys back, he has another chance to succeed and feel good about himself.

The following example illustrates constructive and nonconstructive parental responses to a chore done poorly.

SITUATION: Child is taking much too long to do the dishes.

Nonconstructive response: "I'm sick and tired of you taking so long to do these dishes. What's wrong with you? Get them done now! (Ten minutes later). It's easier if I do them myself. Go to your room."

Results: Parent is angry, frustrated, and feeling helpless. The child is criticized, alienated, and getting negative attention. The parent-child relationship is hostile and distant.

Constructive response: Parent enters the kitchen smiling, places a hand on the child's shoulder and says, "Honey, you know the great thing about taking so long to do the dishes is that I always know where you are." Parent hugs the child, says "take your time," and leaves the room.

Results: Parent remains calm, loving, and in charge. Message to the child is, "I believe in you, and you are worth every effort it takes to help you get it right. You are capable, and you can do it." Child's strategy for manipulating the parent fails. If the parent consistently responds in this way, the child will eventually give up her negative behavior. The integrity of the parent-child relationship is maintained.

Offer Suitable Choices

Children grow by making choices and facing the consequences. This is how self-examination, responsibility, and cause-and-effect thinking are learned. This leads to the establishment of an inner voice of accountability and self-control: "I better think about my choices because I'm responsible for the outcome."

Telling your child what to do usually results in control battles. Giving choices reduces the likelihood of power struggles and enhances connections. What motivates us all is the desire to be in charge of our own lives. Since children desire control, why not provide it in a positive way. Sharing in the decision-making process helps children feel important and increases motivation. It also displays respect for your child's right to make decisions. By providing choices you allow your child to do most of the thinking, increase the probability he will be cooperative, and give him the opportunity to learn from his mistakes.

Tips for giving choices:

Give choices that are acceptable to you.

Do not give choices you are not comfortable with. For example, you would not say, "You can have dinner with us, or I'll cook another meal for you later." A better choice is, "You can eat with the family now or fix your own meal later."

Strive for a win-win.

Your goal is to *maintain the integrity of the relationship*—to avoid control battles and destructive conflicts. You win because you are in charge in a firm and loving way. Your child wins because she has the power to make a decision and learn from the consequences.

Stay calm.

Even though this is difficult, it is always best to remain emotionally calm and composed. Don't escalate with your child. Present the choices in a steady, determined, yet calm manner.

The Shoes

Mom and 3-year-old Lizzy would fight about her shoes every day. Mom tried to help put her shoes on. Lizzy would struggle and resist, and they both became angry and stressed-out. Mom was taught to stay calm, get Lizzy's attention, and then give her two choices: "I'll help you with your shoes if you calm down and work with me, or you can fight me, and I won't help you." Lizzy tried to get around without her shoes for a while, and then decided to ask for Mom's help and do it Mom's way. The battle over the shoes stopped. Lizzy learned that Mom was only going to help if she made the choice of cooperating—staying calm and making it easy and fun. Mom felt good about being firm and loving. Lizzy felt more secure respecting Mom rather than manipulating her.

The next examples show the importance of your delivery. Communicating with criticism, contempt, or sarcasm is damaging and ineffective. Your tone of voice, facial expressions, and body language, as well as your words, communicate powerful messages. The first example shows the results of a parent ordering her child, and the second shows the positive results of allowing her child to make a choice and learn from it.

ORDERING.

PARENT: Put your coat on, it's cold outside. (*Covert message:* "I must think for you, you are not smart enough to figure it out.")

CHILD: I don't want a coat; I won't be cold.

PARENT: I said, put your coat on; you are going to be cold!

CHILD: No, I won't.

PARENT: (*yelling*) Yes, you will!

CHILD: (*later*) I'm cold!

PARENT: I told you to bring your coat; if you listened to me, you wouldn't be cold.

Result: Power struggle, hostility, and emotional distance between parent and child. The parent is frustrated and the child's low self-esteem is reinforced.

CHOICES.

PARENT: Honey, it's chilly today. You might want to wear your coat. You decide. (*Covert message:* "You can think for yourself, and I trust you will learn from your experiences.")

CHILD: I don't want a coat; I won't be cold.

PARENT: That's up to you.

CHILD: (*later, whining and complaining*) I'm cold.

PARENT: Gee, Honey, I'm sorry you're cold; I bet you'll bring your coat next time. (*Parent gives empathy and encouragement.*)

Result: Power struggle and negativity is avoided. Instead, the child is more likely to learn from her choice. The parent is an empathetic and supportive resource, and the positive emotional connection is maintained.

Children are often labeled "out-of-control" due to the aftereffects of abuse, neglect, and disrupted attachment. While it is true that maltreatment is damaging, this does not mean your child is incapable of self-control. Time and time again, we have seen wounded children exercise self-control under the right conditions. Children are products of their environment and can learn to make healthy choices. Your job as a healing parent is to provide those right conditions.

Units of Concern

Children are only motivated to solve a problem when they "own" the problem. Without a sense of ownership, there is little concern, accountability, or motivation. Instead, there is avoidance, denial, and blame. Parents who take on too many units of concern for their child's problems are unintentionally teaching him to be irresponsible and helpless.

THE PROBLEM PIE. Let's assume that for any problem in life there are 10 units of concern—10 slices of pie. There is a direct correlation between the number of units a parent has and how many the child accepts. When you take on too many units of concern, your child will take on too little. When you take slices of your child's pie, you are robbing him of valuable experiences that can lead to the learning of life skills, maturity, and wisdom. Wisdom is knowledge applied and can only be learned through personal experience. Wisdom develops from making mistakes, receiving consequences, and learning from them. Often our mistakes become our best teachers. If you remind, rescue, or take responsibility for your child's problems, you are taking slices of his pie. If you take too many slices, your child won't have enough left to succeed. Your child needs all the slices he can get; the more he has, the better off he will be. Consider the following example:

Twelve-year-old Adam was failing in school, not paying attention in class, and not doing his homework. His parents were asked how many units of concern they had for Adam's school problem. Mom said, "I have seven of the 10; I always bug him about homework and call the teachers." Dad replied, "I have the other 3 units; I punish and yell at him." They realized they were very concerned about their son's school problem, and he was not; he had zero units of concern. He had no "ownership" of the problem and, therefore, no desire to fix it. Adam only began doing better in school when he was held accountable for his choices and experienced the natural consequences (e.g., loss of privileges at school; dealing directly with the teachers and principal.)

WHOSE PROBLEM IS WHOSE? This is one of the biggest issues in parent-child, as well as marital, relationships. Ask yourself this question: "Is this my problem or my child's problem?" It is your problem if it impacts upon you or your family directly. For example, messing-up common areas of your home or destroying your property become your problem. Conversely, if your child destroys his own property or doesn't do his homework, this should be his problem. If it is your child's problem, show empathy, offer support and advice (if accepted), and expect him to have the units of concern.

DON'T BE AN ENABLER. What is the best way to be involved with your child to help her succeed? When you take on too much responsibility for solving your child's problems, you rob her of the opportunity to learn and grow. Many parents overcompensate for their child's lack of motivation by "thinking and doing for her." But it is a mistake to think rescuing your child is the best way to show love and concern. It only makes the problem worse, resulting in power struggles and reinforcing your child's sense of inadequacy ("I can't solve my own problems"). Give your child a message of hope and encouragement: "This is your problem and you can solve it; I'll be here to provide support and help; I know you will learn from facing the consequences of your choices."

Consequences versus Punishment

Corporal punishment is as humiliating for him who gives it as for him who receives it. Neither shame nor physical pain have any other effect than a hardening one.

—Ellen Kay

Parents are often unclear about the difference between consequences and punishment. A consequence is the result or direct effect of an action. The goal for giving consequences is to teach a lesson that leads to positive choices. It encourages self-examination, accepting responsibility for ones' actions, the ability to learn from mistakes, and the development of an inner voice of self-control. Consequences give your child the message that he is capable of taking responsibility for problems and can handle them.

The definition of punishment is to cause to suffer. The goal is to inflict hurt, pain, and get even. Punishment causes resentment and rarely teaches a child what you want him to learn. It is characterized by criticism, sarcasm, disapproval, and domination. Punishment teaches that force, intimidation, and revenge are okay. It also teaches a child not to think for himself. This "listen to a voice outside yourself" mentality can lead to a susceptibility to negative peer groups, such as cults and gangs.

Punishment is damaging to your child's self-esteem and does not facilitate secure attachment. Corporal punishment (hitting and paddling) hurts children physically and emotionally. Verbal and emotional punishment (yelling, threatening, criticizing, ridiculing, withdrawing love and attention) is particularly hurtful to children with a traumatic background. Table 3 shows the difference between punishment and consequences.

Table 3. Punishment vs. Consequences

BEHAVIOR	PUNISHMENT	CONSEQUENCES
Backtalking/disrespect	Mouth washed out with soap	Child loses privileges until attitude improves
Chores not done	Goes to bed early	"I'd be glad to give you a ride as soon as your chores are done"
Damaging property	Spanked and grounded	Does extra chores to pay for damage
Misbehavior at dinner table	No TV	Excused from the table
Lying	Sit in corner with face to wall	Must earn trust back by demonstrating honesty
Stealing	Yelled at and lectured	Makes amends to store or person
Fails in school	Grounded at home	Studies rather than playing at recesss

There are a number of reasons parents resort to punishment, as previously stated in Chapter 5. First, it is a convenient way to vent anger and frustration. Second, they are often doing to their children what was done to them when they were young. Third, they don't know what else to do. They lack alternative ideas and parenting skills. Fourth, believing they must maintain control and exert authority, they resort to punishment. Lastly, they want an immediate change in their child's behavior. Children often respond quickly out of fear, but the changes are short-lived.

Why Punishment Doesn't Work

- *It backfires.* Punishment is almost always delivered with anger. Using anger as a tool of discipline will backfire. Wounded children have a high tolerance for negativity, conflict, and chaos. Negativity fuels their defiance and strengthens their sense of power. If you are not in control, then they are. To them, being in control is much more important than any punishment you can impose.

- *It is temporary.* Punishment teaches children to respond out of fear, rather than out of a desire to please or "do the right thing." The child may appear to be compliant, but only in the presence of the "punisher." There is no long-lasting development of an inner compass. This does not lead to self-control or self-discipline.

- *It reinforces the child's negative view of self.* Wounded children see themselves as bad and undeserving of love, and they believe they should be punished. This creates a

self-fulfilling prophecy—*If you believe you are bad and deserve punishment, you will act badly. When you act badly you are more likely to be treated badly. When you are treated badly you become angrier, feel worse about yourself, and escalate oppositional behavior.* This is a vicious cycle provoking additional punishment. Each punitive experience reinforces the child's negative self-esteem and creates an expectation by the child and others of additional bad behavior.

- *It replicates unhealthy relationship patterns.* There is a strong tendency to recreate abusive, neglectful, and hurtful relationships. This drive to repeat familiar patterns, no matter how painful or self-defeating, is very powerful. What we have known is what is familiar. If we have known chaos, conflict, and high levels of stress, that is what we will recreate. Punitive parenting approaches replicate abuser-victim roles from the past; "I am not worthy and deserve to be punished." You need to be a role model of healthy self-control, communication, and conflict-management.

- *It provokes revenge.* Consequences teach children that when they make a choice, they set in motion a set of circumstances for which they are responsible and accountable. With punishment, children are too busy being mad at you to think about what they did wrong. Punishment makes the child feel angry and resentful. When defiant children get angry, they get even. They can be very astute at finding ways to make your life miserable, from oppositional or destructive behaviors to more subtle passive-aggressive strategies. You can count on one thing—your child will make you pay.

- *It maintains emotional distance.* Maltreatment during the early years can make a child fearful of ever trusting and loving again. The experience of abandonment and loss is profoundly disturbing. Wounded children believe they must maintain emotional distance in order to protect themselves from the possibility of future injury; "If I get close, I'll get hurt." Fear of abandonment runs their lives. Punishment feeds into their defenses against being close and reinforces a "me against you" mentality. It is natural to feel bad about those who treat you badly; "If you are mad at me, and I am mad at you, then neither of us will feel like being close." Although there is a great need for closeness, distance is a much more comfortable arrangement.

SPANKING. Spanking is defined as physical force used with the intention of causing pain, but not injury, in order to correct a child's behavior. Numerous studies have found spanking has many harmful aftereffects. Children who are spanked have less trusting and affectionate relationships with parents, feel less guilt about misbehavior and more concern about being caught, are more likely to be physically abused by their parents, are more likely to abuse their own children and spouses when they grow up, are more aggressive, and have a higher rate of antisocial and criminal behavior, both in childhood and adulthood (Gershoff 2002). The longer, harder, and more often children are spanked, the worse the outcome. Almost 33% of parents of 2 to 8 year olds say they paddle their children, a practice also used by schools in many parts of the United States (Harvard Mental Health Letter 2002).

Children who are spanked often feel fear and anger. This causes resentment of the parent rather than benefiting from the discipline. When parents spank, they are sending the message that physical aggression is an acceptable way to solve problems. Children do what we do, not what we say. This is especially dangerous when parents are angry; more than two-thirds of abuse incidents start with corporal punishment (Gershoff 2002).

Spanking is particularly counterproductive with children who have backgrounds of abuse, neglect, and disrupted attachment. They already feel insecure and angry, interpret other people's behavior as hostile, and lack trust in caregivers. Spanking only reinforces and magnifies these emotions and perceptions.

Some parents believe spanking is necessary to keep children from becoming undisciplined and unruly; "They need to know who is boss and fear our authority." These parents have a "spare the rod and spoil the child" mentality. Interestingly, in biblical times, the rod was a stick used by shepherds to gently guide their sheep in the right direction, not used for hitting. Instead of being a tool to inflict punishment, a rod could be interpreted as a means of guiding: "Your rod and your staff they comfort me" (Psalm 23:4).

Natural and Imposed Consequences

The real world operates on the principle of *natural consequences*. There is a direct and logical consequence to each action. If you are late getting to the airport, the ticket agent doesn't take away your television privileges—you miss your flight. If you are irresponsible at work, you aren't grounded for a month—you're fired. Natural consequences are between the child and the rest of the world. For example, your child forgets his jacket and is cold, doesn't eat and is hungry, doesn't sleep enough and is tired, doesn't study and fails the test. Natural consequences are preferable because you do not have to think about coming up with a consequence; your child learns from the "real world."

Blake, age 9, was told to have his parent sign the permission slip to go on a field trip. Blake "forgot" (he has a habit of being irresponsible and then blaming others). Since the problem occurred in school, the teacher provided the consequence; "Sorry Blake, you can't go on the field trip." Mom responded with empathy and reassurance; "How sad, you missed your field trip; I'm sure you'll remember the permission slip next time." Mom did not have to impose a consequence because the consequence occurred naturally in the school setting. It is counterproductive to impose consequences when they happen naturally.

The second type of consequence is imposed—those selected or chosen. Use imposed consequences when your child's actions are a problem for you, others, or a danger to self. Whenever possible, imposed consequences must reflect the actions, be enforceable, and address the problem. Children can sometimes come up with their own consequences; they are often harder on themselves than parents would be. This gives children power in a positive way and teaches resourcefulness. Natural and imposed consequences are portrayed in the following scenarios.

While in the car on the way to a restaurant for lunch, Amy, age 7, had a meltdown. She was kicking the back of the driver's seat, throwing toys, and screaming. This was inappropriate and dangerous behavior. The parents turned the car around, drove to the home of a prearranged respite provider, and dropped Amy off. They said, "We will see you after lunch; feel free to go with us to a restaurant when you are able to control yourself in the car." Their actions spoke louder than words; no threats, arguments, second chances, or pleading for better behavior. They remained calm and imposed a reasonable consequence that was appropriate to the situation. They also gave a message of hopefulness and encouragement about the future by telling Amy she will have another chance to behave better.

Think-It-Over Time

This is a very constructive imposed consequence. It is similar to "time-out" in that you and your child take a break, which can de-escalate a tense situation. This is very different from an early attachment parenting philosophy that advocated "strong sitting;" sit cross-legged, back straight, and facing ahead or at a wall without moving. The goal was to assert parental control and achieve capitulation to parental authority. Children typically view this approach as punitive and unkind, and it does not lead to long-term positive change. The goal of think-it-over time, however, is to help your child learn, communicate, and achieve positive change. There are three steps:

1. **Tell your child to sit for a brief time to think about her behaviors and choices.**

   One to two minutes for each year of age is adequate. Don't overdo it; this is not meant to be punitive. The think-it-over spot should be quiet, but not isolating your child.

2. **When you are ready, not when your child demands, go to your child.**

   Ask her the following questions: "*What did you do?*" It is important she takes responsibility and tells the truth ("I hit my brother"). "*What were you thinking and feeling then?"* This helps to understand and communicate her perceptions and emotions ("I was mad because he took my toy"). *"What's a better choice next time?"* Help her find better solutions for the future ("Next time I can ask you for help"). Remain calm, don't lecture, and listen well.

3. **If your child responds appropriately (honest, not blaming others, genuine), give praise, a big hug and smile, and all is forgiven. If your child does not respond appropriately, say "I guess you need more time to think about it; I'll be back soon."**

Some children refuse to comply. Either they won't sit to think it over, or they keep getting up and annoying others. It is best to calmly give choices: "Honey, you can choose to listen to me and think it over, and everything will go well, or you can choose to not listen, and you will have a consequence. What is your choice?" Let the chips fall where they may.

> *Three-and-a-half-year-old Tommy refuses to sit and think it over. Mom says, "I'll be happy to give you your Legos as soon as you think it over and we talk; let me know when you are ready."*

> *Tina, age 8, keeps getting up from the think-it-over spot and engages family members in conversation. Dad says, "You can sit 5 minutes my way or 10 minutes your way. Either way is fine with me." Dad is calm and steadfast no matter what the child decides.*

> *Julie, age 11, flatly refuses to think it over. Mom says, "Bad choice, Honey." The parent does not engage in a power struggle with her child but withdraws all privileges until the task is completed. "Take your time; just get it done before you ask me for anything."*

How to Deliver a Consequence

The way you deliver the consequence—*your style of communication*—will determine how effective and constructive you are. The following is a list of tips for successfully giving a consequence.

Connect with eye contact.

This is a key to gaining your child's attention, giving and receiving clear messages, and creating an emotional connection. Significant, but not constant, eye contact is acceptable.

Be aware of nonverbal messages.

Your body language, facial expressions, and tone of voice send powerful messages. Gently touch your child's arm or shoulder; have a firm, yet empathic, tone and look. Get down to her level, eye-to-eye, rather than in an intimidating position, such as standing over her. Your goal is to teach and connect, not intimidate or control.

Set the stage.

Eliminate distractions. Take the time to find a quiet space where you can focus on your child. Make sure you are in the right mood so your child is more likely to be receptive.

Focus on the behavior, not the child.

Convey the message, "I dislike your choice and behavior, not you." You want your child to learn from the experience rather than feel criticized, rejected, or ashamed—all feelings that confirm his already low self-esteem.

Work as a team.

Parents may have different tolerance levels for what is acceptable or unacceptable. Make sure you and your partner talk about behavior and consequences so you are on the same page.

Be consistent.

Don't ignore your child's behavior one time and give a consequence another time. Your child will do best when you are consistent and predictable.

Don't lecture.

Be brief. Never tell your child something she already knows. Let her tell you why she has a consequence. "I don't know" is not acceptable. Instead, she can take a guess or ask for help.

Control your anger.

Children learn more when adults are firm, yet calm. Yelling, criticizing, lecturing, and losing your cool do not provide a positive role model of coping and communication, and sends the message that your child is in control of your emotional reactions.

Don't threaten or give warnings.

Repeated warnings undermine your authority: "I told you five times to clean your room. If you don't do it now, you can't watch TV!" You are basically teaching your child not to listen the first four times. A single warning can be effective: "Honey, you can continue being rude and get a consequence, or stop now and not get a consequence." This allows your child to correct his behavior, make a better choice, and feel successful.

Give positives.

It is very important to give your child positive "consequences" for good behavior and choices. The best rewards are emotional—smiles, hugs, words of appreciation, and praise: "I really like the way you helped clean up. How about a hug."

Make it relevant.

The consequence should mean something to your child. Parents sometimes say: "My child doesn't care about any consequence; nothing works." Don't believe it. Your child cares more than you realize. This is usually a game of manipulation and control.

It doesn't have to be immediate.

Giving a consequence right after a behavior occurs is only necessary with young children who have short attention spans. For most children over five years old, however, you can delay the consequence. This gives you time to calm down, think about it, and consult with your spouse or partner: "That was a bad choice. Dad and I will let you know about your consequence a little later." This also gives your child time to ponder her choices and actions.

Don't overdo it.

Consequences that are given too often lose their effectiveness. Your goal is not to give consequences 24/7, but to communicate your child is accountable for his choices and actions. Also, consequences should not be too severe. Give the smallest consequence that is effective. Consequences that are too big ("You're grounded for a month") can cause your child to feel perpetually punished, become hopeless, and have no motivation to change.

Don't give up.

Remember, it takes time to change. Don't be discouraged if providing consequences doesn't appear to be working right away. The key is consistency over time. A slight variation in a pattern can result in significant change over time. This is called the "ripple effect."

Being a Secure Base

Fear and discomfort activate attachment needs in babies and young children. When frightened, lonely, and feeling stress, children rely on their caregivers for protection and need-fulfillment. You are being a secure base when you are *emotionally available, sensitive, responsive,* and *helpful*. Your child's fear and stress are reduced. She learns to associate closeness with safety and security. This is the essence of secure attachment.

What happens to babies and young children when there is no secure base, with no reliable and emotionally available caregiver to depend on? This child must face anxiety and stress alone. With little or no support, the child is overwhelmed with stress. She associates closeness with pain and fear and concludes she is better off alone. This is the essence of attachment disorder.

It is crucial that you are a secure base for your child. He will push you away and act as if he doesn't need you. Don't believe it. He does need you, but is afraid to trust, love, and be vulnerable. The elements necessary for a caregiver to have in order to provide a secure base are:

- *emotional availability*—accessible, dependable, self-aware (does not personalize, knows own triggers), mature, good role model;

- *sensitivity*—attuned to your child's feelings, needs, anxieties, and defenses; empathic, nurturing, patient, and loving;

- *responsiveness*—responds appropriately to current behavior and underlying needs; firm and loving; does not ignore negative behaviors; proactive, not reactive; promotes safety not fear; provides consistent, predictable, and developmentally appropriate structure and support; and

- *helpfulness*—mindset of opportunity rather than crisis; helps child learn coping skills, such as anger management, communication, and problem solving; understands the role and attitude of a healing parent.

Don't Take It Personally

No parenting techniques seem to work well with Bobby because we do not believe he has accepted us as his parents. Giving out praise brings on bragging and boasting, and punishment brings on defiance. He refuses to stay in time-out or to be grounded. Rewards for good behavior worked at first, but now the reward has to be so large in comparison to the behavior—it is ineffective and sets a bad precedent. Denying him a favorite toy or refusing to let him play sports is about the only techniques that are marginally effective in gaining his compliance. Bobby doesn't seem to care one way or another about parental approval or disapproval of his behavior or actions. He calls us "the enemy."
—Frustrated Mother

This is easier said than done. Parents often tell us, "It happens so quickly; before I know it I'm yelling, frightened, or just wanting to leave. I know I should do better, but I just can't seem to control my self when my child acts up." Although common, these emotional reactions get in the way of being a healing parent.

In order to be a healing parent, you need to look in the mirror. Knowing yourself is the first step toward creating a healing environment (see *Life Script* in Chapter Four). Be aware of your:

- *mindset*—your belief system or internal working model;

- *self-talk*—what you tell yourself about yourself, others, and situations;

- *emotional reactions*—feelings that are triggered;

- *attachment history*—relationship patterns learned in the past;

- *body signals*—physical reactions, especially in response to threat and stress; and

- *coping strategies*—typical ways you respond to situations, such as rejection, confrontation, anger, disappointment, and frustration.

Know Your Triggers

Emotional triggers are strong reactions associated with past experiences and memories. You cannot avoid bringing emotional baggage into your relationships with your children. Your parenting style, attitudes, and reactions are heavily influenced by your own attachment history—including expectations, patterns of relating, and unresolved wounds. Your own issues can get in the way of being a healing parent. For example, if you experienced a good deal of rejection during childhood, you might overreact when your child emotionally pushes you away. If you were abused as a child, you might panic when your child is aggressive.

Wounded children are experts at provoking reactions from parents—*pushing your buttons.* Getting you angry, frustrated, or scared heightens their feelings of power and control, and keeps you at an emotional distance. There are three ways to know if you are being triggered.

1. Reactions are excessive and out-of-proportion to the situation.

When we enter adulthood, we bring along our unresolved conflicts, fears, hurts, and expectations. These old feelings become indistinguishable from current emotional reactions. A "stacking" of emotions can occur, whereby an event in a current relationship triggers old feelings, creating a confusion of powerful old hurts and new ones. If your emotions in a situation are greater than what the situation calls for, you are probably bringing up an old hurt.

> *Sue's father was emotionally distant and cold when she was a child. Her brother was Dad's favorite and received what little positive attention was available. Sue and her husband adopted Josh. When Josh got into trouble, he quickly learned how to divert attention away from what he did. All Josh would have to say is, "You're not my real mom!" All of Sue's old pain regarding abandonment and rejection flooded to the surface. She took Josh's statement personally and become flustered, hurt, and withdrawn. Sue further complicated the situation by not giving Josh a consequence, for fear of alienating him even more. A more effective approach would have been to remain calm and in a neutral voice say, "Thanks for sharing, Josh," and then proceed to give him a consequence for his inappropriate behavior. This would give Josh a clear message his attempts to manipulate will not work, and he is held accountable for his actions. Sue's ability to guide Josh toward healing will be difficult unless she can separate her past wounds from present responses.*

2. Reactions are a knee-jerk response.

At times we all have intense and abrupt responses to a situation. If you trace a knee-jerk reaction to its root, you will often find a past experience or trauma. What sets a knee-jerk reaction apart from other triggers is the immediacy of your response. The impulsive nature of your reaction does not allow for a well thought-out response.

> *Let's refer back to Josh's family—Sue's husband, Ron, grew up in a family where respect for parents was insisted on. When Ron came home from work and was told about Josh's disrespectful comments to his mother, he flew into a rage. He was in reaction before he knew it. His inner voice said, "No son of mine is going to be disrespectful." Ron's deeply ingrained value system could not tolerate Josh's behavior. Ron proceeded to lecture, scream, and then ground him for a week. None of these interventions were effective in changing Josh's behavior. It was much more rewarding for Josh to be in control of both his parents.*

3. Patterns are continually repeating, even though you consciously desire another outcome.

The tendency to unconsciously repeat patterns based on the past is called *reenactment*. This drive to repeat familiar patterns, no matter how painful or self-defeating, is very powerful. It is no coincidence we often find ourselves in situations similar to the scenarios we grew up in. For example, adult children of alcoholics frequently marry alcoholics. Abused children often grow up and create familiar levels of high stress and conflict in their marriages and with their children. Parents of wounded children also repeat negative patterns because of secondary traumatic stress (STS). They become depressed, hopeless, and burned-out.

> *Christy grew up in a family where her mother and stepfather were both alcoholics. She was the oldest of five children and assumed the role of "parent" to her siblings, which involved being controlling and overresponsible. Christy carried this pattern into her adult life, believing she had to take care of everyone. She and her husband adopted a 5-year-old boy from a Russian orphanage. By the time Sergi was 12 years old Christy was burned-out. She was triggered by his refusal to let her control, rescue, and enable him. In addition, Christy was exhausted from 7 years of defiance and rejection. She was stuck in a pattern of only seeing the negative in her son, thus reacting with constant anger and punishment.*

Look Beyond Behavior

Early experiences with caregivers shape a child's core beliefs about self, others, and life in general. Wounded children see caregivers as rejecting, punitive, and unreliable. They see themselves as bad, helpless, and unlovable. Negative mindsets cause children to misinterpret a parent's behavior, viewing you as controlling and threatening rather than helpful and supportive. This is called a *hostile attributional bias;* misperceiving others as threatening and controlling when, in fact, they are trying to help.

New relationship experiences can change your child's belief system and subsequent behavior. By looking beyond behavior and understanding her point of view, you can help her develop a more trusting, positive, and healthy mindset. *Your goal is to help your child anticipate something new; to expect positive responses, such as empathy, support, honesty, and firm limits.* Slowly, over time, as she is unable to provoke hostility or rejection, her core beliefs will change, trust will grow, and behavior will improve.

Change your focus. Instead of focusing only on your child's negative behaviors, understand the core beliefs that are at the root of those behaviors. Illustrated next is the difference between a behavior focus and a core belief focus.

Behavior focus:
   PARENT: You need a time-out.
   CHILD: You're mean; you hate me.
   PARENT: (*in an angry voice*) I said go to your room!

Core belief focus:
   PARENT: You need to take some time to think about your choices.

CHILD: You're mean; you hate me.

PARENT: I understand why you see me that way; I'm not angry with you, but you still need to think it over; we will talk about this in a little while.

Know Your Child's Defenses

Children without a secure base develop defensive coping strategies in order to survive in a world they see as unsafe. Defenses are self-protective strategies to minimize fear and emotional pain. So much energy goes into self-protection that there is little left for healthy activities, such as exploration and learning, which hampers the child's development. Common defensive strategies are:

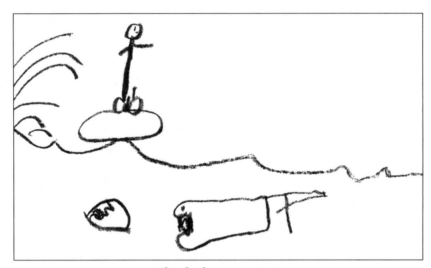

The sharks are coming!

- *emotional numbing*—shuts feelings out of conscious awareness; no language of emotions; "I don't know what I feel;"

- *denial*—refuses to acknowledge the reality of thoughts, feelings, and needs; "Since my needs were not met, I'll deny that I have any;"

- *control*—uses manipulation and dominating others in an effort to feel safe; "I have power when I control you;"

- *projection*—attributes to another person own feelings from the past; "You (adoptive mother) will abandon me just like my birth mother did;"

- *blaming*—avoids personal responsibility by accusing someone else; "It's your fault I got angry;"

- *splitting*—sees some people as all good and others as all bad. Also, seeing the two extremes in the same person at different times; "Birth mom is good, adoptive mom is bad"; "You love me, you hate me;"

- *aggressor identification*—acts abusive toward a person because someone was abusive to him; children who have been abused will expect abuse and attack their new caregiver before they get attacked; "I'll push you away before you hurt me;"

- *reaction formation*—does the opposite of what he feels; "I'll smile so nobody knows I'm scared;" "I'll be nice so you won't see my anger and reject me again;"

- *anger internalization*—feels anger toward someone but taking it out on self; "I hate my birth parents for leaving me and want to hurt myself;"

- *emotional exclusion*—removes from conscious awareness specific feelings to keep a caregiver close; "I won't show you that I am needy or angry, and then maybe you won't leave me;"

- *idealization*—overvalues someone to avoid the pain of the truth; "My birth mom is great, and she will come and get me someday;"

- *dissociation*—is unaware of whole aspects of self; mentally and emotionally "leaves" during severe trauma, such as sexual abuse; "You can't hurt me if my mind is gone;" and

- *pseudoindependence*—acts self-sufficient to hide fear and neediness; "I don't need your help or love; I can do it myself."

Change the Pattern

You don't have a relationship with your child; you have a relationship with your child's defenses. He will *project* his fears, pain, and negative expectations onto you. If he is able to pull you into his "dance" —mold the current relationship into a familiar pattern from the past—then you are not providing a healing environment. When you offer a different response than you child is used to, you create the opportunity for change. New relationship experiences lead to new expectations and behavior.

> *Cindy's adopted son from a Russian orphanage would say, "I hate you, you're not my real mom." She couldn't take the rejection because her own mother abandoned her at age eight. Cindy would give in to her son's demands to avoid his rejection, only making matters worse. When Cindy realized and dealt with how her past was affecting her parenting, she changed; she set limits, gave consequences, and helped her son deal with the loss of his birth mother. He could now change because Cindy responded differently—she "changed the dance."*

Your child will unconsciously *arrange the circumstances to perpetuate familiar patterns from the past*. For example, if your daughter felt unloved, she will attempt to get you to reject her and then say, "See, you don't love me either; nobody loves me!" Another example is common among infants placed in foster care because of abuse and neglect; they fuss, cry, and arch-away from their foster moms, anticipating more neglect or harsh treatment. If the foster mom backs off, the baby experiences a familiar (but damaging) attachment pattern. Wounded children go through an expect-project-defend pattern.

- *Expect*—child anticipates harsh treatment from you because of his negative core beliefs.

- *Project*—child displaces his fear, pain, and anger onto you; he sets you up to do the old "dance," the familiar pattern from the past.

- *Defend*—child uses defensive strategies for self-protection: pushes you away, blames, clings, or avoids.

Reactive parents are manipulated into old and destructive patterns. They become angry and rejecting, take it personally, and feel hopeless and demoralized. *Healing parents* are not manipulated into old patterns. They offer new and helpful responses, including firm limits, constructive communication, empathy, and models of healthy anger management. They do not take it personally. *Change the dance, change the outcome.*

Staying Calm

There is nothing stronger than gentleness.
—**Abraham Lincoln**

It is difficult to stay calm when you are threatened, angry, or frustrated. However, this is the most important time to do so, especially when dealing with your wounded children. Losing your temper and overreacting only leads to saying or doing something you regret later. Staying calm allows you to think before you act. Your child will respect you and see you as a positive role model, and you will feel better about yourself. The three steps to staying calm include: stop, tune-in, and act.

1. **Stop.**

   Don't act impulsively. Take a deep breath. Relax your body. Calm your mind.

2. **Tune-in.**

   Be aware of your *self-talk* and your *body signals.* Your self-talk will either agitate you or calm you down. No one *makes* us angry. Anger is always a *choice.* You can choose to be angry or choose not to be angry. Whenever your anger escalates, you are saying something to yourself that is making you angrier. For example, if you say to yourself, "My child will never learn to listen and respect me," you will feel hopeless and give up. Be aware of your body signals, such as shallow breathing, elevated heart beat, clenched jaws, and flushed cheeks. Your body is telling you that you are physically and emotionally escalating.

3. **Act.**

   Once you are calmed down and in control you are much more likely to think logically, resulting in constructive problem solving. You can now share your thoughts and feelings in a clear, honest, and appropriate way, or decide on another course of action that will be helpful to your child. When in doubt, say nothing. If you are not sure how to respond, defer until later. You can say, "I'll get back to you later; Dad and I will discuss this and let you know."

Jamie, age 6, always interrupted Mom when she was on the phone. Mom would first try to ignore her, then yell and spank her. Jamie got negative attention and enjoyed Mom losing control. Mom, feeling discouraged and overwhelmed, became aware of her self-talk: "Why does she keep doing this to me? She'll never learn; I feel like wringing her neck." This self-talk, as well as her tense body, escalated her anger and punitive reaction. Then, Mom changed her self-talk: "She is just trying to get my goat; I won't allow her to control me; I'm calming down; she will eventually learn, and I can help her." This self-talk calmed Mom's mind and body. It is impossible to be angry and relaxed at the same time. Mom was now ready to communicate her expectations to Jamie in a calm and firm manner. Eventually Jamie learned to respect Mom's space and exercise self-control.

Respond Therapeutically

There are two ways of reacting to your child that increases anger and conflict. A *mutual reaction* occurs when you behave the same way as your child. For example, your child yells and threatens, and you yell and threaten back. Hostility increases hostility. A *complementary reaction* occurs when you give-in to your child's demands or threats. This includes backing down out of fear (emotional blackmail), giving warnings, and pleading for good behavior. Mutual and complementary reactions are nontherapeutic; your child becomes more manipulative, you feel helpless and hopeless, and your relationship is based entirely on conflict.

Healing parents give therapeutic responses. You remain calm, yet in a firm and serious way convey the following message: "I will not accept your behavior, will do all in my power to help you change, and I will not become aggressive or abusive." *Your goal is connection, not control.* When you only think in terms of "Who is the boss?" you invite control battles and power struggles. You want to convey your parental authority, but not at the expense of the relationship. Your determined and calm tone of voice, facial expressions, body language, and words will be transmitted to your child, and his anger, aggression, and agitation will slowly subside.

Down-Regulating Your Child

When your child feels threatened and emotionally aroused, the Reticular Activation System (RAS) in his brain switches the limbic system into high gear: fight-flight-freeze. Your job is to help your child calm down, switching his brain out of survival mode (limbic system) into reasonable thinking (cerebral cortex), and slowing the flow of stress hormones through his brain and body.

You down-regulate a baby by gently touching, massaging, rocking, and speaking softly, which conveys safety and protection. You down-regulate an older child by your calm demeanor, firm and reasonable boundaries and limits, and model of patience, empathy, and confidence.

Emotion reinforces behavior. Stay emotionally neutral when responding to your child's provocations. However, express a great deal of positive emotion when responding to healthy choices and attitudes. Get excited about the things she does right! The example below shows a parent emotionally reactive, or "taking the hook," compared to a parent remaining calm, "not taking the hook."

> **Taking the hook:** *Five-year-old Dana puts her shoes on the wrong feet every morning. Mom gets frustrated and angry, then criticizes and lectures. Dana has a complete meltdown; yells, kicks, and bites. Mom screams even louder and hits back. They are both out-of-control—in their limbic stress responses.*

> **Not taking the hook:** *Mom says to Dana, in a calm and caring way, "I notice you decided to put your shoes on backwards. I'm sure you'll figure out how to do it right, because you are a smart girl." Mom sets the emotional tone. Her calm and supportive message helps Dana remain calm and not feel threatened. Dana does not respond from her limbic brain and is able to use her thinking abilities.*

Use One-Liners

> *A man was walking along a street when from the other side of a wall he heard someone shout, "Fifty-two!" He stopped, and again he heard, "Fifty-two!" Unable to overcome his curiosity, the man stood on a box that he found at the spot, peeked over, and a boy hit him with a handful of clay and shouted, "Fifty-three!"*

One-liners are an excellent way to avoid negative interactions with your child. They keep you from being "hooked" into arguments and allow you to stay calm. One-liners are brief phrases and expressions that focus the problem back to your child, leaving him without a means to continue arguing and engaging negatively. It allows you to maintain the integrity of the relationship with calmness, while avoiding your child's attempts to manipulate and control. One-liners should always be expressed with empathy and humor. They will not work if expressed with anger, sarcasm, or criticism. They call for no reply, but encourage your child to think. Table 4 shows how the use of one-liners avoids negative interactions and maintains calm. Additional appropriate one-liners are as follows:

- "I'm sorry you feel that way."
- "Thank you for sharing."

- "That's an interesting thought."

- "Nice try, Honey."

- "What do you think I think?"

- "Bad choice, Honey."

Table 4: One-Liners

CHILD	PARENT: HOOKED	PARENT: ONE-LINERS
"You don't love me."	"Of course I love you. Look at all the things I do for you …"	"I'm sorry you feel that way."
"That's not fair."	"What do you mean that I'm not fair? I always try to be fair with you."	"Thank you for sharing."
"You don't care about how I feel."	"Yes, I do."	
"No, you don't." "No, you don't."	"Yes, I do." "Yes, I do.	"That's an interesting thought."
"I don't know how to do it."	"How many times do I have to show you!"	"You'll figure it out; you're smart."

Engaging Positively

Relationships involve ongoing and circular patterns—a "dance." One person triggers a reaction, which triggers a counter-reaction in the first person. Escalating with your child only leads to more anger and control battles. Not escalating—engaging positively—increases the chances your child will calm down, and you will be a healing parent. Tips for engaging positively:

Know your triggers.

The more you know yourself the less likely you are to become emotionally triggered. For example, if you grew up in a family where honesty was an important value, you might get angry and upset when your son lies.

Don't take it personally.

It is crucial to avoid taking your child's negative actions and attitudes personally. Remember, this is about your child's fears and negative expectations, not about you. Continuing with the previous example, realizing you are very sensitive to the issue of honesty, you can remain calm and focused on creative solutions. You are *proactive*, not emotionally reactive!

Be prepared.

Having the knowledge and skills of CAP enables you to offer your child learning opportunities. You are providing a healthy balance of love and limits and serving as a good role model. Knowing what to do leads to success. A successful parent is a confident parent, and confidence breeds even more success.

Practice patience.

Slow and steady. Change takes ongoing practice over time. Persevere towards your goals. Each child changes in his or her own time. Know the unique needs and timetable of your child.

The scenarios below show examples of engaging negatively and positively.

Engaging negatively:

PARENT: Clean your room.

CHILD: No, and you can't make me.

PARENT: (*angry and yells*) You better clean your room or you're in big trouble.

CHILD: (*louder*) I hate you! (*runs away*)

Engaging positively:

PARENT: I need you to clean your room.

CHILD: No, and you can't make me.

PARENT: (*remains calm*) You have a choice, clean your room and come swimming with us later, or don't clean your room, and you will not join us for swimming. Either one is okay with me. Which do you want to do?

Praise

Praise is one of the most basic methods parents use to encourage good behavior and positive self-esteem. Praise, however, must be used cautiously. Children will only accept positive comments if consistent with their self-image. Unconditional praise and approval ("You're such a great kid") is only constructive when a child has a positive self-image. This type of general praise backfires with wounded children who have negative core beliefs. Unconditional messages of praise contradict this child's view of himself, and two reactions may occur: you lose your credibility ("You are stupid; you don't know the real me"); your child's acting-out increases ("I'll show you how wrong you are"). Try these tips for praising a child with a negative self-image.

Praise the behavior, not the child.

Give your child praise and approval for specific actions, attitudes, and tasks completed. For example, say, "I like the way you cleaned the kitchen table—thanks for pitching in" rather than "You're such a great kid."

Praise should be genuine.

Never praise your child if you don't mean it. She can tell when you are faking it. Do not praise for the sake of praising, this just dilutes the significance of truly deserved praise. Make sure your tone and body language match your words.

Find some behavior to praise.

It is easy to be pessimistic and critical with challenging children, but it is best to focus on the positive. Noticing and validating little successes eventually lead to bigger successes. Catch your child doing something right!

Eight-year-old Tim struck out at bat in the baseball game. Dad tried unconditional praise; "That was a great try." Tim didn't think it was a great try and became angry. It is better to use empathy ("You must really be disappointed"), followed by praise of a specific behavior ("I liked the way you put a lot of energy into your swing") and encouragement ("I bet you'll get it one of these times").

Humor

Humor is often an effective tool to reduce tension, sidestep conflict, and diffuse escalation of negative behavior. Humor can catch children off guard, divert their attention, break through resistance, and make them more receptive to a change of attitude. Wounded children generally lack a well-developed sense of humor. They may laugh inappropriately, laugh at people and not with them, and feel ridiculed by other's humor. Humor should never be used at the expense of another. Do not laugh at your child or use sarcasm. Sarcasm is hostility in disguise. Humor can help to transform energy. Consider the following story:

Recently, I was standing in a long line at the post office. Only two of the eight windows were open. Everyone waiting was getting more frustrated by the minute. One of the clerks said, "It's time for a break," and walked away. Everyone began moaning and complaining. Seeing the crowd's displeasure, the remaining clerk said, "Sorry, it's time for my break too." Everyone became even more upset. The clerk smiled at the line of people and said, "Gotcha." Everyone laughed and began joking and talking with one another. The energy in the room was dramatically transformed by the clerk's humor (Frederick 2005).

Play

Play is not only fun, it is crucial to children's cognitive, physical, social, and emotional development. From infancy, babies use play to learn about how their world works. Through play, they learn communication, creativity, problem solving, morality, and social skills essential to success in family, school, and life.

Play is a primary way for children and caregivers to connect. Through play, you learn about your child's special needs and talents, convey love and support, and

build a positive and enjoyable relationship. Sadly, most children with backgrounds of maltreatment and disrupted attachment have had little or no experience with play and have not had caregivers who engaged with them in playful ways. They have not had "play partnerships" with safe and supportive caregivers, and therefore, don't know how to play (Comfort 2005).

Young children in foster care or adoptive families have a number of problems regarding play: isolate and play alone; do not know what to do with toys or games; lack curiosity and imagination—don't know how to play "pretend;" have very short attention spans; play with toys designed for younger children; become destructive with toys or aggressive with other children; lose self-control; purposefully sabotage playtime; show no respect for the rules and rights of others; cheat for personal gain; sulk and get angry when losing; and try to control. Wounded children need to be taught how to play. Teaching your child how to play will take time, but with patience, support, and perseverance, she will eventually learn to play by the rules, cooperate, and even have fun.

Below are examples of how you can engage positively with your child in play for learning, fun, and attachment (ZERO TO THREE 2004).

BIRTH TO 12 MONTHS. Engage all of your baby's senses as you play; he learns to reach, grasp, and use his body for discovery. He learns "cause and effect" by about nine months; "I push the button and hear the music." She learns object constancy—things you can't see still exist; "I call for Mom when she leaves the room." Games—such as, back and forth (imitate baby's sounds and she responds), peek-a-boo, sing and dance, rolling a ball—help your baby learn communication, self-worth ("Mom enjoys me"), eye-hand coordination, and language. These reciprocal "give and take" interactions promote sensitivity and responsiveness to your child's cues. Smiling and clapping together create a pleasure bond that encourages affection, security, and trust. Your child's emotional stability and self-image is nurtured by the consistent and pleasurable experience of close contact and undivided attention.

12 TO 24 MONTHS. Toddlers are learning more complex communication, starting to walk and climb, and exploring more. Get to know your child's preferences; does he like action or more calm and quiet play? Toddlers use their imagination and enter the world of make-believe. Action games, like "Ring around the Rosie" and "London Bridge" encourage moving, singing, and learning social skills (cooperation, taking turns). They enjoy and benefit from repetition; singing the same song and reading the same book helps them learn, develop self-confidence, and feel secure. Your toddler can imitate words and melodies; sing songs and read books with rhyming words as she joins in. Young children love to make things work; use toys, clay, finger paint, and other things they can manipulate and explore.

24 TO 36 MONTHS. Younger toddlers play side-by-side ("parallel play"), but as toddlers get older they want and need playmates to interact with. This is important for learning social skills. They spend considerable time in pretend play with friends. Make sure your child has playdates at home or in the park. Be a coach to help him learn to share and work out conflicts. Dance and musical games ("hokey-pokey") provide exercise and help children learn to follow directions. Encourage creativity and fantasy play, such as dress-up. Allow for quiet time—stories, books, art—which is relaxing and comforting.

As a healing parent, you can help your child learn, connect, and have fun through play. Join your child in her play. Showing pleasure in her discoveries leads to becoming an eager learner. Try to understand what he is trying to do and figure out. Give the right amount of help and support so she can accomplish her goal. Present new challenges when he is ready. Have fun! Playing should be enjoyable for you and your child.

OLDER CHILDREN. We used to believe once the window of opportunity for the development of neural pathways has passed new learning was improbable. We now know the brain is very *plastic* and pathways can be created throughout life. What this means is we can use play to help children learn what they didn't get right the first time.

Teaching through play is particularly challenging with a self-centered child who ignores or manipulates rules, sulks or quits when losing, boasts when winning, lies and cheats. Children are much more likely to remember a lesson through play than through lecture or criticism. Through simple games we can model traits such as honesty, fairness, humor, generosity, compliance, and healthy competitiveness.

Wounded children want to avoid connecting at all costs. The more time they can interact with television, computers, or video games, the less time they will have to interact with you. Play combats isolation. Create opportunities to open the door to positive connections with lighthearted, cheerful, and positive play. Play is about connections. It is a way to be close and to reestablish closeness after conflict. The development of a comfortable relationship through empathic and structured fun helps create reciprocity. As the relationship improves, cooperation increases and positive behavior grows.

Proactive, Not Reactive

Many wounded children never learned to identify, regulate, or communicate their emotions constructively. They are out of touch with their feelings. When you ask, "What are you feeling?" the typical response is, "I don't know." They are overwhelmed by fear, anger, grief, and shame, but do not know how to manage or talk about these emotions. A common defensive strategy to avoid being vulnerable is to hide fear and pain under anger, threats, and "game playing." It is safer to push you away than face their feelings, be vulnerable, or allow emotional closeness.

You create the emotional climate in your family when you are proactive and take the initiative. Your child creates the emotional climate when you are reactive. Reacting to your child places him in a position of control; he is in control, and you are not!

To be proactive, you must know your goals and persevere towards those goals. As you get to know your child, you notice his responses are very predictable. For example, he will react to limits, tasks, and group activities in the same way over and over. Being proactive means you are prepared to deal constructively with your child's predictable behavior—you have a game plan. Next are examples of a father being reactive and proactive.

> **Reactive parent:** *Every time 10-year-old Kyle plays Monopoly with the family, he tries to control the game and throws a temper tantrum if he doesn't win. Dad gets upset, yells at Kyle, sends him to his room, and the game is ruined for everyone.*

> **Proactive parent:** *Before the game begins, Dad tells Kyle, "I notice you get very upset when we play this game, so at the first sign of losing your temper, you will be given a time-out to think about your choices and calm down." Kyle knows what to expect and the consequences of his actions. If he loses his temper and receives a consequence, it can be a learning experience. Over time, he will learn new and better ways to cope with his frustration, while building a healthy bond with his father. By being proactive, Dad is prepared, and the game is not ruined for everyone.*

Having constructive skills and tools helps you to be proactive. There are two particularly essential skills—anger management and problem solving. You can use these skills for yourself, your adult relationships, and with your children.

Anger Management

Anger is a normal emotion everyone experiences, young and old. However, anger can be very destructive when acted-out against others or turned inward against oneself. Unchecked, anger can lead to violence, aggression, and the destruction of relationships—parent-child, marital, family, friendships, and work.

A primary goal is to learn to manage anger constructively—to achieve appropriate self-control and to be able to cope effectively. Before anger can be managed, however, it must be understood. Anger is an emotion that often results from your *thinking*: your attitude and beliefs about anger and conflict, early messages you received from role models, and your "self-talk" that determines your feelings and actions.

Anger is typically a *secondary emotion*; it covers up other emotions, such as fear, loss, rejection, and sadness. For example, anger often results from unresolved grief. Children who lost birth parents often act out anger toward their foster and adoptive parents. This covers their pain about loss and grief and provides protection against future loss ("I'll push you away before you reject me").

Anger often results from feeling threatened. Children with backgrounds of maltreatment and compromised attachment feel threatened when they perceive a loss of control. Early trauma and lack of secure attachment also results in changes in the *developing brain* that makes it difficult to handle impulses, arousal, and anger. These children lack frustration tolerance and flexibility, and easily become distressed, agitated, and angry. A child's *physical condition* is also important to understand. High levels of stress caused by lack of sleep, poor diet, and lack of exercise can lead to anger. For example, a drop in blood sugar (hypoglycemia) or too much sugar in the blood both can trigger stress and anger.

Anger management is a skill and can be learned by both children and parents. Learning involves practice. First, practice your skills in a safe setting via role-playing. Next, practice these same skills in a real-life situation. We all need "strokes;" give your child plenty of positive feedback for trying new skills. Help your child (and yourself) to view setbacks as opportunities for learning and growth, not as failures.

Learning to manage anger is only the beginning. Once your child is handling his anger better, then the door is opened for the mastery of other developmental tasks (e.g., impulse-control, frustration tolerance, and empathy) and for a healthier parent-child relationship. Anger management includes the following skills and steps: identify and address underlying emotions, be aware of external and internal triggers, understand early messages received from role models, recognize self-talk, know your anger sequence, be aware of body signals and body language, and identify your conflict style. The following describes each step and skill and provides a task for you to complete.

Identify and Address Underlying Emotions

- Anger is often just the tip of the iceberg; there are other emotions beneath the surface.

Task: practice identifying the emotions under your anger. Describe a situation in which you became angry and name your underlying emotions.

Situation/anger _____

Emotions below surface _____

Be Aware of External and Internal Triggers

- There are certain situations or actions that trigger angry feelings and behavior. When someone pushes your buttons, you always have a choice as to how you respond; you have control over, and are responsible for, your own behavior.

Task: describe what triggered your anger in a specific situation.

Situation/anger _____

The trigger _____

Understand Early Messages Received from Role Models

- People often behave in the same ways they were taught, based on messages received and behaviors demonstrated by role models early in life. You have a choice; which messages and values about anger do you want to keep or let go of?

- Examples of anger messages:
  - "Violence is OK."
  - "Don't be angry."
  - "Talk or don't talk about your anger."
  - "Men can be angry, but not women."
  - "Anger leads to abuse and pain."

Task: identify the anger messages you received from important role models.

Role model _____

1. What did he or she teach you about anger and handling anger? _____

_____

2. Describe a memory about this person's anger. _____

_____

3. What messages and values do you want to keep or reject? _____

_____

Recognize Self-talk

- Self-talk is what you tell yourself about yourself, others, and situations. These preconceived ideas and beliefs have a major influence on how you deal with conflict and anger because feelings follow thoughts. Self-talk can be positive ("I can do this") or negative ("I'll never succeed"). Increasing your positive "scripts" will lead to more positive attitudes and behaviors.

Task: Describe a situation in which you got very angry. Now describe your self-talk before, during, and after that situation. Include self-talk about yourself, the person you were angry with, and other self-talk (e.g., others, the world in general).

Know Your Anger Sequence

- Anger often feels like a sudden explosion, but as you have realized there are specific thoughts and feelings that come before anger. Knowing your thoughts (self-talk) and emotions will allow you to de-escalate before you explode.

Task: complete the chart below for a number of situations that involved anger.

SITUATION	THOUGHTS	FEELINGS	ACTIONS

Be Aware of Body Signals and Body Language

- Anger is usually a reaction to a perceived threat. All animals have physiological reactions for self-protection and to be able to respond—fight-flight-freeze.

Task 1: identify physical cues so you know when your anger is escalating.

- Fast heart beat
- Can't catch your breath
- Clenched jaws
- Headache
- Flushed face
- Knots in your stomach
- Clenched fists
- Sweaty palms
- Shaking arms or legs
- Feet tapping
- Crying
- Others _____

Task 2: Know your *body language*. Nonverbal communication often conveys more than your words. Is your body language physically or emotionally threatening? Do your nonverbal signals convey a lack of caring or interest in resolving conflict? Your goal is to send messages that help others feel more comfortable and safe and lead to conflict resolution.

Identify Your Conflict Style

- There are four styles of dealing with conflict and anger.
1. *Passive:* You are anxious, inhibited, indirect, and do not speak up for your rights. You are often ignored or taken advantage of. Anger builds up inside, and you may become depressed, develop anxiety and physical symptoms (e.g., headaches, stomachaches), or explode. You find it hard to say, "No," avoid and feel immobilized with conflict, often assume you are wrong, and feel resentful of others.

2. *Passive-Aggressive:* You don't address problems directly, but retaliate by hurting them without drawing attention to yourself. You sulk, pout, make negative comments behind the person's back, give the silent treatment, hold a grudge, or get even.

3. *Aggressive:* You are dominating, threatening, and attacking toward others. You may get your way, but do not gain other's respect. You may speak loudly and yell, get into physical fights, ignore other's feelings, interrupt, be sarcastic, never admit you're wrong, and blame.

4. *Assertive:* You are confident, send clear messages, and are in control of your emotions. You stand up for your rights and respect the rights of others. You tend to use "I messages," make good eye contact, listen to other's point of view, say, "No," and set healthy boundaries, offer solutions rather than complaints, accept criticism without becoming defensive, and apologize when you know you are wrong.

Task: identify your style of handling conflict. Make a plan of how you will be assertive, and create a constructive and positive style of dealing with conflict and anger.

Ten-year-old Matt does not follow instructions well and has a difficult time obeying rules or taking guidance from adults. He often overreacts emotionally to minor things by screaming, stomping, or throwing objects. After dinner, Dad asked Matt to take out the trash. Matt responded by throwing a fit and stating, "I don't have to, and you can't make me."

The next thing Dad knows he is overcome with anger. He becomes beet red, grabs Matt by the collar and screams, "Don't you talk to me that way, young man. I'm sick and tired of your crap. You're grounded for a month!" Dad felt personally attacked and responded by attacking back. Remember, when you feel attacked, your body responds by producing adrenalin for use as a defense against the perceived threat. Focus is directed toward self-protection, leaving little energy for clear thinking and good decision-making. Instead of brushing off the remark and responding calmly, Dad felt he had no alternative but to attack.

Dad learned to be conscious of his escalating self-talk. He was then able to take a deep breath and change his self-talk to a more constructive inner dialogue; "This is not about me. I am not getting upset. He is just trying to take control because he feels unsafe. I choose to respond with compassion and understanding. I am in control of my emotions."

Over time, Dad became more and more astute. Eventually, his positive self-statements became automatic responses. By not escalating, Dad was able to stay calm and respond with true power, becoming a safe and comforting influence on his son. He was being the kind of person he wanted his son to become.

Problem Solving

Since problems are a natural and inevitable part of life, it is in your best interest to learn effective ways to solve them. Having effective problem-solving skills leads to feelings of competency and hope, and enhances family relationships. Ineffective strategies result in feelings of inadequacy and hopelessness, and intensify relationship conflicts.

It is important to understand and follow a sequence of problem-solving steps. First, however, it is helpful to know the seven *basic principles of problem solving*. These basic principles will enable you to have a positive mindset and attitude about problem solving. Following these basic principles will help you to be successful by avoiding common pitfalls and self-defeating strategies. Then you can implement an effective problem-solving method, described later in this section.

Basic Principles of Problem Solving

1. Problems are natural.

It is not "bad" to have problems, and it is not a sign of "weakness." Accepting problems as an inevitable part of life allows you to be more open-minded and less cynical when confronted with conflicts. Seeing problems as "bad" leads to denial, avoidance, and feelings of shame or guilt, which prevents effective problem solving.

2. Don't jump to solutions.

It is usually not a good idea to act on the first solution to a problem that comes to mind. Think about the nature of the problem, brainstorm alternative solutions, evaluate each option, and then select the best course of action.

3. Most problems have solutions.

People sometimes feel helpless and hopeless and throw in the towel before even trying to solve a problem. This is especially common when dealing with the frustrations of parenting challenging children. Having effective problem-solving skills, however, will increase your confidence, positive expectations, and satisfactory results.

4. Take responsibility.

You can only solve a problem when you take responsibility for your part in it. This does not mean blaming, criticizing, or "guilting" yourselves. It does mean recognizing your contributions and reactions to problems and your ability to change. You can change yourself, but have little or no control over others.

5. Focus on what you can do, not on what you can't do.

Be positive rather than negative. Having a goal and positive alternatives increases motivation and provides direction. For example, family members who constantly argue may decide to avoid one another; "We can't talk." A more positive solution is to learn communication skills, including effective sharing and listening; "We can learn to handle our conflicts more effectively."

6. Solutions must be within your power and ability.

You will experience failure if you use solutions that are *beyond* your power and ability. For example, parents commonly try to control their children's behavior. You cannot make your child behave in a certain way. You can offer information, make requests, and provide choices and consequences. Ultimately, your child will only change when he wants to.

7. Solutions must be legal and socially acceptable.

Sometimes, out of frustration and desperation, parents try solutions that push the limits of what is legal and socially acceptable. For example, some parents have become neglectful or abusive in reaction to their challenging children. Their lives were then complicated by social services and criminal justice system investigations.

Problem-Solving Method

1. Set the tone.

Creating the right atmosphere is crucial in order to get off on the right foot. For personal problems, prepare and relax your mind and body; make sure it's the best time and place. If this is a relationship problem, state positive intentions: "I appreciate your willingness to work this out with me."

2. Identify the problem.

Recognizing a problem early in its development, before it becomes extreme and overwhelming, makes it more manageable. Your self-awareness skills—being in touch with your thoughts, feelings, and behaviors—enable you to recognize the existence of a problem before things get-out-of-hand.

Define the problem thoroughly, including all surface and underlying emotional issues. A problem defined in a vague or incorrect way cannot be solved. Define the problem in such a way that it can be solved, including:

- *Situation*—who, what, where, when?

- *Reactions*—thoughts, triggers, emotions, way of perceiving problem.

- *"How-to" statement*—place "how to" in front of your desire or goal. For example, "How to get my child to respect me." Remember, you cannot control behaviors of others. The question is, "How can I increase my positive impact on my child to increase respect?"

  If you are unable to solve your problem, maybe you are trying to solve the wrong problem. Perhaps you have not identified the real problem.

3. Generate alternative solutions.

Be creative; don't just rely on solutions you have tried before. Keep an open mind, and keep the problem you have identified in mind. Solutions should address the current problem and also prevent the problem from occurring in the future. There are three methods for generating alternatives.

- *Use brainstorming*—Think-up and write down many alternatives; don't worry about if they seem good, reasonable, or far-fetched.

- *Change your frame of reference*—See the problem from someone else's perspective. You may find a new solution by viewing the problem from a fresh vantage point. Ask yourself, "What would so-and-so do in this situation?"

- *Adapt a solution from a similar problem*—Remember and use prior successful solutions. Effective past solutions can sometimes be applied to your present situation.

4. Evaluate your alternatives.

Choose the best solution based on the following criteria: 1) Is this something I can realistically do; is it within my power and ability? 2) Does it coincide with my needs, style, and values? 3) Is it sensitive to others? 4) What are the costs and benefits of the alternative you choose?

Make a list of pros and cons, advantages and disadvantages, of each alternative. Assign a grade to each, "A" to "F." Pick the alternative with the highest grade, keeping in mind the criteria previously listed. If the solution involves communication and negotiation between two parties, the solution should: 1) be acceptable to both parties, 2) state specifically what each person will do, and how and when it will occur, and 3) be balanced, with each person contributing to the resolution.

5. Implement and evaluate results.

If possible, it is always a good idea to rehearse and practice your solutions first. For example, you can role-play what you plan to say or do in order to practice, receive feedback, and get comfortable with new behaviors. Once new ways of thinking and responding have been successfully rehearsed, you will be more confident in the real-life situations.

It is now time to implement your solution and to verify the results. Did you carry it out according to your plan? Did it achieve the desired effect? Did it solve your problem? If *yes*, congratulate yourself. If *no*, either you did not carry it out effectively, or you have not identified the problem correctly (National Resource Center for Youth Services 1987, Bedell & Lennon 1997, Gottlieb 1999).

Sense of Belonging

A sense of belonging to family and community is essential for healthy emotional and social development. Children are social beings. Beginning in infancy, they have a strong need to fit in and find their place in the group. Based on social experiences, they conclude, "This is how I can belong; this is how I can have significance" (Dreikers 1964).

Securely attached children have a deep sense of belonging; they feel connected to parents, extended family, friends, community, and culture. The experience of being a part of a clan, with regular customs and traditions, gives children a feeling of security, a sense of identity, and teaches loyalty and altruism.

When attempts to belong are met with rejection, betrayal, and shame, children do not develop a sense of belonging or identification with family, community, and culture.

No child likes being ignored. To a child, being ignored means oblivion. Children develop several strategies to deal with the lack of belonging. The first is self-protection—avoiding additional hurt and rejection by defending and withdrawing. They isolate and alienate themselves from the group, denying their need to belong; "I don't need anybody; you're all jerks."

The second strategy is to desperately try and fit in by getting attention any way possible. They become superficially charming and engaging, chatter incessantly, constantly ask questions, have tantrums, whine, and make annoying sounds—all attention-getting behaviors to let you know; "I am here, trying to belong." They assume the role of the "bad child," a way to be part of the family, and a reflection of their negative self-image. They soon discover the side benefit of misbehavior—power and control over adults.

Biological children have a natural sense of belonging to their families—sharing similar appearance, genes, temperament, and identity. Foster and adopted children do not share this family inheritance and often feel isolated and alone; "I'm different; I don't feel like a member of the group" (Schofield & Beek 2005). As a healing parent, you discourage your child's misguided attempts to connect and encourage positive ways of belonging.

Routines and Rituals

Family routines and rituals increase your child's sense of belonging. Family *routines*, such as eating dinner, getting dressed, or preparing for bed, are "patterned interactions that occur with predictable regularity in the course of everyday living" (Kubicek 2002). Routines provide a way to accomplish a certain task and an opportunity to connect with your child. They organize family life, reinforce family identity, and enhance a sense of belonging. Research has shown the benefits of family routines. Young children from high-risk families did better cognitively and socially, and were more cooperative and compliant with teachers, when caregivers provided consistent routines (Keltner 1990; Norton 1993). It is important that you take an active role in the routines. Remember, this is a chance to connect with your child.

Family *rituals* are emotionally meaningful and convey the message, "This is who we are; this is what it means to be a part of this family" (Fiese 2002). Rituals foster a sense of belonging and identity and are especially important for children with insecure attachments. Children from families with meaningful rituals do better academically and socially. When rituals are disrupted or lost, children develop behavioral and school problems (Fiese 2000).

Here are some of the benefits offered by family routines and rituals, in addition to enhancing your child's sense of belonging:

- organized family life through structure and predictability;
- defined roles and responsibilities;
- reinforced family identity;
- contributions to family stability;
- strengthened parent-child bonds;
- internalized morality, beliefs, and values of the family;
- improved emotional self-control through safety and comfort;
- reduced stress through predictability; and
- increased trust and sense of security.

Family rituals that enhance a sense of belonging are:

- shared family mealtime;
- enjoyable activities on the weekends (sports, movies);
- family vacations;
- celebrations such as birthdays, anniversaries, reunions;
- religious holidays; and
- cultural traditions that recognize ethnic roots (camps, gatherings, baking ethnic foods).

In addition to routines and rituals, there are other ways to help your child feel like a family member. Tips to increase belonging:

Don't allow isolation.

Start with one-on-one quality time with your child. As she feels more comfortable and trusting, slowly encourage family involvement.

Respect child's background.

Be nonjudgmental, understanding, and respectful about your child's history and background (e.g., cultural and ethnic roots, biological parents and siblings). Give the message, "You can be true to your past, and still connect with us." Be sensitive to lost rituals from prior families or placements.

Focus on the positive.

Acknowledge your child's unique talents and strengths. Emphasize his positive contributions to the family. Notice the little things he does to belong.

Offer encouragement.

Your child needs encouragement to combat depression, hopelessness, and lack of self-confidence. Express your confidence in his ability to succeed.

Take pleasure.

Take pleasure in your child's accomplishments, regardless of how small. Let your child know you enjoy her company. Develop common interests. Find a way to have fun together.

Laugh together.

Humor is a great door opener to help your child feel like a part of your family. The ability to laugh at yourself, life, or a silly joke helps us feel, think, and do better. Laughter also reduces stress, smoothes conflicts, and builds relationships. Parents don't realize the power they have to influence their children. Children tend to mimic the moods of those around them. A sad face evokes sadness; a smile induces more smiles. Laughter is a powerful social signal that conveys involvement and approval. Research has shown the simple act of smiling causes your brain to release chemicals that make you feel good (Niven 2000). Plus, laughter is infectious!

Communicating for Attachment

Our son came home from college for the weekend and I asked him,
"How are things going?"
He said, "Good."
I said, "And the dormitory?"
He said, "Good"
I said, "They've always had a strong football team.
How do you think they'll do this year?"
He said, "Good."
I said, "Have you decided on your major yet?"
He said, "Yes."
I said, "What is it?
He said, "Communications."

—Orben's Current Comedy

Communication is the key to secure attachment. Sharing and understanding emotional information enables us to feel deeply connected. Communication begins even before birth. Pregnancy is the dawn of attachment, the time in which parents and unborn baby begin to communicate and attach. A fetus has well-developed senses and reacts to biochemical and emotional messages from the parents and environment. As early as six weeks old the fetus responds to touch, and by five months will react to the parents' voices. Every sensory system is operative in the womb, and there is ongoing communication between parents (especially mother) and the unborn baby (Verny & Kelly 1981). Mother's physical and emotional states are transmitted to her baby. Is she happy and rubbing her belly in a loving and relaxed way? Is she worried about her future and resentful about being pregnant? Is she feeling unsafe and becoming emotionally numb to protect herself? These thoughts and feelings are communicated via a neurohormonal dialogue—a communication of body and mind—and is preparation for communication after birth (Borysenko & Borysenko 1994).

Reciprocal and collaborative communication is the basis of attachment after birth. *The caregiver's sensitivity to the needs and signals of her baby is the essence of creating secure attachment.* Infants communicate their needs and feelings by crying and body language. The way the primary attachment figure responds determines the type of attachment pattern established (secure, avoidant, resistant-ambivalent, or disorganized-disoriented).

When communication is collaborative the parent and child are working in partnership, tuned into one another. The parent accurately reads her baby's verbal and nonverbal signals and meets those needs in a timely, sensitive, and loving way. A deep, trusting, and secure relationship develops (see Figure 1. First Year of Life Attachment Cycle, page 22). This pattern of communication results in *limbic resonance*, a connecting of hearts, minds, and brains. For example, an attuned mother learns to recognize her baby's different cries—"I'm hungry, lonely, frightened, in pain"—and knows to provide milk, rocking, safety, and soothing comfort. The message received by the baby is, "I am listened to, understood, important, and loveable." The baby has an experience of "feeling felt," which leads to trust, security, and positive self-esteem (Siegel 1999).

As children grow and develop, family communication plays a major role in determining the quality of attachment. This is particularly important for children who need special help because of prior neglect, abuse, and inadequate care. They may push you away, turn against you, and sabotage your efforts to reach out and connect. The way you communicate verbally and nonverbally with your child, your partner, and with other family members is crucial to your success as a healing parent.

For many parents this does not come naturally, because it was not something they learned during their own childhoods. Don't worry; you can learn to communicate effectively and constructively, and you can teach your child to do the same by using the ideas and methods described in the following pages. The how-to of communication will focus on:

- cues of attachment,

- developmental factors,

- listening and sharing skills,

- content and process,

- overt and covert messages,

- thinking and fighting words,

- resource model of questioning, and

- style of communication.

Cues of Attachment

Infants are born prewired to connect, as explained in Chapter 2. Secure attachment will only develop, however, when baby and caregiver communicate using certain cues or signals. This type of communication triggers attachment behaviors and feelings in parent and child (see Figure 1. First Year of Life Attachment Cycle). The cues of attachment are eye contact, smile, touch, in-arms, crying, feeding, and movement.

- *Eye Contact*—Newborns can focus their eyes 7–12 inches; just the right distance to make eye contact with their mothers. The gaze between baby and caregiver is a primary form of communication for attachment. The infant gazes into mother's eyes and receives powerful messages about her emotions and involvement, which influences the baby's feelings of safety and security. Emotions are seen on the face; eye contact is the main source of information about other's feelings. A toddler uses her parent's facial expressions to guide her behavior; "Is it safe to explore this place? Am I safe with this stranger?" This is called *social referencing*. The child visually communicates with caregivers, which influences her actions and emotions.

- *Smile*—By two months old, infants smile when seeing their primary attachment figures. The baby's smile attracts the parent's attention and encourages ongoing involvement; "I'm happy to see you." The parent's smile arouses feelings of safety and security in the baby; "I'm happy to see you, too, and I feel joy in your presence." Positive looks and smiles help the baby's brain grow and lead to pleasurable feelings. Seeing a smile on mother or father's face triggers a biochemical response. Neurotransmitters (beta-endorphin and dopamine) are released into the brain and body, which increases brain growth and produces relaxed and happy feelings (Schore 1994).

- *Touch*—Babies can actually die from lack of touch. In the 19th Century, most institutionalized children died from *marasmus* (failure to thrive) due to the lack of touch and affection. Loving touch influences the baby's immune system; the more gentle and soothing the touch, the more antibodies are created. Sensitive parents are attuned to what their babies like; some babies like gentle stroking, and others respond to a firmer touch. Touch helps children feel calm, secure, and loved.

- *In-Arms*—Being lovingly held is one of the most powerful triggers of secure attachment. This is why the image of Madonna and child has become an icon in so many cultures (Gerhardt 2004). Babies have been held close to their mothers throughout human history. In the arms of a loving caregiver it is safe and warm, and the baby relaxes and feels supported. The parent and baby's nervous systems communicate together. The baby's heart rate synchronizes with the parent's heart rate; when the mom is relaxed, the baby is also relaxed. Mothers who are tender and sensitive when holding their babies during the first three months have infants who are securely attached at one year (Ainsworth et al. 1978).

- *Crying*—A baby communicates needs, arousal, and discomfort by crying; "I'm hungry, lonely, in pain, frightened." Crying also releases stress hormones and reduces tension. Caregivers who respond promptly, sensitively, and consistently to their infant's cries have babies who cry less as they grow older. Some parents worry they will spoil their baby if they always respond. You can't spoil a baby with love and attention. When you meet your baby's needs, he learns he can depend on you. This is how trust and secure attachment develop.

- *Feeding*—Satisfying basic needs involves food and nourishment. The infant associates feeding with loving touch, eye contact, and a soothing smile and voice. Breast-feeding is physically and emotionally important. Breast milk contains nutrients and antibodies that nourish the baby and strengthens her immune system. The closeness felt by baby and mother promotes trust, love, and secure attachment. The feeding ritual, quality of the food, and care with which food is given, influence attachment and later attitudes about food and eating.

- *Movement*—Every time a pregnant mother moves her unborn baby moves. After birth, activities such as rocking and bouncing are important for infant development. Rocking is the most effective way to calm and soothe a baby. Sensitive parents naturally rock and rhythmically sway their babies, promoting stimulation and secure attachment. Our ancestors worked, played, slept, and traveled with their babies swaddled or strapped close to their bodies. They instinctively knew the importance of motion, stimulation, and contact.

Healing parents incorporate these cues of attachment into the communication and interaction with their children. It is important to send the right messages with your eyes, smiles, touch, and body language. It is essential to communicate that you understand what your child needs, and you will meet those needs in a sensitive and consistent way.

Developmental Communication

The essence of creating secure attachment is your sensitivity to your child's needs, feelings, and signals. Therefore, it is essential to understand how your child changes over time. The following is an outline of the first three years of life, describing the child's capabilities and needs, and the appropriate parental response, under healthy conditions and normal childhood development. Remember, children are different and develop at their own pace. The key is to understand your child, his strengths, and where he needs extra help (Parlakian & Seibel 2002, ZERO TO THREE 2003).

0 TO 2 MONTHS.

- *Newborn*—Learns to regulate eating and sleeping patterns, arousal, and emotions. Uses body movements, facial expressions, and sounds to communicate needs and feelings. Connects and "plays" with you by watching your eyes, face, and gestures, and listening to your sounds.

- *Parent*—Help your baby feel comfortable, safe, and secure by responding to her signals and meeting her needs in a loving and timely way—*you can't spoil a baby*; know your baby's different cries: "I'm hungry, tired, bored;" talk to, sing to, and gently massage your baby, and give her things to look at and touch; and mimic sounds to engage in "conversation."

2 TO 6 MONTHS.

- *Infant*—Learns new communication skills, including smiling, cooing, and babbling. Enjoys imitating sounds and gestures (e.g., Mom laughs and baby laughs). Loves to explore through looking, touching, reaching, and putting her mouth on objects. Can roll over and sit with assistance by 4 to 6 months.

- *Parent*—Talk to your baby by smiling, back-and-forth babbling, and speaking "parent-ese." This includes using simple language, with lots of expression on your face and in your voice, and vocalizing slowly in a singsong way. Your baby will pay attention and respond. This early communication is the foundation for language and builds attachment. Invent many fun back-and-forth interactions (e.g., hold out a rattle and encourage him to reach for it and then give it back), lots of smiles, eye contact, and gentle touching. Figure out how your baby signals her needs and feelings, verbally and nonverbally, and the special ways you and your baby enjoy communicating with one another.

6 TO 12 MONTHS.

- *Baby*—Communicates through actions, such as gestures, sounds, and facial expressions. Putting consonants and vowels together to form words ("dada" and "mama"). Begins to understand cause and effect—he can make something happen; "If I cry, Mom will pick me up." Develops "object constancy"—knows when you leave you still exist, leading to protest when separated from the attachment figure. Able to move in new ways (crawl, stand, walk) allowing for more exploration and interaction with his environment.

- *Parent*—Talk a great deal with your baby, even though he doesn't understand at first. His brain is building the connections for language, and you and your baby are creating limbic resonance through empathy and attunement. Play games like "patty-cake" and "peek-a-boo", which teach the give-and-take of communication and reassure him that when you disappear you will reappear. Engage in *circles of communication*—back-and-forth conversations verbally and nonverbally that boost development and attachment. Create a babyproof environment that is safe for exploration and reduces conflicts between you and your baby. Help him learn to handle his feelings. Convey comfort when he cries, and support when anxious and frustrated. Give encouragement to try again, and help him calm down through soothing and nurturing messages (*down-regulate*).

12 TO 18 MONTHS.

- *Toddler*—Learns new words every day, and understands much more than she can speak. Continues to imitate others, but also beginning to understand symbols and ideas, and can do pretend play (e.g., a twig can become an airplane). Able to walk and run, but lacks the impulse control to stay safe.

- *Parent*—Encourage your toddler to use words to communicate needs and feelings; she learns new words as you tell stories, read, and play. Begin to set limits and help her learn to deal with emotions; "I know you are angry because you want to play more at the park, but we need to go. We will come back another day." Communicate with calmness and empathy, while being firm and setting limits. Read often, as it fosters brain and language development and a love of books. Join in her play, and let her direct the play at times, building reciprocity and a sense of mastery. Avoid negative communication, such as saying "No" too often, by diverting your child's attention (e.g., a toy with buttons can replace the TV remote). Use positive messages whenever possible; "Please walk" is better than "Don't run" because it focuses on what *to do* rather than what *not to do*. The way you convey messages to your toddler—eye-to-eye, gently touch, calm, firm, and empathic— will help her learn impulse control and frustration tolerance.

18 TO 36 MONTHS.

- *Toddler and preschooler*—Vocabulary is growing quickly; a 2-year-old can typically speak between 200 and 300 words. Very independent and eager to be in control (Terrible Twos), but still lacking in self-control and an understanding of the consequences of their actions. Play is essential for all areas of development, as is reading with your child and conversation. Very active; wants to run, climb, jump, and explore.

- *Parent*—Expand on what your child says. When she says, "Fall down," you say, "Yes, you fell down on the floor. Are you okay?" Be a good listener and let him know you understand what he is going through; "I know you are upset because you can't find your toy," which will calm him down, model good communication skills, and offer a secure base. Allow him to have some control by giving acceptable choices ("You can have the red or blue cup"), and provide age-appropriate consequences delivered in a calm and caring tone. Be proactive; if your child is getting frustrated calm him down, offer support, or suggest another activity. Communicate your expectations to ease transition times; "In 5 minutes we will be going." Encourage play with other children to help him learn sharing, impulse control, communication, and the pleasures of friendship. Be creative and have fun together; go to the park, play games, do art, go for a walk, collect leaves, make food, read books, tell stories. Be aware of your own feelings: what behaviors of your child are most difficult to handle; how are you triggered; how were you treated as a child; and how does that influence you as a parent?

Active Listening

The ability to *really* listen is the most basic and important of all communication skills. Everyone, regardless of his or her age, has a need to be heard, understood, and validated. A baby feels safe and loved when his caregiver "listens" to his cues and signals. A child feels supported and encouraged when her dad listens to her frustrations about school. A husband and wife feel closeness and trust when they take the time to listen to one another's needs, feelings, and opinions. Instead of listening, however, parents often interrogate, judge, advise, criticize, or misinterpret their child. The result is a rupture in the parent-child relationship, causing both to feel frustrated, angry, and at odds. This only reinforces the child's emotional isolation and lack of trust. Described below are the door openers and door closers for listening (Fanning & McKay 2000).

DOOR OPENERS FOR LISTENING.

- *Be empathic*—To be empathic is to place yourself in your child's shoes; to understand his thoughts and feelings and convey that understanding to him. Looking at the world from your child's point of view, and understanding his feelings, sends valuable messages: "I respect and value your opinion; you are worth understanding and being listened to; I am dependable and invested in you." You can convey understanding and empathy without words: nodding your head to show you are paying attention, having a caring and compassionate look on your face, or gently touching your child's arm or shoulder to signify support and concern. You can convey empathy by active listening, reflecting-back your child's experience without judgment, as described below.

Nonempathic response:

CHILD: It's dark in here.

PARENT: There's nothing to be scared of. You're a big boy. Big boys shouldn't be afraid.

Result: Child feels judged, misunderstood, and discounted. Fear of the dark is not logical for an adult but is perfectly logical for a child.

Empathic response:

CHILD: It's dark in here.

PARENT: You seem kind of upset, huh?

CHILD: I'm scared.

PARENT: I'm sorry you're scared. The dark can be scary sometimes.

CHILD: Yeah.

PARENT: Would you like to hear how I got over being scared when I was your age?

CHILD: Sure.

Result: Child feels understood and acknowledged. Empathic response encourages trust and openness to adult's ideas and direction.

- *Don't judge*—When you evaluate or judge how your child acts, thinks, or feels, you are not listening to your child; you are listening to your own appraisals of your child. To be nonjudgmental is to avoid focusing on right or wrong, good or bad, agree or disagree. Your goal is to understand your child's experience. Children are more likely to change when they feel accepted for who they are. Acceptance helps them feel emotionally safe, which opens the door to trust and the possibility of change.

- *Know yourself*—What nonverbal signals are you sending as you listen? Pay attention to your eye contact, facial expressions, gestures, or body positions. Are you communicating that you are safe to confide in or threatening and should be avoided? Send accepting, understanding, and supportive messages. You must also be aware of your emotional baggage. If you are being emotionally triggered then you are filtering your child's signals through a lens of your own issues and beliefs. When you are self-aware, you can tune into your child and truly connect.

- *Relax*—Maintain a calm mind and body regardless of your child's attitude or behavior. Composure and confidence promote attunement and communicate that you are a secure base. When your child senses your composure she feels safe, which leads to trust in you as someone to confide in.

- *Keep an open mind*—When you are planning your rebuttal, you are listening to your own inner voice, rather than being attuned to your child. Having an open mind also means you are willing to listen to your child's feelings about difficult and sensitive subjects. Even though you do not accept inappropriate behavior, you want to hear your child's feelings and point of view.

DOOR CLOSERS FOR LISTENING.

- *Mind reading*—Trying to figure out what *you believe* he is *really* thinking or feeling, making assumptions.

- *Rehearsing*—Silently preparing your next comment or rebuttal before the other has even finished and not really listening.

- *Filtering*—Selective listening; tuning into only the parts you are comfortable with and tuning out all other messages.

- *Judging*—Assigning blame or placing negative labels.

- *Avoiding*—Your attention may wander (daydreaming) or you may only be partially listening (reading the paper, watching TV); your message is, "You are not very important to me."

- *Identifying*—Self-referential; referring everything back to yourself and your own experience.

- *Advising*—Always trying to "fix it," problem-solve, and offer suggestions.

- *Sparring*—Arguing and debating; must defend your position.

- *Perfectionism*—Being right; go to any length to avoid being less than perfect (defend, lie, or shout).

- *Derailing*—Change the subject or use humor to avoid issues that are uncomfortable.

- *Placating*—Too quick to agree and too concerned with being "nice"; not genuine.

- *Stonewalling*—Refusing to listen (leaving the room, shutting down, giving the silent treatment); usually a passive-aggressive way of dealing with anger and resentment.

Sharing

The way you share your thoughts and feelings, both verbally and nonverbally, determines if your child listens or tunes you out. Here are the door openers and door closers for sharing.

DOOR OPENERS FOR SHARING.

- *Share both thoughts and feelings*—It is important to share your thoughts (opinions, perceptions, ideas) and your feelings (sad, angry, fearful, frustrated, love). Sharing only thoughts comes across as too cerebral and cold, while sharing only feelings can seem overly intense or dramatic. Wounded children do not have a language of emotion and find it difficult to identify and express feelings. Therefore, it is very important to model constructive sharing of emotions.

  - *Make "I statements"*—which allow you to express your own thoughts and feelings, rather than talking about, judging, or blaming your child. "I statements" include: "I feel _____ when _____ because _____." For example, "I feel sad when you run away from me because I am not able to help you;" or "I feel angry when you take my things without asking because this shows disrespect."

    Making "I statements," rather than asking questions, allows you to talk about your own experiences and take responsibility for your own perceptions. "You statements" are often perceived as blaming, accusing, or disapproving, and causes your child to become defensive and shut down.

- *Be clear and concise*—Be specific and concrete, rather than vague or unclear. Give examples. Be brief; lectures, lengthy speeches, or repeating the same message over and over is annoying and will turn your child off. Do not hint or expect your child to mind read. Speak slowly. Communication is not about how much you say; it is about how much is conveyed and understood. People who speak slowly are perceived as more knowledgeable than those who speak quickly.

- *Be assertive*—There are four basic communication styles—*passive, passive-aggressive, aggressive,* and *assertive. Passive* people don't express their thoughts, feelings, or needs. They find it hard to say, "No," and don't stand-up for their rights. Those who use a *passive-aggressive* style are indirect. They get even with others by pouting, giving the silent treatment, holding a grudge, or making hurtful comments. An *aggressive* style of communication involves put-downs, sarcasm, and blame. You express yourself at the expense of other's rights and feelings. Your goal is to use an *assertive* style; make direct statements, requests, and refusals. You stand up for your rights but not at the expense of other's rights or feelings. You convey an aura of confidence and self-assurance, as well as empathy and humility. An assertive statement has three parts: your *perspective, feelings,* and *wants (requests)* regarding a particular situation. Share your thoughts, feelings, and desires in a decisive and positive way. Do not criticize, blame, attack, or complain.

- *Use proper timing*—There is an old Chinese saying, "The ripe melon falls of itself." Timing is everything. *When* you say something is just as important as what you say. For example, it is usually not a good idea to confront your child early in the morning, as he may not be in a good mood, and it starts the day off on a negative tone. Also, it is not productive to bring up issues when you are very angry or frustrated. Your child will be more receptive if you wait until you calm down and then communicate assertively.

- *Get your child's attention*—Eye contact and loving touch are two ways to gain your child's attention. Eye-level shelves in a supermarket are highly prized because advertisers know in order to sell something you must catch the eye of the consumer. Do not talk to your child if she is not looking at you. Touching is a fundamental way to connect; it communicates involvement, concern, and support. You must connect before you can guide. For example, touch your child gently on her shoulder or arm. Her body language (posture, facial expression, eye contact) will let you know if she is listening.

- *Be aware of covert messages*—Communication involves two simultaneous messages: *overt* and *covert*. The *overt* message is the content, topic, or spoken words. The *covert* message is the meaning behind the words. Covert messages are powerful because they carry emotional meaning and go directly to the unconscious mind. Negative covert messages reinforce low self-esteem. Positive covert messages challenge your child's negative self-image, thereby encouraging positive change. The example below shows the difference between negative and positive covert messages.

Negative covert message:

PARENT ASKS: Did you bring your homework home, or did you forget it again?

NEGATIVE COVERT MESSAGE: *I have no faith in you; since you are choosing not to be responsible, I will be responsible for you.*

Result: Creates a lose-lose power struggle and a battle about homework. Maintains a negative emotional relationship in which your child feels like a failure. Parent and child are angry and frustrated.

Positive covert message:

PARENT SAYS: Let me know if you want help with your homework.

POSITIVE COVERT MESSAGE: *You are smart enough to know if you need help and can handle your schoolwork.*

Result: Avoids power struggle and lets your child know he is responsible for homework and school. Maintains a positive emotional climate. Parent remains calm and models healthy boundaries. Child feels validated, supported, and competent.

- *Use thinking, not fighting, words*—Thinking words help your child reflect on his thoughts, feelings, and choices and promote cooperation and responsibility. Fighting words are threatening and demanding and lead to hostility, defiance, and power struggles. Thinking words convey your guidelines and expectations without inviting an altercation (Cline & Fay 1990). Next are examples of thinking and fighting words:

FIGHTING WORDS	THINKING WORDS
"You can't watch TV until your homework's done!"	"Feel free to watch TV as soon as you finish your homework."
"I'm not letting you play until your chores are finished."	"You're welcome to play when your chores are done."
"You can't have any more money until you get your next allowance."	"I'll be glad to give you your allowance on Saturday."
"You better stop that kind of talk immediately!"	"I'll be happy to listen when you calm down."

- *Keep it positive*—A large part of a child's self-esteem is based on how she is perceived by important people. Do you convey positive or negative messages to your child? Parents often fail to notice positive behaviors and focus on negative ones. Defiant children give their parents plenty of negatives to occupy their attention, and it is easy to miss opportunities to validate good behavior because you are either too busy anticipating the next infraction or too angry to care.

  Emotion reinforces behavior. Both positive and negative actions occur more often when reinforced. Thus, it is necessary to remain neutral with negative behavior and show positive emotion for appropriate behavior. *Catch your child doing something right.* Encouragement leads to an expectation of success. When your child makes a mistake, find something positive to communicate as well as attending to the negative. For instance, validate your child's honesty as he tells you what he did wrong; "Thanks for telling me the truth about stealing from school. I really appreciate your honesty, and there will be a consequence."

- *Ask clarifying questions*—Sometimes it is necessary to ask for clarification. Paraphrasing is one of the best ways to gain more information: "What I hear you say is …" Your intention is to learn, understand, and help, not to interrogate or convey your own point of view. Soliciting additional information is an excellent way to gain clarification of your child's point of view and sends the message that you care about what she is saying. For example, "So are you saying …" or "I'm not sure what you mean—can you tell me more?" When you accurately receive your child's message you build a bridge of understanding. Nothing wins over a child more than sending the message that you value her viewpoint.

DOOR CLOSERS FOR SHARING.

- *Say it once*—Parents repeat themselves an average of 7 to 10 times before they get a response (Levy & O'Hanlon 2001). At best, these ignored requests lead to frustration, pleading, and empty threats, which damage your credibility. At worse, the situation can escalate into verbal and physical aggression. When you say things 10 times you are training your child not to listen 9 times. He quickly learns delaying will buy him time to continue what he is doing. The more you remind the less your child will listen.

- *Stop lecturing*—There is no better way to "turn off" your child then to give her a long-winded discourse. Lectures are one-way and often given with reprimands and scolding. The message is, "I know best, and like it or not, you are going to hear about it." This leads to emotional alienation and distance. Opened-mouth parents have closed-ear children. Helpless parents do a great deal of talking, to no avail.

- *Avoid criticism, attacking, and blaming*—Parents cannot win cooperation from children who feel attacked. This only results in defensiveness and counterattack. The more critical you are, the more your child will react negatively. Children often blame rather than take responsibility for their actions. It is impossible to change your child's behavior if you are doing the same. Children do what we do.

- *Refrain from asking why*—Parents routinely ask children why they did something. There are several reasons why they rarely get a satisfactory answer. First, children do not typically know why they do what they do. Much of your child's behavior is in response to motivations that lie deep below conscious awareness. Your child may not have the ability to tune into his feelings and thoughts. He lacks a "language of emotion" and the ability to be self-aware. Second, when he does know why, most likely he is not going to tell you. Holding back the truth is a strategy for maintaining power and control. He may also be afraid of the consequences of telling the truth, such as lecturing, scolding, or loss of privileges. Also, children with compromised attachment characteristically lack honesty and other prosocial values. Third, children are adept at being "parent deaf," feigning ignorance and shutting down. The parent becomes frustrated and angry, which perpetuates a hostile and distant parent-child relationship.

Rather than asking *why*, three other strategies are more productive:

1. Use One-liners.

These are brief messages, delivered with empathy rather than anger or sarcasm, which prevent negative interactions. One-liners focus the problem or issue on the child and remove the parent from a winless power struggle. See page 175 for examples of one-liners.

2. Guess or ask for help.

When your child responds with "I don't know" this closes the door to communication. Instead, saying, "Take your best guess or ask me for help," leads to better results. If your child takes a guess, he is using his brain to problem solve. If he asks for help, he is reaching out, a sign of reciprocity and trust. Either response is preferable to a frustrating power struggle.

3. Go in the back door.

Direct questions rarely get direct answers. Children often perceive inquiries as confrontational, intimidating, and invasive. Changing the context is helpful. You can get a wealth of information during easygoing and enjoyable moments. For instance, your child may spontaneously share more while playing a game or sport with you.

- *Leave the past behind*—Prior hurtful behaviors and offenses should be left in the past. Holding on to previous deeds keeps the past alive and prevents wounds from healing. If consequences were given at the time of the infraction, then the debt has been paid and it is best to forgive and move on. If there were not appropriate consequences, then you must take responsibility for this oversight. Holding onto old resentments in order to be a martyr or to continue to make the child pay will backfire.

- *Be clear and specific*—When listening to someone who talks in circles, it is difficult to keep focused. For children who already have difficulty paying attention, vague and indirect communication is a disaster. They require clear and consistent messages in order to correctly process details. Additionally, wounded children typically misinterpret information. Because they take things the wrong way, it is even more important to be clear and concise. It is often helpful to have your child repeat what you have just said. This is a good way to see if she got it right and to "lock it in."

Nonverbal Messages are Powerful

Your style of communication with your child is crucial. Often *how* you say something is more important than *what* you are saying. Body language tells us more about what someone is really feeling than their words. Nonverbal messages include facial expressions, eye contact, tone of voice, gestures, and body posture. Be aware of the following nonverbal communication tips when delivering your message.

Use a calm tone.

Speak firmly, but in a tranquil and nonthreatening way. Your tone of voice down-regulates your child, reducing physical and emotional arousal and stress.

Make eye contact.

The eyes are "the windows to the soul." Eye contact is a primary trigger of attachment for newborns and parents, and continues to be a vehicle for emotional intimacy throughout life. When your child looks into your eyes you gain her attention and achieve a connection of your minds and emotions.

Use gentle touch.

Gently touching your child's arm or shoulder can be soothing, reassuring, and loving. If your child is *tactilely defensive* (does not like to be touched), introduce touch slowly and respectfully. Be especially careful if your child has had "bad touch," a history of physical or sexual abuse. With time, patience, and dialogue, your child will feel more comfortable with hugs and "healthy touch."

Be aware of body position.

Get down to your child's level: face-to-face, eye-to-eye. This is less intimidating than standing over her. *Your goal is connection, not control.* You want your body position to convey safety, empathy, and connection.

Content and Process

Communication involves both content and process. The content is *what* is being said (words and subject), while the process is how the communication occurs (message sent back and forth). The true meaning of relationships is found in the process, not the content. For example, Mom was having a talk with her 10-year-old son, Josh, about not doing his chores. Josh was silent and would not look at her. The content is the topic (not doing chores); the process is how they were interacting—Mom speaking and Josh avoiding. A *content-to-process shift* is most helpful at a time like this (Fanning & McKay 2000). Mom might say, "I see I'm doing all the talking, and you are being very quiet." Mom merely comments on what she notices—the process. This gives Josh a nonthreatening invitation; he may say, "I know I'm quiet, because I'm afraid I'll get into trouble."

A content-to-process shift is especially useful when escalating into anger. Comment on what is going on between you and your child in a calm way so your message is not perceived as a threat or attack: "I see we are getting upset; this is a real touchy issue." A process comment is more likely to facilitate communication than remaining focused on the content alone.

Resource Model

Rather than lecturing or criticizing, a *resource model of communication* is more constructive when problems arise. This is used when a child needs to go to the think-it-over spot in order to reflect on his choices and actions. After several minutes, you ask your child to answer the following questions:

- Why did you go to the think-it-over spot?
- What were you thinking and feeling at the time?

- How did you handle yourself?

- What were the results of your choices and actions?

- How can you handle the situation differently next time to get a better result? What did you learn?

This method of communication guides your child to think, reflect, and come up with solutions. It also avoids power struggles because you are not telling her what to do. It sends the message, "You are smart, capable, and I know you will figure this out."

Home-School Connection

The single most important influence on a child's development is the family. The second most important is the school. Children whose parents are involved with their school in positive ways have both academic and emotional advantages: higher test scores, better self-esteem and attitudes towards school, improved attendance, and less behavior problems. There is a positive two-way effect: parents implement teacher recommendations at home, and teachers feel more positive toward children in school (McAuliffe 2002, Christenson & Sheridan 2001).

One of the most common complaints we hear from parents is a lack of cooperation and communication with the school. The parents and school personnel are not on the same page. Teachers, counselors, and principals, although well-meaning, do not always have an understanding of these children and the nature of their problems. Consequently, children can play one against the other—turn the school and parents against one another. For example, a child may do well in school even though he or she acts out at home. Teachers and others in the school may assume the child is okay, and it is the parents who have a problem.

> *Gina's foster mom informed the principal not to give her candy as a reward because Gina was on a special diet and rewards are not appropriate for negative behaviors (lying and stealing). The principal used candy as a reward for all children in the school and thought the foster mom was being too hard on Gina. The relationship between the parents and the school became strained to the point that the principal reported the parents to Social Services incorrectly for assuming neglect.*

Children with compromised attachment often direct their pain and anger toward women, due to the loss of the primary attachment figure (birth mother). The majority of young children in school have female teachers, and they commonly project their negative feelings and expectations on their teachers. Research shows babies who are insecurely attached are more likely to be oppositional, aggressive, impulsive, and have more conflicts with peers, during their school years. These children can be hard to control in the classroom and on the playground, placing an enormous burden on the school system's resources.

The best scenario is when the school system, parents, and child welfare professionals are on the same page about developing a unified, realistic, and therapeutic plan of action for the benefit of the child. Children are most likely to learn and grow when the adults in their lives have relationships that involve trust, communication, and respect, and are working towards common goals.

Schools are generally well-equipped to teach the "average" child. However, children with histories of trauma and compromised attachment have special challenges, needs, and difficulties in school. They are commonly behind academically, have social problems with children and teachers, and exhibit behavior patterns that are barriers to learning. The following tips will help you advocate for your child and enhance school success.

Be assertive.

Make sure the school understands your child's academic, social, and emotional challenges, and takes appropriate action. Do so without being aggressive, angry, and alienating school personnel.

Provide information.

Give the teacher enough information about your child's background so he or she understands the special needs and challenges. Regarding confidentiality, the details of past events are less important than how your child is affected.

Foster relationships.

Build a relationship with your child's teacher and do this soon, rather than wait until a problem or crisis occurs. Get to know school personnel (principal, special education, art, music, and gym teachers, librarian, cafeteria workers, bus driver). Volunteer to help; attend school meetings, especially the individualized education program (IEP) review.

Communicate regularly.

Talk frequently with your child's teacher about both positives and negatives; your child can bring home a daily journal where you and the teacher communicate about issues and progress. Discuss discipline with the teacher—consistent, firm, caring, and consequence-driven approaches work best.

Promote understanding.

Help the teacher understand that learning difficulties are associated with lack of stability and security—prior maltreatment, moves, losses, grief, and uncertainties about the future—not necessarily learning disabilities or lack of intelligence. Increase awareness about your child's school history; some children are stereotyped, and do not receive support and services because they are seen as transient. Your child may not be able to complete assignments, such as a family tree, due to lack of information about birth family.

Accentuate success.

Help the teacher encourage your child's success in areas of competence; for example, giving your child responsibility for feeding a classroom pet or handing-out supplies can provide positive attention and boost self-esteem.

Provide resources.

Share books, websites, educational opportunities and activities, and other resources to help the teacher and others learn about attachment, foster care, adoption, and related issues. You are the "quarterback" of the team; make sure your child receives the understanding, support, and services required for success.

Be respectful.

Teachers and other school personnel may feel challenged by a highly involved parent. Be respectful of the teacher's position, many responsibilities, and other children in the class with special needs. Help the teacher see you as a resource who offers to help, not someone who is demanding.

Know your role.

Leave the teaching and learning assignments to the teacher and child; you are an advocate for your child but not a "policewoman" regarding homework and grades. Provide a regular place and time for homework, and offer assistance when requested. The consequence for school-related problems (e.g., misbehavior in class, incomplete assignments) should be dealt with at school.

Individualized Education Program (IEP)

The *Individuals with Disabilities Education Act (IDEA)* states all children are entitled to free and appropriate public education. Therefore, schools must provide children with specially designed instruction to meet their specific needs and challenges. Federal law mandates any student needing special education receive an annual IEP. Every third year a triennial IEP is to be completed which is more comprehensive. The IEP meeting allows for communication between parents and school personnel, *equal partners* in making joint decisions regarding: 1) child's needs and goals; 2) services necessary to achieve goals; and 3) extent to which the child will be involved in the general curriculum, and participate in the regular classroom environment and district/statewide assessments.

The IEP must include the following (Meier 2003):

- *current performance*—present levels of educational performance; describe how the child's disability affects his or her involvement and progress;

- *annual goals*—academic, social, behavioral, physical, and occupational goals that can be reasonably accomplished in a year; include short-term objectives and must be measurable;

- *services*—describes special education and related services, such as counseling, assessment, medical, parent training, physical therapy, psychological, recreational, speech and language, and transportation;

- *participation*—statement regarding amount of time spent with nondisabled students in regular classroom and other activities; participation in, and modifications in administration of, district and statewide tests;

- *time frame*—states when the services will begin, how long they will last, and where and how often they will be provided;

- *transitional services*—starting at age 14, or younger if appropriate, child receives services and support necessary to reach postschool goals, and preparation to leave school; and

- *progress*—statement describing how progress will be measured, and how parents will be informed of that progress. (A source for information about IDEA and IEPs is the *National Information Center for Children and Youth with Disabilities* (NICHCY); www.nichcy.org)

When a child does not fit the criteria for a special education IEP, you might explore the option of services under Section 504 of the Rehabilitation Act of 1973. Eligibility for 504 includes mental or physical impairments, which impact the child's education. The school must evaluate the child and develop and implement the delivery of all needed services for the child.

School Violence

School violence has been increasing; the number of students victimized rose 25% from 1989 to 1995, and since then school violence has increased to a more dangerous and pandemic level (Osborne 2004). Early assessment is essential to preventing many cases of school violence. More than 20% of all students have been found to have diagnosable psychological disorders. The following are warning signs of potential violence (Clark 2002, Breunlin & Cimmarusti 2003):

- social withdrawal, especially if this is a behavior change;

- excessive feelings of rejection;

- increasingly upset about being teased or bullied;

- impulsive or chronic abuse or bullying of others;

- increase in drug and alcohol use;

- personality changes, such as mood swings, angry acting out, or isolating oneself;

- intolerance for differences regarding ethnic and racial background or sexual orientation;

- access to weapons;

- intense interest in violence, including video games, movies, and use of weapons;

- violent feelings expressed through drawing, writing, or fantasy; and

- extreme reactions of anger in response to seemingly minor situations.

Some form of social isolation—family, friends, school, and community—characterizes most cases of school violence. Youth who feel cared about and supported are less likely to act out. The following are conditions in school that prevent violence:

- *sense of belonging*—children participate in and feel like a valuable member of the community;

- *sense of accomplishment*—validate efforts, perseverance, values, and competencies in addition to academics;

- *role models*—a caring adult who each student can trust, turn to for advice, and feel connected to;

- *self-confidence*—encourage children to believe they can be successful and make a difference;

- *responsibility*—convey the message that students are responsible for their decisions; give each student a voice in the learning environment;

- *creativity*—encourage students to question, explore, and be inquisitive;

- *spirit of adventure*—let children know it is okay to try and fail, as well as to succeed; and

- *fun*—learning can be fun; provide interesting and exciting learning experiences.

Frequently Asked Questions

The questions which follow are commonly asked by parents participating in our seminars and therapy programs or contacting us through our website (www.attachmentexperts.com). The answers are based on research findings and clinical experience with children and families and provide practical application of the skills and solutions discussed in this chapter. Issues covered include: lying and dishonesty; food and eating; attachment disorders in biological families; public misbehavior (e.g., supermarket); lack of motivation; sibling conflicts; responding to a crying baby; holiday reactions; role of the father; daycare; media violence; residential treatment centers; and respite care.

Lying and Dishonesty

My child's lying is driving me crazy! We never know when he is telling the truth. What can we do?

All children lie occasionally, to be socially accepted or because they fear the consequences of telling the truth. Some children lie as a way of life. There are several reasons for chronic lying: it prevents closeness, inflates low self-esteem, creates an avenue for power and control, and maintains a habit.

Lying harms relationships. Parents who are lied to feel betrayed, angry, hurt, and disappointed. Many parents feel totally defiled by their child's lies. Wounded children believe closeness leads to pain and rejection and must be avoided. What better way to distance yourself from the possibility of intimacy than to push away the ones who love you?

Chronic liars do not feel good about themselves, and therefore try to boost their self-image by exaggerating their abilities and accomplishments. They also make up stories to gain sympathy or provoke an emotional reaction. They often lie for no apparent reason, even if the truth would serve them better. This provides a sense of excitement and a feeling of having the upper hand. They perceive others as pawns to be manipulated and receive satisfaction in the fact "I know the truth and you don't." Lying is easy when one lacks the morality necessary to feel bad about being deceptive or hurting someone else. Often there is no remorse about lying, only for getting caught.

Pathological liars are addicted to lying; it becomes habitual. Many of their social interactions revolve around lies rather than the truth. These children will often hold onto a lie, even in the face of overwhelming evidence to the contrary. Their deception is intentional and premeditated. Sometimes they may tease you with a little taste of the truth and then lie at strategic times when it serves them.

How do you figure out if your child is telling the truth? You don't! It is way too much work for the average parent to become a lie expert. This is where the "whose-problem-is-whose" rule comes into effect. If you make it your job to figure out the truth then it becomes your problem. If your child lies 6 times out of 10, and tells the truth 4 times, how do you know which one this is? Lying should be your child's problem, not yours. The natural consequence for someone who lies is that they are not believed, even if they are telling the truth. They don't get the privileges that go along with earned trust.

The first step in solving any problem is "owning" it. If your child doesn't feel the consequences of the problem, he will never take responsibility for solving it.

CHILD: I am telling you the truth! Why don't you believe me?

PARENT: Honey, who lies a lot?

CHILD: I do, but I'm not lying now.

PARENT: Well, if it turns out that you are telling the truth, I will be the first to apologize.

Lecturing or punishing will do nothing to stop constant lying. It's much more productive to diminish the advantages your child gets from lying—take away the payoffs. If you don't believe your child, and don't respond with anger and negativity, you will be in control in a positive way and gain your child's respect.

You can say to your child, "When you consistently tell the truth over time, I'll be sure to give you more chances to earn my trust." Even when trying, habitual liars will slip. Offer him a way out with the "Whoops Rule." You can encourage your child to say, "Whoops," as the lie leaves his lips. For example: "Whoops, that wasn't the truth; this is what really happened." Then you respond, "Thanks for catching yourself. Good job."

Food and Eating

My daughter eats very slowly. She picks at her food or refuses to eat at all. We are always waiting for her to finish. What can I do if she won't eat?

It is common for parents and children to have conflicts over food and eating. First, rule out true medical conditions (e.g., stomach disorders) or eating disorders (e.g., Anorexia, Bulimia). Many eating issues revolve around control battles. There is usually a misguided parent behind a child's appetite issues. You will not win a power struggle with your child about what and how to eat. She reads your message—"You are going to eat the way *I* want you to"—as an irresistible challenge. The payoff for your daughter is lots of attention and power. The more you yell, plead, threaten, or bribe the more she is in control. Also, refusing to eat your food is a way to reject nurturance and belonging.

Remember to analyze: "whose problem is whose." It's your child's business to concern herself with her eating, and it's your business to concern yourself with your eating. The more you make her eating your concern, the less she will make it hers. The quickest way to get your daughter to eat is to leave the issue alone. Remain friendly and loving. Let her see she is not able to get an emotional rise out of you. Let her eat at her own pace, but do not wait for her to finish. Go about your business.

Some parents report their children eat enormous portions; "I can't believe how much food can go into that little mouth. She eats more than my husband." Children who are maltreated early in life feel deprived, and their fear of "not getting enough" can manifest in gorging, hoarding, and stealing of food. They find solace in the food itself and not those providing it. Parents must not respond in ways that reinforce this behavior.

Attachment Disorders in Biological Families

Can a child develop an attachment disorder if she was not abused, neglected, or removed from her biological parents?

The most common factors, other than abuse and neglect, which place children at risk for developing attachment problems are: in utero insults, unresolved chronic pain, prematurity, and maternal illness, stress, or depression. Maternal physical or emotional illnesses, such as postpartum depression (PPD), impede the parents' ability to provide the triggers for attachment—comfort, touch, eye contact, smiles, protection, and need-fulfillment.

Besides the obvious detriments of alcohol, drug, and nicotine abuse, the mother's emotional state during pregnancy plays an important part in fetal development. There is a biochemical communication between mother and fetus through which the unborn baby feels what the mother feels. If she is stressed due to financial pressures, domestic violence, or family crises, the fetus responds in kind. After birth, these infants may become irritable, inconsolable, and colicky.

Infants are totally dependent on caregivers to meet their needs. An infant's cries signal distress, a plea for caregivers to eliminate the discomfort. If parents are successful in removing the pain, the child learns caregivers are responsive and trustworthy. But what if a child has chronic pain due to gastrointestinal problems, an inner ear infection, or other medical problems that cannot be "fixed" by parents? First, the infant will protest. Next the baby's cries take on a more disturbing quality as stress and frustration grows. Eventually, the baby feels despair, gives up, and stops relying on the parent to meet her needs.

In the past, babies born prematurely were physically and emotionally isolated. Living in an "isolette" or incubator significantly impedes parents' opportunities for interacting with their baby and providing crucial stimulation through rocking and caressing. Preterm infants don't sleep as well, are less alert and responsive at birth, and are more difficult to feed and soothe. Research has shown, however, preemies who are touched more gain weight faster, are more active and alert, and leave the hospital sooner than untouched babies (Field 1997).

Prematurity also affects the parents' state of mind. Psychologically, parents need the nine months of pregnancy to emotionally prepare for the task ahead. When this natural schedule is cut short parents often feel anxious and unprepared. Anxiety and a lack of confidence can partly account for why parents of premature babies tend to initiate less contact with their infants, smile, talk, and play with them less, and lean toward overprotection.

If a mother is seriously ill during her child's first two years of life, she will not be in a position to adequately meet her child's needs. Mental illness, alcohol-drug abuse, PPD, and high levels of stress hamper a parent's ability to provide the elements leading to secure attachment. It is estimated 10% to 12% of pregnant women suffer from chronic depression that can be directly transmitted to the fetus. Newborns of depressed mothers were found to be harder to comfort and had less developed motor skills (Field 1997).

Roughly 10% of pregnancies result in PPD, which can occur a few days or even months after delivery. At any given time, 400,000 women are experiencing postpartum depression in the United States. Women with a history of depression are at increased risk of relapse after delivery. As many as 60% of women with a history of bipolar disorder have postpartum depression (National Women's Health Information Center 2001). The symptoms of PPD include extreme exhaustion, feelings of inadequacy, excessive concern or disinterest in the baby, and fear of harming the baby or oneself. This results in diminished sensitivity and responsiveness to the infant's needs and a breakdown in the normal attachment cycle.

Public Misbehavior

Every time I take my son to the supermarket he misbehaves. He runs up and down the aisles, demands things, and won't listen. I feel so embarrassed. How can I control him?

While at the supermarket, a man passed a woman whose cart carried a four-year-old girl. He overheard the mother saying, "Take it easy, Emma. I won't be long. We only have two more things to buy."

A few minutes later, he passed the same woman and overheard her say, "It's okay, Emma. We're almost done. Nothing to get upset about. We'll be outside in no time at all."

At the checkout counter, the man said, "Excuse me. I'd like to compliment you on the way you kept little Emma calm." The woman looked puzzled for a moment, and then laughed. "You've got it all wrong. My daughter's name is Sarah. I'm Emma."

Going grocery shopping with a difficult child can be very challenging. He will misbehave if he thinks he's "got you." For example, if he senses you are uncomfortable calling attention to yourself in public, he will manipulate the situation to his advantage.

The key to success is to be proactive, not reactive. Ask yourself, "Does he consistently show the knowledge, skills, judgment, and self-control to behave in the market? If he doesn't, then taking him to the store is a setup for failure. Leave him with your partner, shop while he is at school, or get a babysitter. Although this might be inconvenient in the short-run, it will make life easier in the long-run.

Advertisers understand if you want to sell a product, you must catch the eye of the consumer. Keen marketing minds have created an environment in supermarkets aimed at seducing you into impulse buying. Companies compete for the best shelf space to grasp your attention. It's no accident candy, gum, and toys surround checkout lines. Supermarkets are highly stimulating environments, not the best place for a child who is easily overstimulated, demanding, and disobedient.

If you are going to give him another chance, be prepared and have a plan. Take him to the store when shopping isn't urgent. Use it as a practice run. Be very clear on your expectations for appropriate behavior, and tell your child those expectations prior to going. If he "acts up," give him a choice to change his behavior or receive a consequence. If the behavior continues, leave the store immediately. Stay calm and don't reprimand. Actions speak louder than words. Another option could be to have someone who can take him home prearranged to be in the parking lot. He will soon realize you mean business.

Lack of Motivation

We can't seem to get our son to care about anything. He is not interested in sports or other activities. He would stay in his room all the time if we let him. How can we motivate him?

Parents spend a great deal of time and energy trying to figure out how to motivate their children. They use the carrot and stick approach. When the carrot doesn't work, they get out the stick. Parental influence based on lectures, demands, punishment, or incentives can be deceiving. Your child may appear to be doing better, but problems occur when the outside motivator is removed. You cannot change your child's mind through external motivation. All outside motivation is temporary. You cannot be with your child forever; he eventually will go off on his own. Your job as a parent is to prepare your child for the real world. If your child is not internally motivated, he is left no choice but to find another external motivator or flounder. If you control, enable, or rescue your child, don't expect him to be responsible as a young adult. Self-accountability is a skill that needs to be developed long before leaving home. This might explain why a disturbing number of college freshmen who go away to school don't make it past the first year. They do not possess the self-discipline and inner drive necessary to succeed independently.

You cannot motivate your child, but you can do the things that will improve his attitude and self-motivation. Permanent change requires a shift in attitude. The better your child's attitude, the more likely he is to succeed. Our attitudes are key ingredients in the overall quality of our lives. It's our attitude that motivates us to deal with challenges and accomplish goals. A child with a positive attitude motivates himself. You cannot help a child develop a positive attitude by using put-downs, criticism, and hostility. These only further reinforce his negative mindset.

If you want to change your child's attitude you must help him change how he views himself. Each of us carries a mental image of ourselves defining who we are and what we can do. These core beliefs develop based on early experiences with attachment figures. Our actions, feelings, and abilities are consistent with our self-image. Wounded children have a very damaged sense of self-worth, often feeling worthless, unlovable, and inadequate. Their core underlying feelings are fear and powerlessness. A child who sees himself as a failure will find a way to fail. A child who sees himself as unlikable invites rejection and drives away the very approval he seeks, thus confirming his negative self-image.

Change the self-image and you change the behavior. The self-image is changed for better or worse through experiences. The best way to help your child to change a belief acquired through a life experience is to provide an alternative life experience. Children cannot be taught about love, empathy, and compassion; they must experience it. They can only become what they experience. They require relationships that promote self-worth and dignity, which enables them to reevaluate their beliefs and see themselves in a new light.

To be successful, motivation must come from within, not from the outside. We can only truly be motivated when we feel like we are in charge of our own lives. In learning any task, if the learner feels in control, a wider range of significant learning occurs. True leaders strengthen their followers. They set a positive example and empower those under them. Positive esteem can only be developed in a positive atmosphere, containing safety, trust, connection, and enthusiasm. Positive role models create a climate in which their children feel comfortable being themselves. Children can only change when they feel accepted for who they are. The better they feel about themselves, the more likely they are to do the things that are in their own and others' best interests.

Sibling Conflicts

My children are constantly bickering. It never ends. What can I do?

Sibling fighting is a common cause of parental annoyance and frustration. An enormous amount of time is spent refereeing fights and preaching the merits of getting along. Many parents believe it is their duty to settle disagreements and protect the innocent. Other parents believe it is best to stay out of sibling conflicts. The key is to know *when* to intervene and when *not to*.

Children need coaching in how to resolve conflicts in a healthy way. It is part of your job as a healing parent to model and teach your children communication and problem-solving skills. For example, help your children talk about angry feelings rather than acting out aggressively, and teach tolerance, cooperation, and compassion. However, the heat of the moment is not the ideal time to teach anything. It is best to discuss these things when they are calm and more receptive to learning. It is  not your job to settle disagreements for your children. Intervening might stop fighting temporarily, but it doesn't teach siblings how to resolve conflicts themselves. Give them the support, guidance, and skills, and the opportunity to implement those skills. Consider the following example:

CHILD ONE: Ouch! Mom, she pinched me.

PARENT: (*comes running*) Stop this fighting. You're driving me crazy!

CHILD TWO: She hit me.

CHILD ONE: Well, you cheated; it was my turn.

CHILD TWO: No, it wasn't.

CHILD ONE: It was my turn.

CHILD TWO: You're stupid.

CHILD ONE: Mom, help.

PARENT: Leave your sister alone. Go to your room. You have lost T.V. tonight!

There are always secondary gains when siblings engage in this kind of behavior. Sibling fighting is often for your benefit, to gain your attention. Mother had to stop what she was doing, engage with her children on their terms, and play the role of arbitrator. Her anger and frustration give the children inappropriate power and influence. They are working her like a puppet.

Another consequence of this type of parenting strategy is that it reinforces the roles of "good kid" and "bad kid" in the family. Siblings are very adept at setting each other up. Frequently, the person disciplined is not the one who started the fight. The innocent often use subtle provocations to instigate the conflict. Their yelling and screaming rarely is as bad as it sounds. Remember, the purpose is often to get you to react.

As long as there is a payoff children will continue doing what works. This is why nothing you do seems to end the fighting. If you want to stop the behavior, then you must stop making it appealing. Let's go back to the example. Instead of intervening in the fight, mom realizes the children's dispute is between them. She has made an assessment that no one is in danger of serious injury and says, "I'm sorry you guys are having a problem. I'm sure you will work it out."

The best way to stop sibling fighting is to stay out of it. When parents try to solve the conflict or separate the children, they are depriving them of a valuable opportunity to learn how to resolve conflict. Staying out of it puts the responsibility for solving the problem in the children's lap, where it belongs. Sibling relationships are where we develop skills in conflict management, cooperation, and fair play.

Although you don't want to separate them from each other, you might want to separate them from you. Most parents don't like listening to their children's yelling and screaming. Try "Kids, you're hassling my ears. Please take your disagreement somewhere else where I can't hear it. Feel free to come back when you are both smiling." You will be amazed how quickly they can settle their differences without an audience. This takes the fun out of it.

Abby and Tyler love to go at it every night at the dinner table. "Mom, Tyler's kicking my foot;" "No I'm not;" "Tyler, keep your feet to yourself!" Three minutes later, "Dad, Abby took my napkin." "How many times have I told you two, stop this constant fighting?" Now let's look at this situation another way. The parents decide to be proactive and say to the children before dinner; "You know how you guys are always fighting at the dinner table? Well, Mom and I don't want to get indigestion. So, if you fight at the table, you will be asked to leave the table." Later, when the fighting starts, the parents say, "You have a choice. You can continue to fight and both leave the table, or you can stop and everything will be fine." "We will stop." "Good choice." Two minutes later they start again. "O.K., dinner is over. You are both excused. I hope you make a better decision tomorrow night." Parents don't enter the conflict or choose sides, and they remain calm.

Here is another example. Jon, age 10, is often mean to his younger brother Zach, age 7. He trips him and teases him relentlessly. Zach is continually crying to mom to make Jon stop. "How many times have I told you to leave your brother alone? What's the matter with you?" Sometimes the parents' positive intent to protect the innocent sibling can reinforce his low self-esteem and "victim" mindset. The covert message is, "You are incapable of handling your problems, and I will have to do it for you." It also teaches the child to use helplessness to get others to solve his problems.

Instead of intervening for him, mom might say, "You know, Zach, when I was young, my brother was mean and I decided I wouldn't play with someone who didn't treat me well." "That's not a bad idea, Mom." Zach eventually told Jon he wouldn't play with him unless he was nice. Jon had no one else to play with and soon realized he had to treat his brother better. They both learned a powerful lesson about resolving conflicts in relationships.

At first, your children may not like it when you stay out of their quarrels. They might call you mean or question your love for them. Don't believe it. When left to their own devices, children can take care of themselves much better than you might think. You must know your children. It is your primary job to keep them safe. If a child cannot be trusted to be safe around siblings, then he needs close supervision. An unsafe child should lose the privilege of playing with other siblings until he can act appropriately. There are a small percentage of disturbed children who are a true safety risk for other children. These children may need more structure than a family can reasonably provide and might need a more restrictive environment.

Responding to a Crying Baby

Will I spoil my baby if I always pick her up when she cries? Some books say yes, others say no. I'm confused.

There are two schools of thought regarding how to meet a baby's needs. One is, "don't pick them up all the time; let them cry, or you will spoil them." The second belief is just the opposite, "meet the baby's needs on demand; they will trust you and become securely attached."

In the 1920s, child psychologists warned parents against picking up a crying baby, because the baby would become a demanding and needy child. "Never hug and kiss them; never let them sit on your lap. If you must, kiss them on the forehead or shake their hands," advised behaviorist John Watson in his book on child rearing (Watson 1928). In the 1950s, the pendulum swung the other way. John Bowlby pioneered more "child friendly" ideas. He believed the mother's sensitive and timely responsiveness to the infant's needs was crucial for healthy child development (Bowlby 1988). This has caused a great deal of confusion and misunderstanding as parents try to figure out what to do. Different generations give different advice.

Human infants are the most helpless mammals on earth. A baby's only means of getting his needs met is to signal distress and hope assistance comes. An infant's survival is totally dependent on a responsive caregiver who is attentive to his signals.

Attachment during the first year of life is all about need fulfillment. When you pick up and soothe a crying baby you are opening the window for attachment to occur. When a baby communicates her needs and they are met in a sensitive and timely way, the infant learns several important lessons that can last a lifetime: "I have some influence on my environment; caregivers are reliable and dependable; I am secure and trust that my needs are valid and deserving of being met."

An infant's first attempt to signal caregivers is a cry designed to elicit empathy and a nurturing response. However, if his signals go unanswered, the infant will become irritated and his cries have a more piercing and grating quality. Caregivers who respond promptly and consistently to their infants have babies who cry less in frequency and intensity as they grow older. They also develop frustration tolerance and patience, knowing relief is coming. Infants who do not receive timely responses to their cries may learn not to trust that their needs will be met. They do not see their world as a safe and responsive place. These babies often become more demanding, impatient, needy, and clingy. They can't wait for what they want, fearing it will never come.

After an infant becomes secure in the knowledge her needs will be met some adjustments can be made. After 4 to 6 months of age responses can be less immediate because she has learned to trust. Instead of rushing right over, you can say, "I'm right here, honey. I'll be there in a minute." This will satisfy her for a few minutes. She is learning that waiting is okay; "I will get what I need soon."

During the second year of life the child is interested in exploring the world, and she begins to experience independence and autonomy. This is a time when she will test boundaries and must have appropriate limits. Fully meeting an infant's needs is good for her and good for the parent-child relationship. However, fully meeting the wants and demands of a toddler is not good for anyone. This often results in a demanding and over-indulged toddler.

Holiday Reactions

My adopted child goes "wild" on holidays. Why does he blow it every year?

There are several reasons why wounded children can't handle birthdays and holidays. First, children with compromised attachment are often poorly regulated—impulsive and hyperactive. They simply can't handle the excitement. The more gifts, activities, and guests there are, the greater the stimulation and the greater the overload. Also, the typical birthday fare usually includes large quantities of sugar, cake, ice cream, and soda, which fuel the fire for the children.

Secondly, these children have poor self-esteem. They don't feel like they deserve positive attention. They might unconsciously misbehave to get the party taken away. Canceling the party also relieves the anxiety produced by anticipation; they don't like surprises and change. Third, holidays can trigger a grief reaction. Memories and emotions from the past can bring on sadness, loss, anger, and shame.

Christmas, in particular, is a holiday where problems can be predicted for many of the same reasons. Parents are usually stressed during the holidays. Add to this an

overaroused child and it is not a pretty picture. Children might also behave poorly to distance themselves from family holiday rituals; "I'm not going to be part of this celebration because I'm not part of the family."

Have you noticed your child will go into a "tailspin" at certain times of the year for no apparent reason? This can be an anniversary reaction to some event that has occurred in the past. It may correspond to the time he was relinquished, abused, or experienced some other traumatic event. A song, a particular smell, or a feeling can also trigger memories. If you can get access to case records, it might be helpful to see if there are any correlations between past events and your child's reactions.

For birthdays and holidays in general, it is best to keep gifts to a minimum. Tell friends and family to tone it down. If you have to, dole gifts out over an extended time. The celebration should be simple and low key. Base what you do on what your child can handle. Create a family tradition that is appropriate for your child's emotional needs.

Role of the Father

How important is the father's role as an attachment figure?

For most of our history infants had to remain close to their mothers because of the necessity of breast feeding. The father's primary role was as a provider and protector. Mothers are biologically, emotionally, and socially programmed to bond. They have the hardware for the role of primary attachment figure, including hormones that promote caregiving and attachment. Women are more sensitive to auditory cues—keen hearing to pick up her child's signals—and more sensitive to smell, helpful in being alert to infant distress.

In the past, fathers were not very involved with their children in their early years. More recently, however, fathers have become significant childcare providers and more actively involved in family life. Fathers are attachment figures, socialization agents, and playmates/companions of their children. The shift in fathers' roles began around the time when more women entered the workforce. The percentage of women working outside the home doubled between 1948 and 2001—from less than 33% to more than 60% (Stambor 2005).

Fathers' affection and family involvement help promote their children's social and emotional development. Many experts believe the influence of "father's love" on children is as great as the influence of a mother's love. Babies who have positively involved fathers score better on infant development scales. Children with warm and loving fathers are less likely to develop behavioral or substance abuse problems and become more empathic adults. Fathers provide role models for their sons as to how to be a man and invaluable models to daughters regarding a relationship to males. Fathers provide an important template for meaningful relationships throughout a child's life. Involved fathers are emotionally engaged and physically accessible, behave responsibly toward their child, provide material support to sustain the child's needs, and have influence in child rearing decisions (Pruett 2000).

One of the important ways a father supports his child's development is through play. Young children who are played with regularly by their fathers do better with peer and other relationships and develop more self-confidence. Rough play is not as beneficial, as it leads to more aggressive peer relationships. The amount of time spent is not as important as the quality and the father's sensitivity (Grossman et al. 2002).

A father's importance to his family goes way beyond the father-child relationship. He shares the burden of caregiving, supplies emotional and financial support for the mother, and helps to buffer the child from the mother's "orbit" in order to facilitate healthy autonomy. The father's role is important even before birth; a husband's support during pregnancy reduces the likelihood of complications. His positive presence also quickens the duration of delivery. The more the father is involved during the pregnancy and delivery, and the sooner he holds his infant, the more likely he is to continue a positive involvement (Lamb 2002).

We have seen the damage done to children when they are raised without their fathers. The percentage of children living in fatherless families in the United States continues to grow: 30% of European American, 46% of Hispanic, and 70% of African American children live without their biological fathers. One half of these children either never sees their fathers or sees them less than once per month (Lamb 1997, 2002).

In the court system, judges are not always aware of the important role fathers play in their children's lives. Studies show children whose fathers are more involved with them after divorce do better socially, behaviorally, and academically than those whose fathers are less involved. Children in joint-custody settings have fewer emotional and behavioral problems, higher self-esteem, better family relationships, and do better in school than children living only with their mothers (Stambor 2005).

One of the most important things a father can do to promote attachment is to support his spouse. This is particularly crucial when coparenting a child with attachment issues. Fathers need to realize the maternal figure typically becomes the target for the child's unresolved hurt and pain. Fathers are usually not present when most of the poor behavior occurs. The child turns the smiles and charm on when Dad comes home.

Since he is usually around less, and is not a primary target, his relationship with the child is often easier and less conflictual. Dad doesn't see the problems with the child but does see an exhausted, frustrated, and angry Mom. It's easy for an unaware father to blame mother for the child's problems, further alienating and frustrating her. This is very damaging to the marriage and the parent-child relationship. Parents need to be a "united front" in order to facilitate their child's attachment and healing.

Daycare

How will daycare affect my baby's attachment? How long should I wait before I go back to work? What should I look for in quality daycare?

Since the 1970s, there has been a dramatic increase in the number of infants and toddlers who are in substitute care for 35 or more hours per week. Economic and social factors have made childcare a necessity for most families with children. More than 50% of preschoolers in the United States are being raised for a significant part of the day in childcare facilities, provider homes, and at home with babysitters (Levy & Orans 1998).

The National Institute for Child Health and Human Development conducted the longest running study on childcare. The data showed 4 and a half-year-olds who spent more than 30 hours per week in group childcare had better reading and math skills, but were more demanding, aggressive, and noncompliant than other children. A follow-up study found these same children, now in third grade, continued to score higher in math and reading. Their aggressive behavior had subsided; however, they still had poorer work habits and social skills. Researchers also found the earlier a child enters daycare, the slower the pace of social development. However, the negative effects of childcare were much less significant compared to the damaging effects of insensitive or unresponsive parenting (Lewin 2005).

If your young child must be placed in substitute care, it is important to find the best care available—do your homework. There is a vast consensus among childcare researchers and providers about what quality care is: it is warm and supportive relationships with adults in a safe, clean, structured, and stimulating environment where early education and trusting relationships combine to support a child's physical, social, emotional, and intellectual development.

When seeking daycare, consider the qualifications of the provider. Not just their knowledge, training, and experience, but also their emotional availability and maturity. Assess their ability to provide comfort, nurturance, stimulation, and social interaction. It is also important for providers to be good communicators. Are they interested in hearing about your child and are they willing to keep you informed on how she is doing? Good quality childcare is rich in patterns and routines that support children's cognitive and social development. Routines enhance emotional security and the learning of self-control, and these benefits are transferred to the home.

Consider how many children are in care. For children under the age of three, the preferred provider-to-child ratio is one-to-four, with a maximum group size of eight. Infants and toddlers do best with one consistent, responsive, and loving caregiver. Find a warm and reliable provider to stay with your child. In group facilities, a primary caregiver should be assigned to your child, and this person should remain the same over time.

Media Violence

How should I control and limit the amount of time my child watches television? Does violence in the media really affect children's behavior?

There have been decades of anecdotal evidence and scientific research on the harmful effects to children of TV, movie, and video game violence. The last 40 years of research has shown there are four main effects of viewing media violence: *aggression, desensitization, fear,* and *negative messages* (Murray 2000).

The average American child spends three to five hours per day watching TV; 1,500 hours a year in front of the TV compared to only 900 hours a year in school.

Children's TV shows contain about 25 violent acts per hour; they see about 10,000 violent acts per year. The average child sees 8,000 murders by the end of elementary school and 200,000 acts of violence by age 18. More than 60% of TV programs contain violence; 75% of violent scenes show no punishment for or condemnation of violence. To make matters worse, at-risk children tend to watch more TV than average, and watch more violent shows (Levy & Orlans 1999, 2000a; National Institute of Mental Health 1982).

The first research linking media violence with childhood aggression was by psychologist Albert Bandura in 1961. Bandura suggested children learn through modeling—imitating the actions of others, especially adults. His experiments involved children watching a movie of adults interacting with a large plastic doll that bounced back when hit or pushed. The children who watched the adults being aggressive with the toy figure were more likely to be aggressive with other kids during playtime (Bandura 1961). Subsequent studies have found preschoolers who watch violent cartoons are more likely to hit playmates and disobey teachers, than children who view nonviolent shows. Children between the ages of 6 and 9 who watch a lot of media violence are more aggressive as teens and adults, including spouse abuse and criminal offenses. Men who were "heavy viewers" of TV violence as children were twice as likely to physically abuse their spouses, compared to those who watched less violence as children. The results were similar for women (Levy & Orlans 2000a).

Children who witness considerable media violence can become desensitized—less shocked by violence, less sensitive to the pain and suffering of others, and less likely to show empathy for victims of violence. Many of the popular video games, for example, can desensitize youngsters to violence. These violent video games are similar to modern military training techniques that desensitize soldiers to killing. Only about 20% of soldiers in World War II were able to actually shoot the enemy. During the Vietnam War 90% could shoot and kill with no hesitation. This change was a result of new training procedures; the soldiers would practice shooting human-shaped figures rather than bulls-eyes (Grossman & Siddle 1999). Lifelike video game violence desensitizes children in the same way, and leads to *automaticity*—the overlearning of a behavior to the point it becomes reflexive.

Fear is another result of media violence. Children and adults can become anxious and even traumatized by the violence they see on TV and in movies. One study found 95% of college students reported they were still quite frightened by a movie they saw in their youth. Remember *Jaws*—were you afraid to swim in the ocean after that movie? (Murray 2000) Using MRIs (Magnetic Resonance Imaging) for brain-mapping, we can determine which parts of the brain are activated during exposure to media violence. Studies have found when children, ages 8 to 13, view TV and video violence, the part of the brain activated (right posterior cingulated) is an area used for long-term memory of traumatic events. Just as in nightmares and flashbacks common in PTSD, these violent and fearful memories keep returning to guide or disrupt current behavior (Murray 2000).

Media violence gives children the message that aggression and violence are acceptable solutions to conflicts and problems. In many homes, especially at-risk families, children identify with TV, movie, and video game characters, and look to them as heroes, role models, and parent-figures. A three-year study sponsored by the American Academy of Pediatrics (1995) had alarming findings about how violence is portrayed: almost half of the violent scenes on TV involved attractive, hero-type characters worthy of emulation; 70% of these characters showed no remorse; 50% of the violent scenes showed victims without any pain; and 40% of all violence was combined with humor. The message is that violence is painless and a desirable problem-solving tool. Again, the negative effects of media violence are multiplied for children with frightening and traumatic backgrounds. Their anger, fear, and lack of self-control are easily triggered.

Telling children stories has been part of our heritage since time immortal. Storytelling is still the way primitive cultures pass on the history, traditions, and meaning of their culture. Children naturally love to listen, and are captivated by every word of a good story or fairytale. The story causes the child to turn inside and create mental pictures to correspond with the spoken words. This internal imaging stimulates the child's brain, and is the foundation for the development of *symbolic* thought (how we picture things) and *metaphoric* thought (transforming meaning from one object to another). Exposure to storytelling, reading materials, and conversations form the foundation for a young child's literacy.

Television presents both a verbal and visual image at the same time. Nothing is left to the imagination. The child is deprived of the self-generated imaging required by his developing brain. Without adequate stimulation, the brain does not make new connections (neural fields). To put it simply, watching television doesn't challenge the brain; it actually pacifies the brain and puts it to sleep. The child's television-induced stupor puts his brain on autopilot and impedes the development of imagination.

Unimaginative children are more prone to violence, partly because they have difficulty imagining creative alternatives to their problems.

The following are tips for parents to use when making entertainment choices for their children.

Monitor viewing.

Limit the amount of time children watch TV or other media, and limit the type of exposure.

Set Location.

TVs and computers should be in an area of the house in which parents can monitor and supervise; not in bedrooms.

Encourage reading.

Children watch less TV when they read more, and are more likely to watch educational programs.

Provide guidance.

Parents watch programs with children to foster communication, and reinforce positive messages while buffering negative messages.

Set age limits.

Do not allow children under age 2 to watch TV, as it may hamper language development and social interaction.

Limit commercials.

Use videos and public television to reduce exposure to commercials.

Residential Treatment Centers

When should I consider placing my child in a residential treatment center? What should I look for in such a facility?

Sometimes it is necessary and appropriate to place a child or youth in a residential treatment center (RTC) for a period of time (usually at least one year). This happens most frequently when the child is very angry, aggressive, defiant, and a danger to himself and others. Placing the child will hopefully provide the necessary structure and learning opportunities for the child, and also give the parents and siblings time to heal.

Choosing the right RTC is crucial. Most RTCs rely on behavior modification strategies to control children's behavior. Control-focused approaches do not typically produce long-term positive results with wounded children. Youth with compromised attachment do not trust adults, have no interest in pleasing them, and will reject their efforts. Control-oriented approaches instigate power struggles, and fail to help children develop a sense of personal responsibility for and control over their actions. In an adversarial climate, children feel rejected, victimized, and vulnerable.

In the last decade or so, RTCs have developed programs designed to *connect* with youth, not just contain and control their behavior. The focus is on the *primacy* of relationships—creating and maintaining healthy attachments. They understand the function of anger, aggression, and defiance in the mind of a child with attachment problems. They understand the child's *internal working model*; the core beliefs formed early in life, that cause the child to view adults as threatening and controlling. The therapeutic relationships are the vehicle for changing negative attitudes and beliefs. Thus, the RTC should emphasize one primary attachment relationship over time for the child.

The RTC should identify and accommodate to the unique needs of each child. A "cookie cutter" approach does not work, since attachment is formed based on meeting a child's true emotional needs. A family-focus is important. The RTC should have a *systems* approach; they understand children are part of social systems (family, school, peers, and extended kin). Everyone should be on the same page to help the child and family. Thus, family therapy and parent training are crucial. The child is changing and the family is also changing.

It is important that if you place your child in an RTC you view this as an opportunity for everyone to grow. This is not the end of the road, not a failure on your part. Rather, with time and learning, you can prepare yourself for your child's return, and your child will hopefully develop social skills, connections, and maturity.

Respite Care

I need some time off, but I'm afraid my child will see respite as abandonment. What should I do?

Respite care is temporary relief for primary caregivers to reduce stress, support family stability, prevent destructive interactions, and minimize the need for out-of-home placements. For many parents of children with special needs, however, getting some time off seems like an impossibility.

Depending on where you live, the quality and availability of respite varies widely in type, cost, staffing, and ease of access. It is clear there is a crucial need for good respite services. Research has shown without family support, children with special needs are four times more likely to be victims of abuse and neglect, and parents are much more likely to become burned-out (Green 2002). Respite can prevent you from having severe stress, reduce the damaging effects of anger and demoralization, and give you and your child a necessary time-out.

Here are a few suggestions regarding respite care. Seek respite if you are feeling chronically angry or frightened with your child. Try to find respite *before* you are at the end of your rope, so you can make the best choice and prevent burnout. Respite should support family relationships, not undermine them. Make sure the respite providers maintain the same type of rules, structure, and communication that you have in your home, and that respite is a "learning place," not just a fun place.

It is important that you, as well as the respite provider, send the message that respite is for support and learning, not punishment or rejection. Your child is likely to interpret this as abandonment, but with clear communication you can help your child have a more positive viewpoint. Consistency and predictability are vital, so use the same reliable respite providers over time. Your child will benefit from the consistency and from the ongoing supportive relationships.

Summary

- The skills, strategies, and solutions of *Corrective Attachment Parenting* (CAP) include: healing attitude; constructive limits, choices, and consequences; competency-based parenting; serve as a secure base; avoid negative emotional reactions; change child's core beliefs; stay calm; engage positively; be proactive; enhance sense of belonging; and communicate for attachment.

- Guidelines for providing structure: balance love and limits; based on developmental and emotional needs; is clear, consistent, and realistic.

- Structure provided is based on four competencies: knowledge, skills, self-control, and judgment.

- Hold the bar high. Expect your child to be responsible, respectful, resourceful, and reciprocal.

- Children learn by making choices and facing the consequences. Make sure the choices are acceptable, it is a win-win, and you stay calm.

- The goal for giving a consequence is to teach a lesson. The goal of punishment is to inflict pain and get revenge. Punishment is damaging and does not facilitate secure attachment.

- You are being a *secure base* when you are emotionally available, sensitive, responsive, and helpful.

- Healing parents *look in the mirror,* being aware of mindset, self-talk, emotional reactions, attachment history, body signals, and coping strategies.

- Look beyond behavior to understand your child's core beliefs. Help your child *anticipate something new.*

- Change the pattern; new relationship experiences lead to new expectations and behavior. *Change the dance, change the outcome.*

- Three steps to staying calm: stop, tune-in, and respond constructively. *Your goal is connection, not control.*

- Engage positively via praise, humor, play, and having effective anger-management and problem-solving skills.

- Build a sense of belonging via routines, rituals, respecting your child's background, discouraging isolation, focusing on the positive, taking pleasure in her accomplishments, and having fun together.

- Communication is the key to secure attachment. Healing parents know: the cues of attachment, listening and sharing skills (Attachment Communication Training), overt and covert messages, thinking versus fighting words, resource questions, and an effective verbal and nonverbal communication style.

7

Attachment and the Adoptive Family

Sixty percent of Americans have had personal experiences with adoption. There are 2.1 million adopted children now living in the United States, comprising 2.5% of all children. About 127,000 adoptions take place in the United States every year: 87% of adoptees are born in the United States; 39% are adopted from public child welfare agencies; 46% are private and kinship adoptions; 13% are foreign adoptions. Since the Adoption and Safe Families Act in 1997, with the goal of promoting permanency for children, adoptions from the foster care system increased 78%. There were 50,000 of these adoptions in 2000. Foreign adoptions have tripled in the last decade; 15% of all adopted children are foreign-born, most coming from orphanages and institutions. Korea is now the largest source for international adoptions, accounting for 24% in 2004 (National Adoption Information Clearinghouse 2005; U.S. Census Bureau 2004).

There is a long-standing discussion among mental health professionals as to whether children of adoption have more psychological problems than nonadopted children. Many adopted children, particularly when placed in infancy, develop secure attachments and lead healthy and productive lives (Schaffer & Lindstrom 1989). Many others, however, do not fare as well. Although research results vary, studies have found adoptees have higher rates of academic deficiencies, behavior problems, delinquency, substance abuse, and running away from home (Brodzinsky 1993, Brodzinsky et al. 1998; Feigelman 2000). While only 2% of the children in the United States are adopted, they comprise 33% of the population in residential treatment centers (Jones 1997). Adoptees were found to have more problems when coresiding with the biological children of their adoptive parents (Feigleman 2000). This is because adopted children are vulnerable to diminished self-esteem. They often feel stigmatized by society and insecure about their parent's love, compared to their siblings; "Am I worthy of your loyalty and love as much as your biological children?"

The impact of adoption is lifelong. Adoption issues are significant for both a child and adult in every stage of social and emotional development. As a healing parent you need to be aware of the challenges and tasks required to meet the needs of your child. Years ago parents typically did not talk with their children about adoption; they worried it would be emotionally damaging and lacked information and guidance. Most adoption experts now advise parents to discuss adoption early, between 3 and 4 years of age. Young children need to have an *adoption story,* which provides a sense of meaning and answers the question, "Why was I adopted?" This helps to normalize adoption, enhance a positive self-image, and sets the stage for confiding and communicating with parents.

As children enter the latency stage, at around 7 years of age, their cognitive abilities and awareness expand. Their perspective about adoption changes and they begin to ask questions; "Why did my birth mother give me up?" "Was I bad and it was my fault?" "Do I have brothers and sisters, and where are they?" Children are now trying to understand and deal with the losses inherent in adoption, including the loss of birth parents and family, cultural and racial background, and other prior connections. These losses can cause grief reactions resulting in anger, depression, and emotional withdrawal. Healing parents help their children acknowledge and talk about their intense emotions regarding loss and grief. Answer you child's questions in an honest, sensitive, and age-appropriate way. This is an opportunity for communication and building trust, cornerstones of secure attachment. Sometimes parents' own insecurities prevent open communication; "Do your questions mean you are unhappy with our family, and I'm not a good parent?" Guidance from a mental health professional who specializes in adoption issues may be helpful at these times to prevent conflict and enhance communication (American Academy of Pediatrics 1999; Brodzinsky & Schecter 1990).

A key task of adolescence is the formation of identity. This is particularly challenging for adopted teenagers who must deal with their sense of identity regarding both birth families and adoptive families. The normal process of individuation (i.e., emotionally separating from parents) becomes complicated and can trigger feelings of loss, abandonment, and anxiety; "Who am I, and can I make it in the world?"

Adoption Trends

Increasingly, there are changes in adoption occurring which influence how families are formed and how they function. These changes in adoptive families play an important role in redefining the American family. A generation ago, adoption typically involved a white, two-parent, heterosexual, married couple adopting a white infant. Now there is much more diversity.

The typical American nuclear family consisting of a mother, father, and biological children is a thing of the past. Today, more than 64% of families are considered nontraditional. Over the past decade there has been a steady increase in unmarried couples, single parent, gay-lesbian, stepfamily, transracial, and kinship care households raising children. We are adopting children that don't look like their parents in race and ethnicity, forcing us to redefine the way we view the family. Family life is no longer characterized by stability but by diversity and change. There is no such thing as a perfect family, and there is no one right way to raise a child. The thing that children crave most is a stable family environment, and this can be accomplished in a wide variety of family structures.

International and transracial adoptions are creating more multicultural families and communities. The number of transracial adoptions has doubled in the last decade. Now 17% of adopted children are of a different race than their parents, and 13% of all adopted children are foreign-born. An increasing number of adopted children are being raised in gay and lesbian families. More single mothers and fathers are adoptive parents, a result of the decrease in the social stigma of single parenthood. Kinship adoptions, formal and informal adoption by relatives, have increased significantly to 42%. The practice of open adoptions, where there is some type of contact with birth families, has gained popularity. Adoptive and birth parents have many options to choose from on the open-closed continuum. Couples are forming blended families, parenting children by birth and by adoption. Many parents with biological children who want to expand their families are adopting, often through the foster care system (U.S. Census Bureau 2004; Riley & Singer 2003).

Another trend is toward the *deinstitutionalization* of adoption. Historically, there was an emphasis on institutions in the adoption process, from orphanages to adoption agencies. Currently, adoption methods have changed in ways that rely less on institutions. For example, the Internet has expanded opportunities for birth parents and prospective adoptive parents to select one another without a mediating agency, and then use private attorneys or agencies for the legal process only. The goal of deinstitutionalizing adoption is to have an adoption process that meets the needs of all involved (i.e., adoption triad members), rather than a bureaucratic and rigid approach to adoption as determined by agencies and institutions. This trend does present risks however, such as adoption disruption, and parents must use caution (Weir 2004).

International Adoption

The practice of international adoption began in the United States after World War II. Thousands of Japanese children were brought to this country as Americans responded to the plight of displaced families. After the Korean War, the adoption of foreign-born children became even more common. Americans adopt more children from abroad than the rest of the world combined. More than 40,000 children are adopted each year across national lines, coming mostly to the United States (23,000) and Western Europe (16,000). Korea is the largest source of adopted children (24%), followed by China (11%) and Russia (10%) (National Adoption Information Clearinghouse 2005).

More than two-thirds of children adopted in the United States from overseas have spent all or part of their lives in orphanages. They often suffered neglect, abuse, malnutrition, and inadequate medical care before and after birth. The lack of nurturing and stimulation often leads to behavioral, emotional, and attachment problems after adoption. One study found children raised in Romanian orphanages and later adopted by families in the United Kingdom have substantially more cognitive deficits and attachment problems than children adopted from the United Kingdom (O'Connor et al. 1999).

The care children receive varies. In South Korea the adoption process is quick, well-organized, does not require parents to travel, and birth mothers often provide a family history. China is one of the most stable countries regarding foreign adoption. They match prospective adoptive parents with children through a centrally run orphanage system. Strict population laws make thousands of healthy infants (mostly girls) available. Children from Russia tend to have more medical problems and in utero alcohol exposure, and it is often impossible to get information about family history.

There are a number of reasons parents adopt from overseas. Some people seek foreign adoption to avoid the legal and emotional conflicts that may arise if the child's birth parents fight to reclaim custody. Parents adopt from abroad because the process of adopting foreign children is usually much faster than in the United States. There is often less scrutiny; foreign adoption requirements regarding age, marital status, and sexual orientation are more lax. Finally, the availability of white infants for adoption in the United States has declined due to an increased acceptance of single parenthood and reliable birth control practices. Many parents turn to Eastern Europe for adoption of white babies and children.

The loss of the birth culture is an issue to be addressed. Some adoptive parents expose their children to the birth culture by sending them to language classes and culture camps or making sure they have contact with other internationally adopted children. They may also make a conscious effort to talk with children about discrimination and racism to encourage effective coping skills (Chamberlin 2005). Some children reject their birth culture to deny emotions or fit in.

Transracial Adoption

Transracial adoption involves placing children of one race or ethnicity with adoptive parents of another race or ethnic group. In 1993, 8% of adoptions were transracial.

Currently, 36% of children adopted from foster care are placed in transracial families (Bartlett 2004). Many overseas adoptions are also transracial. The vast majority of transracial adoptions in this country involve white parents adopting black children. Historically, agencies tried to place African American children with African American families. African American and interracial families adopt at a higher rate than any other group in the population. However, due to the high numbers of African American children in need of homes, the minority community has been stretched to its limits. There are a disproportionate number of black children in out-of-home care. Although they represent approximately 15% of the nation's children, they represent 47% of the children waiting to be adopted. Black children are removed from their homes at a higher rate and also remain in out-of-home care for longer periods than white children. The number of black children awaiting adoption continues to climb, greatly outpacing the number of available same-race adoptive homes.

The issue of transracial adoption has generated a great deal of controversy. In the early 1970s, the National Association of Black Social Workers took a strong position against transracial adoption. They still argue that these children are vulnerable to developing poor self-esteem, weakened racial identity, and the lack of coping skills for living in a racist society. Advocates of transracial adoption site numerous long-term studies indicating adoptees in transracial families do as well as those in same-race families. Transracial adoption was not found to be detrimental to adoptees in terms of emotional adjustment, self-esteem, racial identity, academic achievement, peer relationships, and adult or parental relationships (Silverman 1993, Sharma et al. 1996, Brodzinsky et al. 1998, Feigelman 2000, Burrow & Finley 2004). Transracial adoptees adjust as successfully as their interracially-placed counterparts, and racial differences between parents and adoptees were not found to harm the normal development of children.

Transracial adoption challenges our beliefs about race, family, and the nature of love. In a perfect world, same-race placements may seem ideal. Considering the reality of so many children waiting to be adopted, however, the goal should be to serve the best interests of children. A belief in adoption as a "colorblind" process allows more children to enjoy the benefits of family life without race being a sole or major factor for consideration (Bartlett 2004).

Kinship Adoption

Kinship care occurs when grandparents, aunts and uncles, siblings, or other extended family take responsibility for raising a child in the absence of the birth parents. Informal kinship adoptions are not formalized legally. It is most often the maternal grandmother who takes over the care. Many families have a strong tradition of intergenerational caregiving and see no need to formalize the adoption. They may also feel that formalizing would be an act of betrayal to the birth parents and are thinking it may be temporary. Relatives usually pursue legal custody to attain rights, financial assistance, or medical care for the child.

Almost 50% of all adoptions each year are by relatives. There are advantages and disadvantages to kinship adoption. Benefits for children include greater placement stability, closer connection with immediate family members, increased likelihood of being placed with siblings, and less difficult identity issues and chance of maltreatment. Further, children often remain tied to their cultures and communities, and kin typically feel a strong commitment to the child and to encouraging the child's relationship with the birth family. There may be an opportunity to have contact with birth parents that may assume a role in the child's life even though they lack the ability to parent the child full-time.

Kinship care also has drawbacks. These children are less likely to be reunified with their birth parents, are usually in care longer before reunification occurs, are less likely to be adopted, and are less likely to receive mental health and medical services. Also, there are concerns about the ability of relatives, especially grandparents, to set appropriate boundaries with birth parents and to adequately protect children. Despite these concerns, the preference for children to be placed with relatives is now federal policy. Studies show adoptions by kin have more positive outcomes than other adoption types (Howard & Smith 2003, Dubowitz et al. 1993).

Gay and Lesbian Adoption

An increasing number of adopted children are being raised in gay and lesbian households. The most recent data available reveal that nearly 600,000 same-sex couples live in the United States, almost equally divided between male couples and female couples; and 25% of these couple are raising children (U.S. Census Bureau 2003). Many of these couples are raising children from prior heterosexual relationships. Surrogacy and donor insemination are also increasingly used as a route to parenting.

Until recently, adoption was not an option for gay and lesbian singles and couples, but that has been changing. There are 23 states in which homosexuals have successfully adopted, and 60% of adoption agencies now accept applications from these prospective parents. Public agencies, as well as those trying to place special needs children, are most willing to consider gay and lesbian parents. The challenges of finding homes for hard to place children have forced agencies to broaden their pool of parents to include those that were previously excluded (Weir 2004).

The issue of same-sex parenting has escalated into a national debate, with mental health and adoption professionals, sociologists, politicians, religious leaders, and talk-show hosts all giving opinions about what makes a good parent. The social conservatives believe creating motherless or fatherless families is not in a child's best interest. They are concerned about children seeing an "abnormal" sexual relationship as normal and believe there is a homosexual agenda to win acceptance in society. Proponents of same-sex parenting believe family-building should not be a political issue, and that because we have so many children waiting for adoption, we should welcome and support all qualified people who have a loving heart and the ability to provide a safe and caring home for a child. The American Academy of Pediatrics, often conservative in its policies, endorsed same-sex parenting, concluding that children's optimal development is influenced more by the nature of the relationships within the family than by the particular structural form it takes (Dingfelder 2005).

Three decades of research has shown children of gay or lesbian parents are as successful and healthy as their peers. Studies have found no difference between children of same-sex and heterosexual families in cognitive development, academic performance, self-esteem, social and psychological adjustment, family functioning, behavior problems, or sexual orientation (Kreisher 2002, Gartrell et al. 2005, Erich et al. 2005). Good parenting, not a parent's sexual orientation, leads to mentally healthy children, the studies have found. Children who reported secure and loving relationships with their parents were the most emotionally healthy and did the best in school (Wainright et al. 2004).

Children of same-sex parents commonly are targeted for homophobic teasing, discrimination, and stigmatization from other children, which can result in psychological distress. Sensitive parents help their children deal with their feelings through open and supportive communication. Support is also available in the form of gay parents' groups that provide parenting tips, information, and referral services. National groups, such as Children of Lesbians and Gays Everywhere (COLAGE) and Parents, Families, and Friends of Lesbians and Gays (PFLAG) support parents and children.

Single-Parent Adoption

Sixty percent of children in the United States will spend some time in a single parent family. The number of single parent homes has doubled in the last 25 years. Births to unmarried mothers account for 30% of all births, and single fathers raising children is on the rise. As the social stigma of single parenthood has decreased in our society, more single parents are raising adopted children (U.S. Census Bureau 2004).

Single parents are often under stress trying to handle the responsibilities traditionally taken care of by two parents. The median income for single mothers is an average 33% that of the income for a married couple with children. Single parents are also at an emotional disadvantage, as the stress of dealing with a challenging child alone can be overwhelming. There is no one else to offer a hand or an ear. Working single parents must use childcare for their younger children. Often childcare does not go well for these children. The quality of childcare is a significant contributor to a child's emotional, social, and intellectual development.

Many single parents try their best to be both father and mother to their children. Unfortunately, this can only go so far. Psychologically, children need both parents. Mothers and fathers give children a reference point to define their gender identities. When a same-sex parent is not available, the influence of substitute same-sex role models becomes important. Although single parent families face many challenges, it is the quality of the relationship with your child that really matters. Good parenting can compensate for a great deal of stress and hardship. It is important that single parents take good care of themselves to avoid burnout. Having a reliable support system offering encouragement and support is crucial.

Open Adoption

Another change is related to the secrecy that characterized adoption in the past. Due to changes in policies in many states, adoptions tend to be much more open than in past years when records were sealed and adopted children and adults had no access to their personal histories. Increasing numbers of families are arranging *open adoptions* in which some type of contact occurs between members of the birth family and the adoptive family. In one California study, 60% of adoptive parents met birth parents prior to the adoption. Many families continue contact for years, including letters, photos, phone calls, and personal contact (Riley & Singer 2003).

The goals of open adoption are to minimize loss, maintain attachments, enhance identity, and reduce loyalty conflicts. Many experts believe it is beneficial to connect children to their birth family to reduce their sense of loss and acknowledge their birth family as an important part of their identity. In addition, ongoing contact may help the child to understand why she was adopted and accept the reality that the birth parents could not meet her needs (Silverstein & Roszia 1999). A 20-year study found higher degrees of collaboration and communication between a child's adoptive parents and birth mothers resulted in better adjustment in the children as they grew older (Grotevant & McRoy 1998).

Most of the practice of open adoption focuses on non-special-needs adoption of infants. When children come to adoption as a result of maltreatment and disrupted attachment, open adoption is not typically recommended due to the possibility of additional harm that may occur to the child and adoptive family.

Blended Adoptive Family

A blended or stepfamily is created by remarriage, when either one or both spouses bring at least one child from a previous marriage or relationship. Stepfamilies are the fastest growing family structure due to high divorce and remarriage rates. Almost 60% of marriages end in divorce, 75% of divorces include children, and most adults remarry. One of two Americans is a member of a blended family, and stepfamilies are predicted to be the predominant family structure in the United States by 2010 (Berger 1998; Visher & Visher 1996).

Parents are forming blended families with both biological and adoptive children. Couples with biological children may choose to foster or adopt a child, also forming a blended family. When parents are mature, equipped with effective parenting skills, and sensitive to their children's unique needs, these families can function well. Due to the stresses and complications of blended families, however, problems are common. Blended families commonly have a complex structure, vague boundaries, and unclear roles. They include children with multiple parental figures and loyalties. Ambiguous boundaries are a major issue. For example, it is impossible to create a boundary around the marriage when a child plays one parent against the other (*triangulation*) or one parent has no authority over the child. Wounded children are often resentful toward and jealous of siblings who are biological offspring. Seeing the bonds of trust and love between parents and their birth children can be painful for an adoptive child who is unable to achieve close and secure attachments.

Blended families are at risk for stress, instability, and conflict. Having the right knowledge and skills, however, can make all the difference. The following tips will help reduce common conflicts:

Discuss, plan, and agree.

Agree in advance about each parent's role, rules of the home, and methods of discipline.

Have a strong marital bond.

Place a priority on your marriage. Have quality time together, and operate as a team.

Be consistent.

Parents must agree on the rules, acceptable behavior, and consequences of behavior that is not acceptable. Maintain a consistent and predictable environment.

Support one another.

Avoid giving in, allowing manipulation, or undermining the other parent. No taking sides or disagreeing in front of the children.

No "badmouthing."

Do not speak against a child's prior attachment figures. This can damage a child's self-esteem, place the child in a position of defending a parent, and is destructive to family relationships.

Adopting the Wounded Child

Children adopted from the foster care system or foreign orphanages have often experienced abuse, neglect, multiple moves and caregivers, and disrupted attachment. They enter their adoptive families having serious problems with self-control, accepting rules and limits, caring about others, and forming trusting and loving relationships. Traits and symptoms commonly displayed include: anger, aggression, oppositional behavior, controlling nature, manipulative, selfishness, lying, stealing, depression, and lack of remorse.

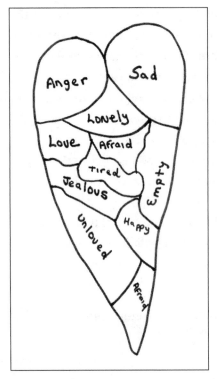

What's in my heart?

There are five *key factors* that influence an adopted child's emotional development and attachment to the adoptive family:

1. Prenatal experience.

Lack of proper prenatal care, poor diet and nutrition, severe maternal stress, and exposure to drugs and alcohol affect the fetus as well as a child's long-term development. Attachment begins during pregnancy; mother and father convey their love and connection to their unborn baby with gentle touch and soothing tones (Brazelton & Cramer 1990). Mothers who want their babies and express positive feelings have easier pregnancies and healthier infants than those with unwanted pregnancies (Verny & Kelly 1981).

2. Age and stage at placement.

Children adopted at older ages, compared with those placed at birth or in early infancy, have more difficulties adjusting and developing secure attachments to their adoptive parents and families. As the placement age increases so does the risk for psychological, behavioral, and educational problems (Brodzinsky & Schecter 1990). Sixty-six percent of babies adopted from Romanian orphanages at 4 months old developed secure attachments to their adoptive parents, while only 37% were securely attached when in the orphanage for 8 months (Chisholm 1998). Infants placed in foster homes after 12 months of age were more likely to have insecure attachments than those placed earlier (Stovall & Dozier 2000). Each developmental stage presents unique needs and challenges. Children do best when parents understand and respond appropriately to those needs.

3. History of maltreatment.

Abuse and neglect causes emotional and neurobiological damage that results in a myriad of problems over the course of a child's life. Children adopted from foster care have commonly experienced years of maltreatment, multiple placements, and unresolved losses. Children adopted from foreign orphanages have endured deprivation, lack of stimulation, many different caregivers, and the loss of families and cultures. Adoptive parents are generally unable to get full disclosure about their child's history.

4. Prior attachments.

The quality of previous caregiving, the number of different caregivers, and the types of attachments formed influence a child's psychological and social development as well as attachment to adoptive parents. Children with insecure and disorganized-disoriented attachment patterns lack trust, are extremely defensive and controlling, and misinterpret parent's motives and behaviors. One primary key is place early and don't move; moves are traumatizing and increase the risk of compromised attachment. Attachment problems, including reactive attachment disorder, are the most common reasons for adoption disruption and dissolution (Riley & Singer 2003).

5. Postadoption parenting.

Parents who receive education, support, helpful resources, and effective family therapy are better able to cope with their personal, child, and family challenges. Healing parents acquire the knowledge, skills, and confidence to effectively deal with their children's problems and create secure attachments. As with any family of a child with special needs, this is a daunting task and taxes emotional and financial resources.

Negative Core Beliefs

Early experiences with caregivers shape the development of a child's *internal working models*—core beliefs about self, caregivers, and life in general. Adopted children who have experienced maltreatment and compromised attachment generally have negative core beliefs. Their view of themselves is: "I am bad, defective, and unlovable." They have cynical perceptions of caregivers; "Parents are rejecting, punitive, and untrustworthy."

Children with these negative mindsets regularly misinterpret parental efforts. Rather than seeing you as helpful, supportive, or trying to be instructive, your child views you as threatening, punitive, and controlling. She is likely to expect harsh and insensitive treatment from you, just as she received in the past. A vicious cycle occurs: the child projects her negative expectations on to the parent, and the parent unknowingly reinforces the child's negative beliefs. For example, your child may try to get you to reject or abuse him to confirm his core belief ("I'm not worth loving; you will abandon me too") by misbehaving. You might take the bait, becoming angry and withdrawing attention and love.

As a healing parent you must *respond rather than react;* maintain your composure, set limits, and provide appropriate consequences. You don't react by emotionally escalating or yielding to your child's demands. You realize that new relationship experiences will lead to positive changes in your child's core beliefs and subsequent behavior. Your relationship with your child is the key to healing. Your goal is connection, not control.

Loss and Grief

Are you there, Mother?

M other, are you gone forever to a land so bright and fair? While your children weep unstopping, can you hear us? Do you care? Do you hear us, Mother, do you hear us? I hope you do. Are you there, Mother, are you, are you? Please say you are, Mother, please say you are. We miss you so much, Mother. I hope it is not too long before we are with you again.

Children, adoptive parents, and birth parents—*the adoption triad*—commonly experience loss and grief. Children lost their genetic and birth bonds with biological parents. Genetic bonds involve common ancestry, shared genetic background, and inherited char-

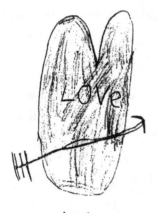

acteristics. Birth bonding is the primal emotional experience shared by mother and baby throughout pregnancy, as well as during and immediately after birth. Neglectful or abusive parenting does not diminish the profound sense of loss children feel when separated from birth mothers and fathers, a *primal wound* (Verrier 1994). The emotional and actual searching done by many adoptees—trying to connect with birth parents/family by actually looking for them, or by mentally and emotionally fixating on the loss, and trying to fill the emptiness—is driven by this loss (Brodzinsky & Schecter 1990). Adopted children experience additional losses: siblings and extended kin; culture, customs, language, and community; identity and self-worth ("Why did they give me up? Why was I not worth keeping?"); relationships with foster parents and families; and the losses due to prior failed adoptions.

Adoptive parents have their own losses to deal with. Many have chosen to adopt due to infertility, which can lead to feelings of inadequacy, marital stress, and the loss of a wished-for biological child. Some parents are still struggling with their own unresolved childhood losses, triggered and magnified by their child's issues. There is often a feeling of loss because the fantasy of the child and family planned is very different from the reality—a child who pushes away your love and a family burdened with severe stress and conflict.

Tanya was abandoned immediately after birth and spent her first year of life in a Russian hospital. She was then moved to an orphanage where she remained until age 2 and a half. The caregivers were all female; she never even saw a man. The orphanage was crowded and had very few caregivers.

Wendy and James desperately wanted children, but Wendy had four miscarriages and was told she could never have a biological child. She felt enormous grief over this loss. They decided to adopt; "If we can't have our own child, we will save a child who has no one." Wendy imagined a loving relationship and a wonderful family life with the girl they would adopt.

Then reality happened. Tanya was screaming and kicking as they were taking her out of the orphanage; she was terrified of these strangers taking her away and tried to run to the nurse she considered her "mom." They had to medicate her on the airplane to keep her calm. She continued to scream, kick, and bite for the next year, while the parents consulted with one doctor after another to find a solution to this puzzling and painful situation. Wendy was devastated, vacillating between severe depression and intense anger. James felt sorry for the little girl and was caught in the middle between his wife and child.

Birth parents experience the loss of their biological child and the pain associated with relinquishment or removal by social services. Some birth parents do not feel much or anything at all due to substance abuse, mental illness, or never wanting the child in the first place. Many birth parents have suffered maltreatment, unresolved losses, and severe attachment disorders in their own childhoods, resulting in their inability to care for their offspring.

Grief is a natural reaction to loss. A child's adaptation to her adoptive family is influenced by the nature of prior attachments and her reaction to separation and loss. Unresolved loss and grief block the development of secure attachment with adoptive parents.

Children go through three stages when separated from an attachment figure: *protest, despair,* and *detachment.* Protest, including intense crying and other expressions of dissatisfaction, occurs initially when basic needs go unmet. Children who feel despair are depressed but still yearning for their loved one and have not yet given up. Detached children, however, have emotionally "shut down," having lost all hope for a safe and secure caregiver. These children have not grieved their losses, and when placed in adoptive families, will not emotionally connect. Their ability to trust has been damaged, and they are afraid to love, anticipating more abandonment or abuse. Fear and a deep-seated need for attachment are concealed under a veil of angry, defensive, and controlling behavior.

There are a number of common emotional reactions children have to loss including anxiety, anger, sadness, depression, and mood swings. Other reactions include denial, shock, numbness, confusion, irritability, nightmares, changes in eating and sleeping patterns, fear of being alone, and physical ailments (e.g., headaches, stomach aches, and fatigue). Some children have difficulty concentrating, school problems, loss of interest in activities, hyperactivity, guilt over failing to prevent the loss, and regressive behaviors (e.g., bedwetting, thumb-sucking, baby talk).

Loss is always stressful and difficult, and it is normal for children to have sad, angry, and painful reactions. Helping children cope with loss is an important job for healing parents. You are coaching them through the trauma and teaching crucial life skills. You can't take away the loss, but you can listen, affirm, and support. Remember, the human psyche has tremendous capacity for recovery and growth. Below are parenting tips to help your children cope with loss and grief.

Be patient and listen.

Children need time to grieve. Don't push them to talk, but let them know you're available to listen when they are ready.

Encourage communication.

Help them talk about all feelings. Validate emotions as normal, and offer support and reassurance.

Use appropriate honesty.

Answer questions about loss honestly and simply (e.g., avoid expressions such as "went to sleep," when referring to death, which may be confusing). Offer only details they can handle.

Understand physical and repetitive behaviors.

Emotions are often expressed through children's bodies, play, and actions—their "language of grief." It can take a long time to recover, and emotions may revisit in cycles over many years. Reminders, such as the anniversary of a loss, can trigger grief.

Think preventively.

Anxiety and fear are normal when security is threatened. Dealing with loss-related feelings will prevent later emotional problems.

Be a good role model.

What ideas and skills do you have about dealing with loss? What are you teaching your child by example? Parents must demonstrate healthy coping skills and communication.

Offer healing opportunities.

Time doesn't heal wounds; wounds heal over time as a result of our actions. Offer options to express grief (plant a tree, pray, look at photos, draw pictures, share feelings).

Grieve as part of a family.

Beyond the loss of a person, children have feelings about the changed behavior and environment of family and friends. Routines and consistency are important to reduce insecurity. Children must feel safe to express emotions without fear of judgment or criticism.

Loyalty Conflicts

Adopted children have connections to at least two families—one by biology and the other by day-to-day interaction and parenting. Children struggle with confusing and conflicting loyalties that can prevent secure attachments from developing with adoptive parents. Many adoptees have not come to terms with the loss of their birth parents, foster parents, or other caregivers, and their devotion to those prior attachment figures often remains. They frequently idealize abusive and neglectful birth parents, placing them on a pedestal, and fantasizing about a "happy-ever-after" reunion. They often blame their adoptive parents for taking them away from birth parents, remaining angry and distant.

The triangle of child, birth parents, and adoptive parents seems like an insurmountable problem for some parents. It is important to know why children feel disloyal to birth parents if they become close with their adoptive parents. First, as previously stated, it is very difficult to grieve the loss of birth mother, and remaining loyal is a way of dealing with and denying that pain. Second, children were often in the role of *parental child,* responsible for taking care of their birth mothers or siblings. Maintaining loyalty is their way of keeping those bonds alive. Lastly, children fantasize about *fixing* their birth parents, thereby reducing their shame and creating a positive sense of self: "I am now worthwhile and loveable."

Adoptive parents often feel confused and threatened by their child's desire to maintain ties with prior attachment figures. The following tips for parents will help you deal constructively with loyalty conflicts.

Understand your child's struggle.

Healing parents understand and accept the place of birth parents and other prior caregivers in their children's emotional life. Help your child acknowledge and normalize his thoughts and feelings, and talk about missing, yearning, anger, sadness, and other emotions relating to loss. Children need help in accepting reality and placing responsibility where it belongs: "It was not my fault; my birth parents hurt me, and they are responsible."

Be aware of your messages.

Direct or indirect messages that it is wrong to maintain prior loyalties will backfire. Your child will feel misunderstood, become defensive, and pull away even more. Patience, empathy, and support create a healing environment in which your child can resolve feelings of loss and conflicted loyalties.

Know when contact is appropriate.

There are times when ongoing contact with birth parents and relatives (e.g., grandparents) is beneficial. This occurs when birth parents and extended kin are emotionally mature enough to support the child's current attachments with the adoptive family. These ties, when appropriate and supervised if necessary, can reduce the child's emotional conflict, enhance self-identity, and enrich relationships in the adoptive family. Conversely, there are times when ongoing contact with prior attachment figures is harmful and ill-advised. Birth parents and relatives who are not emotionally healthy will typically reinforce loyalty conflicts and destructive ways of relating, thereby sabotaging the child's current attachments. Although some birth parents improve following the loss of their children, many do not. Foster and adoptive parents commonly report it is not beneficial for their children to maintain contact. Many children are angry, defiant, and depressed following visitation and it may take a long time for them to settle down. Children must be protected from damaging influences and adult conflicts and rivalries, such as legal battles (e.g., custody, visitation, termination of parental rights) and emotional battles. In many cases termination of contact is in the best interests of the child.

Parenting Your Adopted Child

Parenting your adopted child requires an understanding of the emotional issues and family dynamics, as well as having constructive skills and strategies. Described next are three primary areas to focus on, with examples of children's typical behavior and constructive parental responses (see Weitzman & Avni-Singer 2005; Dozier et al. 2002a).

1. When children push away your love and support.

Rather than show their need for love, support, and guidance, wounded children tend to alienate parents, sending the message, "I don't need you, go away." Securely attached children have received sensitive and responsive care and expect more of the same in the future. They trust caregivers and can display their emotional needs, especially when feeling most vulnerable. Many children adopted from orphanages and foster care are fearful of caregivers, due to abuse, neglect, and multiple disruptions. They protect themselves from anticipated hurt and disappointment by hiding their needs, not allowing vulnerability or connection. They turn against parents with anger and aggression, turn away by rejecting their parent's attempts to provide love and support, or turn inward by being clingy and enmeshed.

Parents make a common mistake. When their child acts as if she doesn't need them, they respond in-kind by pulling away or getting angry. This only reinforces their child's negative mindset and feelings about caregivers. As a healing parent you *look beyond behavior,* realizing your child does need your love and support but is afraid to let you know. Instead of taking it personally, you understand that the antagonistic behaviors you see reflect your child's negative core beliefs—lack of trust in and fear of caregivers. You challenge those beliefs and expectations by being proactive not reactive, firm yet nurturing. Over time your child will learn to view you and himself in new and positive ways, and develop a more open and trusting relationship.

2. When children need help coping with emotion and stress.

A primary function of secure attachment is to help infants and young children manage stress and develop self-control. The absence of a dependable and sensitive caregiver leaves children alone to deal with stress, which becomes unmanageable and overwhelming. Lacking a safe and supportive caregiver, children do not develop the ability to regulate their impulses, emotions, and distress. Their brains and bodies are flooded with stress hormones that increase anxiety and hyperactivity. They have temper tantrums and meltdowns when faced with even minimal challenges and pressure.

Healing parents provide a calm, consistent, and predictable environment in order to increase security and decrease stress. Understanding your child's emotional and physical needs, and meeting those needs in a sensitive and consistent way, helps your child feel safe and secure. Remaining calm and not escalating sends the message that you are safe to rely on and trust. Your confident and composed demeanor soothes your child's nervous system. Your ability to exercise self-control and effective anger management provide a model of constructive coping skills. With time your child learns to trust, internalizes your positive messages, and develops self-control.

3. When you become emotionally triggered.

Parenting is a challenging job. Parenting children with histories of maltreatment, unresolved loss, and compromised attachment is considerably more difficult. Many adoptive parents are dealing with their own loss and grief regarding infertility, failed pregnancies, and the pain of not having the child and family they imagined. Parents also frequently have emotional baggage from their childhoods, unresolved losses and attachment wounds that affect their attitudes and behavior. It is common to have strong negative emotional reactions, including anger, fear, and hopelessness, as parents try to cope with their challenging children.

Healing parents look in the mirror—are aware of their sensitivities, old patterns of thinking and relating, and current emotional "buttons." Parents who are mindful and have healthy relationships in their lives (e.g., marriage, friendships, extended family) are more likely to have children with secure attachments. By being self-aware you provide thoughtful and helpful responses, rather than impulsive, knee-jerk emotional reactions. You find a way to offer the nurturance, compassion, and limits your child really needs. You are in control of the emotional climate of your relationship with your child.

The Adoptive Family System

As we have been emphasizing throughout this book, it is crucial for the parent to *look in the mirror*—to know oneself. In this regard, there are a number of issues to focus on: parent's history prior to adoption; reasons for adoption; how prepared parents are; and the expectations, hopes, and dreams for their children.

In Chapter 4, *Know Yourself*, we explained why it is so important for parents to understand their attachment history, parenting concepts and attitudes, and current emotional and relationship life. Parents who are able to reflect on their own emotions and family backgrounds are more likely to have children with secure attachments. The question to ask is: "What was my life like before adoption, and what emotions, mindset, and patterns of relating do I bring into my current situation?"

There are three primary reasons why people adopt. The first is due to infertility. More than 5 million couples in the United States are affected by infertility (Bain 2004). After years of frustration many couples turn to adoption. It is essential that the couple deal with the emotional issues regarding their inability to conceive. They must grieve the loss of the dream of bearing their own offspring before adopting; otherwise the unresolved loss can negatively influence their parenting. Parents who do not have biological children are often not able to determine what "normal" behavior is. If their adopted child exhibits behaviors indicating emotional and attachment problems, inexperienced parents may not recognize those "red flag" behaviors or know how to respond. This can lead to a feeling of personal fault or inadequacy; "I must be doing something wrong."

Expanding the family is another reason for adoption. Some parents believe by adopting they are helping a child as well as expanding and enriching their family. Perhaps they had girls and want a boy, or visa versa. Some couples had biological children and then encountered medical difficulties that made another pregnancy impossible. Others adopted because of infertility and later were able to conceive. Families with a mix of biological and adopted children have their own unique challenges. Sibling conflicts, jealousies, attention-seeking behavior, fairness issues, and resentments are often magnified.

Sometimes mature couples or individuals have completed raising biological children and want to do a good thing for a child in need. These "second-time-arounders" are frequently at the tail end of, or have completed their careers, and have the time and financial resources to adopt. They often have plenty of parenting experience, but not necessarily with a wounded child having special needs. As a healing parent it is vitally important to be aware of your motivation to adopt, how your decision was made, and the extent to which loss and grief was involved in that decision.

Adoptive parents are generally well-meaning, hoping to provide a loving home for a child in need. Unfortunately, they are often unprepared to deal with their child's enormous emotional and behavioral problems. Parents regularly tell us that prior to adoption they were not informed about the nature and severity of their child's problems, not educated about the possible consequences of maltreatment and compromised attachment, and not given appropriate parenting training. Following adoption, they report there was a lack of support, parenting information and skills training, or effective therapeutic services for their child and family. Over time these parents experience severe stress and typically feel helpless and hopeless.

Traumatized Adoptive Family

In our therapy program for adoptive families, as well as in seminars with numerous parents, we have seen the devastating effects of family stress and conflict. The environment of the *traumatized adoptive family* is characterized by the following (Levy & Orlans 2000b):

- *Emotional climate*—There is much anger, frustration, and despair. Wounded children compulsively repeat negative behaviors and patterns of relating learned in their past.

Parents feel rejected, unappreciated, and inadequate, and become angry and punitive or depressed and withdrawn. Parents with their own unresolved attachment issues become even more emotionally reactive. Many parents and siblings develop *secondary traumatic stress disorder* (STSD), the symptoms that result from years of conflict and tension (e.g., depression, anxiety, medical illnesses). The result is emotional exhaustion and family burnout—the breakdown of family members' ability to work together toward common goals (Figley 1998).

- *Isolation and lack of support*—Parents commonly feel alone, misunderstood, and blamed for the child's problems. They feel unsupported by extended kin, school, and the mental health and child welfare systems. For example, grandparents may not understand the child's problems and blame the parents, thereby undermining their authority. Parents often report they cannot turn to adoption agencies or social services for help following adoption. Parents feel isolated and alone at a time when they have a huge need for support, understanding, and practical help.

- *Control battles*—Wounded children sought power and control to survive under harsh conditions. They bring this need to control people and situations into their adoptive families, resulting in ongoing power struggles and control battles with their parents. Parents are extremely frustrated and angry because they are not able to get their child to listen and follow the rules. Healing parents understand how to effectively deal with children who believe their survival depends on coercion, manipulation, and control.

- *Triangulation*—Wounded children are adept at "playing one against the other," a common form of manipulation. The child may be hostile and defiant with mom but charming and cooperative with dad when he comes home. A child may be oppositional at home but compliant at school. While it is true children act differently in various settings, this change in attitude and behavior is frequently a way to maintain control and avoid closeness. It is crucial that the adults in the child's life, such as parents, teachers, relatives, and counselors, are on the same page so that triangulation does not occur.

- *Marital conflict*—Couples are challenged by the demands and stress of dealing with wounded children. When the child plays mom against dad it is particularly important to remain united as a team. Couples who have marital problems prior to adoption are at risk for severe conflict due to the added stress. Healing parents know the importance of good communication, effective problem-solving skills, teamwork, and maintaining affection and emotional closeness in their marriages.

- *Sibling relationships*—Sibling conflicts are magnified and a constant source of irritation and frustration for parents. Wounded children are generally abusive, manipulative, jealous, and resentful toward siblings, especially if these are biological offspring. They resent the loving connection between parents and their biological children and believe they are not capable of such an attachment ("I'm not good enough to love"). Siblings are often neglected because the parents devote most of their time and energy to the "problem child." An emotional conflict occurs; siblings resent the other child and their parents, but feel guilty because they also want to be helpful and supportive. Family life frequently becomes restricted. For example, siblings may stop inviting friends to their home, fearing conflict and embarrassment. Family activities are curtailed, as they no longer are able to enjoy time as a family.

Adopting Siblings

Sibling relationships can last a lifetime, even more enduring than parent-child or marital relationships. Sibling relationships have a significant influence on children's emotional and social development. Lessons about sharing, compromising, conflict-resolution, competition, and empathy are generally learned with siblings.

Adopting a sibling group is a controversial subject, with arguments on both sides of the issue. For example, the general rule in child welfare is that, whenever possible, siblings should be placed together. The belief is the familiarity of the sibling relationship increases a sense of permanency, helps children cope with loss, and reduces stress, and separating siblings leads to further traumatization (Schooler 1997). This is true under certain circumstances, including with children who have secure attachments.

A number of studies have identified circumstances when sibling placements are problematic. Serious emotional and behavioral problems were more common for children adopted from Romanian orphanages when two or more children were adopted simultaneously (Ames 1997). Several studies found sibling placements were more likely to result in adoption disruption than single-child placements (Barth 2000, Rosenthal 1993). Adoptive parents report adopting a sibling group is one of the risk factors that lead to disruption (Howard & Smith 2003). Our own research on treatment effectiveness found children improved more when they were not adopted as a sibling group.

There are four factors to consider when determining whether or not a sibling group placement is appropriate.

1. Severity of emotional, behavioral, and attachment problems.

Parents reported significant stress related to their adoptee's mood, level of demanding behavior, unwillingness to adapt, and lack of compliance to parental authority. Traits identified as particularly stressful were lying, stealing, verbal and physical aggression, tantrums, and hyperactivity (Groze 1996). These are traits and symptoms common among children with compromised attachments. Sibling groups that display these symptoms are emotionally and financially taxing and increase the risk of negative outcomes for these families.

2. Pathology of the sibling relationship.

Siblings with pathological patterns of relating (e.g., physical and sexual abuse) bring these unhealthy behaviors into the adoptive family. This is extremely disturbing and overwhelming for the family and prevents the development of secure attachment with the parents. It is common for one member of the sibling group to perform a parenting role with younger siblings. Sibling loyalties can create an "us against you" mentality and block new family relationships from forming. Separation of siblings is usually warranted when there is a history of sexual abuse. Even the most diligent parents cannot watch their children 24/7, and the abused sibling is at risk for further victimization.

3. Strengths of the family.

A thorough assessment should be made of the parent's strengths, resources, and deficits, including: parent's attachment histories; quality of the marital relationship; family cohesion; parent's ability to manage stress and adversity; and support systems available. Do the parents have supportive friends and extended family? Do they have a faith to sustain them? What is the extent of their parenting knowledge and skills? How open are they to learn new and constructive skills?

4. Pre- and postadoption services.

Parents frequently do not receive sufficient information about the harm their children have suffered and how those problems will manifest in the adoptive family. Parents need to know what they are dealing with so that they can have realistic expectations and seek the right type of help. Families need ongoing support and counseling, especially in the first year following placement. What services are available to minimize stress, enhance parenting skills, promote family cohesion, and address the children's psychosocial problems?

An Adoption Story

Casey entered a foster home the day after her birth. One week later Bud and Grace Eden took her home. Grace was not able to have a biological child due to medical problems. As an infant Casey would not allow her adoptive parents to comfort her. Her mom reported, "She would cry for hours at a time and finally fall asleep in a sweaty heap in her crib. She would not let me cuddle her unless she was sick." As a preschooler she refused to follow rules and tested limits constantly. She was referred to as a "high energy" child. In first grade she was diagnosed with ADHD and took Ritalin with moderate results. During her elementary school years Casey was monitored very closely at home and at school. Her grades were fairly good and she excelled in athletics. The Edens assumed that she would outgrow her behavior problems.

In 7th grade Casey's oppositional and defiant behavior intensified. She became unruly at school, increased impulsive and daredevil behavior, and became more aggressive at home. The parenting techniques that worked with their older daughter, such as behavioral contracts and removal of privileges, were failing miserably with Casey. Mom reported, "Nothing we tried has ever worked." In 9th grade the Edens placed Casey in a residential treatment center (RTC) in an effort to "save her from herself." After completion of this program, Casey returned home where things improved for a while, but soon many of the same old problems returned. The Edens then boarded Casey at a private Christian high school. It did not take long for Casey to be asked to leave the school. The Edens then tried sending Casey to a close family friend who lived in a rural community.

After this failed, at age 15, she returned home and showed some improvement. She was home-schooled, taking medication, and developed a relationship with a "good kid." Casey seemed happier and more settled. Her behavior changed abruptly for the worse right after Christmas, when her boyfriend gave her a ring. She broke up with him and fled into the "wrong crowd," drug use, and extreme defiance. Casey was again returned to the RTC. Here is a poem Casey wrote at age 15:

I am the Red Hibiscus
Vibrant and Vivid
Outstanding
Proud
Distinguished
Like None Other

gloomy
the weeping willow am i
dreary
melancholy
ashamed
embarrassed
shy
detached
the weeping willow am i

I am the Great Ocean
Calm and Pleasant
Easy to Confide in
Listening
Understanding
Occasional Breaks
Yet Never a Falter

i am fire
eating
killing
stealing
blazing not caring
untrusted

The Birth Parents

Casey's birth mom was 17 years old when she gave birth to her. She was herself the product of an unwed mother, had a long history of substance abuse and volatile relationships, and was an admitted "party girl." She was described as pretty, intelligent, outgoing, impulsive, and artistic. She had a hot temper, was demanding, and could lash out if she didn't get her way. Less is known about Casey's birth father. He was a few years older than birth mom, good with mechanics, and worked as a handyman. He also was a "party person" but more passive, quiet, and serious.

Birth mom used alcohol and marijuana during the early part of her pregnancy but discontinued use when the pregnancy was confirmed. Casey was born full-term and healthy. Birth mom chose the family she wanted to adopt her child. She requested a stay-at-home mom and a family with strong moral values and religious beliefs. Birth mom did see Casey after delivery and was extremely saddened that she could not keep her.

The Adoptive Parents and Family

Grace and Bud met in grade school, began dating in high school, and after a brief split, reunited and were married 1 and a half years later. They have been married for 31 years. Grace is a stay-at-home mom and Bud is a successful businessman. They consider themselves to have a strong marriage, deep religious convictions, conservative views, and an active involvement in community and church. Besides Casey, they have another daughter, Christine, age 23, adopted at 18 days old. Christine recently graduated from college and married her high school sweetheart. She has always been a responsible, organized, and goal-directed child.

Grace described herself as artistic, neat, demanding of herself, organized, and a perfectionist. Orderliness is very important to Grace. Eldest daughter Christine is very similar to mom—serious, determined, and well organized. Casey, on the other hand, is far from organized. The parents reported, "She is never where she is supposed to be when she is supposed to be there. She loses everything (wallets, jewelry, books)." Mother and Casey have butted heads for years, neither able to back off from conflicts. Grace was engaging in constant power struggles over the smallest things and was anxious, angry, hurt, and helpless in the face of Casey's defiance.

Bud described himself as a peacemaker. He has high expectations of himself, tends to be philosophical, and considers himself sensitive, responsible, and a leader. He is often stunned by Casey's outright refusal to accept parental authority. The Edens were severely traumatized by the loss of the dream of what they thought these years would be.

The Family Dance

The parents were having a great deal of conflict over differences in their approach to Casey and her problems. This was creating alienation and frustration in their marriage.

Their parenting views were greatly influenced by the lessons they learned in their respective childhoods.

Grace grew up in a family where problems were not dealt with directly. The unspoken rule was, "If you ignore it, it will go away." Her father's philosophy was, "There is my way or the wrong way." Grace attempted to gain her father's approval by being compliant, responsible, and an overachiever. Her mother had fragile health, depression, and was passive as a wife and parent.

Bud's father was a successful businessman who was characterized as quiet, stern, and fun-loving. Bud could not remember anyone in his family dealing directly with conflicts. His mother was described as overindulgent; she died when he was 16. At the same time as his mother's death, his older brother initiated a nasty lawsuit against his father over the family business. This tore the family apart, and they never spoke again.

Neither Grace nor Bud was prepared to deal with Casey's challenges. They had never learned how to deal with relationship conflicts in their families-of-origin. Whenever Casey and Grace had a conflict, Bud would become extremely anxious and take his daughter's side against his wife in order to end the conflict. Bud learned while growing up that conflict and stress led to the death of his family. He was trying to save his family, but in actuality was destroying it. Grace never learned how to express her needs and adopted her mother's approach of internalizing her pain and becoming physically ill. Grace felt like a victim of her daughter and her husband. Casey was an expert at playing her parents against one another. She would stir the pot, then sit back and watch her parents argue, thus diverting attention from what she had done.

Steps to Healing

There were several things the Edens needed to change in order to increase Casey's opportunities for healing. Grace and Bud needed to be on the same page, operating as a united parental team. As long as Casey was able to triangulate her parents (work one against the other) she would never respect them or trust them to be safe authority figures. They must see the "same" child and respond to Casey with consistency. In order to accomplish these goals they had to become mindful of their emotional triggers from the past.

They also had to understand Casey on a deeper level; they had to *look beyond the behavior.* Grace and Bud understandably viewed Casey as rebellious, ungrateful, angry, and uncaring. The truth was she was a deeply wounded child who was pushing her parents away in an attempt to protect herself from anticipated hurt and rejection. The way you see a problem determines how you deal with it. The Edens needed to truly understand Casey and what made her "tick" which would enable them stop taking her behaviors personally. They needed to be educated in the special ways of parenting teens that have experienced attachment traumas. They had to stop using punitive and controlling parenting methods, which were undermining their ability to be positive influences for Casey. They had to adopt a new parenting structure based on mutual respect, clear expectations, and natural consequences. This approach must include a "buy in" for Casey, something that motivates her to participate. Described below is how the Eden's achieved these goals.

Attachment Communication Training

Attachment Communication Training (ACT; described on pages 101–104) was used with Bud and Grace. Information from their *Life Scripts* was incorporated into the ACT so that they could acknowledge and change patterns of relating. Open and honest communication allowed them to be aware of the contribution past patterns and beliefs have on their marital and parenting conflicts. At key points in the communication we (referred to as TL and MO in the following dialog) functioned as "alter egos," standing behind Bud or Grace to help clarify emotional messages and offer insights for discussion. To begin the session, Grace and Bud were asked to sit knee-to-knee, face-to-face, and follow the guidelines of effective communication. Grace appeared anxious and defensive. Bud was leaning backward, arms crossed, with a scowl on his face.

> BUD: I think I have helped you when you're struggling but I wish you would lighten up a little bit. But I know you can't because you're you. I guess I need to be more sensitive to things that are important to you that are not important to me. Your stress level affects Casey. That's my big concern. Your stress level brought on by what you think needs to get done looks to Casey like anger towards her.
>
> THERAPIST (TL): What do you hear Bud saying?
>
> GRACE: My stress, whether it's real or made up in my own mind, spills over into how I deal with everybody, especially Casey.
>
> TL: I think he is saying more than that.
>
> BUD: Exactly. It's so unfair. Casey is sensitive, and it frustrates me when there are times that I think you are not as sensitive.
>
> TL: I think what you are really saying to your wife is—if Casey has problems, it just might well be your fault. Your anxiety and your stress are going to create the very thing you fear most. Casey's problems are your fault and I'm going to blame you.
>
> BUD: I'm not going to say it, but that is just how I feel.
>
> THERAPIST (MO): You need to share with Bud your reaction to his message of blame. What do you think about it and how do you feel about it?
>
> GRACE: I resent feeling like it's all on me. I didn't cause Casey to make all her poor decisions. You've given me the message to lighten up, don't make Casey mad and everything will be fine; well, things are not fine. Your giving in to her hasn't helped the situation either. I feel like the biggest responsibility should be on Casey. I'm sensing from you that the greatest responsibility is mine, not hers.
>
> BUD: You're right. That is what I am thinking.

TL (*for GRACE*): "I'm sick and tired of this splitting. It's you and Casey against me. You're siding with her and I'm alone in left field. You tell me not to be nervous. I'm real nervous, because if something goes wrong, it will be in my lap."

BUD: We are at an impasse on this one. I feel helpless about what to do now. I can't solve it.

TL: Casey gets dragged into this impasse. It's not good for your marriage and it's not good for Casey. Especially at her age, it's not wise to give her the message that if there are problems it's Mom's fault.

MO (*for BUD*): "When you get all angry and stressed out, it really triggers my childhood and all those uncomfortable feelings. All I want to do is go away."

BUD: (Nods his head in agreement.) Yeah, it triggers all that strife. All that living that I had to do for years and years with turmoil. I saw it as unnecessary then and I saw the damage that it did. I want to stop the bleeding, because I'm still bleeding after all these years. Wow! I guess I'm really scared of conflict and what it did to me when I was a kid. My family broke up. (Grace smiles. Bud leans forward and takes Grace's hands). I don't want to lose you and I don't want to lose Casey. I did that once and I don't want to do that again. I love you.

MO (*for BUD*): "I avoid the conflict in our family to prevent it from escalating because I am overly sensitive to conflict as a result of what happened in my family."

BUD: That is absolutely right. That is exactly what is going on with me. I'm just on pins and needles waiting, waiting for the next thing to happen. I can tell by the tone of your voice if I have to go down the hall and settle the situation.

TL: Bud, now do you want to reevaluate your statement, 'I'm pretty laid back in my family relationships?'

BUD: (*deep sob, leaning forward*). I would like to reconsider. I'm carrying as much responsibility as you for this but for different reasons. I'm relieved to find out what I have been doing to you and why I have been doing it to you. You're the last person I want to put any additional pressure on. I love you dearly and I want to change it.

GRACE: I feel total relief. I always anticipate everyone telling me it's my fault and how I have to do things differently. I finally feel your support and understanding.

This experience was the catalyst that took the Edens marriage and parenting in positive direction. Bud truly realized what he was doing and began backing up and supporting his wife. The dance had changed. Now they can move on to effective parenting.

Attachment and Adolescence

Adolescence is typically a difficult time of life for teens and their parents. Most experts agree this is an extremely complex stage of development, further complicated by the challenges posed by a teenager with attachment problems. Teens are transitioning between the dependence and restrictions of childhood and the independence and freedoms of adulthood. They don't really fit in either and are expected to adopt adult-like values and standards without having adult maturity.

The essential tasks of adolescence are to form self-identity, learn self-control, and develop independence. Some teens are still so wounded by early maltreatment and compromised attachment that they fail to establish healthy autonomy. Experiencing successes as a result of good judgment, self-control, and constructive relationship skills develops self-esteem. Teens with a history of disrupted attachments commonly have low self-esteem; they are impulsive, have low frustration tolerance, make poor judgments, and have difficulty maintaining healthy relationships. They appear to be independent, but are actually uncertain and anxious on the inside. They demand independence and freedom, yet demonstrate little ability to manage their lives constructively.

A particular concern of the Edens was Casey's choice of friends. Mom said, "She gravitates toward the risktakers, rejects, and rebels. She loves to live on the edge." Adolescents are attracted to other children who they can relate to and feel accepted by. We all have a deep need to belong and feel more comfortable around others who think like us. A teen who thinks she is a "loser" is not going to hang out with "winners." The peer group replaces the parents as the place where they test out behaviors and get feedback about themselves. This is where they further explore self-identity and social standards. The parents tried to control Casey's choice of friends. They did not realize that Casey would naturally move toward healthier friends as she felt better about herself.

Casey never really felt like she belonged in her family. Her defiant behavior in and outside the home was her way of asserting power, alienating her parents (distance is safer), and rejecting their teachings. As their authority was weakening, in desperation, they resorted to punishment, bribery, or surrender, all of which further damaged their influence with Casey. The more ineffective her parents became, the more Casey lost respect and trust in their ability to be good managers. Although Casey appeared boastful and self-assured, she was really covering up a very fragile self-identity. Here is how Casey described herself:

"I never really let people get close. When they try, I push away with everything I have. I think it's because I'm afraid. I don't know if it's rejection, hurt, or just being vulnerable. I need to get the guts to let someone in. Namely my parents. I know in my heart they would never hurt me but my head is saying something else. I don't feel like I'm important to anybody. I have a little game with myself to see how I can get other kids to do what I want. I always need to be in control. I'm sweet and charming with people. Sometimes I get fed up with charming and go straight to mean. With friends I don't have to deal with criticism or not being liked. I have had some good friends but they probably liked me for the person I pretended to be. I'm afraid if I show them the real me, they won't like me. I cover up so people don't see my hurt and what I'm really feeling."

A New Parenting Approach:
The Autonomy Circle

The Edens admitted that they micromanaged their children. This approach seemed to work for older daughter, Christine, who was an "easy" child. Children adopt very different strategies to deal with loss and abandonment. One is a tendency toward passivity and compliance; "If I don't make waves, you won't reject me." Christine fit into the family by being the "good girl." Casey's strategy was to push away the very connection she needed; "I will reject you before you reject me." Her more aggressive disposition led her toward the family battlefield. Casey perceived any parental involvement as an attempt to control her. The parents' frustration led to increased confrontations, which compounded her feelings of isolation and inadequacy.

The parents' main method of discipline was behavioral, involving the removal or earning of privileges and behavioral contracts. Unfortunately, this approach failed with Casey because she did not care what her parents did to her. Making them angry and frustrated was well worth the cost, as she maintained distance and control. She didn't care about earning privileges because she would do what she wanted anyway. Contracts are only as good as the integrity of those entering into them. Casey would agree to anything to get what she wanted, then not follow through after she got it.

Grace and Casey were constantly in control battles, which increased Casey's aggressive and oppositional behavior. The more controlling Mom attempted to be and the more Dad sided with Casey, the more severe Casey's behavior became. Hitting and shoving her mom was not uncommon. There were many spiraling arguments over cleaning her room, homework, appropriate dress, school, attitude, boys, phone usage, and social activities. All became mini wars. Casey described her mom as a "perfection freak." She said that she never feels good enough for her mom and that it is difficult for her to agree with her mom about anything. She sees herself as not fitting the mold of what is expected of her. Here are Casey's words:

> "I'm realizing that my rage comes from hurt. I have a hard time showing hurt because it makes me vulnerable. I've used anger for a long time because it puts me in control. I don't have to deal with the real problem when I throw a fit and scare everyone away. If I'm violent or have bizarre threats they won't want to get close. I am defiant to hurt them back. I know that disregard for rules makes my parents angry and hurt. So when I feel hurt, I break rules to hurt them back. I also have to admit that breaking something also helps me to vent. I have felt a lot of hurt over not being understood by my parents. I think the reason they don't understand me is because I never let them in."

The definition of escalation is to cause an increase in intensity, to make worse. Put simply, what you want to do as a healing parent is to reduce the frequency and intensity of negative encounters with your children and increase the positive and healing interactions. There are two major ways parents fuel the fire of escalating negativity. Grace used one, and Bud, the other. The first involves meeting hostility with hostility (reciprocal escalation). As the child escalates, the parent responds by escalating. Mother and Casey had an endless stream of control battles with each trying to impose their will on the other. This resulted in a buildup of anger and resentment leading to a climate of adversity and distance. The second way that parents increase the likelihood of escalation is by giving-in. Father was trying to avoid escalating conflicts, but instead was increasing them. He would lecture, explain, plead, and submit his way to peace in the family.

The parents had to learn how to stop trying to control Casey's behavior. Only Casey is in control of her behavior. You cannot force a child to do it your way, but you can use an approach that increases the likelihood that you will have a positive influence. The following is an example of the frustrating power struggles between Grace and Casey:

MOM: Casey, take your car and go to the pharmacy. I need you to pick up some medication for me now.

(*30 minutes later*)

MOM: Casey! I've told you three times. I'm not going to tell you again. I need that medication. Get to the store now!

CASEY: You're such a bitch! Get your own damn stuff.

MOM: Don't you talk to me that way, young lady. You will be sorry. Get to your room now!

CASEY: No way, you can't make me.

Results: Mom uses confronting words, which causes Casey to "dig in her heels." When Mom's attempt to demand compliance fails, she escalates, which triggers an escalation by her daughter. Mom's authority is eroded further, leading to feelings of helplessness. Casey's false sense of self ("I am all powerful") and her true self ("I am defective and worthless") are reinforced. The relationship is adversarial and negative.

The Autonomy Circle provides a road map for achieving a "win-win" in families (see page 148). All teens have an inherent need to be in control of their lives. Teens with attachment issues believe that complying with authority is not in their best interest, particularly *parental* authority. Teens must see the benefits to themselves in acting a certain way in order to be motivated. They can be very driven in getting what they want. They can argue, demand, or defy their way to freedom, or they can learn a way to earn it. The Autonomy Circle gives them a positive way to earn freedom and privileges. The Edens used the Autonomy Circle to explain the new competency-based structure to Casey. She was told that her freedoms and privileges would be based on how successful she was at demonstrating four competencies consistently over time—knowledge, judgment, skills, and self-control. The more freedom she handled, the more she would get. If she wanted a particular privilege, she knew exactly what it would take to get it. If she made a mistake, she would have a natural consequence and eventually be given another opportunity to try again.

This new approach gave Casey control in a positive way and transformed the nature of the parent-child relationships. Instead of viewing her parents as "the enemy," an obstacle to her freedom, they were now seen as supportive of her goal to achieve autonomy and empathic when she wavered. They no longer found it necessary to judge and criticize Casey's choices, reducing the defiance, antagonism, and power struggles. Grace and Bud made no attempts to control Casey's behavior and were respectful of her right to make decisions and deal with the consequences. Casey began to see herself as someone who could achieve positive goals and feel good about acting responsibly.

The changes in the marital relationship, the family "dance," the parenting approach, as well as counseling for Casey's emotional wounds, resulted in a positive outcome. It is now 10 years later. Casey is a well-adjusted young adult. She is happily married, emotionally close with her parents, and an active member of her community. Bud and Grace report their marriage is "better than ever." The challenges of raising Casey gave them an opportunity to look in the mirror, which was a vehicle for personal and family growth.

Summary

- Sixty percent of Americans have personal experiences with adoption.

- Adoption has a lifelong impact, and adoptees have significant challenges due to loss and grief, loyalty conflicts, unclear identities, histories of maltreatment and compromised attachment, complicated family dynamics, and stigmatization in society.

- Adoptive families are characterized by diversity, including international, transracial, gay and lesbian, single-parent, kinship, blended, and open adoptions.

- Key factors that influence attachment of adopted children: prenatal experience, age and stage at placement, history of maltreatment, prior attachments, and postadoption parenting.

- Adopted children commonly have negative internal working models—negative core beliefs about self, caregivers, and life—and unresolved loss and grief.

- Loyalty conflicts can prevent secure attachments from developing with adoptive parents.

- Adoptive parents need effective strategies to deal with three primary challenges: your child pushing away your love and support; helping your child cope with emotions and stress; and managing your own emotional reactions.

- The traumatized adoptive family is characterized by a tense and negative emotional climate, isolation and lack of support, control battles, triangulation, marital conflicts, and sibling conflicts.

- Factors to consider regarding placement of a sibling group: severity of emotional, behavioral, and attachment problems; pathology of the sibling relationships; strengths of the family; and pre- and postadoption services.

8

Attachment and Foster Care

*Yesterday was my first day of school. I'm in the 2nd grade. My teacher's name is
Mrs. Felber and my teacher is very nice. I had a hot dog for lunch today.
Today I was a very good boy. I wonder if my mom had a good mom. I would like to
know a lot about my mom. I really love my mom. I hope we can find my mom. I sorta
remember my mom but I barely remember what she looks like. I miss my mom very much
and I wish she were here. I would tell her I love her very much. I would ask her to never
leave me again. If she did I would be very sad. My foster dad, John, bought me a new
book and three pair of long pants. My best friend Kyle from last year is in my class.
I love my mom very much but my mom smoked too much and she did drugs too much.
Today I had a fun day and then I went home. I guess that's all.*

—Billy, 7, foster child

Over the last 50 years we have accomplished amazing things. We have cured
diseases, landed men on the moon, figured out DNA, split the atom, and
invented the computer and the Internet. There have been great strides in
technology, medicine, space exploration, and other realms due to the priority placed on
those endeavors and the vast human and financial resources applied. Sadly, we have not
placed such a priority on children and families, as evidenced by the increases in child
maltreatment and out-of-home placements.

As long as there are parents who do not nurture, love, and protect their children,
there will be a need for foster care. As long as there are chronic social problems that
lead to high-risk children and families, we will need foster homes as temporary or
longer-term placements. These family and social problems include the increasing number of children who are victims of abuse and neglect, the growing number of high-
stress single-parent households, poverty and homelessness, the cycle of violence in
families, and the reactionary way in which child welfare is funded.

Foster Care System: A Brief History

In order to understand the current state of our foster care system it is helpful to appreciate how it began and changed over time. Initially, there was no organized approach

for dealing with child welfare in the United States. Beginning in the early 19th Century, public concern and policy for maltreated and dependent children came from private and secular agencies. Only the state of Indiana had a governmental body concerning child welfare. Abandoned and unwanted babies were placed in foundling hospitals and large orphanages, where many were neglected and even died from lack of nurturing and human contact.

Our current foster care system originated with two contrasting models. The New York City Children's Aid Society, started in 1853, was created to protect the community from children whose behavior was viewed as threatening. Violent and antisocial children from the city were placed with rural western families; 100,000 of these children were placed between 1854 and 1921. The ties to their families and communities were completely severed.

A new and different approach to foster care began in 1886 with the Boston Children's Aid Society, which focused on the needs of the child and the importance of maintaining ties with the biological family. The foster home was meant to be a temporary placement with the goal of reunification. They were also the first to emphasize prevention in order to avoid the need for out-of-home placement. This approach to foster care was endorsed by the first White House Conference on Children in 1909, and family foster care became favored as an alternative to institutional care.

The Child Welfare League of America (CWLA) was founded in 1920. They helped to standardize child welfare programs, stressing the need for temporary out-of-home placements, family preservation, and reunification. The Social Security Act of 1935 marked the federal government's first attempt to fund child welfare services. Grant money was provided to states for children lacking parental support, to pay for foster care, but not for services involving biological families. From the 1930s, child welfare services moved from a punitive, law enforcement model to a rehabilitation approach.

There was a huge increase in foster care placements, as well as federal funding for social service programs, in the 1960s and 1970s (177,000 in 1961 to 500,000 by 1977). This was a result of the increased public awareness of child abuse and neglect, and the new laws requiring child care professionals to report maltreatment. Additional factors also led to the vast increase in foster care: poverty, increased minority population, single-mother households, alcohol and drug abuse, homelessness, and how the federal government funded child welfare.

The foster care system has been *reactionary* on the federal level in its efforts to respond to the needs of at-risk children and families. The Child Abuse Prevention and Treatment Act in 1974 was passed as a reaction to the growing awareness of child maltreatment. The result was an enormous increase in foster care placements, more time spent in foster care, and more moves from home-to-home. In 1980, Congress passed the Adoption Assistance and Child Welfare Act, a reaction to the ballooning foster care population. The goal now was "permanency planning," an effort to prevent removal, place children in adoptive homes quickly, and reunify families. The term "special needs" was introduced, and agencies tried to find homes for hard-to-adopt children (e.g., older, sibling groups, physically and mentally disabled, varying racial backgrounds).

Adoption agencies and social service programs were not prepared to deal with the extensive needs of children and families. In 1989, a government report entitled *No

Place to Call Home: Discarded Children in America exposed the nation's failure to really help high-risk children and families. The report concluded, "...children bounce from one overwhelmed system to another, and fail to receive the counseling and safeguards necessary to enable them to find permanent families and essential services" (U.S. Select Committee on C.Y.F 1989).

Congress responded once again in 1993 with funding for intensive family preservation and reunification services. However, child welfare services continued to be overwhelmed by large caseloads, high burnout and turnover of staff and foster parents, and increasing numbers of disturbed children remaining in long-term placement. The Adoption and Safe Families Act of 1997 was designed to improve the safety of children and move them more quickly from foster care to adoptive homes. Placing needy children in permanent adoptive homes was, of course, a worthwhile goal, but two problems resulted: lack of necessary preplacement services (assessment, effective transitioning of children, training and support of parents); and lack of crucial postplacement services (treatment and support for children and families), which left many adoptive parents unable to manage their special needs children. Meanwhile, the foster care population continued to increase (Levy & Orlans 1998).

To date, not much has changed. The federal government is currently conducting Child and Family Service Reviews, designed to evaluate the safety, permanency, and well-being of vulnerable children in our foster care system. Affected are nearly 550,000 children in foster care and approximately a half million others living at home under state supervision. These reviews are looking at such things as whether children continue to bounce from foster home to foster home, are siblings kept together or separated, are children being abused after entering the system, how long is it taking states to finalize adoptions or send children back home, and are parents receiving promised services? The reviews so far indicate that not a single state has passed the test in its ability to protect children from child abuse and to find permanent homes. It is the same old story; Human Services Departments are not providing the case management, assessment and treatment, and other services that these children and families desperately need (Webb 2006).

This is not meant to be an indictment of the many dedicated and hardworking people in the foster care system—foster parents, case workers, administrators, mental health professionals. These people have their hands tied. Children and families continue to be a low priority among those who make funding decisions.

Our society is being "penny wise and pound foolish." We fail to realize that by providing real help to high-risk children and families today, we are likely to prevent more serious problems and the need for considerably more services tomorrow. On an economic level, it does not make much sense. By not allocating the appropriate funding, we are creating a much larger financial burden on society when these children become adults.

Foster Care System

On any given day, half a million children are in foster care in the United States. During the 1980s, about 260,000 children were in out-of-home care. By 1999, that figure increased to

Now what?

568,000 (U.S. Department of Health & Human Services 2002). Not only did the numbers of high-risk children and families increase, but the severity of their problems increased as well. Around 75% of children entering foster care have a family history of mental illness or drug and alcohol abuse (Chernoff et al. 1994). Children in foster care are 10 times more likely to have mental health problems than other Medicaid eligible children (Harmon et al. 2000). These children have high rates of emotional and behavioral problems due to early maltreatment, attachment disruptions, and the instability of the foster care system itself (McIntyre & Keesler 1986).

Foster care is a term for children living in out-of-home care, mostly as a result of abuse and neglect. There are four types of foster care: *family* foster care (nonrelative), *kinship* care (relative), therapeutic foster care (treatment or specialized), and *residential group* care (not actually foster care, but these children are considered in national statistics as living in foster care). Most children live in family foster care (50%) or kinship care (42%), while less are in therapeutic foster care (2%) (Curtis et al. 1999).

Therapeutic foster care, also called treatment or specialized foster care, is designed to have the following characteristics: 1) foster parents are considered professionals; 2) small number of children under the foster parents' care (one or two preferably); 3) case managers also have small caseloads; 4) special training and skills needed for foster parents; 5) child has specific treatment plan implemented by foster parents; 6) emotional and professional support given to foster parents; 7) crisis intervention services are available to parent 24 hours a day; 8) emphasis is on assessment and fulfillment of the child's educational needs; and 9) each child has a coordinated system of care. These are ideals that are not often followed in many foster care programs (Curtis et al. 1999).

Although thousands of foster parents provide conscientious and heart-felt care, the *system* often fails the very children it's supposed to protect. Foster care was originally set up to furnish safe and temporary homes for children. The reality is many children stay in foster care for years, often until they "age out" as young adults. Stability and safety are also often lacking, as children are commonly moved from one home to another. A statewide study in Wisconsin found children had an average of 4.6 different placements, and stayed in the system for an average of 5.5 years. Children raised in multiple homes are more likely to have severe emotional, behavioral, and academic problems. Children in long-term foster care are more likely to become adults who are homeless, unemployed, and suffer from debilitating psychological problems (Newton et al. 2000).

While the number of children in foster care has increased, the number of foster parents has declined. There are several reasons why people do not want to become foster parents and are leaving foster care: inadequate salaries; lack of recognition, training, and support; the poor image of the foster care system; the increased needs and problems of foster children; and role confusion (CWLA 1995; Klee et al. 1997). Foster parents often say they do not feel valued, are not adequately trained to handle challenging children, and are involved in a system with a tarnished reputation. They are often unclear about the roles they play with children—are they parents, short-term guardians, attachment figures, coaches, preadoptive parents, or therapists? Depending on agency philosophy and personal choice, they take on some or all of these roles.

Despite the challenges and frustrations, learning to be a therapeutic and healing foster parent can be rewarding and beneficial. Studies show the benefits of mature, sensitive, and responsive parenting. Infants and young children, victims of abuse, neglect and multiple disruptions, were able to make substantial emotional, cognitive, social, and physical improvements when placed in stable and loving homes. Infants placed in foster care during the first 20 months of life were studied. These babies had a history of abuse, neglect, and up to five changes in caregivers. The results give us hope. These babies were able to develop secure attachments as long as they had *autonomous* foster moms. Autonomous state of mind means that the mothers value attachment and are able to make sense of or come to terms with their own attachment histories (Dozier et al. 2001).

Another study shows the importance of skill-based training. Low-income mothers of irritable infants were taught to be more sensitive and responsive to their babies' needs. After nine months, these babies were significantly more likely to be securely attached than those with mothers who were not trained. At 3.5 years old, these mothers and children were still doing well regarding maternal sensitivity, attachment security, and mother-child cooperation. The fathers became better parents as well, even though they were not specifically trained (Van den Boom 1994, 1995). Toddlers fostered or adopted from orphanages in Romania and other countries, where they experienced extreme neglect, have been able to change their attachment behavior over time. Many of these traumatized children learned to trust and depend on foster and adoptive parents who were sensitive, responsive, and consistently *healing* parents (Chisholm 1998; O'Conner et al. 1999).

Foster Youth Speak Out

Current and former foster care youths have shared important ideas about their needs and ways to improve the system (Knipe & Warren 1999). These young adults have had personal journeys through the foster care system and have a lot to teach us. Here are their recommendations:

- Train foster parents and kinship care providers in how to assist youths.

- Include children and teens in decisions about their futures.

- Hire workers who have a background in child and youth development.

- Provide adopted youths with all available information about their biological family, including medical history.

- Create a program for younger youths with older and emancipated young adults as mentors.

- Establish a rental assistance fund for youths leaving foster care.

- Create a mechanism for holding social workers accountable if they do not promptly return youths' calls. Provide youths with a list of phone numbers of people to contact if the workers are unavailable.

- Inform youths about programs available to them.

- Allow youths to evaluate their social workers, placements, and foster homes.

- Assist teens and young adults with transportation to and from work.

- Help youths obtain proper clothing for job interviews.

- Be certain youths understand their medical needs, how to utilize their medical insurance, and how to access health care providers.

Children in Foster Care

As a result of neglect, abuse, the absence of secure attachments, losses that led to out-of-home placements, and the trauma of removal from their homes, foster children have numerous medical, emotional, social, and behavioral problems. Studies of foster children have found between 50% to 96% show signs of psychological problems and developmental delays, such as depression, aggression, and learning and language disorders. Children placed in foster homes after two years of age had more of these problems than children entering the homes at a younger age. More than 80% of children in foster care have at least one serious and chronic medical condition, such as asthma or infections. Infants have an average of almost three medical conditions (Harmon et al. 2000).

The worst thing that has happened in my life.

Even though children entering foster care are suffering from serious medical and psychological problems, they commonly do not receive the diagnostic or treatment services they need. Often, the foster care agencies and local social services departments lack the necessary financial and professional resources. So the children who need desperately to be evaluated, and are at greatest risk for developing even more problems over time, are left without services. This same situation holds true for the foster parents; they lack sufficient information, training, and support.

It is common for children in foster care to have multiple diagnoses, including ODD, conduct disorder, depression, anxiety disorder, PTSD, ADHD, and reactive attachment disorder. These children are victims of high-risk families, characterized by abuse and neglect, poverty, substance abuse, violence, and parents with severe psychological problems and maltreatment in their own childhoods. Up to 80% of high-risk families cause severe attachment problems in their children (Lyons-Ruth 1996). The foster care system is overwhelmed with these traumatized children. Consider the following statistics regarding children in foster care (Leslie et al. 2003).

- A family history of mental illness or drug and alcohol abuse is found in 75% of cases.
- More than 80% have developmental, emotional, and behavioral problems.
- More than 30% show symptoms of antisocial behaviors.
- Nearly 50% have cognitive or learning disabilities.
- More than 82% have at least one serious medical condition, such as asthma, malnutrition, infections, or failure to thrive.
- Prenatal drug or alcohol exposure occurs in 62% of cases.

Foster children also have many educational challenges. Schools are generally equipped to teach and manage the "average" child. Children in foster care, however, typically have a wider range of school-related problems. They perform lower on standardized achievement tests, earn lower grades, have trouble getting along with teachers and other children, have higher rates of absenteeism and disciplinary referrals, and are more likely to repeat a grade (Zetlin 2002). A recent study showed the educational plight of children in foster care with the following results (Meier 2003):

- *grade level*—43% were not performing at grade level;
- *special education services*—38% were receiving special education services, and many others needed these services;
- *multiple moves*—80% had lived in a different school district prior to their current foster home;
- *mental health services*—63% were receiving mental health services, and they had many more suspensions and expulsions than peers receiving mental health services; and
- *advocate services*—40% of foster parents were not aware of the "parent surrogate" role in order to advocate for their children to receive special services.

Attachment, Loss, and Foster Care

When children with unresolved grief and loss enter a foster home they bring their pain with them, and their main priority is self-protection against future loss and vulnerability. They avoid intimacy, closeness, and dependence at all costs. They are fearful of ever loving again, leading to a profound sense of loneliness and mistrust; "If I get close, I'll get hurt," or "If I get close, you will see me for who I really am, someone unlovable and not good enough." Wounded children can only deal with the intense fear of abandonment by armoring themselves against it. They shut down their hearts to love both physically and psychologically. Fear of abandonment is a force that runs their lives. Even though they maintain elaborate defenses against experiencing closeness, they still have a great need for it. They are also motivated by a desperate need for power and control ("If I'm in control, I'm safe") because they cannot trust others to be in charge. They can manipulate through helplessness, open hostility, and defiance.

Internal working models, or core beliefs, are formed early in life based on how caregivers behave toward children. Sensitive and responsive parenting results in positive core beliefs. The child feels safe, loved, learns to trust, and views himself in a positive way; "I am worthwhile, competent, and loveable." Abusive, neglectful, and otherwise frightening parenting leads to negative core beliefs. The child is afraid of and does not trust his caregiver and views himself negatively; "I am bad, helpless, and unlovable."

Most children are placed in foster care because of neglect, abuse, and abandonment, often associated with parental substance abuse. Maltreatment and multiple caregivers generally lead to insecure and compromised attachment styles. A recent study of children five years and younger in foster care found 86% were avoidantly attached, regardless of the type of maltreatment they experienced in their biological families (McWey 2004). Children in foster care have negative core beliefs. They expect caregivers will not meet their needs and develop defensive strategies for protection: *no trust, a profound need to control others, and never rely or depend on caregivers.*

These are survival strategies learned in order to adapt to past unhealthy caregivers and adverse conditions. When placed they view foster care in a mistrustful way and are generally resistant to accepting care, guidance, and support. They turn away from the caregivers, sending the message, "I don't need you; I can take care of myself." Foster parents often report the more they attempt to offer comfort and care, the more mistrustful and angry the children become. They are protecting themselves from anticipated hurt by rejecting and alienating the foster parent. Infants show this defensive and rejecting behavior to even the most sensitive and loving foster parent. The problem is magnified with older foster children due to long-term exposure to maltreatment, the likelihood of multiple moves and previous placement failures, and unresolved emotional issues with their birth families (e.g., loyalty conflicts) (Schofield & Beek 2005).

Many children enter foster care in their early years when brain growth and development is most active. During the first several years of life the parts of the brain that govern learning, self-control, coping with stress and emotions, and personality traits are established. The neural connections formed during those critical years are significantly influenced by abuse, neglect, and attachment disruptions (American Academy of Pediatrics 1999). Early separation and loss causes babies and young children to become behaviorally and biochemically dysregulated (Fisher et al. 2000). The absence of consistent and supportive attachment figures leaves children alone in dealing with stress. This results in children who are anxious, impulsive, lack self-control, and cannot manage their emotions and stress.

Moves

Children need consistent and predictable relationships with caregivers in order to develop properly. Due to severe emotional and behavioral problems, however, children regularly move from foster home to foster home. Children with insecure attachments have more foster care placements. This is a vicious cycle: maltreatment and loss lead to negative core beliefs; mistrust and defensiveness cause children to push parents away, refuse to be cared for, and act in angry, aggressive, and defiant ways; this causes foster parents to remove these children from their homes. With each move, children experience more loss and abandonment, feel more worthless, inadequate, and unlovable, and are less likely to trust caregivers and form secure attachments in the future.

Adults often do not understand how traumatic it is for children to move. Although they might appear unaffected, every move children endure results in further anxiety, anger, and mistrust. As an adult, imagine how you would feel if some arbitrary person told you that tomorrow you would leave your home and live with complete strangers.

Children do best in foster care when they are placed early in life and remain in one home. When a child must be moved, appropriate preplacement planning can ease the transition. It is crucial that the prospective foster parents know the child, including: medical, family, and psychological history; number and results of prior moves; and emotional triggers (e.g., anniversary reactions). They need a clear understanding of therapeutic plans and goals. Knowing the child can also help determine the right match in a foster family. The better the fit, the better the chances for success. The following factors should be considered before moving a child into a foster home: match in temperaments; ages and issues of other children in the home; parent's ability to manage high-risk behavior; and parent's sensitivity to cultural and ethnic background.

Foster parents must understand the child's defensive attitude and behavior when first coming into their homes. There is an adjustment period when children are grieving prior losses and trying to deal with many changes—new school, new family rules, and new relationships. It is not uncommon for children to "honeymoon" for days, weeks, or even months. During this time, they are assessing the strengths and weaknesses of the parents and family and preparing a strategy to protect themselves and cope with their new environment. Children may be superficially close and compliant, but begin to act out in angry and defiant ways when the honeymoon is over. Table 5 describes ways to minimize the trauma of moves based on the age and developmental stage of the child.

Table 5. Minimizing the Trauma of Moves: Developmental Considerations

1. **Infants:** Emphasis on transferring attachment and caregiving routines during preplacement contacts. Maintain as many routines as possible in new setting. After move, provide consistency and *meet needs on demand.*

2. **Toddlers:** Preplacement preparation is crucial to reduce long-term anxiety and fear regarding separation, loss, and lack of safety with caregivers. Primary goal during moving process is to transfer attachment; best facilitated by cooperative contact between parents the child is leaving and new parents or caregivers. Provide support and understanding if regression occurs after move; undue pressure may have negative long-term effects. Note events surrounding the move on the child's permanent record, as this information may help caregivers and helping professionals understand the child's future actions and issues.

3. **Preschool Years:** Explaining in "child-friendly" language what is occurring and why reduces magical thinking and helps the child attain a sense of control over events. Magical thinking refers to the fantasies and unrealistic expectations and conclusions of children in early developmental stages. Children may misinterpret events; such as believing they are responsible for loss or abuse. Preplacement services aid in transferring attachment to new caregivers and initiating the process of grieving. Identifying and modifying the child's negative perceptions ("It is my fault I lost my mom") prevents future emotional problems. As child develops increased cognitive skills, around 8 or 9 years old, caregivers or helpers need to review the past, so that the child is not misinterpreting those events.

4. **Grade School Age:** Despite increased cognitive and verbal skills, it remains necessary to identify and correct magical thinking and misperceptions. It is important to help the child understand what is happening, and to provide aid in identifying and constructively expressing emotions. Adults are responsible for decision-making, but the child is encouraged to share feelings, worries, and desires regarding the transition. After the move, discussions about grief-related (or other) feelings helps the child free-up energy for social, academic, and additional activities and accomplishments.

5. **Adolescence:** Moves during early adolescence (ages 12 to 14) are more difficult than in later adolescence because individuation is a major developmental task of this stage. It is difficult to encourage attachment to new caregivers when the child is in the process of emotionally separating from family. Parents need to be sensitive to these development issues; children do best with a clear and concrete commitment, or "contract," to the new caregivers. Adolescents need to have input into decision-making about their lives and future, consistent with their need to have increasing control over life events in general. They should be a part of the process of deciding where to live, except in special situations (e.g., displaying poor judgment). Commitments and contracts are helpful in clarifying and attaining goals. Parents, caregivers, and helping professionals can assist the adolescent come to terms with prior losses and trauma, and encourage a healthy balance of dependence and independence [adapted from Fahlberg 1991].

Outcomes for Foster Youths

About 20,000 youths leave the foster care system (*age out*) each year, usually when they turn 18. They are often unprepared and unconnected. Due to the lack of support typically provided for the transition to adulthood, combined with unresolved psychological problems, these young adults have severe difficulties after exiting foster care. Douglas Nelson, president of the Annie E. Casey Foundation, wrote "…no group in the United States is more predictably headed for unhappy outcomes than young people who spend their adolescence in foster care. This litany of failure constitutes a national shame" (Annie E. Casey Foundation 2001).

The quality of a youngster's life after out-of-home care is usually assessed in four realms: self-sufficiency, behavioral adjustment, family and social support, and sense of well-being. Adults formerly in care have more than their share of problems. Physical and mental health problems are severe and often untreated; homelessness and academic failure are commonplace; gainful employment is elusive. Consider the following circumstances for many former foster youths (Annie E. Casey Foundation 2001):

- Between 25% and 41% of former foster youths spend time in prison. One study found the arrest rate 67% higher for youths previously in the child welfare system compared to those never in that system.

- Severe emotional problems presented in 38%, with a much higher rate of serious disorders (e.g., schizophrenia, depression, personality disorders) and use of psychotropic medication.

- Illegal drugs used by 50%; 30% of males and 15% of females report using drugs or alcohol daily.

- Between 24% to 35% experience homelessness; representing more than half of young adults using federally-funded shelters.

- Up to 46% have not completed high school within 4 years after leaving foster care. Only 48% graduate from high school compared to 85% in the general population. Only 1% goes to college compared to 42% of the general population.

- Unemployment rates of 35% to 51% within two to four years after leaving the system. Those who do work earn considerably less than others, many with incomes under the poverty line; 24% report selling drugs and 11% report having sex to support themselves.

- Women who had been in care are more likely to get pregnant (and at a younger age) than comparisons; 42% of prior foster care youths become parents within 2.5 to 4 years after exiting care. Serious parenting failures were found in 51% of these young adults compared to 11% of those never in the system (McDonald et al. 1996; Annie E. Casey Foundation 2001; Courtney et al. 2001).

To summarize, children in the foster care system have a myriad of challenges. The aftereffects of maltreatment, losses, and compromised attachment have produced the following needs and issues:

- profound loss prior to placement;

- unresolved loss and grief often expressed as anger, defiance, or depression;

- expectation that caregivers will abuse them or dismiss their needs; lacked trust;

- avoidance of closeness with and dependence on caregivers while still having a pronounced need for nurturance and support;

- fear abandonment and protect themselves by pushing parents away;

- power and control sought to compensate for a lack of secure attachment;

- appearance of self-reliance, but under this façade they are insecure, needy, and fearful;

- inability to cope with stress and employ self-control; dysregulated behaviorally, emotionally, and biochemically;

- self-perception as unlovable, inadequate, and powerless;

- preoccupation about birth families, although might not talk about them;

- loyalty conflicts felt; reluctant to voice feelings about birth parents and other prior caregivers;

- painful memories and negative behaviors triggered by birthdays and other anniversary dates;

- feelings of self as different, defective, and ashamed; and

- presentation of severe psychological and social problems as adults.

Foster Parents: Needs and Goals

Many in the child welfare field refer to the *foster care crisis* as a way to describe the many difficulties of the foster care system today. What are some of these challenges? First, there has been a dramatic increase in the number of children placed in foster homes. There were nearly 600,000 children in the foster care system in 2002, a number that doubled since 1987 (Leslie et al. 2003). Second, the children placed in foster homes are more challenging, having more serious and complex problems and needs. Third, the role of the foster parent has changed, making it more complicated and stressful. For example, foster parents are expected to be therapeutic parents, minus the extra training, support, and pay. Also, foster parents often have to deal with the ongoing contact between birthparents and foster children (inclusive foster care), which provokes unresolved grief and acting out in the children.

Foster parents have two major frustrations regarding their role. The first is *all foster parents are therapeutic parents,* because of the severe problems of the children they have under their care. The second is even parents that are identified as therapeutic foster parents often are *not sufficiently trained and supported*. It is easy to understand why all foster parents must function in a therapeutic capacity when you look at the wounded children who enter the foster care system. The milieu of the foster home *must* be therapeutic. By providing a role model of healthy values and behavior, and offering a safe, nurturing, and predictable environment, foster parents can help children heal emotional wounds and achieve many positive changes (Baker et al. 1996).

It is becoming more difficult to keep foster parents in the current system. When asked directly, foster parents site the following reasons for leaving (Hudson & Levasseur, 2002; Jorgenson & Schooler, 2002):

- *Role ambiguity*—a lack of clarity about their roles and responsibilities. In exit interviews foster parents say, "We were unclear what the agency and social workers expected of us."

- *Insufficient training*—a lack of sufficient preparation in the preservice orientation, as well as a lack of relevant ongoing training and supervision. "My orientation training did not prepare me for the *realities* of being a foster parent;" "We were not trained to deal with the serious problems of the children in our home;" "There is no way for the agency to identify my training needs."

- *Lack of respect and positive regard*—a central theme involving the need for more respect, recognition, and acknowledgement (recognizing and valuing the foster parents' contribution). "We were never included in case planning;" "Records and information were kept from me;" "Our ideas were minimized and treated as unimportant."

- *Lack of support*—a need for a high level of parental support, coming from a variety of sources, to effectively deal with very challenging children and day-to-day responsibilities. "I never see my child's social worker, only an aide who is not able to answer my questions;" "I feel isolated and alone in the agency—having more contact and support from other parents would help;" "We were told to arrange our own respite, as the agency would not provide that for us."

Support of various kinds—practical and emotional—is necessary for successful foster parenting. Support comes in three forms. *Concrete* support involves adequate income, available respite, and proper training. Second is *crisis assistance* which includes advice on how to handle difficult situations, not only someone handling the situation for them. One survey found 90% of foster parents wanted support within 24 hours of a crisis in order to remain with the agency (CWLA 1995). The third category is *emotional* support, including the need for respect and recognition. Emotional support includes:

- expressing gratitude for doing a difficult job;

- returning phone calls in a timely manner and letting you know your questions and concerns matter;

- not blaming the parent when a child acts out or runs away;

- debriefing after moving a child;

- honesty in the parent-agency relationship, including honest feedback regarding strengths and weaknesses to increase the parents' competencies; and

- having a role in developing and reviewing the child's plan of care.

Key Principles of Success

The foster care system needs to make a transition—from an overburdened system which does not meet the needs of its children or parents, to a place where parents and families are valued for the crucial role they play in the lives of children and society. The following are the keys to providing quality foster care and retaining experienced foster parents (Jorgenson & Schooler 2002):

- *Recruitment*—agency must fully explain the application and training process and other expectations.

- *Assessment*—parents must look in the mirror to see an honest assessment of their own motivations, qualifications, and abilities regarding this challenging job.

- *Preservice training*—agency provides competency-based training that teaches the concepts and skills required to be successful with specific children in their homes.

- *Communication and support*—mutual sharing of information between parents and agency. Support, respect, and positive regard in relationships with case managers, social workers, other foster parents, respite providers, school and mental health professionals. Parents are treated as valued members of the treatment team.

- *Clear roles*—agency provides clear and consistent definition to the parents of their roles and responsibilities as a team member.

- *Ongoing training*—agency provides competency-based training relevant to the challenges and requirements of therapeutic foster parenting. Includes training and supervision focusing on the emotional challenges foster parents face when dealing day-to-day with challenging children.

Role of Foster Parents

Foster parents are the most influential adults in the lives of many wounded children, as they have the most direct, day-to-day contact and the greatest opportunity to impact children emotionally, socially, and morally. All interactions in the foster home have the potential to be therapeutic, an opportunity for *Corrective Attachment Parenting* and corrective emotional experiences. Foster parents are therapeutic parents, agents of healing and change. Through their actions, reactions, and the creation of a safe, consistent, and loving environment, they provide a context in which children can make numerous positive changes, including the following:

- develop secure attachments, which will benefit children in all future relationships and endeavors;

- improve self-image and develop positive core beliefs;

- learn constructive coping skills, such as anger management, stress management, communication, and problem solving;

- achieve impulse control and emotional self-control;

- cultivate intrinsic motivation;

- create mastery over prior trauma and loss;

- become responsible and accountable;

- learn to use good judgment; and

- acquire prosocial values, ethics, and morality, including honesty, compassion, and tolerance.

Goals and Solutions

Foster parents are agents of change and healing. By maintaining a positive attitude and healing environment, you provide an opportunity for children to learn and grow. The following list offers guidelines and practical suggestions in order to heal emotional wounds and to facilitate secure attachment in the foster home.

1. Understand Core Beliefs.

Your child's early experiences with caregivers shaped his core beliefs about self, relationships, and life in general. Children with negative core beliefs perceive parents as rejecting, punitive, untrustworthy, and threatening. Therapeutic parenting can change your child's core beliefs and subsequent behavior.

Look beyond behavior—see rejection and resistance as your child's strategy to cope with prior loss. Give approval and praise for specific behavior (e.g., "Thanks for feeding the dog")—unconditional praise does not match your child's self-image. And do not take your child's negative attitude and actions personally; wounded children have negative expectations about caregivers.

2. Provide a Balance of Connection and Structure

Therapeutic parenting is a balance of love and limits. Connecting with your child (empathy, support, nurturing) must be balanced with the necessary structure to engender respect, security, and trust. Parenting approaches that exclusively focus on control instigate power struggles and an adversarial climate.

Instead, be nurturing even when your child behaves in alienating ways. Create a positive emotional climate by being proactive, not reactive. Nonpunitive responses and lots of hugs are essential. Model caring, nonjudgmental, sensitive, and positive emotions and behavior. Provide clear and consistent limits and consequences. Give choices, not commands. And maintain consistent and predictable routines and rituals.

3. Teach Reciprocity.

Children with histories of compromised attachment generally are self-centered, demanding, and unable to give and receive in relationships. They avoid needing others and being vulnerable, due to a lack of trust and belief that they are unworthy of love and caring.

To teach how to give and receive, encourage your child to ask for help and specific need-fulfillment. Your child must contribute to the family. Doing chores allows your child to be a part of the family, have a feeling of accomplishment, and receive praise and appreciation. Engage with your child in reciprocal interactions through play, rituals, homework, and other activities done cooperatively. And negotiate conflicts; teach problem solving, communication, and the acceptance of individual differences.

4. Meet Individual Needs.

Understand the unique needs, core beliefs, and attachment patterns of each child. Caregiver attunement to the needs and signals of children facilitates secure attachment. Know your child: history, patterns, triggers (e.g., anniversary reactions), and underlying needs. By fulfilling deep emotional needs you promote attachment (support, empathy, love). Look beyond negative behavior into the deeper needs and emotions. And build trust by successful completion of the *Attachment Cycle* (see Figure 1, page 22).

5. Look In the Mirror.

Caregivers cannot avoid bringing their own mindsets and emotional baggage into relationships with their children. Healing parents must be aware of their own histories and issues. Solutions are dictated by the way you frame the problem, and your mindset is formed by prior relationship experiences.

To understand your mindset, complete your own *Life Script*, a self-report tool that generates awareness of one's relationship history (see pages 96–100). Be aware of common reactions, such as anger, fear, withdrawal, rejection, depression, and helplessness. Don't forget to take good care of yourself. Be aware of stress levels and personal needs (physical, emotional, social, and spiritual).

6. Managing Emotions.

Children experience and express intense anger, fear, sadness, shame, and pain due to unresolved loss and maltreatment. They had never learned to identify, regulate, and effectively communicate their emotions. They often mask fear and pain under a response of anger and avoidance in order to reduce vulnerability.

When conflicts arise, do not escalate. Remain emotionally neutral in response to negative behaviors, but show pleasure and excitement in response to positive behavior. Encourage communication about feelings. Teach your child to label and talk about her emotions in a safe and empathic context. Be a model of healthy emotional management and communication. Promote positive emotions, such as joy, fun, love, pleasure, pride, and sense of accomplishment.

7. Sense of Belonging.

The primary experience of foster children is loss and abandonment. They have lost connections with family, cultural background, and community, and need to feel a part of your family and community. You can encourage participation as a member of your family and community through ongoing routines and rituals. Respect your child's cultural and ethnic background as well as prior relationships with her biological family. And help your child feel a sense of belonging, which has a stabilizing and reassuring effect.

Summary

- More than 500,000 children are in foster care in the United States.

- The number of foster parents has declined due to: inadequate pay; lack of recognition, training, and support; the poor image of the foster care system; role confusion; and the increased problems of foster children.

- Children in foster care have serious medical, psychological, and behavioral problems: 75% have a family history of mental illness or substance abuse; more than 80% have severe developmental and emotional problems.

- Unresolved losses and disrupted attachments are common among foster children; they act out and are moved from home to home.

- Many children enter foster care early in life when brain growth and development is most active, which affects learning, self-control, and stress-related conditions.

- Facilitating secure attachment involves: understanding core beliefs; a balance of connection and structure; teaching reciprocity; meeting individual needs; looking in the mirror; managing emotions; and enhancing a child's sense of belonging.

9

Epilogue

It is now well known that attachment is vital to healthy development. Secure attachment is associated with mental, emotional, social, and moral well-being. We are also familiar with the damage done to children, families, and society as a result of compromised attachment. We have explained throughout this book how parents can create secure attachment from the beginning and how to help wounded children improve when attachment goes wrong. You, the healing parent, can be the emotional guide that holds the key.

Relationships are the foundation of humanity. As a healing parent, you not only can have a positive impact on your child, but are also helping the next generation and society in general. Maltreatment and disrupted attachment are pathways to antisocial thinking and behavior. Many of these children grow up without an internal guidance system that enables them to accept responsibility, follow rules, and care for others. They continue this negative cycle with their own children, contribute to the breakdown of the family, and often end up in treatment facilities or prisons. By providing your children with a sense of connectedness, belonging, and trust, you can make a difference.

We hope that this book has given you the information, skills, support, self-awareness, and optimism necessary to help your child and family. We have invited you to look at yourself and your family in a different way—being a mindful parent, deeply understanding your child's thoughts, feelings, and needs, and creating positive family relationships. We wish you all the best on your journey toward health and healing.

About the Authors

MICHAEL ORLANS, M.A., D.A.P.A., B.C.F.E.

Michael Orlans is an internationally renowned author and trainer who has taught throughout the United States, Canada, Great Britain, and Japan. Mr. Orlans is a Certified Master Therapist with more than 32 years of clinical experience working with children, adults, and families in public mental health, the criminal justice system, and private practice. He is codirector of the Evergreen Psychotherapy Center and the Attachment Treatment and Training Institute. A pioneer in the treatment of children, adolescents, and adults with compromised attachment, he is the developer of Corrective Attachment Therapy and innovator of the two-week intensive treatment approach. He served on the faculty or lectured at several universities; and is a presenter for the National Foster Parent Association and a consultant to foster care programs and child welfare agencies around the world. Mr. Orlans is a cofounder of the Association for Treatment and Training in the Attachment of Children (ATTACh). He is a member of the Founding Executive Board of Directors of the American Psychotherapy Association, Association for Treatment and Training in the Attachment of Children, and the National Alliance for Rational Children's Policy. He is a Board Certified Forensic Examiner and Fellow of the College of the American College of Forensic Examiners; Diplomate in Psychotherapy—the American Psychotherapy Association; and a Certified Criminal Justice Specialist, Master Addictions Specialist—American College of Certified Forensic Counselors. He is a member of Colorado Psychotherapy Association and an honorary lifetime member of the Colorado Society for the Study of Traumatic Stress and Dissociation. Mr. Orlans has contributed to numerous books, journals, and other publications. With Dr. Levy, he coauthored the bestseller, *Attachment, Trauma, and Healing* (1998, Child Welfare League of America).

TERRY M. LEVY, Ph.D., D.A.P.A., B.C.F.E.

Dr. Terry Levy has been a psychotherapist, trainer, supervisor, and consultant for more than 30 years. Dr. Levy is a Licensed Clinical Psychologist in Colorado and Florida, a Board Certified Forensic Examiner, and a Diplomate and Master Therapist of the American Psychotherapy Association. He is a clinical member of the American, Colorado, and Florida Psychological Associations, American and Colorado Associations of Marriage and Family Therapy, American Family Therapy Academy, and the National Register of Health Service Providers in Psychology. Dr. Levy was previously founder and Director of the Family Life Center (Florida) and the Miami Psychotherapy Institute, which offered family systems treatment and training. He was cofounder and past president of the Board of Directors of the Association for Treatment and Training in the Attachment of Children (ATTACh), an international organization dedicated to attachment and its critical importance to human development. Dr. Levy has taught clinical and therapeutic parenting seminars for the American Psychological Association, American Professional Society on the Abuse of Children, Association for Pre- and Perinatal Psychology and Health, American Academy of Psychotherapists, American Association of Marriage and Family Therapy, Child Welfare League of America, National Foster Parents Association, and numerous mental health, child welfare, and school systems nationally and in Canada, Europe, and Asia. He is coauthor of the best seller *Attachment, Trauma & Healing* (1998, Child Welfare League of America), and editor of *Handbook of Attachment Interventions* (2000, Elsevier Press). Dr. Levy is currently codirector of the Evergreen Psychotherapy Center and the Attachment Treatment and Training Institute in Evergreen, Colorado.

Evergreen Psychotherapy Center, pllc
Attachment Treatment and Training Institute
32065 Castle Court, #325 • Evergreen, CO 80439
www.attachmentexperts.com/attiepc@aol.com
Fax: 303-674-4078 • Phone: 303-674-4029
(Dr. Levy x103) (Mr. Orlans x101) (Dr. Coster x102)

References

Adelson, R. (2005). Only the lonely. *Monitor on Psychology, 36*(5), 26–27.

Ainsworth, M.D.S., Blehar, M., Waters, E. & Wall, S. (1978). *Patterns of attachment.* Hillsdale, NJ: Lawrence Erlbaum Associates.

American Academy of Pediatrics. (1995). Media violence. *Pediatrics, 95,* 949–951.

American Academy of Pediatrics. (1999). *Adoption: Guidelines for parents.* Elk Grove Village, IL: American Academy of Pediatrics Publications.

American Psychiatric Association. (2000). *Diagnostic and statistical manual of mental disorders.* (4th ed., text rev.). Washington, DC: Author.

Ames, E.W. (1997). *The development of Romanian orphanage children adopted to Canada.* Burnaby, British Columbia: Simon Fraser University.

Annie E. Casey Foundation. (2001). *Fostered or forgotten? A special report on foster teens in transition. AdvoCasey, 3*(2).

Annie E. Casey Foundation. (2004). KIDS COUNT Data Book. Baltimore, MD: Author. Available online at www.aecf.org/kidscount/databook/index04.htm.

Atkinson, W. (2005). Food and mood: Feeding problem behaviors. *Children's Voice, 14*(4), 18–21.

Baker, C.B., Burke, R.V., Herron, R.W., & Mott, M.A. (1996). *Rebuilding children's lives: A blueprint for treatment foster parents.* Boys Town, NE: Boys Town Press.

Bain, J.W. (2004). *Infertility: Learn to take charge of your condition.* New York: Barnes & Noble Books.

Bandura, A. (1961). Transmission of aggression through imitation of aggressive models. *Journal of Abnormal and Social Psychology, 66,* 3–11.

Barth, R. (2000). What works in permanency planning: Adoption. In M. Kluger, G. Alexander, and P. Curtis (Eds.), *What works in child welfare* (pp. 217–226). Washington, DC: Child Welfare League of America.

Bartlett, C.V. (2004). Transracial adoption: A triumph of love over race. *Family Therapy Magazine, 1*(10), 17–21.

Bedell, J.R., & Lennon, S. (1997). *Handbook for communication and problem-solving skills training.* New York: John Wiley & Sons.

Bell, C.C., & Jenkins, E.J. (1993). Community violence and children on Chicago's southside. *Psychiatry, 56,* 46–54.

Benson, H. (2000). *The relaxation response.* New York: Avon Books.

Berger, R. (1998). *Stepfamilies: A multi-dimensional perspective.* New York: Haworth Press.

Berkman, L.F. (1995). The role of social relations in health promotion. *Psychosomatic Medicine, 57,* 245–254.

Birmaher, B. (2004). *New hope for children and teens with bipolar disorder.* New York: Three Rivers Press.

Borysenko, J., & Borysenko, M. (1994). *The power of the mind to heal.* Carson, CA: The Hay House, Inc.

Bowlby, J. (1969). *Attachment and loss. Vol. 1: Attachment.* New York: Basic Books.

Bowlby, J. (1980). *Attachment and loss. Vol. 3: Loss, sadness and depression.* New York: Basic Books.

Bowlby, J. (1988). *A secure base: Parent-child attachment and healthy human development.* New York: Basic Books.

Brazelton, T.B., & Cramer, B.G. (1990). *The earliest relationship.* New York: Addison-Wesley.

Breggin, P.R. (1999). *Reclaiming our children.* Cambridge, MA: Perseus Books.

Breunlin, D.C., & Cimmarusti, R. (2003). A systemic approach to changing school climate: A necessary component of a comprehensive violence prevention program. *AFTA Newsletter, 88*(2), 20–22.

Bridges, A. (2006, February 9). Deaths, heart woes tied to ADD drugs. *Denver Post,* 6.

Brodzinsky, D.M. (1993). Long-term outcomes in adoption. *The Future of Children, 3*(1), 153–166.

Brodzinsky, D.M., & Schechter, M.D. (1990). *The psychology of adoption.* New York: Oxford University Press.

Brodzinsky, D.M., Schechter, M.D. & Henig, R.M. (1992). *Being adopted: The lifelong search for self.* New York, NY: Doubleday.

Brodzinsky, D.M., Smith, D.W., & Brodzinsky, A.B. (1998). Children's adjustment to adoption. *Developmental Clinical Psychology and Psychiatry, 38,* 10–20.

Brohl, K. (1996). *Working with traumatized children: A handbook for healing.* Washington, DC: CWLA Press.

Brooks, R., & Goldstein, S. (2001). *Raising resilient children.* Chicago: Contemporary Books.

Burrow, A.L., & Finley, G.E. (2004). Transracial, same-race adoptions, and the need for multiple measures of adolescent adjustment. *American Journal of Orthopsychiatry, 74*(4), 577–583.

Chamberlin, J. (2005). Adopting a new American family. *Monitor on Psychology, 36*(11), 70–72.

Chamberlin, J. (2006). Into the mouths of babes. *Monitor on Psychology, 37*(2), 32–33.

Chernoff, R., Combs-Orne, T., Risley-Curtiss, C., & Heisler, A. (1994). Assessing the health status of children entering foster care. *Pediatrics, 93,* 594–601.

Children's Defense Fund. (1997). *The state of America's children: Yearbook 1997.* Washington, DC: Author.

Child Welfare League of America. (1995). *Foster parent retention and recruitment.* Washington, DC: Author.

Chisholm, K. (1998). A three year follow-up of attachment and indiscriminate friendliness in children adopted from Romanian orphanages. *Child Development. 69*(4), 1092–1106.

Christenson, S.L., & Sheridan, S.M. (2001). *Schools and families: Creating essential connections for learning.* New York: Guilford Press.

Cicchetti, D. (2004). An odyssey of discovery: Lessons learned through three decades of research on child maltreatment. *American Psychologist, 59*(8), 731–741.

Clark, M.A. (2002). Reaching potentially violent youth in schools: A guide to collaborative assessment, alertness, atmosphere, and accountability. In G. McAuliffe (Ed.), *Working with troubled youth in schools* (pp. 19–30), Westport, CT: Bergin & Garvey.

Cline, F., & Fay, J. (1990). *Parenting with love and logic.* Colorado Springs, CO: Pinon Press.

Clinton, W.J. (2005, September 25). We must act now. *Parade Magazine,* 4–5.

Cohen, S. (1988). Psychosocial models of the role of social support in the etiology of physical disease. *Health Psychology, 7,* 269–297.

Comfort, R.L. (2005). Learning to play: Play deprivation among young children in foster care. *Zero To Three, 25*(4), 50–53.

Cooper, G. (2005). British children go off antidepressants. *Psychotherapy Networker, 29*(6), 21–22.

Courtney, M.E., Piliavin, I., Grogan-Kaylor, A., & Nesmith, A. (2001). Foster youth transitions to adulthood: A longitudinal view of youth leaving foster care. *Child Welfare, 80*(6), 685–717.

Crittendon, P.M., & Ainsworth, M.D.S. (1989). Child maltreatment and attachment theory. In D. Cicchetti and V. Carlson (Eds.), *Child maltreatment: Theory and research on the causes and consequences of child abuse and neglect* (pp. 432–463). New York: Cambridge University Press.

Curtis, P.A., Dale, G., & Kendall, J.C. (Eds.) (1999). *The foster care crisis: Translating research into policy and practice.* Lincoln, NE: University of Nebraska Press.

DeAngelis, T. (2004). Should our children be taking psychotropics? *Monitor on Psychology, 35*(11), 42.

Dadoly, A.M. (Ed.) (2002). *Stress control: Techniques for preventing and easing stress.* Available online at www.health.harvard.edu/special_health_reports/Stress_Control.htm. Boston, MA: Harvard Health Publications.

DeCasper, A., & Fifer, W. (1980). Of human bonding: Infants prefer their mother's voices. *Science, 208,* 1174–1176.

Dingfelder, S. (2005). The 21st century American family: The kids are all right. *Monitor on Psychology, 36*(11), 66–68.

Dozier, M., Albus, K.E., Stovall, K.C., & Bates, B.C. (2001). Foster infants' attachment quality: The role of foster mother's state of mind. *Child Development, 72*(5), 1467–1477.

Dozier, M., Albus, K.E., Higley, E., & Nutter, A.B. (2002a). Intervention services for foster and adoptive parents: Targeting three critical needs. *Infant Mental Health Journal, 25,* 541–554.

Dozier, M., Dozier, D., & Manni, M. (2002b). Attachment and biobehavioral catch-up: The ABC's of helping infants in foster care cope with early adversity. *ZERO TO THREE, 22*(5), 7–13.

Dubowitz, H., Feigelman, S., & Zuravin, S.C. (1993). A profile of kinship care. *Child Welfare, 72,* 153–169.

Durkheim, E. (1951). *Suicide.* Glencoe, IL: Free Press.

Egeland, B., Yates, T., Appleyard, K., & Dulmen, M. (2002). The long-term consequences of maltreatment in the early years: A developmental pathway model to antisocial behavior. *Children's Services, 5*(4), 249–260.

Egolf, B., Lasker, J., Wolf, S., & Pavin, L. (1992). Featuring health risks and mortality: The Roseto effect. *American Journal of Public Health, 82*(8), 1089–1092.

Erickson, M., Egeland, B., & Pianta, R. (1989). The effects of maltreatment on the development of young children. In D. Cicchetti & V. Carlson (Eds.), *Child maltreatment: Theory and research on the causes and consequences of child abuse and neglect* (pp. 647–684). New York: Cambridge University Press.

Erickson, M.F., & Egeland, B. (1996). Child neglect. In J. Briere, L. Berliner, J.A. Buckley, C. Jenny, & T. Reid (Eds.), *APSAC handbook on child maltreatment* (pp. 4–20). Thousand Oaks, CA: Sage.

Erich, S., Leung, P., & Kindle, P. (2005). A comparative analysis of adoptive family functioning with gay, lesbian, and heterosexual parents and their children. *Journal of GLBT Family Studies, 1*(4), 43–60.

Fahlberg, V. (1991). *A child's journey through placement*. Indianapolis, IN: Perspective Press.

Fanning, P., & McKay, M. (2000). *Family guide to emotional wellness*. Oakland, CA: New Harbinger Publications.

Feigelman, W. (2000). Adjustments of transracially and inracially adopted children. *Journal of Child and Adolescent Social Work, 17,* 165–184.

Field, T. (1997). The treatment of depressed mothers and their infants. In L. Murray and P.J. Cooper (Eds.), *Postpartum Depression and Child Development* (pp. 221–236). New York: Guilford.

Field, T., Grizzle, N., Scafidi, F., & Abrams, S. (1996). Massage therapy for infants of depressed mothers. *Infant Behavior and Development, 19,* 107–112.

Fiese, B.H. (2000). Family matters: A systems view of family effects on children's cognitive health. In R.J. Sternberg & E.J. Grigorenko (Eds.), *Environmental effects on cognitive abilities* (pp.39–57). Mahwah, NJ: Lawrence Erlbaum Associates.

Fiese, B.H. (2002). Routines of daily living in family life. *ZERO TO THREE, 22*(4), 10–13.

Figley, C. (1998). *Burnout in families: The systemic cost of caring*. New York: CRC Press.

Figley, C. (1999). Compassion fatigue: Toward a new understanding of the costs of caring. In B. Stamm (Ed.), *Secondary traumatic stress: Self-care issues for clinicians, researchers, and educators*. Lutherford, MD: Sidren Press.

Finkelhor, D., Hotaling, G., Lewis, I.A., & Smith, C. (1990). Sexual abuse in a national survey of adult men and women: Prevalence, characteristics, and risk factors. *Child Abuse & Neglect, 14,* 19–28.

Finn, C.D. (2003). Cultural models for early caring. *ZERO TO THREE, 23*(5), 40–45.

Fisher, P.A., Gunnar, M.R., Chamberlain, P., & Reid, J.B. (2000). Preventive intervention for maltreated preschoolers: Impact on children's behavior, neuroendocrine activity, and foster parent functioning. *Journal of the American Academy of Child and Adolescent Psychiatry, 39,* 1355–1364.

Fonagy, P., Steele, H., & Steele, M. (1991). Maternal representations of attachment during pregnancy predict the organization of infant-mother attachment at one year of age. *Child Development, 62,* 891–905.

Frederick, S. (2005, March/April). Energy-saving techniques to elevate any situation. *Nexus,* 11–12.

Gartrell, N., Deck, A., Rodas, C., Peyser, H., & Banks, A. (2005). The national lesbian family study: 4. Interviews with the 10-year old children. *American Journal of Orthopsychiatry, 75,* 518–524.

Gerhardt, S. (2004). *Why love matters*. New York: Brunner-Routledge.

Gershoff, E.T. (2002). Corporal punishment by parents and associated child behaviors and experiences: A meta-analytic and theoretical review. *Psychological Bulletin, 128*(4), 539–579.

Gerwood, J., LeBlanc, M., & Piazza, N. (1998). The purpose in life and religious denomination. *Journal of Clinical Psychology, 54,* 49–55.

Goleman, D. (1995). *Emotional intelligence*. New York: Bantam.

Gottlieb, M.M. (1999). *The angry self*. Phoenix, AZ: Zieg, Tucker & Co.

Gottman, J.M. (1999). *The seven principles for making marriage work*. New York: Three Rivers Press.

Green, M. (2002). Care for the caregivers. *Children's Voice, 11*(3), 8–13.

Greenspan, S. (1999). *Building healthy minds: The six experiences that create intelligence and emotional growth in babies and young children*. Cambridge, MA: Perseus Publishing.

Grossman, D., & Siddle, P. (1999). Combat. In L. Kurtz (Ed.), *The Encyclopedia of Violence, Peace, and Conflict* (pp. 93–114). Orlando, FL: Academic Press.

Grossmann, K., Grossmann, K.E., Fremmer-Bombik, E., Kindler, H., Scheuerer-Englisch, H., & Zimmerman, P. (2002). The uniqueness of the child-father attachment relationship: Fathers' sensitive and challenging play as a pivotal variable in a 16-year longitudinal study. *Social Development, 11*, 307–331.

Grotevant, H.D., & McRoy, R.G. (1998). *Openness in adoption: Exploring family connections*. Thousand Oaks, CA: Sage.

Groze, V. (1996). *Successful adoptive families: A longitudinal study of special needs adoption*. Westport, CT: Praeger.

Hafen, B.Q., Karren, K.J., Frandsen, K.J., & Smith, N.L. (1996). *Mind/body health*. MA: Allyn and Bacon.

Hansen, C. (2003). Are our children what they eat? *Children's Voice, 12*(2), 30–33.

Harlow, H. (1958). The nature of love. *The American Psychologist, 3,* 673–685.

Harmon, J., Childs, G., & Kelleher, K. (2000). Mental health care utilization and expenditures by children in foster care. *Archives of Pediatrics and Adolescent Medicine, 154*, 1114–1117.

Harvard Mental Health Letter. (2002). The spanking debate. *19*(5), 1–3. Boston, MA: Harvard Health Publications, Author.

Harvard Mental Health Letter. (2004). Alcohol before birth. *21*(3), 1–3. Boston, MA: Harvard Health Publications, Author.

Hawkins, D. K. (2002). *Power vs. force*. Carlsbad, CA: Hay House.

Hesse, E., Main, M., Abrams, K.Y., & Rifkin, A. (2003). Unresolved states regarding loss or abuse can have "second-generation" effect: Disorganized, role-inversion and frightening ideation in the offspring of traumatized nonmaltreating parents. In D.J. Siegel & M.F. Solomon (Eds.), *Healing trauma: Attachment, mind, body and brain,* (pp. 57–106). New York: Norton.

Howard, J.A., & Smith, S.L. (2003). *After adoption: The needs of adopted youth*. Washington, DC: Child Welfare League of America.

Howard, P.J. (1994) *The owner's manual for the brain: Everyday applications from mind-brain research*. Austin, TX: Leornian Press.

Hudson, P., & Levasseur, K. (2002). Supporting foster parents: Caring voices. *Child Welfare, 81*, 853–877.

Huston, A.C., Donnerstein, E., Fairchild, H., Feshbach, N.D., Katz, P.A., Murray, J.P., Rubinstein, E.A., Wilcox, B.L., & Zuckerman, D. (1992). *Big world, small screen: The role of television in American society*. Lincoln: University of Nebraska Press.

Ingersoll, E.W., & Thomas, E.B. (1994). The breathing bear: Effects on respiration in premature infants. *Physiology and behavior, 56*(5), 855–859.

Institute for American Values. (2003). *Hardwired to connect.* (A report to the nation from the Commission on Children at Risk). New York: Author.

Jaudes, P.K., & Ekwo, E.E. (1997). Outcomes for infants exposed in utero to illicit drugs. *Child Welfare, 77*(4), 521–534.

Johnson, R.M., Kotch, J.B., & Catellier, D.J. (2002). Adverse behavioral and emotional outcomes from child abuse and witnessed violence. *Child Maltreatment, 7*(3), 179–186.

Jones, A. (1997). Issues relevant to therapy with adoptees. *Psychotherapy, 34*(1), 64–68.

Jorgenson, K., & Schooler, J. (2002, Spring). What makes foster parents come and stay? *National Advocate, 2,* 4–6.

Kaplan, G.A., Salonen, J.T., & Cohen, R.D., (1988). Social connections and mortality from all causes and from cardiovascular disease: Prospective evidence from eastern Finland. *American Journal of Epidemiology, 128*(2), 370–380.

Keltner, B. (1990). Family characteristics of preschool social competence among black children in a Head Start program. *Child Psychiatry and Human Development, 21*(2), 95–108.

Kendall-Tackett, K.A., Williams, L.M., & Finkelhor, D. (1993). Impact of sexual abuse on children: A review and synthesis of recent empirical studies. *Psychological Bulletin, 113,* 164–180.

Kessler, R.C. (2005). Prevalence and treatment of mental disorders, 1990 to 2003. *New England Journal of Medicine, 62*(6), 603–613.

Klee, L., Kronstadt, D., & Zlotnick, C. (1997). Foster care's youngest: A preliminary report. *American Journal of Orthopsychiatry, 67*(2), 290–299.

Knipe, J., & Warren, J. (1999). *Foster youth share their ideas for change.* Washington, DC: Child Welfare League of America Press.

Kreisher, K. (2002). Gay adoption. *Children's Voice, 11*(1), 12–15.

Kubicek, L. F. (2002). Fresh perspectives on young children and family routines. *ZERO TO THREE, 22*(4), 4–9.

Kutulak, R. (1996). *Inside the brain.* Kansas City: Andrews McMeel.

Lamb, M.E. (1997). *The role of the father in child development* (3rd Ed.). New York: Wiley.

Lamb, M.E. (2002). Infant-father attachments and their impact on child development. In C. Tamis-LeMonda & N. Cabrera (Eds.), *Handbook of father involvement* (pp. 93–117). Hillside, NJ: Erlbaum.

Leslie, L.K., Kelleher, K.J., Burns, B.J., Landsverk, J., & Rolls, J.A. (2003). Foster care and Medicaid managed care. *Child Welfare, 88*(3), 367–392.

Levy, T., (Ed.) (2000). *Handbook of attachment interventions.* San Diego: Academic Press.

Levy, T., (2001). Successful marriage. *Professional Update, 3*(1), 1–2.

Levy, T., & Orlans, M. (1998). *Attachment, trauma and healing: Understanding and treating attachment disorder in children and families.* Washington, DC: Child Welfare League of America Press.

Levy, T., & Orlans, M. (1999). Kids who kill: Attachment disorder, antisocial personality, and violence. *The Forensic Examiner, 8*(3 & 4).

Levy, T., & Orlans, M. (2000a). Attachment disorder as an antecedent to violence and antisocial patterns in children. In T. Levy (Ed.), *Handbook of attachment interventions* (pp.1–26). San Diego: Academic Press.

Levy, T., & Orlans, M. (2000b). Attachment disorder and the adoptive family. In T. Levy (Ed.), *Handbook of attachment interventions* (pp. 243–259). San Diego: Academic Press.

Levy, R., & O'Hanlon, W. (2001). *Try and make me: Simple strategies that turn off the temper tantrums and create cooperation.* Emmaus, PA: Rodale.

Lewin, T. (2005, November 1). Data suggests positive and negative effects of child care. *New York Times,* 21–22.

Lewis, T., Amini, F., & Lannon, R. (2000). *A general theory of love.* New York: Vintage Books.

Lynch, J.J. (1977). *The broken heart: Medical consequences of loneliness.* New York: Basic Books.

Lyons-Ruth, K. (1996). Attachment relationships among children with aggressive behavior problems: The role of disorganized early attachment patterns. *Journal of Consulting and Clinical Psychology, 64*(1), 64–73.

Lyons-Ruth, K., & Jacobvitz, D. (1999). Attachment disorganization: Unresolved loss, relational violence and lapses in behavioral and attentional strategies. In J. Cassidy & P. R. Shaver (Eds.), *Handbook of attachment,* (pp. 520–554). New York: Guilford Press.

Lyons-Ruth, K., Repacholi B., McLeod, S., & Silva, E. (1991). Disorganized attachment behavior in infancy: Short-term stability, maternal and infant correlates, and risk-related subtypes. *Development and Psychopathology, 3,* 377–396.

MacLean, P. (1990). *The triune brain in evolution.* New York: Plenum Press.

Main, M., Kaplan, N., & Cassidy, J. (1985). Security in infancy, childhood and adulthood: A move to the level of representation. In I. Bretherton & E. Waters (Eds.), Growing points of attachment theory and research. *Monographs of the Society for Research in Child Development, 50,* (1–2, Serial No. 209), 66–104.

Maltz, M. (1960). *Psycho-Cybernetics.* New York: Pocket Books.

McAuliffe, G. (Ed.). (2002). *Working with troubled youth in schools.* Westport, CT: Bergin & Garvey.

McCreight, B. (1997). *Recognizing and managing children with fetal alcohol syndrome/fetal alcohol effects.* Washington, DC: Child Welfare League of America.

McDonald, T., Allen, R., Westerfelt, A., & Piliavin, I. (1996). *Assessing the long-term effects of foster care: A research synthesis.* Washington, DC: Child Welfare League of America.

McIntyre, A., & Keesler, T.Y. (1986). Psychological disorders among foster children. *Journal of Clinical Child Psychology, 15,* 297–303.

McKay, M., Davis, M., & Fanning, P. (1995). *Messages: The communication skills book.* Oakland, CA: New Harbinger Publications.

McLeer, S.V., Deblinger, E., Atkins, M.S., Ralphe, D.L., & Foa, E. (1988). Posttraumatic stress disorder in sexually abused children. *Journal of the American Academy of Child and Adolescent Psychiatry, 27,* 650–654.

McWey, L.M. (2004). Predictors of attachment styles of children in foster care: An attachment theory model for working with families. *Journal of Marital and Family Therapy, 30*(4), 439–452.

Medalie, J.H., & Goldbourt, U. (1976). Angina pectoris among 10,000 men. *American Journal of Medicine, 60*(6), 910–921.

Medhus, E. (2001). *Raising children who think for themselves.* Hillsboro, OR: Beyond Words Publishing.

Meier, P. (2003, Summer). Training foster parents to help children with special educational needs. *National Advocate, 3,* 6–7.

Murray, J.P. (2000). Media effects. In A. Kazdin (Ed.), *Encyclopedia of Psychology* (pp. 153–155). New York: Oxford University Press.

Murray, M., & Pizzorno, J. (1998). *Encyclopedia of natural medicine.* Roseville, CA: Prima Publishing.

National Center on Child Abuse and Neglect (NCCAN). (1995). *National child abuse and neglect data systems. Third national incidence study of child maltreatment.* Washington, DC: U.S. Government Printing Office.

National Institute of Mental Health. (1982). *Television and behavior: Vol. 1 Ten years of progress and implications for the eighties.* Washington, DC: U.S. Government Printing Office.

National Research Council and Institute of Medicine. (2000). *From neurons to neighborhoods: The science of early childhood development.* Committee on Integrating the Science of Early Childhood Development. Jack P. Shonkoff and Deborah A. Phillips (Eds.) Board on Children, Youth, and Families, Commission on Behavioral and Social Sciences and Education. Washington, DC: National Academy Press.

National Resource Center for Youth Services. (1987). *Conflict resolution: A curriculum for youth providers.* Tulsa, OK: University of Oklahoma.

National Women's Health Information Center. (2001). *Postpartum depression fact sheet.* Retrieve from www.wrongdiagnosis.com/artic/postpartum_depression_fact_sheet_nwhic.

Nelson-Gardell, D., & Harris, D. (2003). Childhood abuse history, secondary traumatic stress, and child welfare workers. *Child Welfare, 87*(1), 5–26.

Newton, R.R., Litrownik, A.J., & Landsverk, J.A. (2000). Children and youth in foster care. *Child Abuse and Neglect, 24,* 1363–1374.

Niven, D. (2000). *The 100 simple secrets of happy people.* San Francisco, CA: Harper.

Norton, D. (1993). Diversity, early socialization, and temporal development: The dual perspective revisited. *Social Work, 38*(1), 82–90.

Null, G. (2000). *The food-mood-body connection.* New York: Seven Stories Press.

O'Connor, T.G., Bredenkamp, D., Rutter, M., and The English and Romanian Adoptees (ERA) Study Team (1999). Attachment disturbances and disorders in children exposed to early severe deprivation. *Infant Mental Health Journal, 20*(1), 10–29.

Ornish, D. (1998). *Love and survival: The scientific basis for the healing power of intimacy.* New York: Harper Collins.

Ornstein, R., & Sobel, D. (1987). *The healing brain.* New York: Simon & Schuster, 195–196.

Osborne, J.S. (2004). Identification with academics and violence in schools. *Review of General Psychology, 8*(3), 147–162.

Osofsky, J.D. (1995). The effects of exposure to violence on young children. *American Psychologist, 50,* 782–788.

Parlakian, R., & Seibel, N.L. (2002). *Building strong foundations.* Washington, DC: ZERO TO THREE.

Pedersen, F., Yarrow, L., Anderson, B., & Cain, R. (1978). Conceptualization of father influences in the infancy period. In M. Lewis & L.A. Rosenblum (Eds.), *The social network of the developing infant* (pp. 138–165). New York: Plenum.

Phelps, J.L., Belsky, J., & Crnic, K. (1998). Earned security, daily stress, and parenting. *Development and psychopathology, 10,* 21–38.

Pruett, K. (2000). *Fatherneed.* New York: The Free Press.

Quartz, S.R., & Sejnowski, T.J. (2002). *Liars, lovers, and heroes: What the new brain science reveals about how we become who we are.* New York: William Morrow.

Raeburn, P. (2004). *Acquainted with the night: A parent's quest to understand depression and bipolar disorder in his children.* New York: Broadway Books.

Rashid, M. (2000). *Horses never lie.* Boulder, CO: Johnson Books.

Reynolds, P., & Kaplan, G.A. (1990). Social connections and risk for cancer: Prospective evidence from the Alameda County Study. *Behavioral Medicine, 16*(3), 101–110.

Rholes, W.S., & Simpson, J.A. (Eds.). (2004). *Adult attachment.* New York: Guildford Press.

Riley, D., & Singer, E. (2003). Adoption challenges. *Family Therapy Magazine, 2*(1), 37–43.

Roisman, G.I., Padron, E., Sroufe, A., & Egeland, B. (2002). Earned-secure attachment status in retrospect and prospect. *Child development, 73*(4), 1204–1219.

Rosenthal, J. (1993). Outcome of adoption of children with special needs. *The Future of Children, 3*(1), 77–88.

Rowe, J.W., & Kahn, R.L. (1998). *Successful aging.* New York: Dell.

Russek, L.G., & Schwartz, G.E. (1997). Feelings of parental caring predict health status in midlife: A 35-year follow-up of the Harvard Mastery of Stress Study. *Journal of Behavioral Medicine, 20,* 1–13.

Schoenbach, V.J., Kaplan, B.H., Friedman, L., & Kleinbaum, D.G. (1986). Social ties and mortality in Evans County, Georgia. *American Journal of Epidemiology, 123*(4), 577–591.

Schofield, G., & Beek, M. (2005). Providing a secure base: Parenting children in long-term family care. *Attachment and Human Development, 7*(1), 3–25.

Schooler, J. (1997). When siblings are separated. *Adoptive Families, 30*(6), 14–19.

Schore, A. (1994). *Affect regulation and the origin of the self.* Hillsdale, NJ: Lawrence Erlbaum.

Seeman, T.E., & Syme, S.L. (1987). Social networks and coronary artery disease: A comparison of the structure and function of social relations as predictors of disease. *Psychosomatic Medicine, 49*(4), 341–54.

Sharma, A.R., McGue, M.K., & Benson, P.L. (1996). The emotional and behavioral adjustment of United States adopted adolescents. *Children and Youth Services Review, 18,* 83–100.

Siegel D. (1999). *The developing mind: Toward a neurobiology of interpersonal experience.* New York: Guilford Press.

Siegel, D.J., & Hartzell, M. (2003). *Parenting from the inside out.* New York: Tarcher/Putnam.

Silverman, A.R. (1993). Outcomes of transracial adoption. *The Future of Children, 3*(1), 104–118.

Silverstein, D., & Roszia, S.K. (1999). Openness: A critical component of special needs adoption. *Child Welfare, 78,* 637–651.

Simmons, R. (2005, Fall). Burnout prevention. *National Advocate, 8.*

Spitz, R.A. (1945). Hospitalization: An inquiry into the genesis of psychiatric conditions in early childhood. *Psychoanalytic Study of the Child, 1,* 53–74.

Sroufe, L.A. (1983). Infant-caregiver attachment patterns of adaptation in preschool: The roots of maladaptation and competence. In M. Perlmutter (Ed.), *Minnesota symposium in child psychology:* Vol. 16 (pp. 41–81). Hillsdale, NJ: Erlbaum.

Stambor, Z. (2005). Meet the renaissance dad. *Monitor on Psychology, 36*(11), 62–64.

Stein, J.A., Golding, J.M., Siegel, J.M., Burnam, M.A., & Sorensen, S.B. (1988). Long-term psychological sequelae of child sexual abuse: The Los Angeles Epidemiological Catchment Area Study. In G.E. Wyatt & G.J. Powell (Eds.), *The lasting effects of child sexual abuse* (pp. 135–154). Newbury Park, CA: Sage.

Stovall, K.C., & Dozier, M. (2000). The development of attachment in new relationships. *Development and Psychopathology, 12*(2), 133–156.

Suomi, S.J. (1991). Early stress and adult emotional reactivity in rhesus monkeys. *Ciba Foundation Symposium. 156,* 171–183.

Thomas, C.B., & Duszynski, K.R. (1974). Close to parents and the family constellation in a prospective study of five disease states. *John Hopkins Medical Journal, 134,* 251–262.

Trevarthen, C. (1993). The self born in intersubjectivity: The psychology of infant communication. In U. Neisser (Ed.), *The perceived self.* New York: Cambridge University Press.

Tronick, E.Z., & Weinberg, M.K. (1997). Depressed mothers and infants: Failure to form dyadic states of consciousness. In L. Murray & P. Cooper (Eds.), *Postpartum depression and child development* (pp. 54–84). New York: Guilford Press.

U.S. Census Bureau. (2003). *Married couple and unmarried partner household 2000: Census 2000 special reports.* Available online at www.census.gov/prod/2003pubs/censr-5.pdf. Washington, DC: Author.

U.S. Census Bureau. (2004). *Adoption statistics.* Available online at www.census.gov/Press-Release/www/releases/archives/facts_for_features_special_editions/002683.html. Washington, DC: Author.

U.S. Department of Health and Human Services. (2002). *National child abuse and neglect data system: Summary of key findings.* Washington, DC: Author.

U.S. Department of Health and Human Services, Administration on Children, Youth, and Families. (2003). *12 years of reporting: Child maltreatment 2001.* Washington, DC: Author.

U.S. Select Committee on Children, Youth and Families. (1989). *No place to call home: Discarded children in America.* Washington, DC: U.S. House of Representatives.

van den Boom, D.C. (1994). The influence of temperament and mothering on attachment and exploration. *Child Development, 65,* 1457–1477.

van den Boom, D.C. (1995). Do first year intervention effects endure? Follow-up during toddlerhood of a sample of Dutch irritable infants. *Child Development, 66,* 1798–1816.

van IJzendoorn, M.H. (1995). Adult attachment representations, parental responsiveness, and infant attachment: A meta-analysis on the predictive validity of the Adult Attachment Interview. *Psychological Bulletin, 117,* 387–403.

Verny T., & Kelly, J. (1981). *The secret life of the unborn child.* New York: Delta Publishing.

Verrier, N. (1994). *The primal wound: Understanding the adopted child.* Baltimore, MD: Gateway Press.

Visher, E.B., & Visher, J.S. (1996). *Therapy with stepfamilies.* New York: Brunner/Mazel.

Wainright, J.L., Russell, S.T., & Patterson, C.J. (2004). Psychosocial adjustment, school outcomes, and romantic relationships of adolescents with same-sex parents. *Child Development, 75,* 1886–1898.

Watson, J.B. (1928). *Psychological care of infant and child.* New York: Norton.

Webb, N.B. (2006). *Working with traumatized youth in child welfare.* New York: Guilford Press.

Weir, K. (2004). The many faces of adoption. *Family Therapy Magazine, 1*(10), 34–35.

Weitzman, C.C., & Avni-Singer, R. (2005). Building the bonds of Adoption: From separation and deprivation toward integration and continuity. *ZERO TO THREE, 25*(6), 14–20.

Werner, E. (1989). High-risk children in young adulthood: A longitudinal study from birth to 32 years. *American Journal of Orthopsychiatry, 59*(1), 72–81.

Wilens, T.E. (2004). *Straight talk about psychiatric medications for kids.* New York: Guilford Press.

Wooden, J. (2005). *Wooden on leadership.* New York: McGraw-Hill.

Zahn-Waxler, C., Radke-Yarrow, M., Wagner, E., & Chapman, M. (1992). Development of concern for others. *Developmental Psychology, 28,* 126–136.

ZERO TO THREE. (2003). *Charting your child's healthy development.* Washington, DC: Author.

ZERO TO THREE. (2004). The power of play: Learning through play from birth to three. Washington, DC: Author.

Zetlin, A. (2002). Advocating to resolve educational problems of children in foster care. *APSAC Advisor, 14*(1), 11–14.

Zigler, E. (1994). Early intervention to prevent juvenile delinquency. *Harvard Mental Health Letter, 11*(3), 5–7.

Index

A

Accident prone behavior, 68–69

Accountability, 149

Active listening, 196–198

Adolescent attachment, 254–255

Adoption. *See also* Foster care
 birth parent contact, 243–244
 blended family, 236–237
 deinstitutionalization of, 231
 family belonging and, 188
 gay and lesbian, 234–235
 international, 231–232
 kinship, 231, 233–234
 open, 236
 reasons for, 246
 sibling placements, 248–249
 single-parent, 235–236
 transracial, 231, 232–233
 trends in, 230–231
 wounded child and
  emotional and attachment
   factors, 238–239
  emotional focus areas, 244–245
  loss and grief, 239–242
  loyalty conflicts, 242–244
  negative core beliefs, 239

Adoption and Safe Families Act,
 229, 261

Adoption Assistance and Child Welfare
 Act, 260

Adoption statistics, 229–230

Adoption story, 230

Adoption triad, 240

Adoptive families, traumatized, 246–248

Adrenaline rush, 25

Adult attachment
 communication and, 100–101
 patterns of
  dismissing, 94–95
  preoccupied, 95
  secure-autonomous, 93–94
  unresolved, 95–96

Advocacy, in school success, 206–207

African American adoptions, 233

Age, at placement, 238

Aggressive communication style, 199

Aggressive conflict style, 184

Aggressor identification, 171

Alcohol
 limiting, in stress management, 113
 in utero exposure to, 43
 as violence factor, 45

Allergies, 85–86

Allowances, 154

Ambivalent attachment, 20–21, 52

American Academy of Pediatrics, 235

Anger internalization, 171

Anger management, 180–184

Anger sequence, 182–183

Animal cruelty, 47, 58

Antidepressants, suicide link with, 80

Anxious attachment, 40

Assertive communication style, 199

Assertive conflict style, 184

Assessment
 of child
  developmental history, 46
  parent/caregiver attachment
   history, 48

symptom checklist for, 71
symptoms and diagnosis, 46–48
of self, by life script
description of, 96–97
questions for, 97–98
understanding, 98–100
Association for the Treatment and
Training in the Attachment of
Children (ATTACH), 4
Attachment
adolescence and, 254–255
as adoption factor, 238–239
in childhood development, 7
communication in, 191
core beliefs in, 27
crying infant and, 217–218
development of, 17
father's role in, 220–221
in foster children, 263, 266–267
parent's mind-set regarding, 92, 124
secure
animal studies on, 19
benefits of, 9
functions of, 18
in self-regulation, 25
Attachment Communication Training
(ACT)
case study for, 253–254
ground rules of, 102
impact of, 101–102
process, 102–104
Attachment cues, 192–194
Attachment cycle, first year of life, 22*f*
Attachment disorder symptoms and traits
behavioral, 54–63
brain biochemistry, 50–51
in child assessment, 46–48
in cognitive functioning, 61–63
core beliefs, 50
defenses, 49–50
defiance, 51
emotional, 63–64
fear of closeness, 49
lying, 53
physical, 68–69
projection, 52

reenactment, 52
shame, 53–54
social, 64–68
spiritual/moral, 70
Attachment disorders. *See also*
Compromised attachment
ambivalent, 20–21, 52
anxious, 40
avoidant, 20, 52
in biological families, 211–212
concurrent conditions
attention deficit/hyperactivity
disorder, 74–75
bipolar disorder, 76–77
conduct disorder, 73–74
dysthymic disorder, 76
major depression, 75
oppositional defiant disorder,
72–73
posttraumatic stress disorder,
77–79
disorganized-disordered, 21, 40, 52
over-medication of, 82–84
percentage experiencing, 2
prematurity, 212
resistant, 20–21, 52
Attachment separation, 241
Attachment wound, 100
Attention deficit/hyperactivity disorder
(ADHD)
as concurrent condition, 74–75
diet's effect on, 84
medication warnings, 81
Automaticity, 224
Autonomous state of mind, 263
Autonomy circle, 126, 148*f*, 256–258
Avoidant attachment, 20, 52

B

Bedwetting, 47, 59
Behavior, looking beyond, 244, 252, 273
Behavior focus vs. core belief focus,
169–170

Behavioral symptoms and traits, 54–63

Belonging, sense of, 187–188

Binge drinking, 5

Biological factors
bipolar disorder, 76
in child assessment, 69
in violent behavior, 45

Biological families, attachment
disorders in, 211–212

Bipolar disorder, 76–77, 212

Birth bonding, 240

Birth parent contact, 243–244

Blaming of others
as defensive coping strategy, 170
as symptom, 66

Blended adoptive families, 236–237

Body language
in anger escalation, 183
in message communication, 203–204

Body tension, 68

Boston Children's Aid Society, 260

Brain and brain processes
in attachment disorder, 50–51
attachment impact on, 7
development of, 22–24
in down-regulation, 173–174
experience recordation, 26–27
in foster children, 266–267
information exchange in, 24
media violence and, 224
medication use and, 80, 83
in stress response, 141

Brain stem, 23, 140–141

Breast-feeding, 193

Breathing, in stress management, 115

Bullying, 66–67

Burnout prevention, 108

C

Caffeine, 112–113

Calm-oriented parenting, 133, 172–173

Carbohydrates, refined, 113

Caregiver stress, 107–108

Cause and effect thinking, 61

Cerebral cortex, 141

Change principles, 121–123

Character-building coaching, 143

Chattering, as symptom, 60–61

Child Abuse Prevention and Treatment
Act, 260

Child and Family Service Reviews, 261

Child Welfare League of America
(CWLA), 260

Child welfare programs, 260

Childhood development core concepts,
6–8

Children of Lesbians and Gays
Everywhere (COLAGE), 235

China, 232

Choices and consequences
autonomy circle and, 148*f*
limit and structure in, 146–149
modeling, 137–138
parent-child contract in, 149
suitable choices, 156–158
vs. punishment, 138

Chores, 153–156

Christmas melt-down, 219

Clingy behavior, 56–57

Closed-loop system, 24

Coaching-oriented parenting, 142–143

Cognitive appraisal, 42–43

Collaborative communication, 191

Commitment-oriented parenting,
134–135

Communication
active listening, 196–198
of adoption story, 230
in attachment, 191
attachment cues, 192–194
body language, 183
clarification in, 201–202
constructive, 105
content and process in, 204

covert messages in, 200
destructive, 104
developmental, 194–196
fighting vs. thinking words, 201
ground rules of, 102
on loss and grief, 241–242
on loyalty conflicts, 243–244
nonverbal, 203–204
one-liners, 174–175, 202
prenatal, 191
reflective listening, 103
resource model of, 204–205
sharing in
    door closers, 202–203
    door openers, 199–202
Communication attachment training
    (ACT), 101–104
Communication-oriented parenting,
    136–137
Communication styles, 199
Community systems, 9
    in effective parenting, 120–121
    as healing environments, 125–126
    health benefits of, 34–35
Competency-based approach, 148*f*,
    149–150
Complementary reaction, 173
Compromised attachment. *See also*
    Attachment disorders
    causes of, 39
    core beliefs in, 27
    definition of, 3
    internalization in, 29
    as risk factor, 31
    risks associated with, 9
    women as focus of anger in, 205
Conduct disorder, 51, 73–74
Confidence-oriented parenting, 139
Conflict escalation, 256–258
Conflict styles, 183–184
Connection, vs. control, 131*t*
Connection-oriented parenting, 130–132
Conscience, 70
Consequences. *See also* Discipline

delivery of, 164–166
modeling of choices, 137–138
natural and imposed, 162–163
think-it-over time, 163–164
vs. punishment, 159–160
Consistency-oriented parenting, 136
Constructive communication, 105
Content-to-process shift, 204
Control
    in adoptive families, 247
    consequences vs. punishment, 138
    as defensive coping strategy, 170
    in eating issues, 211
    foster children and, 266
    playing dumb, 152
    as symptom, 66
    vs. connection, 131*t*
Cooperation-oriented parenting, 140
Core beliefs
    as adoption factor, 239
    in attachment disorder, 50
    development of, 26–27, 47
    focus on, vs. behavior focus,
    169–170
    in foster children, 266
Corporal punishment, 138, 160, 162
Corrective attachment parenting (CAP)
    loving leadership in, 129
    philosophy of, 9–11
    principles of change in, 121–123
    skills and strategies, 145–146
Cortisol, 26, 146
Covert messages, 200
Creativity-oriented parenting, 140–141
Crying
    as attachment cue, 193
    of infant, response to, 217–218
    in stress management, 115
Cultural niche, 38

D

Daycare, 221–222
Deceitful behavior, 57

Defensive coping strategies
    assessment of, 49–50
    changing pattern of, 171–172
    types of, 170–171

Defiance, 51

Deinstitutionalization of adoption, 231

Demanding behavior, 56–57

Denial, 170

Depression
    diet and, 113
    dysthymic disorder, 76
    major, 75
    medications for, 80
    Omega-3 and, 112
    postpartum, 212
    prenatal transmission of, 212
    sexual abuse and, 42
    as symptom, 63–64

Destructive communication, 104

Developmental communication, 194–196

Developmental history, in assessment, 46

Diet and nutrition
    behavioral impact of, 84–86
    caffeine, 112–113
    in stress management, 112–113

Discipline, in loving leadership, 129. *See also* Consequences

Disease resistance, 33–36

Dismissing adult attachment pattern, 94–95

Disorganized-disoriented attachment, 21, 31, 40, 52

Dissociation, 171

Door closers, 202–203

Door openers, 199–202

Down-regulation, 25, 133, 173–174

Drug use
    by foster children, 269
    statistics on, 5
    in utero exposure to, 43
    as violence factor, 45

Dysthymic disorder, 76

E

Eating habits
    behavioral impact of, 84–86
    conflicts over, 211
    as symptom, 60

Education
    homeschooling, 205–207
    individualized education program, 207–208
    parental advocacy in, 206–207
    school violence, 208–209

Emotional attunement, 29–30

Emotional behavior, as symptom, 63–64

Emotional development, as adoption factor, 238–239

Emotional exclusion, 171

Emotional Intelligence (Goleman), 82

Emotional misattunement, 53

Emotional neglect, 41

Emotional numbing, 170

Emotional triggers, 90, 167–169, 181–182, 245

Empathy, 28

Enabling, 159

Encopresis, 59

Enuresis, 59

Escalation of conflict, 256–258

Exercise, in stress management, 111–112

Expect-project-defend pattern, 172

Explicit memory, 26

Eye contact, 65, 192, 203

F

Failure to thrive syndrome, 18, 41, 192

Family foster care, 262

Family rituals, 188–190

Family systems
    as healing environment, 125–126
    health benefits of, 32–33

violence and, 44

Family systems approach, 4, 9

Father, as attachment figure, 220–221

Fetal alcohol effects (FAE), 43

Fetal alcohol syndrome (FAS), 43

Fight-flight-freeze response, 24, 109, 173

Fighting vs. thinking words, 201

Fire setting, 47

Firearms, 45

Food allergies, 85–86

Foster care. *See also* Adoption
    child and family service reviews, 261
    parental state of mind in, 263
    permanency planning and, 260
    skill-based training in, 263
    types of, 262
    youth recommendations for, 264

Foster care crisis, 270

Foster care history, 259–261

Foster children
    attachment in, 266–267
    educational challenges, 265
    health care issues, 264–265
    move anxiety and, 267–268
    outcome statistics for, 269–271

Foster parents
    goals and solutions for, 273–275
    role of, 272–273
    success principles for, 272
    support needs of, 270–272

G

Gay and lesbian adoptions, 234–235

Genetics. *See* Biological factors

Goal setting, 122, 151–153, 180

Grandiosity, 62–63

Grief and loss, 239–242

Guided imagery, 111

Guns, 45

H

Harnett, George, 135

Health. *See also* Medication
    of foster children, 261–262, 264–265
    stress impact on, 109–110

Health benefits
    of community, 34–35
    of families, 32–33
    of marriage, 35

Heredity. *See* Biological factors

Hoarding, 58

Holiday reactions, 219–220

Homeschooling, 205–207

Homicide rate
    child perpetrators of, 5
    child victims of, 44

Hostile attributional bias, 169

Humor, 177. *See also* Laughter

Hygiene, as symptom, 68

Hyperactivity, as symptom, 59–59

Hypervigilance, as symptom, 61

Hypoglycemia, 113

I

"I" statements, 199

Idealization, 171

Identity formation, 230

Implicit memory, 26

Imposed consequences, 162–163

Impulse control, 54–55

In utero alcohol and drug exposure, 43

Individualized education program (IEP), 207–208

Infertility, 246

Internal working model, 47

Internalization, 29, 171

International adoption, 231–232

Irresponsibility, 56

J

Judgment, 150

K

Kinship adoptions, 231, 233–234

Kinship foster care, 262

Knee-jerk response, 168

Know yourself. *See* Life script; Parenting styles; Self-knowledge

Knowledge, 149

L

Labeling, 125

Language disorders, 62

Laughter. *See also* Humor
    as creative choice, 141
    in stress management, 115

Leadership. *See also* Modeling
    10 Cs of, 129–142
    discipline and, 129
    in horse herd, 132

Learning disorders, 62

Lecturing, 202

Life script
    description of, 96–97
    questions for, 97–98
    understanding, 98–100

Life skills, 120

Limbic resonance, 7, 30, 191

Limbic system, 23–24, 141

Limits, establishing, 126, 146–149

Listening, active, 196–198

Loneliness, 34

Loss and grief, 239–242

Loyalty conflicts, 242–244

Lying, 53, 209–211

M

Magical thinking, 268

Major depression, 75. *See also* Depression

Maltreatment, 40–41
    as adoption factor, 238

Managed care, over-medication and, 81

Manic-depressive illness. *See* Bipolar disorder

Manipulative behavior, 67–68

Marasmus. *See* Failure to thrive syndrome

Marriage
    characteristics of successful, 106–107
    health benefits of, 35
    mother-infant attachment and, 125
    stepfamilies, 236–237

Media violence, 45, 222–225

Medication
    brain chemistry and, 80
    managed care and, 81
    over-use of, 82–84
    symptom-focused treatment and, 81–82

Meditation, in stress management, 110

Memory, explicit and implicit, 26

Mentoring, 142–143

Metaphoric thought, 224

Mindful parenting, 89

Modeling. *See also* Leadership; Resource model
    of anger messages, 182
    of change, 121–122
    of competencies, 149
    of cooperation, 140
    by media violence, 223
    mentoring, 142
    in moral development, 28–29
    by offering choices, 138
    by parents, 29, 91, 128
    of respect, 152

Mood disorders, 75

Mood swings, as symptom, 64

Moral behavior, as symptom, 70

Morality development, 27–30, 154

Motivation, 122, 213–215

Move anxiety, 267–268

Muscle relaxation, 110–111

Mutual reaction, 173

N

National Association of Black Social
    Workers, 233

Natural consequences, 162–163

Nature and nurture, 7–8, 23

Neglect, 41–42

Neocortex, 23–24

New York Children's Aid Society, 260

*No Place to Call Home: Discarded Children
    in America,* 260–261

Nonverbal messages, 203–204

Nutrition. *See* Diet

O

Object constancy, 195

O'Hare, Butch, 135

Omega-3 supplements, 84, 112

One-liners, 174–175, 202

Open adoption, 236

Open-loop system, 24

Opportunity vs. crisis, 127

Oppositional behavior, 59

Oppositional defiant disorder (ODD), 51,
    72–73

Overt messages, 200

Oxytocin, 7, 24

P

Pain tolerance, 69

Parallel play, 179

Parental child, 243

Parenting styles
    dismissing, 94–95
    preoccupied, 95
    secure-autonomous, 94
    unresolved, 96

Parenting tips. *See also* Corrective
        attachment parenting
    crying baby, 217–218
    for foster parents, 273–275
    holiday reactions, 219–220
    know yourself, 124–125, 167,
        245, 274
    loss and grief, 241–242
    loyalty conflicts, 243–244
    media violence, 222–225
    move trauma, 268
    sibling conflicts, 215–217

Parents, Families, and friends of Lesbians
    and Gays (PFLAG), 235

Parents/caregivers
    attachment history of, in
        assessment, 48
    coping with losses of, 240–241
    father's role as, 220–221
    loyalty conflicts and, 242–244
    prior attachments to, 238–239
    as secure base, 166–167
    toxic, 54
    women as focus of anger, 205

Passive-aggressive communication style,
    199

Passive-aggressive conflict style, 184

Passive communication style, 199

Passive conflict style, 183

Pathological lying, 210

Peer relationships, 65–66

Personalizing, 167

Placebo effect, 119–120

Placement age, 238

Play, 177–179, 220–221

Positive engagement, 175–176

Postpartum depression, 212

Posttraumatic stress disorder (PTSD)
    as concurrent condition, 77–79
    symptoms of, 78–79
    violence as factor in, 44

Power struggles, as symptom, 66

Praise, 176–177

Prayer, in stress management, 115

Pregnancy, in foster youths, 269

Prematurity, 212

Prenatal communication, 191

Prenatal experience, as adoption factor,
    238

Preoccupied adult attachment pattern, 95

Prevention of Childhood Obesity Act, 85

Primal wound, 240

Prior attachments, 238–239

Proactive vs. reactive parenting, 127–128,
    179–180

Problem pie, 158–159

Problem solving, 184–187

Progressive muscle relaxation, 110–111

Projection, 52, 170

Property destruction, 55

Prosocial morality, 27–30

Protective factors. *See also* Risk factors
    change and, 123
    developmental role of, 8
    resilience and, 31
    types of, 31

Pseudoindependence, 171

Psychological punishment, 138, 160

Public misbehavior, 213

Punishment
    ineffectiveness of, 161–162
    reactive nature of, 138
    spanking as, 162
    vs. consequences, 159–160

R

Reacting therapeutically, 173

Reaction formation, 171

Reactive parenting, 127–128, 138

Reciprocal communication, 191

Reciprocal escalation, 257

Reciprocity
    as competency, 153
    in foster parenting, 274
    in moral development, 29–30
    in trust development, 21–22

Reenactment, 52

Reflective listening, 103

Relaxation response, 110

Religion, 128

Residential group foster care, 262

Residential treatment centers (RTC),
    225–226

Resilience, 30–32

Resistant attachment, 20–21, 52

Resource model. *See also* Modeling
    of communication, 204–205
    in corrective parenting, 121–122
    in offering choices, 138

Resourcefulness, 152–153

Respectfulness, 151–152

Respite care, 226–227

Responsibility
    goal setting for, 151
    units of concern and, 158–159

Reticular activation system (RAS), 141,
    173–174

Risk factors. *See also* Protective factors
    change and, 123
    developmental role of, 8
    resilience and, 31

Rituals, 122, 188–190

Rocking, 193

Role models. *See* Modeling

Romania, 238, 263

Russia, 232

S

Same-sex parenting, 234–235

School violence, 208–209

Secondary traumatic stress, 107–108, 169, 247

Secure attachment. *See also* Attachment
animal studies on, 19
benefits of, 9
communication central to, 137
core beliefs in, 27
functions of, 18
health benefits of, 33
as protective factor, 31
in self-regulation, 25

Secure-autonomous adult attachment pattern, 93–94

Secure bases, 19, 166–167

Self-blame, 54

Self-efficacy, 20

Self-fulfilling prophecy, 161

Self-identity, 30

Self-injury, 55

Self-knowledge, 124–125, 167, 245, 274

Self-regulation
as competency, 150
developmental role of, 8
stress response and, 25–26

Self-talk
recognizing, 182
steps in reducing, 114

Sense of belonging, 187–188

Seroquel, 75

Serotonin, 84

Sexual abuse, 42–43

Sexual inappropriateness, 58

Shame, as symptom, 53–54

Sharing
door closers, 202–203
door openers, 199–202

Sibling conflicts

parental response to, 215–217
in traumatized adoptive family, 247–248

Sibling placements, 248–249

Single-parent adoptions, 235–236

Sleep disturbances
stress and, 114–115
as symptom, 58–59

Smiling, as attachment cue, 192

Smoking, in utero effects of, 43

Social behavior, as symptom, 64–68

Social Security Act, 260

South Korea, 232

Spanking, 162. *See also* Corporal punishment

Special needs (term), 260

Specialized care. *See* Therapeutic foster care

Speech impediments, 62

Spiritual behavior, as symptom, 70

Spirituality, 128

State of mind, 92, 124, 263

Stealing, 57

Stepfamilies, 236–237

Storytelling, 224

Stranger anxiety, 19

Strangers, affection towards, 65

Stress, and stress management
adoption and, 244–245
for caregiver, 107–108
in children, 146–147
diet and nutrition in, 112–113
relaxation response, 110
sleep's impact on, 114–115
visualization, 111
warning signs of, 109–110

Stress response
health risks of, 109
limbic system and, 141
self-regulation and, 25–26

Structure, 147

Sugar consumption, 84–85, 113

Suicide
  antidepressant link to, 80
  by children, 5
  married vs. unmarried, 35
  sexual abuse and, 42

Support systems, 14

Symbolic thought, 224

Symptom checklist, 71

Symptom-focused treatment, 81–82

Symptoms and traits of
      attachment disorder
  behavioral, 54–63
  brain biochemistry, 50–51
  in child assessment, 46–48
  in cognitive functioning, 61–63
  core beliefs, 50
  defenses, 49–50
  defiance, 51
  emotional, 63–64
  fear of closeness, 49
  lying, 53
  physical, 68–69
  projection, 52
  reenactment, 52
  shame, 53–54
  social, 64–68
  spiritual/moral, 70

T

Teenagers, attachment and, 254–255

Temper tantrums, as symptom, 63

Therapeutic foster care, 262

Therapeutic response, 173

Therapy
  therapist selection, 88
  treatment recommendations, 87
  types of, 86–87

Think-it-over time, 163–164

Time management, in stress
      management, 115

Time-out, 163

Touch
  as attachment cue, 192
  in nonverbal communication, 204

Toxic parenting, 54

Traits of attachment disorder. *See*
  Symptoms and traits

Transracial adoptions, 231, 232–233

Traumatic stress, secondary, 107–108,
  169, 247

Traumatized adoptive families, 246–248

Treatment care. *See* Therapeutic foster
  care

Triangulation, 237, 247, 252

Trigger avoidance, 90, 167–169,
  181–182, 245

Triune brain, 23

Trust
  lack of, as symptom, 67
  reciprocal partnership in, 21–22

U

Unemployment rates, 269

Units of concern, 158–159

Unresolved adult attachment pattern,
  95–96

Up-regulation, 25, 133

V

Verbal aggression, 56

Victimization, 62, 67

Violence
  aggressor identification, 171
  causes of, 44–45
  inappropriate interest in, 60
  maltreatment as risk factor for, 40
  in media, 45, 222–225

in schools, 208–209
as symptom, 55

Visualization, in stress management, 111

W

White House Conference on Children of
1909, 260

Women, as focus of anger, 205

Wooden, John, 142–143

Wounded children, 2

Y

Yoga, in stress management, 111